COMMERCIAL NETWORKS AND
EUROPEAN CITIES, 1400–1800

Perspectives in Economic and Social History

Series Editors: Andrew August
Jari Eloranta

Titles in this Series

FORTHCOMING TITLES

COMMERCIAL NETWORKS AND EUROPEAN CITIES, 1400–1800

EDITED BY

Andrea Caracausi and Christof Jeggle

Routledge
Taylor & Francis Group

LONDON AND NEW YORK

First published 2014 by Pickering & Chatto (Publishers) Limited

Published 2016 by Routledge
2 Park Square, Milton Park, Abingdon, Oxfordshire OX14 4RN
711 Third Avenue, New York, NY 10017, USA

First issued in paperback 2015

Routledge is an imprint of the Taylor & Francis Group, an informa business

BRITISH LIBRARY CATALOGUING IN PUBLICATION DATA

Commercial networks and European cities, 1400–1800. – (Perspectives in economic and social history)
1. Europe – Commerce – History – 16th century. 2. Europe – Commerce – History – 17th century. 3. Europe – Economic conditions – 16th century. 4. Europe
– Economic conditions – 17th century. 5. Cities and towns – Europe – History
– 16th century. 6. Cities and towns – Europe – History – 17th century.
I. Series II. Caracausi, Andrea editor of compilation. III. Jeggle, Christof editor
of compilation.
381'.094'09031-dc23

ISBN-13: 978-1-138-66309-1 (pbk)
ISBN-13: 978-1-8489-3450-4 (hbk)

Typeset by Pickering & Chatto (Publishers) Limited

CONTENTS

ACKNOWLEDGEMENTS

This book is the result of a long period of discussion with colleagues and friends on various occasions, whom we would gratefully like to thank for sharing their ideas. This book has been realized within the framework of the research projects 'Forms of Statehood between the Middle Ages and Early Modern Times: The Mediterranean Dimension and the Dominion of the Mainland in the Venetian Model' (PRIN2009W4PHLJ_003) and 'Maritime Borders in the Mediterranean: How Permeable Are They? Exchange, Control and Denial of Access' (FIRB2012RBFR12GBQZ_002) financed by the Italian Ministry of Instruction, University and Research. We would like to thank Giuseppe Gullino, who was the local coordinator of the first project, for trusting in the book project and supporting a meeting of the editors, authors and commentators in Padua on 24–5 May 2013, which facilitated the preparation of the final versions of the chapters. Special thanks go to Maria Fusaro, Cinzia Lorandini, Claudio Marsilio and Amélia Polónia, who participated in the workshop as discussants, for taking the time and for providing us and the authors with their ideas to improve the book. Some chapters have also been presented during sessions and conferences within the framework of the European Association for Urban History (Ghent, 2010) and the European Business History Association (Glasgow, 2010), and during a workshop held at the Ca' Foscari University of Venice in June 2010. We would like to thank all the participants of these meetings for their useful comments, in particular Salvatore Ciriacono, Giovanni Favero, Anna Moretti, Franz-Julius Morche, Paola Lanaro, Michele Tamma and Francesco Vianello. Finally we like to thank Philip Good for giving us the chance to publish the book at Pickering & Chatto and for his patient advice during the editing process, Janka Romero for her kind assistance in the copy-editing process and Alvise Vivenza for improving the figures.

LIST OF CONTRIBUTORS

Francesco Ammannati is Research Fellow at the Carlo F. Dondena Centre for Research on Social Dynamics, Bocconi University, and Adjunct Professor of Economic History at the University of Florence. He obtained his PhD in economic history at the University of Bari (2007) for his dissertation 'L'Arte della Lana a Firenze nel XVI secolo – Analisi comparativa di produzione e produttività attraverso i registri contabili delle Compagnie Busini'. His main research field is pre-industrial European economic history (thirteenth to eighteenth centuries). His scientific interests include the history of manufacture and trade, with a focus on guilds, labour markets and international merchant networks.

Mike Burkhardt received his MA at the University of Kiel and his PhD at the University of Copenhagen (2007). He has previously lectured at the universities of Copenhagen (2006–2008) and Kassel (2008–2012), and he currently works as a teacher in high school service. He has published a book entitled *Der hansische Bergenhandel im Spätmittelalter: Handel, Kaufleute, Netzwerke* (Cologne: Böhlau, 2009), one edited volume and several articles on Hanseatic history.

Andrea Caracausi is Assistant Professor of Early Modern History at the University of Padua. He received a BA in history (University of Padua) and a PhD in economic and social history (Bocconi University). He was Adjunct Professor in Business History and Economic History at the universities of Bocconi, Trieste, Venice and Verona. His field of research is the social and economic history of Italy and the Mediterranean world, with a focus on labour market, guilds, institutions and legal proceedings in the early modern period. On these topics, he has published two monographs, five co-edited books and several essays and articles in Italian and international books and journals.

David Carvajal de la Vega is a researcher at the University of Valladolid, where he received his PhD (2013) with the dissertation 'Crédito privado y deuda en Castilla (1480–1521)'. His research topics are Castilian economic history (fifteenth and sixteenth centuries), private credit, financial instruments, debts, litigation and relations between institutions and economic growth. He has edited books on social networks (*Redes sociales y económicas en el mundo bajome-dieval* (Valladolid: Castilla Ediciones, 2011)) and merchants (*Los negocios del hombre: negocio y rentas en Castilla (siglos XV–XVI)* (Valladolid: Castilla Edi-ciones, forthcoming)).

Benedetta Crivelli is a postdoctoral fellow at the University of Milan and a fellow of the Luigi De Rosa Scholarship at the Bank of Naples Foundation. She gained a PhD in economic history at the University of Verona. Her main research interests are the history of credit and the merchant communities of the Iberian world in the sixteenth and seventeenth centuries. She has carried out her research activities mainly in Spain and Portugal. Her publications include 'La Carreira da India nel corso dell'età moderna: problemi e riflessioni storiogra-fiche', *Storia Economica*, 3 (2011), pp. 507–41, and 'From Lisbon to Venice: The Network of Pepper Commerce in the Second Half of the Sixteenth Century', *Journal of European Economic History*, forthcoming.

Blanca González Talavera received her PhD in art history from the University of Florence and the University of Granada for her co-supervised thesis, 'Pres-ence and Spanish Patronage Medici in Florence: From Cosimo I to Fernando I'. Her career is supported by the fulfilment of predoctoral and doctoral fellow-ships: the Start Fellowship for Research, the Collaboration Fellowship and the Predoctoral FPU Fellowship (Teacher Training College) from the Ministry of Education and Science, Spain (2007–11). She has taught in the Department of Art History at the University of Granada and was responsible for various core subjects for graduate studies in history, art history and architecture. Her publi-cations include 'Imagen y poder español en la Florencia medicea: La Capilla de los Españoles de Santa María Novella', in J. L. Castellano and M. L. López-Gua-dalupe Muñoz (eds), *Actas de la XI Reunión Científica de la Fundación Española de Historia Moderna*, Volume 1 (2012), pp. 361–72, and 'Presencia y mecenazgo español en la Florencia medicea del Quinientos', *Anales de Historia del Arte*, 23 (2013), pp. 395–406.

Francesco Guidi-Bruscoli is Assistant Professor at the University of Florence, where he teaches economic history. He is also an honorary fellow of the uni-versities of London (Queen Mary), Bristol and York, and a fellow of the Royal Historical Society. In 1999 his PhD thesis was awarded the Young Scholar Prize by the European Association for Banking History; in 2007 he was *Enseignant invité* at the Université Paris 7; and in 2010 he was a fellow of the Beinecke Library, Yale University. He specializes in the history of trade and banking in the Renaissance and is currently involved in several international research projects. His publications include numerous articles in scientific journals, collections of essays and a volume entitled *Papal Banking in Renaissance Rome* (Aldershot:

Ashgate, 2007). His book on Bartolomeo Marchionni, a Florentine merchant in Lisbon in the age of the European expansion, is currently in press.

Christof Jeggle is Research Associate at the University of Bamberg and of the ANR-research project 'Les privilèges économiques en Europe, XVᵉ–XIXᵉ siècles: étude quantitative et comparative', Université Paris 1, Panthéon–Sorbonne/ ENS Lyon. He received his MA (1992) and his PhD ('Linen from Münster: Westphalia in the Sixteenth and Seventeenth Centuries', 2009) in modern history at the Free University of Berlin. He has co-edited three books and published thirty essays and articles on the topics of pre-industrial production and commerce, the social constitution of markets and the cultures of economies, including the article 'Pre-industrial Worlds of Production: Conventions, Institutions and Organizations' in R. Diaz-Bone and R. Salais (eds), 'Conventions and Institutions from a Historical Perspective', a special issue of *Historische Sozialforschung/Historical Social Research*, 36:4 (2011), pp. 125–49.

Evelyn Korsch is Research Associate of the DFG-project *Material Culture and Consumption in Early Modern Europe*. After receiving her PhD in history at the University of Zurich in 2009 (*Bilder der Macht. Venezianische Repräsentationsstrategien beim Staatsbesuch Heinrichs III. (1574)*, Berlin: Akademie, 2013), she worked in several research projects on early modern markets and is currently engaged in research on Armenian trading networks during the seventeenth and eighteenth centuries.

Heinrich Lang is holding a *Gerda Henkel Foundation*-research grant and is Lecturer on Early Modern History at the University of Bamberg. He obtained his PhD in 2006 on 'Cosimo de' Medici il vecchio, the Orators and the Condottieri. Diplomacy and Wars of the Florentine Republic in the Middle of the 15th Century', published as *Cosimo de' Medici, die Gesandten und die Condottieri. Diplomatie und Kriege der Republik Florenz im 15. Jahrhundert.* (Paderborn: Schöningh, 2009). He worked in several research projects on commercial history at the University of Bamberg and has published several articles on Renaissance military and economic history, and on South German and Florentine merchant bankers active in Lyon.

Flávio Miranda is a postdoctoral researcher at the Nova University of Lisbon (Instituto de Estudos Medievais), University of Porto (CITCEM) and University of Cambridge (Faculty of Economics), and works on merchant communities and economic institutions in the later Middle Ages. He received his PhD at the University of Porto for his dissertation 'Portugal and the Medieval Atlantic: Commercial Diplomacy, Merchants, and Trade, 1143–1488'. He has published articles on Portuguese commercial networks and books on the history of Porto.

Stefania Montemezzo is completing her PhD in economic history at the University of Verona. Her research lies in the fields of economic and social history, with a special focus on merchants' networks during the Renaissance. She edited the book *Giovanni Foscari. Viaggi di Fiandra, 1463–1464 e 1467–1468* (Venice: La Malcontenta, 2012). She is currently engaged in research on the Venetian trade system between Northern Europe and Asia during the late fifteenth century.

Angela Orlandi is Associate Professor at the University of Florence. Her research includes studies on merchants in the Mediterranean and the Atlantic during the late medieval and early modern periods, with a focus on networks and institutions. She has focused in particular on Tuscan colonies, financial and insurance mechanisms and economic and juridical relationships. She is the author of *Le Grand Parti. Fiorentini a Lione e il debito pubblico francese nel XVI secolo* (Florence: L. S. Olschki, 2002) and 'Les précurseurs des voyageurs et représentants de commerce parmi les hommes d'affaires toscans de la Renaissance (fin XIVe-début XVIe siècle)', *Entreprises et Histoire*, 66 (2012), pp. 22–36.

LIST OF FIGURES AND TABLES

INTRODUCTION

Andrea Caracausi and Christof Jeggle

The Aim of the Book

This volume deals with commercial networks and how they were related to cities in the late medieval and early modern periods. Over the last few decades a number of books and articles have been published on trade, merchants and commercial institutions, encompassing European and – especially – non-European countries, showing the complexity of trading mechanisms, and discussing the constitution of groups, formal or informal associations, cross-cultural relations and religious boundaries across the world. Despite this rich amount of studies, the formation of networks, the exchanges between various networks and their relation to local or supra-local institutions, and the ways networks have influenced the territories they encompassed is still an open debate. This book therefore aims to contribute to this debate by presenting in-depth research on various parts of Europe mostly during the period at the beginning of overseas expansion, and demonstrating the opportunities of using the methodologies of social network analysis.

The paradigm of networks is well established for the study of merchants as well as for research in the social and economic history of the medieval and early modern periods. Networks generated by situated social interactions are increasingly being considered the base of studying social organization. The approach of multiple networks allows for linking commercial and other social interactions taking place in the cities. Cities and commerce were closely linked, and most large cities can be described as nodes, hubs and gateways of commercial relations. Thus the essays in this volume take as their starting point cities that were commercial centres. On this basis, the essays aim to reflect the state of research of different aspects of network study in commercial history, and to focus on the ways commercial networks were structured, what kinds of structural patterns they formed, and how different structures of networks were linked to specific commercial practices and to the social and economic development of medieval and early modern cities. The volume thus presents exemplary case studies presently being done on commercial networks related to different cities and offers a comparative view of the ways merchant networks influenced urban life, and how the specific forms of social and cultural life at certain places shaped commercial networks. Merchant networks generated the flow of material goods, money and other values. They constituted the core of urban economies and markets, influencing the governance of the cities. In addition to commercial exchange, these networks established the infrastructure for the dispersion of cultural artefacts and practices as well as for migration between cities.[1]

Trade is recognized as a key factor in the development of urban economies both on the regional and interregional levels. Since the 'commercial revolution' of the late Middle Ages, commercial networks constituted influential social structures across Europe and beyond the surrounding seas, reaching a global dimension with the expansion of European trade relations.[2] Commercial networks did not simply connect all kinds of merchants with each other. Depending on social and cultural factors such as kinship, origin, religion, local commercial practices, means of transportation and the types of products, different kinds of networks developed that were to some degree separated from each other, while cities offered the locations where interfaces like markets could be established for exchange between different networks. The social coherence of networks influenced the structures of urban societies because the actors constituted social groups – for example merchant communities – within the urban society that were creating or were forced into own infrastructures within the cities.[3]

The present volume does not understand social networks simply as a metaphorical term for describing any kind of social relation; rather, it refers to social network analysis as a tool for the reconstruction and analysis of social relations among merchants. In economic history, different concepts of 'networks' are deployed;[4] within business history, in particular, networks are understood as a specific form of business organization along with firms and markets.[5] However, in this volume the network approach is used as a tool for analysing all kinds of patterns of merchants' social organization, not just forms of business organization.[6] When talking about networks beyond the metaphorical sense, the particular quality of social interaction has to be taken in consideration.[7] The minimum requirements for social networks as an analytical category include frequent social relationships – occasional or singular encounters do not necessarily constitute a network. A network also needs at least three frequently interacting persons, while single pairs of interacting persons do not comprise a network.[8] Streams of goods and values may also be considered network ties, even if not every single transaction can be drawn back to particular persons; in these cases the frequency and volume of exchanges are decisive.[9] As the structural approach of social network analysis has already proven useful for showing the structures of commercial networks, more recent studies have emphasized the different types and qualities of social ties. It has become clear that merchants were tied in multiple networks of kinship, origin, religion and business relations. Hence the essays in the volume focus on approaches that are based on situated social interactions from which these social networks emerge within urban settings.

The State of Research

From the beginnings of commercial history as a field of study in the nineteenth century, the ties maintained by merchants in respect of business relations and social surrounding have been investigated as a strategy of research.[10] In this way some merchants or merchant families such as the Medici,[11] Francesco Datini[12] or Jakob and Anton Fugger[13] and others became quite prominent. After social network analysis was developed and established in the social sciences from the 1960s onwards,[14] the notion of the 'network' began to appear in commercial history studies in the 1990s.[15] The term became popular in the field, with many publications somehow referring to networks; this makes it difficult to distinguish those studies that are actually based on a systematic analysis of the patterns of commercial or merchant networks.

Among the first who applied the approach of social network analysis in the late 1990s were Leos Müller, who included a quantifying correspondence analysis in his examination of merchant networks,[16] and Mark Häberlein, who based his network analysis of the Weyer in Augsburg on the categories of kinship and legal interaction.[17] About ten years later, several studies appeared which may be taken as an indication that social network analysis slowly became established not only as a metaphorical term but also as an approach for the structured analysis of networks.[18] Eberhard Crailsheim decided to analyse the private and commercial networks within the French and Flemish merchant communities in Seville for four periods between 1580 and 1640 with the aid of social network analysis because of the large volume of data.[19] Long-term developments of social change were studied by Quentin Van Dooselaere on the base of thousands of Genoese notarial records from 1150 to 1435, which provided data on about 20,000 commercial relations covering business partnerships, credit networks and insurances.[20] Maximilian Kalus tried to improve the existing banks for collecting network data by developing a semantic databank with which he analysed the data of the sixteenth-century European-Asiatic trade of merchants from Southern Germany.[21] Besides general considerations of how the quantitative analysis of historical business networks might look like,[22] Sheryllyne Haggerty showed that kinship ties were not always helpful for operating in eighteenth-century transatlantic networks.[23] Ana Sofia Vieira Ribeiro conducted a series of social network analyses of the different networks of the influential Spanish merchant Simon Ruiz who was based in sixteenth-century Medina del Campo.[24] For the

French Atlantic trade in the eighteenth century, Pierre Gervais analysed business accounts and reconstructed the links between the people registered, thus showing the ties between the transfer of goods and credit relations.[25] Based on the transactions presented in the commercial handbook of C. F. Gaignat de l'Aulnais entitled *Guide de commerce* (1773), Cheryl S. McWatters and Yannick Lemarchand analysed the structure and density of the business networks behind the entries in the accounts.[26]

While these studies remain rather singular, for the Hanse area several studies have appeared. During the Middle Ages large centralized merchant companies did not appear in the Hanse area, and trade within networks is considered a typical characteristic of Hanseatic commerce. While Ulf Christian Ewert and Stephan Selzer developed a theoretical economic model,[27] several studies aimed to reconstruct the network structures of the Hanse merchants.[28] Carsten Jahnke analysed the networks of the merchants Bernd Pal III and Hans Selhorst and the change of business practices in Reval around 1500.[29] The most extensive systematic work to date was done by Mike Burkhardt with his analysis of the changing structures of networks of the fifteenth-century *Bergenfahrer*.[30] Dietrich Poeck also collected extensive data about the delegates of the Hanse diets in 1379 and 1418;[31] however, while Poeck's book impressively shows how the delegates were linked by all kinds of ties, and provides numerous graphics of network stars centred around single delegates, a through network analysis of the social structures was not conducted.[32]

The fact that many authors still include rather detailed introductions to social network analysis in their research shows that certain standards for applying the approach have not yet been established. Yet the basic idea all authors share is to focus not on single merchants, as the heroic historiographies of single merchants and companies have often done, but on relations between people. The kinds of relations become increasingly more differentiated, while the scope of possible types of ties is closely linked to the data available in the documents. While looking to the relatedness of people as an approach for doing historical research may now go well go beyond the field of analysing commercial networks, the possibilities for conducting social network analyses have to be seen in light of their premises and limitations. A certain volume of consistent data is necessary to be able to start reconstructing social networks. As the available studies show, this is not a question of the historical period or place but of the quality of the extant historical material. The historical documents can set limits in respect of making a social network analysis, and they may turn out as insufficient for going beyond a reconstruction of rather accidental relations of single persons while the systematic reconstruction and analysis of networks remains impossible.[33] Thus serial material seems to be of advantage; otherwise it can be difficult to collect a significant volume of data of a consistent quality that allows for connecting a significant number of people based on equivalent criteria. At the same time, commercial history looks back on a long tradition of prosopographical and genealogical research, and collecting and preparing dispersed data seems to be more a question of obtainable resources in respect of time for research and databank technologies.

All studies of commercial networks highlight the fact that social network analysis is ultimately a tool for making the structural aspects of webs of actors visible; the structural patterns themselves need to be interpreted to give them explanatory value. Indeed, many authors have emphasized the limited explanatory range of quantitative network analyses. The factors that have been analysed by the few quantitative studies are average connectivity, density, centrality, betweenness and path length, and in some cases also clusters. Here some common approaches of research seem to develop. Quantitative analyses only make sense if the volume of data is large enough to provide some statistical relevance. This is not always the case, but the idea of social network analysis can also be used for mapping the often intricate ties of commercial actors and the streams of goods and values. Patterns such as structural holes or central nodes can also be detected without quantifying, and these can give important hints about the structures of social interaction.[34] It also has to be recognized that the quantitative analysis of networks originates from those approaches to social network analysis that were directed on social structures as given frameworks of social action. These approaches have already been criticized by Harrison C. White, a protagonist of mathematical network analysis, and others since the early 1990s; meanwhile pragmatic approaches for a relational interaction sociology have been introduced,[35] wherein social network structures are taken not as a framework but as a result of social interaction, and patterns of multiple networks give indications for repertoires and practices of interacting.[36] These approaches deserve more attention for working with the concept of social networks as the result, not the premise, of social interaction. The idea of relational sociology also offers the opportunity for systematically linking different kinds of interacting, like exchanging goods, communicating or different fields of interaction beyond business operations.[37] Within this framework, the French approach of the *économie des conventions*, the actor network theory and the sociology of markets should also find more reception in commercial history.[38] The essays included in this volume provide case studies featuring network analysis as a tool for qualitative analysis of commercial interaction.

The Parts and Chapters

The book is organized into four parts that offer different perspectives on the study of economic history using social network analysis. The first part, 'Approaches', discusses the conceptual approaches, tools and methods applied by network analysis, which might be useful for the study of economic history. The second part provides different perspectives on 'Merchants', analysing firms, their internal cohesion and their formal associations. The third part on 'Markets and Institutions' is about commercial networks and the institutional frameworks of markets. The final part focuses on 'Products' in order to examine commercial networks as networks of production and distribution.

These essays discuss a set of basic questions that were taken as the point of departure:

- What were the social and economic structures of commercial networks?
- What kinds of interfaces connected different networks? Which factors constituted boundaries, and how were different networks connected, for example for the transfer of goods and values?
- What kind of impact did commercial networks have on urban life, and did urban life influence commercial networks?

The first point that emerges from the volume is the variety of social and economic structures of networks. The first step in working with networks as an analytical approach is to define the networks under investigation. Hence each essay defines its concept of 'network' and the particular social and economic data on which it is based, while some basic assumptions are shared across the volume: networks are based on voluntary participation without formal membership or organization, and the participants aim at a shared goal with the help of the network. The participants must expect some advantages deriving from the transfer of resources throughout the network, even if they fail in practice. At least three people have to interact frequently, and each actor within the network must have at least two ties to other participants.

Networks emerge from different forms of economic and social interactions. Commercial and financial transactions make up different relationships such as exchange operations, single-venture arrangements, short- and medium-term loans and limited liability contracts. As shown in several essays (especially those by Mike Burkhardt, Heinrich Lang, David Carvajal de la Vega and Benedetta Crivelli), commercial networks are not only based on business relations, they are also embedded in multiple and synergetic structures that reach beyond business. Distinct layers of networks – commerce, banking, knowledge – are entangled with relationships of special qualities such as kinship, business partnerships, common origin, political partisanship and shared economic interests. Long-distance merchants usually were only retailers on the side, and their main occupation was business-to-business trade with other merchants. Thus some social and cultural coherence may have developed and stabilized businesses and networks. The success of the enterprise depended greatly on the specific qualities of these networks – in some cases networks as a resource outside markets were sufficient to counterbalance economic difficulties. Although the agents involved in financial and trading activities structured their networks around ties based on kinship, origin and friendships, their actions demonstrated a desire to extend such ties in order to be able to react in cases of structural weakness that could cause the collapse of the complex system in which they operated. The cases of the Portuguese merchants analysed by Flávio Miranda and the Datini companies examined by Angela Orlandi show that the different solutions applied depend greatly on the particular situation. Merchants did not necessarily form new mechanisms of commerce, but they were able to take advantage of pre-existing trade routes, markets and institutions, adopting short-term commercial linkages and trading contacts that usually involved agents and other middlemen. As Miranda shows, these circumstances determined whether merchants acted as network takers, in trying to form links with already established networks, or as network makers, by attempting to set up networks of their own. Commercial networks were not always stories of success, as Lang shows. Shifts in interests could result in processes of exclusion and retreat. Yet unlike institutions that may collapse or at least require reorganization if one of the partners leaves or is excluded, in the case of the network the partners could withdraw their engagement without much conflict.

In respect of commercial networks, different dimensions have to be distinguished. Merchants need something to offer; they need sources for these products; and they need someone who is interested in buying these things. This may sound mundane, but it makes clear that merchants are destined to link different kinds of people, often at different times and in different places. At the same time, merchants are carriers of goods and values. Since merchandise and payments are not necessarily being transported by the merchants themselves, further relations emerge. Therefore different kinds of ties have to be considered: those of the direct interaction of merchants when they are communicating, negotiating or joining business enterprises; those ties that come up with the exchange, processing and distribution of goods; and those for compensating the costs by transferring payments and which balance the transfers of goods. Another dimension is introduced in directing long-distance trade from the office by communicating with agents and commissions by letter. The art of operating the business was also the art of coordinating successfully these various dimensions of network ties, as failure in one dimension could affect the others. Though it would be important to study all these parallel ties, the essays here show that often only a selection can be investigated. In this case the other kinds of ties have to be taken into consideration as possible factors that may influence those being observed. There is no sale of goods without payment and no transfer of payment without reason, and merchants usually did not travel to far-off places just to socialize.

The different dimensions of network ties demanded a variety of competences. Depending on the kinds of goods they were dealing with, merchants needed a specialized connoisseurship of their products.[39] Therefore merchants usually specialized in a certain selection of goods because they needed a substantial knowledge of production processes, while the product qualities were also closely linked to the particular practices of trade on specialized markets. From the perspective of commercial networks, it may be more advantageous not to consider general markets, maybe subdivided in segments but covering all kinds of goods, and instead to think of specialized markets made up of merchants who considered themselves as being equivalent actors dealing with equivalent goods. In terms of products and their qualities, networks might appear much more differentiated because merchants operated within a particular logic necessary to trade certain goods successfully. Markets are interfaces within the networks of production and distribution: they offer a form of exchange that allows the connection of different sub-networks along a product line without the necessity of maintaining social ties between the agents of the different networks. This aspect is especially important when we consider transcultural trade relations where cultural restraints restricted the emergence of social ties but both sides were interested in exchanging goods.

As seen in the following essays, payments not only served as compensation for delivered goods, credits also created their own networks of obligation. Merchants needed substantial competences to participate in the practices of payment, which were manifold. In many cases the payments occurred in quite different ways to the goods, which increased the complexity of commercial networks, while the merchants had to take care that their accounts were balanced in the long run. In many essays another aspect of financial ties is revealed: often merchants gave to political authorities, which usually were in permanent need of money. Besides speculating on good returns for these investments, when merchants provided loans to political authorities it was often with the intention of reaching some other goal, for example access to the nobility or the improvement of their own immigrant status.

Business history is often focused on single firms, but their significance varies in the essays: while some take firms as a point of reference for their case studies, in others they are not central. Although there has been some debate on firms as vertically integrated organizations and networks as alternative, horizontal forms of business organization, this distinction is not very explicitly discussed. In the case of the Datini group, Orlandi considers both internal and external networks and thus integrates the network into the structures of the firm. In other essays it is not always clear whether people acted on their own or as representatives of their companies. Perhaps this is due the small size of many merchant companies, which were often made up of only a few people; and all kinds of delegated or commissioned trade make it even more difficult to distinguish the roles of the actors. While it seems easy to differentiate between firms and networks on a theoretical level, in the situation of social interaction it needs to be figured out whom people were representing in their interactions with others. As conflicts have shown, even the actors themselves were not always sure about the status of their business partners.

Most of the essays indicate that relations of kinship likely constituted the most important networks of social interaction for merchants, as most of their businesses were based on their kin group.[40] Merchant capital was often based on the collective property of a kinship network.[41] These networks developed a large variety of businesses, depending on size, kind and location.[42] Kinship networks structured the social relations of the merchant communities both within and between cities (see for example Carvajal de la Vega's essay on merchant networks in the cities of Castile). Within the cities, kinship networks often constituted influential factions of political life; between cities, they made up the framework for commercial relations but also for diplomacy. Despite the great relevance of kinship, it should not be overestimated because merchants often realized that the people to whom they were related were not always advantageous to their business. As Orlandi discusses, Francesco Datini seems to have been reluctant to draw too much on relatives, and Mike Burkhardt also shows the declining relevance of kinship ties among the *Bergenfahrer*. Hence even in the Middle Ages kinship and business ties were already seen as rather distinct qualities of social relationships. On the other hand, as Evelyn Korsch shows, the early modern Armenians built their businesses primarily on kinship ties. Here the perspective of network analysis makes it clear that there was no general relevance of kinship ties for merchants; the importance of these ties depended on the particular situation and social circumstances. Another aspect that deserves more attention when looking at kinship ties is the involvement of the women, who often provided both part of the capital and access to urban or noble elites.

Communication is one of the essential components of social networks, and the importance of language for the formation and evolution of networks is discussed in a number of the essays. This important competence for communicating has often been ignored by historical studies on commercial networks.[43] Francesco Guidi-Bruscoli examines how merchants carried out their trade in spite of the obstacles of operating with foreign languages; different languages therefore did not mean insuperable barriers. Speaking a language fluently could be an important way to bridge the communication gap and avoid the services of brokers or translators who could distort meanings. When trading was impossible because the merchants could not communicate, different solutions had to be found; this gave factors and agents who were members of the same community in places abroad further relevance. The Datini group, as shown in Orlandi's essay, was largely operated by Tuscan merchants who communicated through the exchange of letters. When they tried to expand their business, they began to learn the local idioms in order to be able to communicate with Catalan merchants. On the other hand, the merchants travelling from Venice to north-western Europe, analysed in Stefania Montemezzo's essay, were usually rather young and made their journeys on state galleys to unknown cities, without access to established webs of correspondents and with limited knowledge of the local language. They were forced to rely on networks of agents – often of the same origin – who would be willing to help by sharing their resources and local contacts. Whereas some languages, like Italian, were important for business communication, merchants would try to have agents who were able to communicate in the local language; the use of interpreters, however, was a choice to be made with care because of the danger of disclosure of information to third parties. In addition to professional interpreters, there were other authorities whose linguistic expertise could compensate for the merchants' shortcomings: brokers, notaries, scriveners and others could bring different parties together and act as agents in the strengthening of the network-building process.

The second point the volume analyses concerns the kinds of interfaces between different networks. The new institutional economics has long discussed whether goods and values were preferably exchanged on markets or within hierarchies or networks.[44] Thus the essays focus on the ways in which goods and values were transferred between different networks, either on the basis of direct exchange or through markets that could be established as an open interface at the edges of different networks in order to bridge cultural differences (see the essay by Christof Jeggle in particular). Hence the focus on the organization of exchanges between different networks became crucial. Some essays, especially those by Francesco Ammannati and Blanca González Talavera, David Carvajal de la Vega, Flávio Miranda and Stefania Montemezzo, show how the institutional framework in some cities could help and influence the establishment of networks. Institutions like consulates can be considered as devices that facilitated merchant networks by collecting taxes, providing assistance, being guarantors and brokers, and acting as agents, especially in the case of travelling or mobile merchants. This was particularly true when networks depended on the rules of institutional behaviour imposed by the states, such as in the case of the Venetian consuls who acted as intermediaries for several payments by letters of exchange during the galley voyages. The characteristics of the urban infrastructures can influence the constitutions of networks, especially in the case of travelling merchants. If the cities were well organized, with a strong institutional presence, travelling merchants could rely on more expert compatriots who hosted and guided them in their contact with native traders. Institutional design and urban policies could also influence the kind and volume of exchanges, where actors of trade were more subject to strict regulation, as in the case of England and Flanders at the end of the fifteenth century. In many commercial centres (discussed in the contributions by Andrea Caracausi and Evelyn Korsch), commercial exchanges and urban policies influenced each other reciprocally. Privileges and grants attracted the flow of goods and the relocation of merchants but also sustained technological dissemination and migrations flows.[45] The case of the Scerimans during the eighteenth century is emblematic because it shows how movement across cities followed the economic trends of the centres involved and the opportunities that those places offered in terms of economic pursuits.

Finally, the third point being analysed in the volume is the impact of merchants on the urban environment and especially the relations between commercial and production networks. Research on trade history has normally underlined the role of merchants in disseminating merchandise, especially new novelties and fashionable objects. Nevertheless, as many essays demonstrate, the movement of goods was only one side of the story. Commercial networks radically influenced the rise and fall of manufacturing activities as well as the migration of people. Markets emerged as a form of social interaction that is far more complex than simply considering the two parties of supply and demand, without recognizing the dimension of quality in respect of the actors and the products. The production and distribution of goods are closely linked and should be analysed in their interrelations. Distinguishing different kinds of markets allows for a better understanding of business practices and strategies in relation to different kinds of product qualities. In particular, the essays by Caracausi, and Ammannati and González show the predominance of commercial (and financial) capital on production markets. The rise and decline of local industries relied largely on decisions made in terms of investment flows (in the form of raw materials) by those merchants who controlled the commercial routes. Combining production and distribution markets, merchant-entrepreneurs of the early modern period were able to influence production and urban politics, disseminating human capital as well as product and process innovations across cities. Commercial history should be seen as an element of a comprehensive analysis of historical economies, which comprise agriculture and manufacturing in their entanglement with commerce.

With their focus on the commercial relations between the Mediterranean and the Central and Northern parts of Europe, these case studies complement each other, offering a long-term perspective on the changing structures of commercial networks across European cities. The Mediterranean and Western Europe constitute the core region being studied in the essays included here. In recent decades much research has been done on overseas trade, looking at the relations going outside of Europe, and for some time the decreasing importance of the Mediterranean for European commerce has been emphasized. In our opinion it remains important to present and analyse new research on Continental commerce, on which, ultimately, European global commerce was based. The studies in this volume offer a number of links and interfaces for connecting (and comparing) with research on other regions; indeed, almost all of the developments of Continental commerce can only be fully understood within a global framework.[46] These case studies show exemplary parts of a wider globalizing economy, and they are focused on transnational flows going beyond political borders. Furthermore, recent research in the field of global history also has shown the relevance of the Mediterranean region during the early modern period in transmitting consumption models and human capital, but also in influencing global patterns.[47] Even in today's globalized world, the region is subject to an intense discussion, not as a prime economic player but as a hub between three continents that has to be taken into serious consideration in many respects.

1 NETWORKS AS SOCIAL STRUCTURES IN LATE MEDIEVAL AND EARLY MODERN TOWNS: A THEORETICAL APPROACH TO HISTORICAL NETWORK ANALYSIS

Mike Burkhardt

Historical Network Analysis

Network is a popular term in contemporary historical research papers and articles. It is rare to find a journal without at least one article that to some extent discusses networks which are found in the relations between the subjects being investigated. However, when we take a closer look at these networks, they often turn out to be nothing more than a couple of relations between a certain person and his/her surroundings. Thus the word network is merely used as a metaphor, a trendy term to attract potential readers. With its vagueness and lack of a determined definition, it is regarded as suitable to describe a huge variety of social relations that otherwise are hard to define. Ylva Hasselberg pinpointed this tendency when she observed: 'If the people that we are working with don't belong to a class or professional group, maybe it is a network!?'[1] When I started my research project on the web of economic and social ties between Hanse merchants on the Norwegian market about ten years ago, I decided to work with the term network as the overall description for this phenomenon. In the year 2001 this term and approach sounded very reasonable, as network was already established as a concept used in many scientific and intellectual discourses. Social sciences and economics had at that time paved the methodological pathway to investigating networks, and even in the humanities the term was widely used in many contexts.

As I was asked for a more theoretical essay about the problems and benefits of network research in historical contexts, I reconsidered many of the arguments in favour of the network theory proposed by many historians, myself included. The core conclusion to emerge from my re-evaluation was that the approach still is worth research efforts, but that the term is no longer useful in all fields of historical research.

Some ten years back the term network was mainly used as a technical description for organized meshes. No matter what field of research was involved, the aim of network theory was always to show genuine structural patterns of networks which could be quantitatively analysed. However, in the meantime the term has changed its meaning. In the common adoption, the term network often means a metaphorical sphere of more or less loose relations between people, thoughts or even technical units. This change did not occur all of a sudden, as the use of the term in this way was already common in the field of history in the 1990s. If a historian could not define the group he or she was investigating precisely, the attractive, loosely defined term network was always available and often misused. Hitherto we have found it in many contexts which do not describe networks and which specifically lack an empirically based line of argument for coming to the conclusion that a network is indeed being investigated.

Social network analysis is a field of research in the social sciences. Its methods and theory had already been established by the first half of the twentieth century. However, over the last thirty years the volume of network studies has increased immensely; and with computers becoming more powerful and easy to use, the technical conditions required to run a large-scale analysis have improved significantly.

In contrast to other fields of research in the social sciences, network analysis is not directed towards the attributes of the agents. It is focused on their relations.[2] For example, the network analyst does not ask how a person is affected by his or her profession or social status, but rather what consequences relations with other people have in terms of success or failure, the sense of well- or ill-being, influence or powerlessness and so on.

Formally a network is a structure or system that can be described mathematically by a graph.[3] The centre points of the graph are linked according to existing relations between the system components. This mathematical-technical definition is also the basis of definitions of social networks.[4] However, a number of adjustments and extensions are needed in order to obtain a definition that we can work with in an investigation of social relations and their networks. Taking into account the special characteristics of social relations and organization, the following definition may be used as the foundation of social network analysis.

A social network is a group of actors that all are connected to at least two other actors in the group. The foundation of the network is a flow of resources, which are important to all members of the network in order to enable them to reach their goal(s). A social network is a type of social organization where the position of the individual within the group is not determined by hierarchically stipulated patterns, but only by his or her access to resources that are important in the network, and by the qualitative and quantitative strength of its connections to other members of the network. A social network is a dynamic pattern.

Its size, structure, social influence and goals may vary and change. It will disintegrate when the common goal, which is shared by its members, is achieved or regarded as no longer achievable with the network.[5]

If we decide to work with networks as an analytical approach, the first and foremost step is to define the network under investigation very thoroughly. The social sciences and economics have provided us with several useful definitions and methods regarding network analysis. However, since our data sources are very different from modern empirical investigations, we should not hesitate to change and adapt these definitions to our own methodological approaches. First of all, though, it is necessary to find out whether we are really focusing on a network or not.

The best negative example here is the classical model of social network analysis – a school class. School classes are often described as perfect examples of networks. They are convenient to study, since it is very easy to define the boundaries of the network. However, according to standard definitions of networks in the social sciences, a school class is not a network. There is no common voluntary goal that pupils try to reach when cooperating with other pupils in their school class (if they have any goal at all). There is no possibility for a pupil to voluntarily enter or leave the 'network'. Thus school classes are enforced communities, with a limited choice of connections and relations. This example shows how problematic and misleading the use of the term network can be.

Theoretically and methodologically there are certain criteria that have to be met in order to allow us to speak of networks. A network has at least to meet the following criteria:

- Participation must be voluntary.
- There must be a shared goal which participants aim at with the help of the network.
- There must be advantages deriving from transfer of resources throughout the network.
- They must have flat hierarchies.
- Each actor within the network must have at least two ties to other participants in the network.
- There must be no formal membership or organization.

If these criteria are met, we might be on the verge of detecting a network. Still, there is a long way to go to be sure that there is (or was) a network with a certain endeavour. As network analysts, we sometimes feel tempted to accept every relation a person has as part of his or her social network. Historians in particular tend to do so, as we often lack adequate data to provide our actors with a sufficient number of relevant contacts. Still, the woman at the bakery, who sells bread to me and whom I talk to every morning, does not necessarily belong to my social network, not to mention my economic, political or ecological network.

In this example another problem becomes apparent. Every person is part of several networks. According to the aims and goals that people are interested in, we might even detect networks of which the agents under investigation were not actively aware. This means that we draw artificial borders and boundaries based on our scientific interpretations for research purposes. On the one hand this approach constitutes reasonable scientific practice, while on the other hand it is contrary to the realm of experience of our agents. It also makes it very difficult to decide whether a certain contact might be part of one network or another.

Since sources on particular individuals are often very scarce, the time frame of our networks will often turn up another problem. Usually network diagrams are images of a moment in time. Affinities and goals might change overnight, and thus a network may look different every day. In the case of historical studies, a network diagram might cover several years because information is only available for periods of time. Thus some of the members of our virtual network might already have died or left the network for various reasons when others entered. However, within a more structural approach this method might still lead to new answers. For example through their institutionalized *memoria*, medieval urban religious brotherhoods can be understood as a network of many people, both dead and living, which lasted for generations and was reproduced by certain rituals over a very long time.

Another problematic point is the measurement of quality within a person's relations. Even modern social network analysis has its difficulties in defining the strength of ties between two individuals, though most sociologists would disagree with me on this statement. But as the historian's questions depend on sources that have survived rather accidentally, it is far more difficult for us to find out how close people felt to each other, how frequently they really met and how intense their interactions might have been. The details of interaction are lost and only the written documents survive – at least for the period being considered here. Thus the contacts we find documented are rather occasional. Business papers, last wills, letters, tax registers and membership rolls provide only highly selective information. In many cases this problem remains unsolvable, but the written documentation prevents us from intentionally manipulating information about the actors being studied during the survey and the results of our studies. What is found in the sources has been recorded in particular historical situations which have to be taken into consideration in order to evaluate the data. In contrast to the social sciences, we cannot ask our actors questions that might lead to misleading or hushed answers.

With all these problems and obstacles in mind, and particularly with regard to the very strict requirements a network has to satisfy in order to be subject to social network analysis, I would like to suggest the use of another term for most of the social webs in historical investigations. If we are quite sure that a network has existed, but we do not have enough empirical evidence to meet all of the criteria, the term 'linkage' would be more reasonable.[6] An advantage of this term would be that it is not as loaded with ideas and prejudices as the term network, and it is already used by social network analysis to describe weaker bonds in between a group of agents. Despite of all the difficulties mentioned, I still regard historical network analysis as very promising and worth applying to research.

Important terms in network analysis are *nodes*, the dots which represent a single individual or object in the pattern; *diads*, which signify the connection between two nodes; and *triads*, which describe three nodes that are connected with each other, thus creating a triangle and representing the smallest possible unit of a network. *Stars* are important nodes with a lot of relations in the network; *clusters* are groups of nodes which are densely connected with each other; and a *broker* is a node that is the only one in the mesh that has a relation to a part of another network. Thus a broker is able to decide which resources flow from one to the other network.[7]

The expert in the field of social network analysis might find this short introduction far too incomplete and immature. Several essential terms such as density, centrality, cores and cliques are not mentioned, nor are any of the structural conclusions which are drawn from a network analysis explained. As the main objective of this essay is to show how network analysis can be applied to historical studies, the reader may refer to textbooks and articles specially focusing on the methods and techniques of social network analysis for explanations of the abovementioned terms.[8]

All of the problems mentioned earlier need to be taken into consideration before we go into a detailed network study. The first part of such an operation must always be the extremely demanding and difficult task of prosopographical and biographical research. It is absolutely necessary to collect hundreds or even thousands of pieces of data and to integrate them into a system of matrices and categories before we can move on from talking of a network in a merely metaphorical sense to historical network analysis in the proper sense. It is not enough to have the feeling that there might be a network or a linkage. If I talk about a network, I need to be able to prove that it existed. And the base of proof for a network analysis is found in empirical data collection. After collecting the data, we have various options to choose for our research focus. We can decide to carry out our research on the macro, meso or micro level.[9]

Often we will find that networks on the macro scale are too large and complex to provide us with useful information other than that a very large network existed. The macro level takes into account all links and relations within a certain network. Thus the structures which result from such research can be huge and consequently confusing. Still, they provide us with proof that a network actually existed, as opposed to merely a large number of connections leading from or to a certain individual.

On the meso level, investigations concerning core groups and clusters within the larger network structures are useful. Here we can analyse means of resource transfer as well as the combination of critical positions within networks and powerful positions within a certain society or group. Furthermore we might be able to determine whether connections between members of a core group only consist of a certain kind of relation (political, economic, religious, etc.) or whether there was a multiplicity of different ties between these people.

On the micro level, sociometric stars can be analysed. A variety of possible questions can also be posed. We may ask about contacts based on relations of power or resources and the quality of these ties compared to others, or we can investigate regional, social or economic boundaries and their influence in network-building processes, to name just two possibilities.

Finally, a combined macro-meso-micro analysis seems to me to be the most intriguing methodological approach. Here we can combine the strengths of all three levels and compensate for some of the weaknesses of each.

One very important reason for network research is the simple fact that we need to find out whether there were networks, linkages or other structures which performed resource transfer processes within a certain society and historical period. We need a better understanding of the dynamics and structures behind human decision-making in the past, and network theory is one among many approaches to explaining it. Networks and other kinds of social formation do not exclude each other *per se*. Thus we can also investigate the importance of formal and informal codes and contacts, especially on the political and economic levels. Many historians like to see political structures and hierarchies as the driving forces in political and social developments. Here network analysis can provide us with useful information about influence over decisions and resource flows determined outside the established structures of the political organization of governments. This is not only true for the Middle Ages – during which cooperative elements formed an essential part of the organization of society, especially in towns and cities – but for all kinds of societies as well.

A point of criticism often directed against historical network analysis is the argument that it risks assigning people to networks who might not even have been aware themselves of being a member of that network. However, this is a rather weak argument, since this requires an idea of membership of an organization which *per se* runs contrary to the network concept. A person may very well be part of a network without identifying herself with the network. She might only gather small parts of the information that she requires from the network. However, she is still included in the network structure and might even be – albeit unknowingly – a vital source of information for other participants. Here we enter the macro level, where personal identity and consciousness give way to other concepts and ideas that might be beyond individual awareness. Thus a person might act as an agent in a smaller or larger network without being aware of doing so. Still, as a result of research, we can prove that she is part of this network, which after all would mark the difference between a scientific analysis and random guesswork.

So far most of my considerations have been concerned with the difficulties and perils of historical network analysis. Nevertheless, this should not discourage network research with historical sources. This field of research is still relatively new and undeveloped; we need to be careful and critical in order to make network analysis a successful and useful research tool within historical research as a whole. Municipal archives in particular offer a great variety of sources for network analysis. For each part of the social, economic or political relations of their inhabitants – whether rich or poor, powerful or outsiders – there is enough source material to find linkages and networks alongside and beneath the hierarchical structures that have already been acknowledged by research.

A Case Study: The Networks of the *Bergenfahrer*

The group that I have investigated in my research are the merchants that were active in the stockfish market of the Norwegian town of Bergen in the Late Middle Ages.[10] I have focused on three periods, covering the years 1360–1400, 1440–70 and 1490–1510. These reference periods were chosen due to the availability of source material and political background. In view of the available sources and given the important position of the Hanse merchants in the Bergen trade during the fourteenth and fifteenth centuries, the main focus of my work is these merchants, first and foremost those sailing from Lübeck.

I was able to verify a total of 882 merchants who were active in the Bergen market over the three periods, to which a further 120 should be added. With all their connections in the Baltic and North Sea region, a total of about 1,650 people had to be taken into account. Such a large number of individuals is hard to incorporate into any kind of network analysis. I therefore chose to split the total network up into different meshes, which each represent a certain type of relation. The main groups are the economic and social networks. Economic networks regard trade companies, short-term business connections, loans, and joint customs clearance and charter parties. In the last two cases only those merchants that appeared in the registers could be recognized. Concerning social relations, I examined kinship and friendship, last wills, sureties, membership of merchant corporations, guilds and closed societies, political activities, and investments in the Lübeck property market. For all these aspects of relations I found relatively dense patterns that merit the description as networks. Even after cutting out all of the dead links that did not meet the requirement of at least two connections to other parts of the mesh, in most cases a large number of nodes and relations remained.

After combining all the different 'part' networks, I found extremely large networks in all three periods: indeed, so large that it is impossible to obtain any useful information from the corresponding graphs. For this reason I decided first to analyse smaller meshes in order to present an intelligible picture of the many sub-networks which make up the complex 'entire' networks.

Economic Networks

I will start the description with some examples of the economic networks that made up the foundations of the Hansard's powerful position in the Norwegian market throughout the Late Middle Ages. When we look at the graph which shows the relations between trading companies that were run with at least one *Bergenfahrer* in the second half of the fourteenth century (Figure 1.1), we see a lot of small networks. Most of the merchants had one or two partnerships, which carried the main part of their Bergen trade. Many of the partners bear the same family names, indicating that they were relatives. Two larger structures, however, show that there was a tendency towards more complex holdings. Both larger networks are dominated by kin groups, one made up mainly of the Gronau, the other of the Paal and Wartberch. Obviously kin relations were a very important factor at the time when merchants wished to establish longer-lasting trading partnerships.

In the middle of the fifteenth century we can see a similar pattern with many triads and small networks (Figure 1.2). The biggest difference is that business partners no longer seem to be related by kin. Although we still have a sufficient number of quite dense networks, some of them consisting of five or more actors, and a very long cluster chain with Hinrik Moller as a regional star, kinship ties are no longer a dominant factor in the choice of corporate business partners. Only a few partners could be proved to be members of the same kin group. In most cases the choice of partners was influenced by factors other than common origin or descent. Even in the somewhat larger network centred around Hans Wulff and Sander Wentmeyer, for most of the merchants it is not possible to prove kinship links.

A totally different picture can be observed at the end of the fifteenth century (Figure 1.3). The whole network structure of corporate business partnerships disintegrated. The largest relational pattern found during this phase consisted of five merchants. None of the many triads could be connected to any of the others. Once again kinship did not play a significant role in partner selection.

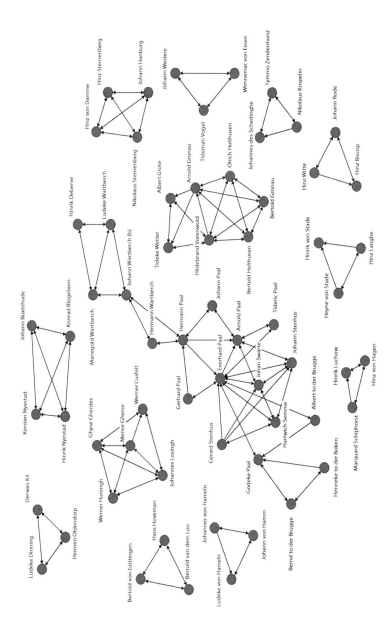

Figure 1.1: Network of companies with at least one *Bergenfahrer* as partner, 1360–1400.

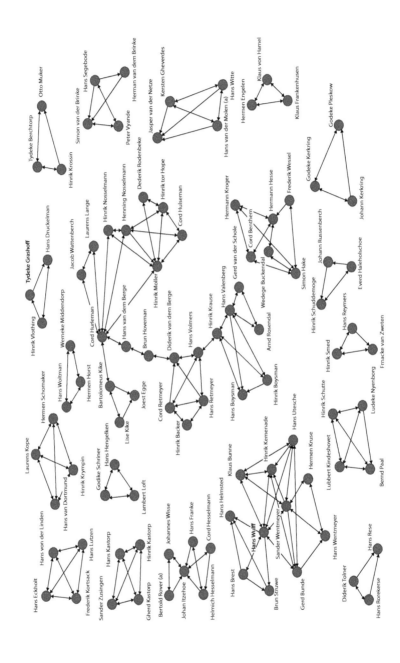

Figure 1.2: Network of companies with at least one *Bergenfahrer* as partner, 1440–70.

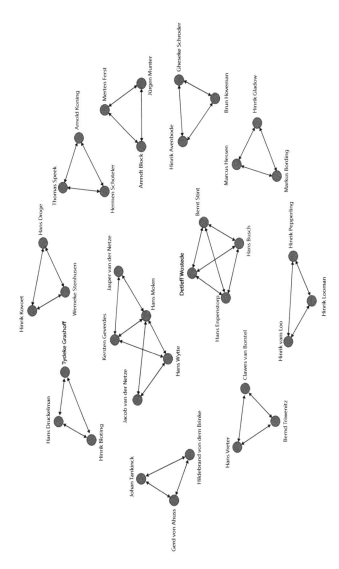

Figure 1.3: Network of companies with at least one *Bergenfahrer* as partner, 1490–1510.

A gradual change can be seen in the way the *Bergenfahrer* organized their long-term business partnerships in the late Middle Ages. While in the last half of the fourteenth century trade corporations were family businesses with a considerable degree of interlocking, kinship ties were not of great importance in the choice of company partners in the second half of the fifteenth and at the turn of the fifteenth to the sixteenth century. An interlocking of trade companies was nearly impossible to prove for the last reference period, in contrast to the first one, where a lot of companies were connected to other trade corporations by the dual engagement of one of the partners.

When examining short-term business contacts, a different situation clearly emerges. Beside a network of six people, which resulted from one single transaction, only one larger mesh of relations can be detected in the second half of the fourteenth century (Figure 1.4). Interestingly, it is concentrated around Everhard Paal, who is also the star of one of the two kin group networks related to corporate business. This provides us with the opportunity to compare both types of relations maintained by one single person. It may be observed that Paal conducted his short-term business transactions mainly with people with whom he did not have kinship ties. The other larger network of short-term trade contacts that is to be found in this period also did not show any kin relations between any of the six members. Thus we may conclude that in the fourteenth century kinship was much less important for participating in short-term transactions than it was in the establishment of long-lasting partnerships.

A much denser pattern of relations regarding short-term business contacts can be observed in the reference period between 1440 and 1470 (Figure 1.5). Several smaller patterns of relations and a larger chain integrating no less than forty-one merchants lead to the assumption that short-term business contacts between unrelated merchants became much more common in the middle of the fifteenth century compared to the situation in the late fourteenth century. Still, most of the contacts were very weak from a network analytical point of view. Several merchants, especially Cord Hurleman and Hinrik Moller, held decisive positions. Their disappearance would have caused the loss of a large number of agents in the resource distribution chain. Thus in this case we cannot speak of a network. Nevertheless, we see many chains of relationships that might be proven to be parts of networks if our source base were larger.

At the turn of the fifteenth to the sixteenth century an even more complex picture is observed (Figure 1.6). Many nodes are linked to each other by different actions, thus creating a stable and dense network of short-term business relations. Here we see a fully fledged network with several central agents and very strong integration of many participants with more than two links to other merchants. Again kinship was only a marginal factor in the establishment of this type of relation.

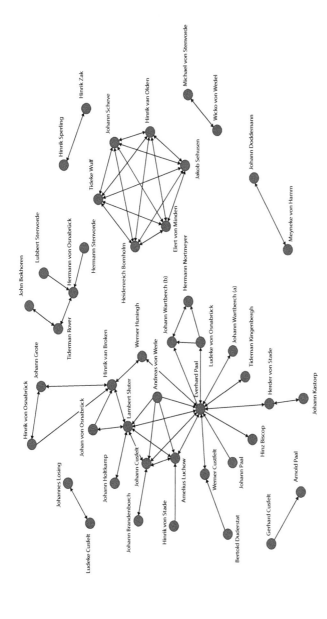

Figure 1.4: Network of the *Bergenfahrer*'s short-term business deals, 1360–1400.

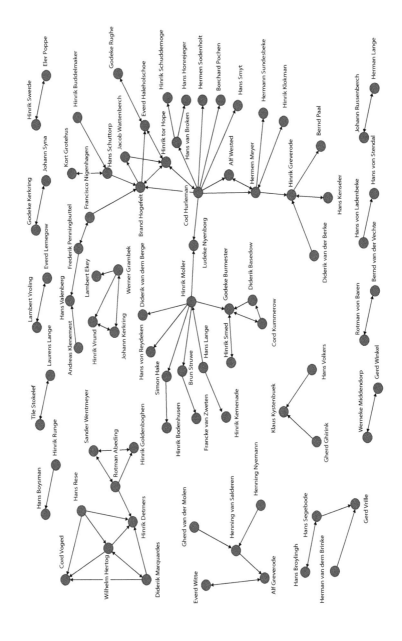

Figure 1.5: Network of the *Bergenfahrer*'s short-term business deals, 1440–70.

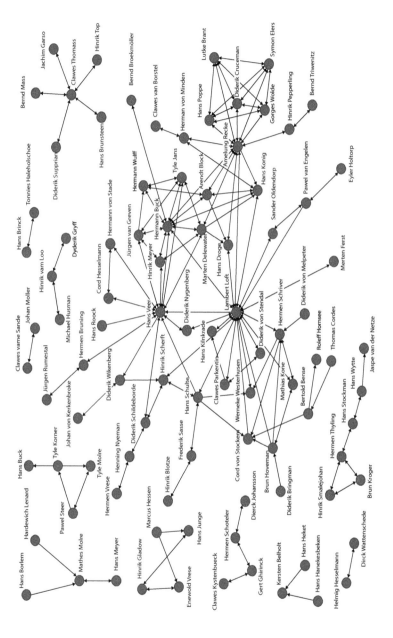

Figure 1.6: Network of the *Bergenfahrer's* short-term business deals, 1490–1510.

On the basis of the data presented, it is possible to identify a change in the way *Bergenfahrer* organized their trade in the late Middle Ages. In the second half of the fourteenth century, kinship seemed to be very important in establishing a long-term business partnership. Merchants without kinship relations in the trade mostly entered into short-term business contacts, and only in some cases did these cooperations lead to the establishment of a permanent corporate business. In the middle of the fifteenth and the beginning of the sixteenth centuries the market was much more open to non-kinship-based business relations. If a merchant wanted to start a business, it was no longer necessary to draw on relatives as partners. Hanse merchants had established other means of social control in order to ensure contract security. One of these was the principle of *Treu und Glauben*.[11] Another was tighter integration of the individual into social organizations, brotherhoods and guilds. A change in economic attitudes might also be discerned, a greater willingness to take on risks, which made it possible to start a company with any other merchant. The breaking up of the rigid company system and the use of more flexible forms of cooperation were perhaps a response to the success of Dutch and English competitors and offered higher returns and the capacity to react much more quickly to changes in markets or the political situation.

Another important constituent part of a medieval merchant's economic linkage was made up by loans. In this regard the *Bergenfahrer* were very active, especially in the capital market in Lübeck, the main financial centre in the Baltic region. Table 1.1 shows that between 1360 and 1400, ten *Bergenfahrer* were debtors to non-*Bergenfahrer*. Seven loans were raised the other way round, and in seven cases *Bergenfahrer* borrowed money from a merchant who also was active in the Bergen market. The average amount of the loans was slightly higher for loans taken out by *Bergenfahrer* than for those made by them, while between *Bergenfahrer* much more money was borrowed. In the period between 1440 and 1470, seventy-two *Bergenfahrer* raised a loan from non-*Bergenfahrer* and 107 gave money to a person who did not invest in the Bergen market. Loans were made to other *Bergenfahrer* eighty times.

Table 1.1: Number and average amount (in *Mark lübsch* – *m.l.*) of loans in the Lübeck capital market with the proven participation of *Bergenfahrer*. Source: Archiv der Hansestadt Lübeck, Niederstadtbücher 1360–1510.

	Loans taken by *Bergenfahrer* from non-*Bergenfahrer*	Loans taken by non-*Bergenfahrer* from *Bergenfahrer*	Loans between *Bergenfahrer*
1360–1400	10 (167.14 *m.l.*)	7 (118.33 *m.l.*)	7 (489.00 *m.l.*)
1440–70	72 (169.30 *m.l.*)	107 (279.40 *m.l.*)	80 (386.71 *m.l.*)
1490–1510	14 (71.75 *m.l.*)	16 (1,103.00 *m.l.*)	35 (803.00 *m.l.*)

While the average loan from non-*Bergenfahrer* in the middle of the fifteenth century was nearly as high as in the second half of the fourteenth century, the amount of loans made to them became much higher. Loans between *Bergenfahrer* amounted to the highest average sum. At the turn of the fifteenth to the sixteenth century, fewer loans outside the *Bergenfahrer* circle could be established. The average amount of loans taken from non-*Bergenfahrer* became very low, while the amount of money that was lent to non-*Bergenfahrer* rose considerably, and the average amount of loans between *Bergenfahrer* increased significantly during the period as well.

For the period from 1440 to 1470, we also have enough data for loans to see when the main financial business was done in Lübeck (Figure 1.7). Loans to non-*Bergenfahrer* were mainly made in the spring and late summer. Loans from them were made in winter and late summer, while loans between *Bergenfahrer* were mainly taken between March and August.

The *Bergenfahrer* were active in the Lübeck capital market all year round. Most lending was done in the spring, when all merchants had to make their investments, and the summer, when the profits from voyages earlier in the year came in and were available for another round of investments. The *Bergenfahrer* had access to large amounts of capital and were active players on the Lübeck capital market, both as borrowers and to at least an equal extent as lenders too.

Social Networks

Besides economic relations, a medieval merchant had many social contacts. Although some of these were necessary for maintaining economic success, care must be taken not to reduce people to their professional sphere. Social contacts were also important in terms of exerting influence on the opinion-building process within the community and, last but not least, people's well-being. One group of documents which provides us with a large amount of information about the position of an individual within the community are last wills. Wills not only preserve the memory of many individuals who can thereby be connected to the testator, but also provide information as they show the choice of executor, which indicates the importance of a person and the relations he could draw on.

In the three periods selected there is a large imbalance in the number of last wills that can be ascribed to *Bergenfahrer*. For the period between 1360 and 1400, we have fifty-two wills made by forty-three different merchants, while for the period in the middle of the fifteenth century, fifty-eight wills were made by fifty-four people. In the period between 1490 and 1510, in contrast, only eight wills were found. These data have been supplemented by information from other sources, yet it is still difficult to compare the last phase with the other two.

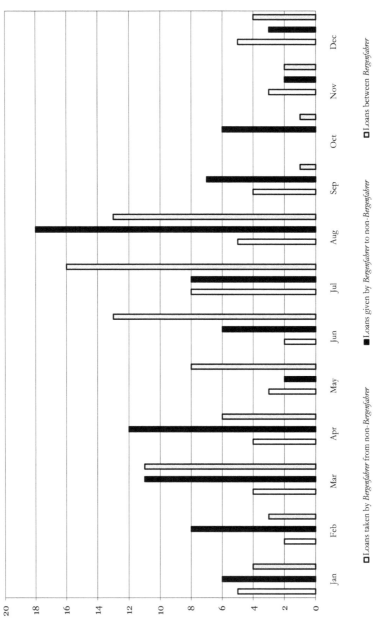

Figure 1.7: Distribution of loans with the participation of at least one *Bergenfahrer* on the Lübeck capital market, 1440–70.

□ Loans taken by *Bergenfahrer* from non-*Bergenfahrer*   ■ Loans given by *Bergenfahrer* to non-*Bergenfahrer*   □ Loans between *Bergenfahrer*

Nevertheless, we shall now look at the meshes constituted by the *Bergenfahrer*'s choice of executors of their wills.

The second half of the fourteenth century shows a very balanced graph, in which some nodes are slightly more central than others (Figure 1.8). Merchants who were also important in other respects, such as Everhard Paal, Lambert Sluter or Ludeke von Osnabrück, were chosen as executors of last wills several times. However, several unknown individuals were chosen as executors by several *Bergenfahrer*, thus creating a solid, densely interwoven network. Interestingly, kin relations seem to have been of no importance in the choice of executors of last wills. This can partly be explained by the fact that relatives were usually among the beneficiaries and that non-kin executors could be independent and were often considered authorities. If they feared a sudden death, people might have taken the first trustworthy people available as executors. One reason for this difference from trading companies may be that wills were made later in life. By that time the merchant concerned had a much wider network of relations within the community compared to the beginning of his career, when he established long-lasting trading companies and had to fall back on relatives because of the lack of other reliable contacts.[12]

A similar pattern can be detected in the middle of the fifteenth century, although the network is now more focused on Brun Struwe as a strong regional star (Figure 1.9). Brun Struwe is known to us as an important *Bergenfahrer*. He served as Elderman of the *kontor* in Bergen in 1451–2[13] and as its delegate in one of the numerous quarrels of the *kontor*'s merchants with the German shoemakers in Bergen in 1451.[14] He was also highly integrated into the social fabric of mid-fifteenth-century Lübeck, as his position as Elderman of the *Hl. Leichnams-Bruderschaft* in 1444[15] and 1451[16] indicates. For other regional stars in the network of executors of last wills, such as Hans Lange, Claus Parkentin and Lambert Wykinghoff, however, there is hardly more source evidence than their engagement as last will executors. They did not seem to have had a strong impact on Lübeck's or the *kontor*'s social and political life. Thus, even for the middle of the fifteenth century, we can conclude that an important position within the town's society was not the only reason why a person was chosen by *Bergenfahrer* to execute their last will. Personal trustworthiness, a good reputation and insight into the *Bergenfahrer*'s business were at least as important.

The graph for the last reference period differs significantly (Figure 1.10). However, considering that only eight last wills could be examined, the network is quite well developed. Many *Bergenfahrer* could choose influential merchants to become executors of their last wills. However, the source material is too limited to provide any evidence for interwoven meshes in the choice of executors of last wills during the period.

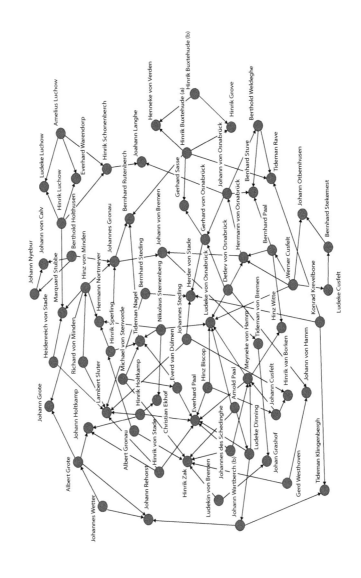

Figure 1.8: Network of the *Bergenfahrer's* last wills based on the choice of executor, 1360–1400.

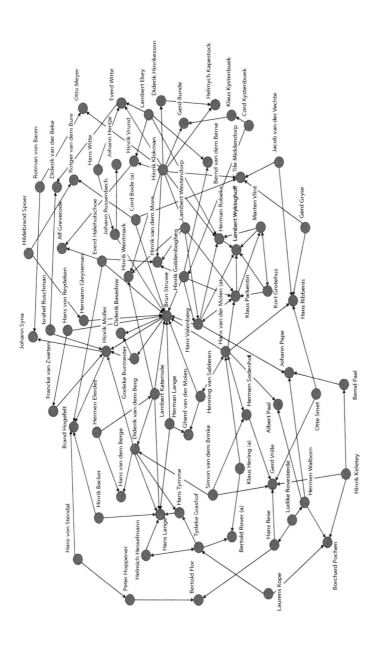

Figure 1.9: Network of the *Bergenfahrer*'s last wills based on the choice of executor, 1440–70.

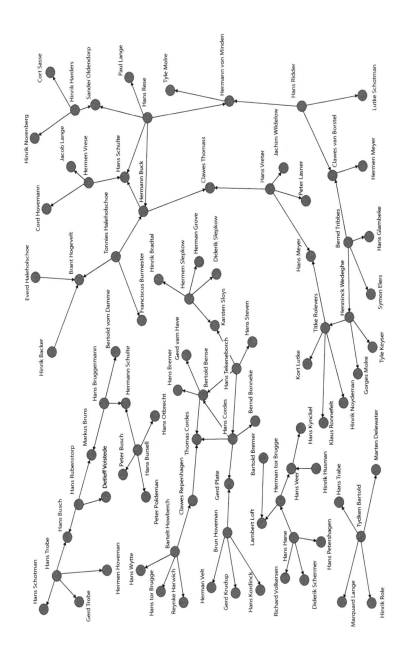

Figure 1.10: Network of the *Bergenfahrer*'s last wills based on the choice of executor, 1490–1510.

An examination of the *Bergenfahrer's* last wills shows that traders who were active in the Bergen market were very well connected to the most powerful groups in Lübeck. In all three reference periods, not only were they able to appoint a considerable number of people to act as executors. Moreover, many of these were respected and influential members of the late medieval town society in Lübeck who were also successful merchants in commercial fields other than the Bergen trade.

The *Bergenfahrer* were members of the Bergen traders' corporation and other merchant corporations, but we also find them among the members of the most respected of the town's more than seventy guilds. A lot of *Bergenfahrer* were members in the *Heiliger Leichnams, St Antonius* and *St Leonhards* brotherhoods.[17] Six *Bergenfahrer* became members of the *Greveradenkompanie*, which was founded in the 1450s, and between 1379 and 1510, seventeen *Bergenfahrer* were admitted to the *Zirkelgesellschaft*, the town's most exclusive and powerful association.[18] In all of these corporations, *Bergenfahrer* could obtain important information about social, economic and political developments which they passed on during the meetings of the *Bergenfahrer's* corporation. Thus, both for the single Bergen trader and the *Bergenfahrer* as a group, memberships of these groups were essential in order to keep abreast in the incessant competition for market shares and best prices.

In addition, between 1350 and 1510 there were twenty-five *Bergenfahrer* who served as councilmen in Lübeck (Figure 1.11). This figure means that almost 10 per cent of all those who became councillors in this period were active in Bergen trade. If we examine the long-term trend, the influence of the *Bergenfahrer* becomes even more visible. Between 1360 and 1510 there was no single year in which at least one *Bergenfahrer* was not a member of the city council. Their representation culminated in the first half of the fifteenth century, but also in the other periods of the late Middle Ages they always made their voice heard in political decision-making processes. Thus the often-made statement that the Lübeck *Bergenfahrer* were not such an influential merchant group with a poor reputation needs to be revised.[19]

Finally, we shall take a brief look at the activities of the *Bergenfahrer* in Lübeck's property market.[20] Contrary to the traditional partition of the town along parish borders, I divided Lübeck into four quarters according to their importance to long-distance merchants. The first quarter, area A, is made up of the streets that surrounded the town hall, St Mary's Church and the market, and those streets which lead from there directly to the harbour at the river Trave. The second quarter, area B, covers the streets leading from the top of the hill in westward direction to the northern part of the Trave. Quarter three, area C, is made up of the streets south of the most important area. They lead to the southern part of the river Trave. Area four, D, encompasses all the streets leading eastwards towards the river Wackenitz. Here mostly craftsmen had their homes and workshops.

Figure 1.11: Members of the Lübeck town council with proven activity in the Bergen market, 1350–1510.

As we can see in the diagrams in all three periods, *Bergenfahrer* purchased houses mainly in the most reputable quarters, with a view to both long- and short-term investments (Figures 1.12–17). Nevertheless, they still made shorter-term purchases of buildings in areas C and D. Specifically, houses in the craftsmen's quarter of the town accounted for about 20 per cent of all building purchases by *Bergenfahrer* in the late Middle Ages. However, when *Bergenfahrer* owned houses for a longer time, these were mostly situated in the best and consequently most expensive areas, where councillors and other rich merchants also had their residences. The ability of the *Bergenfahrer* to buy residences in the most prestigious quarters of Lübeck is not only a sign of their economic success. It also makes clear that one main prerequisite for the establishment of long-term relations was spatial proximity. By using the same institutions, attending the same church services and meeting every day in the street, the merchants who lived in the same quarters had more in common than just doing business. This led on the one hand to a sense of unity, and on the other hand made it easier to assess other people's economical and personal liability. In the end these conditions made two merchants living in the same quarter of the town more likely to become business partners than others.

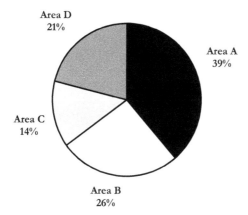

Figure 1.12: The *Bergenfahrer*'s purchases of property in Lübeck, 1360–1400.

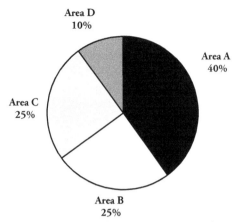

Figure 1.13: The *Bergenfahrer*'s long-term purchases of property in Lübeck, 1360–1400.

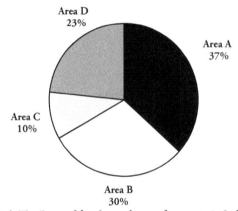

Figure 1.14: The *Bergenfahrer*'s purchases of property in Lübeck, 1440–80.

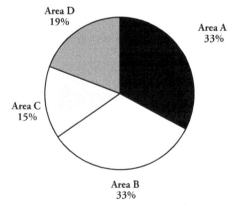

Figure 1.15: The *Bergenfahrer*'s long-term purchases of property in Lübeck, 1440–80.

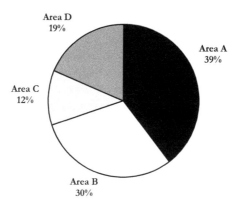

Figure 1.16: The *Bergenfahrer*'s purchases of property in Lübeck, 1490–1510.

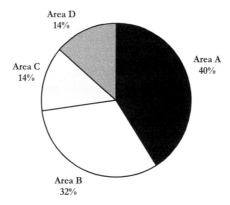

Figure 1.17: The *Bergenfahrer*'s long-term purchases of property in Lübeck, 1490–1510.

Macro Scale Networks

In this essay I have only been able to present a number of snapshots of the networks of social and economic relations that it has been possible to find in the investigation about merchants in the late medieval Bergen market. Some aspects, which are as equally important as those presented here, had to be left out. One difficulty that was impossible to overcome was finding evidence in the sources provided for the outside of the Hanse area. I could prove about twenty-five personal economic contacts between Hansards and merchants from other areas, like England, Holland and Southern Germany. Additionally there are about a dozen other documents that mention such relations, but they all are too weak to be connected to the trading network of the Hanse merchants.

If we are looking at all of the networks showing all the *Bergenfahrer*'s relations to other merchants that it was possible to find in the sources, we see very dense patterns for all three periods (Figures 1.18–20; while the sheer size and complexity of these networks render the individual names indiscernible, the figures have been included here to provide a visual portrayal of the dense mesh of the macro networks). Very dense clusters at the centre surround regional stars, and some peripheral clusters make the networks very stable. Even the more loosely connected nodes at the edges often have more than two connections to other parts of the network. Thus the loss of one agent would not exclude many others from the resource flow in the mesh.

We can see that the *Bergenfahrer* were able to obtain information and other important resources through different channels, and they had the ability to contact a large number of other merchants. Social and economic networks overlapped each other but were not identical. Furthermore, the *Bergenfahrer* were able to exert influence over the political decision-making process in Lübeck through their membership of reputable religious guilds, societies and the town council, as well as their manifold personal relations with other influential people and groups in the town.

Such a dense network made it unnecessary for them to create large, cost-intensive firms, as were to be found in Italy and Southern Germany in the late Middle Ages. Business success was more about efficient communication and cooperation than the type of organization.[21] The strength of the Hanse merchant was his inclusion within a large merchant network that gave him access to important information and potential trade partners, and vice versa.

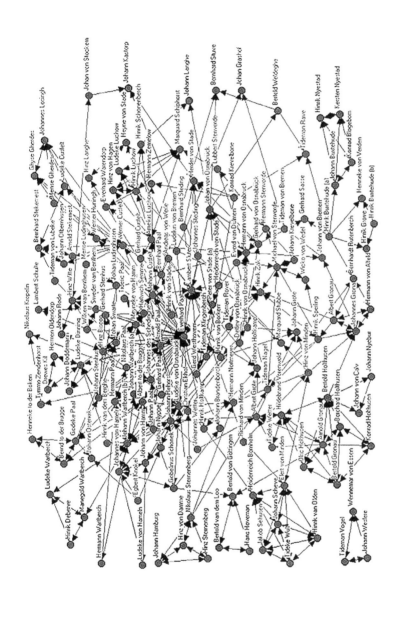

Figure 1.18: The *Bergenfahrer* network, 1360–1400.

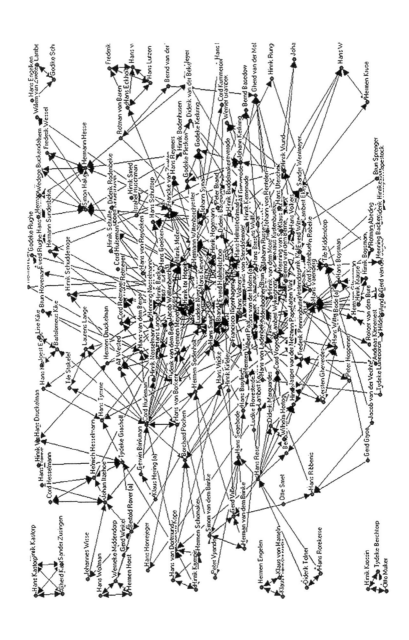

Figure 1.19: The *Bergenfahrer* network, 1440–70.

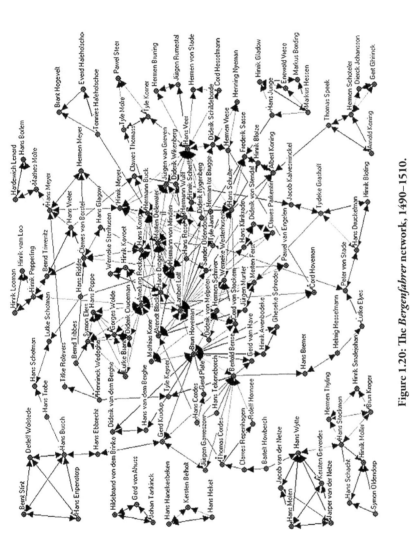

Figure 1.20: The *Bergenfahrer* network, 1490–1510.

2 INTERACTIONS, NETWORKS, DISCOURSES AND MARKETS

Christof Jeggle

Introduction

In commercial history, networks emerged as an important analytical tool for analysing the interaction of its protagonists. The perspective of networks is based on different kinds of social and cultural criteria, such as business relations, merchant companies, 'nations' or kinship.[1] Many studies on merchants are not primarily directed to commercial practices but on the social relations of merchants; hence the emergence of markets from networks has not been subject to research. Therefore some approaches that have been developed by economic sociology will be introduced and discussed in respect of analysing markets within historical commercial networks. After a short outline of the conceptual backgrounds, the spatial dimension of markets will be considered. The social relations will be explored in several steps, starting with defining markets as situated social configurations and the distinction of some basic categories of market organization. How markets emerge from networks will be discussed in three steps: first, the basic categories will be assembled to a more comprehensive model based on the French *économie des conventions*; in a second step, the relevant factors for establishing a market will be considered; and finally in the third step, Harrison C. White's model for production markets will be discussed as an approach for analysing markets within commercial networks. The conclusion emphasizes the necessity of considering the qualities of products and actors that constitute different types of markets. It also shows that markets as a particular form of social interaction for exchanging goods and values do not link all kinds of network ties at one single knot; this is because markets are closely tied to the chains and ties of production and distribution networks, and their networks need to be analysed in a differentiated way.

Networks and Markets in Commercial History

In economic history as well, markets have been studied in many respects, but not as a form of social interaction emerging from networks.[2] Markets are usually regarded as locations where commercial exchange takes place, while the practices of exchange have not been considered systematically in respect of how they consti-tuted markets as a form of situated social interaction. One of the reasons might be the tradition of defining markets as specific places where suppliers and demanders meet and negotiate price as an indicator of the valuation of the exchanged goods. This definition of markets originated in the Middle Ages, and it remained the basis of standard economic theory. Until the nineteenth century and the rise of neoclassical economic theory, markets were taken as social events where 'market prices' were negotiated by the participants and were influenced by social and moral criteria. In the late nineteenth century, theorists aimed at eliminating social fac-tors and finding abstract categories beyond the varieties of individual interaction. They tried to develop an 'objective' and calculable perspective on the economy. Prices were now the result of abstract balances of supply and demand that indicate the state of the market, and standard economic theory was based on the analysis of models of equilibriums of supply and demand.[3] This theoretical mainstream has been accompanied by several streams of institutional economics that tried to bring in social factors.[4] The approach of new institutional economics has been the most successful in economic history.[5] It is based on the hypothesis of utility maximization of all individual choices of an individualized and rational actor that is restrained by institutions. Social relations are taken as contractual relations on property rights, and the impact of social factors on economic transactions is con-sidered as transaction costs. In this approach, markets are taken as a form of social organization where contractual relations are being made; but a theory on the social dynamics of markets has not been developed.[6]

The structural and functionalist approaches of social history could deal well with this kind of model, and it considered itself a complement to economic analysis. The new economic history of the 1960s tried to give the neoclassi-cal analysis of economic trends a historical perspective. Series of prices and wages were collected and interpreted as indicators for economic development and as a scale for measuring the integration of dispersed markets.[7] While these collections certainly were of great advantage for providing some idea of the quantitative dimensions of economic development, the discussion on the inter-pretation of the data made obvious the necessity of considering the social and cultural circumstances from which the empirical findings emerged.[8] In 1979 Fernand Braudel, in his monumental three-volume work *Civilisation matérielle, économie et capitalisme, XVe–XVIIIe siècles*, tried to link quantitative and cul-tural perspectives on economic history. Braudel also emphasized the distinction between market economies and capitalist economies and tried to show that historical economies were based on markets.[9]

After a period of great enthusiasm for quantitative approaches in historical research from the 1960s onwards, a critical assessment on the social and cultural implications of statistical categories emerged in the 1980s, especially in France, where research on the categories of socio-economic statistics laid the basis for new sociological approaches for economic analysis.[10] Since the 1980s in France and the United States, different streams of a 'new' economic sociology developed which still have not found much reception in economic history.[11]

At the same time the structural functionalist approaches in the social sciences and social history were increasingly debated because they would operate with aggregated ideal types of social actors, while the individual perspective of the actors with their particular experiences would get lost. A long debate on how social interactions would constitute societies emerged. Social network analysis became increasingly important within these debates, but it has to be recognized that there are different streams of social network analysis. On the one side, social network analysis is also based on a structural statistical approach that takes social networks as the structural framework for actors. On the other, another stream of research considers networks as emerging from social interaction.[12] Networks are not taken as a given structural framework, and their analysis is directed to finding patterns or repertoires of social interaction within the varieties of situated social interaction.[13]

In the field of commercial history, the notion of the network has been employed quite early on.[14] In commercial history personal relations were always considered important, and there is a long tradition of prosopographical research on merchants. Though the term 'network' has been adopted and widely dispersed in commercial history, there are still not many studies in the field that employ social network analysis as an approach for systematic analysis of the configuration of networks.[15] Thus the idea that markets as a particular form of social interaction emerging from networks has also not yet been considered. Meanwhile current approaches for historical research, which are directed to the situated social interaction of the actors, almost necessarily need to be based on some kind of network analysis for contextualizing single interactions in a social surrounding. The focus on structured social interaction also opens new opportunities for dealing with markets as a specific form of social interaction. One of the pioneers of social network analysis, Harrison C. White, introduced his first version of a model for markets in 1981 when he put forward the question, 'Where do markets come from?'[16] In his book *Markets from Networks* he elaborated his approach, which will be discussed below.[17] First, however, some basic ideas on the social and cultural constitution of markets will be introduced.

Spatial Dimensions of Markets

Most markets take place in clearly defined places. Since the early Middle Ages, in many cases marketplaces were privileged by the authorities in order to protect the participants of already established markets or to attract potential actors for establishing new markets. In setting up arenas of commercial exchange, authorities considered these as a source of income through the raising of fees, tolls and taxes, and as a means for developing the local economy, which in turn would improve the economic situation of the population and also contribute to the fiscal income of the government.[18] While markets were taking place, many marketplaces were subject to a special, often temporary, legal order and jurisdiction to ensure a protected, peaceful arena of exchange and to settle conflicts instantly. The aim to attract markets by providing some infrastructure still remains one of the important strategies of economic policy today. In addition to the interests of political and fiscal control, marketplaces are not only arenas for exchanging material goods but also arenas of communication. In 1560 merchants in Nuremberg asked for a bell in the marketplace to establish fixed time periods for doing business and to ensure that all participants would be in the marketplace at the same time.[19] Even today, despite the advent of electronic media, face-to-face communication is still considered necessary for business operations. As the many travels of merchants and the piles of commercial letters show, communication has always been essential for commercial exchange, and it is the base of many ties of the networks from which markets emerge. Since communication can bridge distances, participants in a market do not necessarily need to meet in one spot such as a local marketplace; but they do need to be able to observe each other, like producers dispersed in one town who were offering their products in their shops. It was rather the aim of the authorities, like urban governments or guilds, to locate particular markets in defined places in order to have transparency and to control the paying of taxes, tolls and fees, the inspection of product quality, and the regulation of access to the markets, which could be privileged or delimited to certain groups of actors. Irregular markets also needed some infrastructure of communication and space to exist; they were based on the difference that they were designed to take place beyond the control of the authorities.[20] Other important aspects of the privileges of marketplaces were the legal regulations and the courts for settling conflicts among the visitors of the marketplace quickly, and which based on professional knowledge of commercial practices.[21] Thus specified locations alone do not make up markets; they emerge from particular forms of social interaction. Not all kinds of exchange constitute markets, and markets need to be defined as a particular form of social interaction.

Markets as Social Configurations

Economic sociologists have defined markets as complex figurations of social interaction where the actors compete for the opportunity of exchange.[22] Competition as a particular quality of markets is also emphasized by standard economic theory. Thus in order to constitute a market, at least three participants are necessary.[23] Markets can be characterized as social figurations for the exchange of rights.[24] They allow the evaluating of persons and firms, their performance and services as well as their products with their particular qualities to negotiate prices.[25] Based on these valuations, the transactions between the participants of the market take place. The actors on markets have to cope with several uncertainties that can be specified as three problems of coordination: competition, cooperation and valuation.[26] While competing for the chance for exchange, actors have to cooperate for maintaining a viable market. They have to find a balance between their particular interests and the economic potential of their competitors. Markets on which the actors do not find such a balance may not be viable and tend to unravel.

While standard economic theory tends to eliminate particular qualities of actors and goods – it generally considers the actors to be driven by utility maximization, and the goods are implicitly taken as being of equivalent quality[27] – sociological analyses have shown that different qualities of actors and products constitute different forms of markets.

Based on the constellations of the actors, two basic forms markets can be distinguished: 'exchange markets' and 'role markets'. In exchange markets the participants act as buyers and sellers on the same market, switching their roles, which is particularly the case in financial markets.[28] This also true for historical practices in payment systems where actors often changed roles within one chain of transactions while dealing with payment transfers. More common are markets that can be classified as role markets because in these markets for goods and services, as well as in labour markets, the roles of buyers and sellers are fixed. Suppliers and demanders may clearly be distinguished as different groups.

The quality of products generates two further basic distinctions: for trading, goods made with fixed quality norms guaranteeing particular quality standards for the product is more important than the personal qualities of the seller. The markets for these goods can be classified as 'standard markets'. If the exchanged goods do not have standardized qualities or the standardization of quality is delimited like for animals or foodstuffs, the value of the exchanged goods is dependent on the social status of the market participants and not restricted to formal product qualities. These markets can be classified as 'status markets', which also comprise labour markets.[29] The repeatedly discussed 'economy of the bazaar' coincides with this kind of market.[30]

These two basic types of markets can also be found in pre-industrial economies, and the categories are useful to analyse historical markets. Merchants doing
business in long-distance trade, like those presented in the following chapters,
particularly operated on specialized markets depending on the kinds of goods
they were trading. The base of medieval and early modern long-distance trade
was not made up by single pieces of some kind of product, but by the trade with
bulk ware like textiles, raw and semi-finished materials, grain, salt, wine, beer,
wood and the like. Merchants usually directed their business on a portfolio
of certain goods, because for successfully operating on different markets they
needed specialized knowledge about the practices of trade, product qualities and
potential business partners.[31] Often the merchants were also engaged in financing and organizing production processes as an investment and for obtaining
certain kinds of goods, especially in the textile and mining industries.[32] During the early modern period the sugar industry became increasingly important.[33]
Besides these goods, some merchants also dealt with small batches of occasional
goods or single items like luxury goods or art.[34]

In dealing with goods, merchants were involved in the transfer of payments.
While the techniques of accounting and cashless payments are quite well known,
the often complex relationships between the transfer of goods and the employment of services and their compensation through some kind of payment deserves
further research.[35] Often the goods were not just simply paid, but the payments
themselves were also made up of their own networks of obligation, which could
constitute their own markets for financial obligations. As special types of accounting books show, it is clear that merchants engaged in banking business; but their
business practices still need to be explored. Thus in the following discussion,
mainly product markets are considered while factor markets are only mentioned.
A network approach to analysing markets allows for literally linking these different
kinds of markets, which would be necessary as commerce, services and finances
were closely related; but the kinds of links and the constitution of factor markets
as elements of commercial networks still require further research.

Different kinds of markets were generated not only by different types of products
but also by the ways in which these were produced. Most trade done on the markets of
long-distance trade was business-to-business trade among merchants, while the business-to-customer retail sale took place at the edges of commercial networks and was
also run by local dealers who were not participating in long-distance trade. The following essays in this volume mainly deal with exchanges between long-distance merchants,
which constituted other types of markets than those for retail sale. Retailers had to
sell their goods to single customers who usually needed very limited volumes. Local
customers who wanted to use the products they were buying for their personal purposes had to rely on the sellers in respect of the qualities of the goods. For consumers,
many of the quality labels of large-scale trade were not relevant because they were not

buying whole rolls of textiles or barrels with foodstuff or metalware but single pieces out of these packages. This kind of business thus constituted status markets.[36] In long-distance trade, goods were traded as bulk ware in bundles, rolls and barrels that often contained defined volumes of goods with specified product qualities. These packages could be certified with labels and thus be traded as branded goods. Merchants could order these goods and could expect to receive certain kinds of goods without specifying every single piece that fits the categories of standard markets.[37]

Markets Emerging from Networks

Merchants were linked by different kinds of networks based on social attributes like kinship, 'nation', place of origin, religion, etc. These networks were important for the social framework of the merchants while they were operating on markets. For constituting markets as arenas of exchange, the streams of goods generated by commerce were essential because markets were the interfaces within the networks of production and distribution systems. Here it is useful to refer to the model of the product line that traces the metamorphosis of a product, starting with its raw materials and going through the production processes to the different stages of its uses until its final dissolution.[38] The transfer of goods could take place between the members of a certain network or among the partners and agents of a merchant company. While the actors of a merchant company operated within the institutional framework of the company, a network is made up of the frequent interaction of its agents. In these cases the transfer of goods is based on the institutionalized or frequent social interaction of the actors. Markets offer the opportunity of exchanging goods without necessarily generating social ties that go beyond each single act of exchange, because the participants compete for the most favourable opportunity of exchange and the involved partners may change or only exchange goods once.

Empirical research on contemporary markets has shown that not all sellers and buyers of one kind of good consider themselves to be participants in the same market. Markets are constituted by actors who consider themselves and their products to be equivalent in some respects, and the specific qualities of actors and products are basic elements for the constitution of specialized markets.[39] They arrange themselves within a certain quality frame that has to be maintained for stabilizing the market over time.[40]

These observations provide important suggestions for analysing medieval and early modern markets. On these markets we have to consider a rather limited degree of reliable up-to-date information concerning the overall situation of long-distance trade relations and the potential actors on a marketplace, especially at the commercial centres, despite all communication by letters and increasingly by the publication of economic information. The better the knowledge about other merchants and their goods, which not always were present on the spot but were being dealt by commissioners and on order, the easier the constitution of a market could take place. For constituting a market, at least three participants were necessary to have competition on at least one side of the suppliers or the customers. It is reasonable to expect some more actors on most markets. Only in the case of a monopsony or a monopoly is there just one actor on one of the sides of the market. For elementary exchange relations like small local markets which are not integrated in supra-local commercial networks, it may be sufficient to consider a market as being constituted by an arena where a supply and a demand side meet and some kind of barter takes place.

In his sociology of markets, Harrison C. White has elaborated the common model of a two-sided exchange market and introduced the model of a production market which takes into consideration the fact that most actors are operating in production and distribution networks and somehow change the condition of the goods they deal with. In this model the producers are situated within the stream of products between their suppliers upstream and their customers downstream. White also speaks of 'processor markets', which are based on the tripartite distinction of roles as procurement, transformation and sale.[41] While it is obvious that producers within a production chain may significantly change the qualities of a product, it also has to be considered that merchants often changed some of the qualities of a good as a traded commodity by assembling single pieces into packages or repacking goods, by labelling and relabelling, and by moving goods through time and space.

When looking at the merchants as actors operating within a product line that had to deal with suppliers upstream and customers downstream, the basic models for differentiating markets introduced above can be refined by referring to the French approach of the *économie des conventions*.[42] As already emphasized, merchants had to give their products certain characteristics for reducing the uncertainties when goods were exchanged to make their economic interactions more calculable. The characteristics of the products provide the base to coordinate the production, the distribution and the practices of interaction with suppliers and customers. The distinction between standard and status markets has already shown that products of similar qualities and those of specialized qualities generate different types of markets.

Products that were expected to represent similar qualities posed a difficult task to pre-industrial economies because the manufacture of generic products under the circumstances of artisan production with only very limited machinery met many obstacles. One of the solutions to getting batches of very similar products was selecting pieces that would fit together.[43] Connected with the problem of providing fixed quality standards were frequent reclamations on the quality of products. It seemed to have been a rather common strategy to negotiate reductions of the stipulated prices after the merchandise had been received.[44] Another problem was the volume of goods because buyers of generic goods expected to find these goods in a volume that would satisfy their demand. The obstacles of pre-industrial production – like restricted production capacities and logistics, especially the limited speed of transportation of information and goods – often made it difficult to meet unexpected demand.[45] Nevertheless the idea of dealing with more or less generic products was already present since the Middle Ages. Merchants tried to consolidate their markets by satisfying the demand of a large number of customers which could be unknown to them, while the customers expected to find these products on permanent offer, at least when the markets specializing in these goods took place. Since production was often based on agrarian seasons and transport often depended on seasonal circumstances, most markets were part of a multilevel system, covering local and regional markets as well as large fairs, in a temporal order of cyclical markets. The customers chose these products according to their prices, and the producers competed on their shares of these product markets based on an economy of scale, which means the volume of traded goods was more important than the particular quality of single pieces or batches. The markets for mass-produced textiles, like many sorts of plain linens that did not follow fashions, but also for raw materials, half-finished goods and bulk ware of all kinds, were organized by a convention of serial production. This combines the convention of consolidation, since the products are directed to markets composed of undifferentiated demands, with the convention of standardization, where the producers fabricate serial products based on codified norms of product quality and production technology. When dealing with the producers, the merchants had to take care that these standards were kept.[46] The products are substitutable and may be transferred between persons, places or other social figurations without limitations. The uncertainty of dealing with these products is considered as predictable risk.[47]

Besides generic products of permanent demand, there were standardized generic products dedicated to the special demand of customers and following their expressions of demand. The buyers expected immediate satisfaction, and the suppliers competed on the ability of rapid delivery as well as on the price. Suppliers had to deal with the uncertainty and unpredictability of future developments of prices and quantity of demand, while the buyers expected producers to respond immediately to their desires. This convention was important for the trade with textiles that followed fashions and other fashionable goods, which became increasingly important during the early modern period.[48]

There were also specialized products designed to meet individual demand. These products were unique and made for customers who were looking for suppliers who were able to meet their particular demands. The suppliers designed their products in close interaction with the customer, trying to satisfy her or his particular demand. This convention of an interpersonal world of production is based on products dedicated to a certain person or group, and their qualities were unique. Thus the evaluation is limited to the actors involved because suppliers and customers are linked by the mutual understanding of a shared experience to which they may refer, without the intention of finding general standards for products. The quality of the product remains unique without reference; therefore suppliers and buyers need to find a 'common language' for defining the product and the way it is made. The only modality for evaluation accessible from the outside was the price that was negotiated. The uncertainty of interaction requires mutual understanding of the meaning of actions taken or requirements expressed.[49]

This convention is often taken as a standard of pre-industrial economies, which is true for most cases of business-to-customer relations in retail trade. In retail trade, customers bought many things on occasion when these were offered, and when buying products for everyday use they chose what they considered the best offer for their purposes at that time. Looking at how markets were related to networks, it becomes clear that these kinds of markets were situated at the edges of business-to-business production and distribution networks because retail sale to end-consumers was not based on further commercial network relations. The suppliers of the goods constituted the markets for the goods they were selling to the customers, and they were linked to their suppliers of the production and distribution network on the other side. If only those goods were sold which the suppliers had produced themselves without being backed up by a production network, they were operating on a basic market for exchanging goods that was not part of a larger production or commercial network. In both cases, occasional relations with the buyers did not constitute commercial networks.

In respect of payment, people on local markets were often linked by networks of crediting each other. These networks may have provided the base for operating retail markets by making financing available, but their ties were based on social relations and reputation that went beyond the immediate commercial interaction on the market.[50] Local retail markets were entangled with the surrounding urban society in many respects, and their multiple networks deserve their own investigations.[51]

In respect of their social embedding, these markets have to be distinguished from those of business-to-business exchange that were mainly connected to urban society by the merchants of long-distance trade and their networks with urban and economic elites. A painting of the main marketplace of Nuremberg by Lorenz Strauch from 1594 makes this obvious. In the houses along the edges of the wide squared marketplace, many shops are located, offering goods in their windows. At the centre of the place, agrarian goods and groceries are offered, which are being sold out of baskets; there are no booths or tables. On the upper left side of the painting, well-dressed male citizens in black are seen, many of them assembled in small groups. These men are the wholesale merchants assembling on the marketplace to negotiate their worldwide business; they are clearly distinguished from the other markets operating in the place. Until the nineteenth century, different spaces in the marketplace were indicated by different names that were related to the kind of market taking place there. The seemingly coherent single marketplace was divided up into several marketplaces for different specialized markets.[52] The same observations could be made for probably all commercial centres. This distinction certainly did not keep wholesalers from selling some of their goods, especially those local dealers could not provide, in retail; but this was usually not their main business and could cause troubles with local dealers who suspected irregular competition.

The ratio between standardized and generic goods in long-distance commerce has not yet been estimated, but it seems probable that standardized goods made up the main part. Along with the goods they were trading on a large scale, many merchants seem to have traded in small batches of goods or single pieces for which they expected to make a good business, especially in the case of high-price products. Besides exclusive single pieces, these goods could be of a more standardized kind meeting some fashionable demand; introducing new goods could also provide some first mover advantage, like in the case of colonial goods. This kind of commerce has not yet found much systematic interest, but most likely it was the base of disseminating a large variety of goods.[53]

A segment that has been increasingly recognized in recent research is the trade with high-value luxury goods among the European elites.[54] Representing social status and political power was closely linked to the magnificence and splendour of monuments and objects. The objects for showing splendour were subject to permanent competition, among the elites themselves but also with other strata of the society that aimed to imitate these forms of material representation. The competition for showing adequate and exclusive luxury objects became one of the driving forces of the early modern development of European economies.[55] Even if the volume of these goods remained comparatively small, they were the basis for generating new kinds of products and thus of markets. Merchants were important agents of providing these goods, and this kind of commerce created networks between the political elites and the merchants. The markets for these goods were not only part of production and distribution networks but also have to be seen within a framework of political and commercial networks.[56]

These distinctions show there was not just a market as such on a marketplace, but a marketplace or a commercial centre has rather to be imagined as an assembly of specialized markets that were shaped by the particular qualities of the products and the related processes of production and distribution. Merchants have to decide between conventions of consolidation or irreducible demands for constructing a market, which means choosing between generic or dedicated product qualities and the devices to serve an economy of scale or an economy of variety. More generally it becomes obvious that commercial history should take the close links between production processes and distribution chains much more into consideration, because the practices of commercial exchanges are determined by the particular demands of production processes for most parts of the distribution chains and their markets, and only at the end by immediate consumer demand.

Making Markets

How do markets emerge when merchants came together in the different centres of commerce? Due to the varieties of local governance and the spatial and institutional facilities of infrastructure that made up most marketplaces and provided a framework for markets as a form of social interaction, there were different local environments for making markets.[57] Though the pre-industrial European economies knew quite a large variety of products, merchants usually specialized in a certain portfolio.[58] For the better part, these selections were guided by supply and demand of the markets on which the merchants were doing business. This observation may be taken as commonplace; but in comparison with present-day industries, with frequent allocations of production sites worldwide, pre-industrial production was tied much more closely to natural resources. Long-distance trade was hence directed to three basic problems of distribution: the provisioning of industries with raw materials and semi-finished products; the distribution of manufactured products beyond local markets; and the provisioning with foodstuffs which could be dealt for necessary needs caused by deficient local supply, like in the case of the grain trade, or as a kind of luxury consumer good, as was the case with the global spice trade and the distribution of Italian specialities in German territories after the Thirty Years' War.[59] In terms of product lines, many pre-industrial industries were operating on a trans-European or even global scale. In the long run industries could shift between locations, for which the silk industry is a good example. Originating from Asia, it was introduced in medieval Europe, and Lucca in Italy became one of the first rather exclusive centres of production. During the following centuries, silk industries successively disseminated throughout Europe, which caused substantial shifts in the commerce with all kinds of silk products.[60] Merchants had to cope with these dynamics and shifts to create viable markets.

Looking at the emergence of markets, the difference has to be distinguished between joining established markets and creating new markets. In established markets the actors had some knowledge about each other and their products. While newcomers to these markets brought in some uncertainty, these merchants could focus on making the best deals within an established surrounding.

The emergence of new markets was more difficult because potential actors had to identify each other and required knowledge about the qualities of the goods. Since the qualities of goods are closely linked with conventions of production and distribution and their related business strategies, markets can only be organized for products that were considered equivalent.

Markets usually do not just happen; they get established by interested actors.[61] As already mentioned, medieval and early modern markets were almost generally governed by political authorities. Markets had to be created within these frameworks, and when new actors arrived at certain places or merchants tried to introduce new products, they had to negotiate with the authorities on the regulations and governance of this particular market. Authorities tried to establish markets at certain places by privilege and the prohibition of setting up markets elsewhere. Depending on the range of political power, restricted areas could be set up. Institutions for labelling goods like textiles were often also designed to attract markets for trading the branded goods. Thus the political framework and the governance of markets were often closely linked with certain kinds of products and their qualities. These frameworks were subjected to political negotiations because different groups of actors tried to influence the governance of markets to their advantage, as the example of labelling textiles shows.[62] The political intention of establishing a market by providing a framework alone did not always turn out to be a satisfactory strategy. Without a sufficient number of capable and interested actors, it was impossible to set up a market and the designated marketplace would stay empty.

These regulations did not prevent markets from emerging in medieval and early modern economies. New products and suppliers could establish themselves rather quickly if they were finding sufficient demand, but obstacles were often set up by local traders. In many cases it is important to find out if these protests were really directed against potential competitors on already established markets or against potential changes in the economic structures by the introduction of new kinds of goods that the established local actors did not offer. This seems to be the case with the Italian merchants who immigrated to central Europe after the Thirty Years' War and were dealing with specialities, mainly foodstuffs, called 'Italian goods', and colonial goods like coffee and cacao. In many German cities they came into conflict with local traders, though it is not always clear if they were really competing on the same kinds of markets.[63] Despite all restrictions, the Italian merchants were able to establish themselves in the long run. Thus actors intending to set up a new market had to arrange with the actors on the established markets.

In his study on fashion photography, Patrick Aspers has shown that new service providers may change the structures of markets.[64] This observation seems to be of great interest for early modern markets, where commissioners and correspondents along with published business information became increasingly important. With this shift in commercial practices and opportunities, the potential geographical range of rather small merchant firms was significantly enlarged: they could participate in faraway markets that would have been beyond their reach if they had needed to participate on their own.[65] Looking at the commercial networks from which markets emerge, it is necessary to consider the particular status of the actors because a shift between different types of commercial actors may change the structure of markets.

As the commercial history of late medieval and early modern Europe shows, multiple networks of commercial activities covered the whole continent and the surrounding seas, connecting marketplaces of all kinds and ranges. Hence new markets emerged within the already outlined framework of established practices concerning the qualities of products and actors, institutions and commercial relations. Most changes to existing markets as well as the establishment of new markets came about as a result of processes over time and not as sudden unpredictable changes. Taking these premises, what had to happen to set up a market?

Production Networks and Markets

At the present state of research, the model of Harrison White is the most elaborated approach.[66] As already mentioned, White puts the producer (looking at commerce, this may also be a merchant) at the centre of his model, which includes on the upstream side the suppliers and on the downstream side the customers. A market is first made up by 'producers'. For constituting a market, they have to deal with a kind of product whose qualities and value they consider as being equivalent. This kind of equivalence makes up the quality frame of the market. Producers offering qualities that do not fit that frame are not able to join the market, or as participants may endanger its viability. In respect of their position within the networks of this particular kind of product chain, they need to have equivalent structural ties with their suppliers upstream and their customers downstream. Another aspect is the economic potential of the producers: for constituting a market over a certain period of time, the relations of product volume, investment and revenue have to be considered as equivalent. Since most markets were taking place within some periodical cycle, they were already organized as a series of sessions which may be taken as the period of time a particular figuration of producers constituting a market existed. Producers that produce or, in case of commerce, turn over a certain volume of a certain kind of product based on comparable investments make up the particular profile of the market, where each producer has his position among the others. If the producers differ too much in their performance and do not make up a profile, they will not be able to set up a viable market.[67] Markets are established not by following a theoretical model but by those actors who consider each other as equivalent while operating their business. Usually detailed economic data of a firm are not available for its competitors; therefore the producers have to observe each other and recognize what the other actors are signalling in respect of their business operations.[68] The necessity of observing each other brings in another dimension of the constitution of markets, which are not only made up by the exchange of material goods but also by discourses and communication.[69]

The producers not only observe each other, they also get observed by their customers downstream. The customers consider the producers as equivalent in respect of their demand for a particular product or service. Within the quality frame of the market, the producers compete with varieties of the product quality to distinguish themselves from each other and set up specific niches of quality. The customers observe the market as an arrangement of these niches that may serve their particular demand. The whole setting makes up the identity of the market, which is manifested in discourses about the market.

While the number of producers is limited (White and other researchers consider these to be less than twenty participants[70]) because they have to observe each other, the number of potential customers is unlimited. Therefore the producers are not able to observe each of their potential customers. These are considered as price takers, and the producers can only recognize the volume of their agglomerated demand. Thus White introduced the idea of a semi-permeable mirror through which the agglomerated customers observe each of the producers as they try to find their best opportunity for exchange, while the producers on the other side observe each other in the mirror to receive signals on the development of the market.

Here another dimension of the model becomes relevant. The structure of the market described here, probably the most common, is directed downstream, meaning that the producers compete for the customers downstream while their business relations with their suppliers are considered stable. White argues that producers who try to compete on both sides of the production market would collapse. In the case of products that find stable business relations on the side of the customers – one may think of the provisioning with raw or semi-finished materials – producers are able to compete on the upstream side for their suppliers. Here the suppliers would observe the producers through the semi-permeable mirror. For understanding the operations of the actors on markets, these distinctions are quite substantial and may help to explain different practices. Within a product line, the direction of markets may shift depending on the particular situation of exchange. Markets for services and labour are supplementary markets at the edges of the distribution system. They are also directed upstream and do not have a downstream side.

To establish a viable market, not only do they have to establish a quality frame, they also have to find compromises in respect of valuation and volume of the products between the producers, the suppliers and the customers. One important ratio is how the increase in volume is related to the satisfaction of customers, which indicates the volume sensitivity. The second is the ratio between the sufficiency of the customers when qualities are improved and the cost for the producer. Based on these two ratios, White developed a matrix called 'market plane' that shows different types of markets depending on their position in the matrix. Here only a few basic examples are outlined which can related to the models of the *économie des conventions* introduced above:[71] on 'ordinary' markets, the returns to scale are critical and the producers reduce the volume than the qualities. This kind of market can be related to the convention of generic goods dedicated to the particular demand of customers, like fashionable goods. On 'advanced' markets, the returns to scale are favourable while the customers are expecting certain qualities; this comes close to the convention of serial generic products. 'Paradox' markets are constituted by products of higher quality with comparatively low production costs and decreasing returns to scale. This kind of market can be based on the convention of dedicated, interpersonal production. White also shows that certain types of markets tend to unravel because of the structure of their parameters. For historical research it would not be the aim to precisely identify one of these types of markets as an ideal type, but to be sensitive to different types of markets and to the effects of shifting ratios of cost structures in respect of volume and quality that make up these differences. The strength of White's approach is in providing complex models for the social structures of markets within production and distribution networks, which are based on quantitative factors like costs in relation to product quality and volume. He is not very detailed about the practices of social interaction on the different types of markets he distinguishes. Here the *économie des conventions* provides a much more detailed socio-cultural approach, while it does not provide a comparable model for structuring markets. Therefore it makes sense to combine both approaches for historical research.

Some other aspects of White's model are useful for consideration. The limited number of participants in a market may lead to several parallel markets set up by producers that are distinguished by some of the relevant parameters that make up a market, like a lower or higher quality or different structures of volume and costs. Different parameters make up different identities of markets that allow the customers to distinguish these markets.[72] This approach may help to explain why in some marketplaces different groups of merchants have parallel exchanges with the same kind of goods but not with each other. The dynamics of economic development may cause changes. Markets that appear to be substitutable may merge, while crowded markets or increasing distinctions may lead to the separation of markets. Changes in the figurations of the markets also imply changes to the network structures on the sides of the suppliers and customers.

The viability of a market can be affected when a producer at the corner of the market profile starts to enlarge the volume of his production without a similar increase in investments. If he tries to carry on by producing goods on the lowest level of the quality frame, in consequence these can dissatisfy the customers, who turn off the market. He thus puts other producers under pressure, and a domino effect may be released by forcing the weakest producer on the lower edge of the market profile to reduce quality for a higher volume while dissatisfying his customers. In this situation a market faces the risk of unravelling. To prevent the market from unravelling, the participants may decide to counteract with a guild opt-out to regulate the access to the market. This option offers one explanation why the access to medieval and early modern markets became regulated – not (only) for privileging a certain group of participants as such but for stabilizing the market by protecting its quality frame.[73]

Markets were not permanent figurations; they only could exist for a limited period of time. Each market went through different stages, and in the first phase of orientation, merchants had to find out what kinds of other merchants had assembled on a marketplace, what kind of products these were dealing with, and what their economic potential would look like. In the following phase of contraction, the participants would set up the market and, if necessary, its institutional framework. A phase of cohesion would follow, where they were operating an ordered market. When participants entered or left or changed their parameters, or the kinds of products in demand changed, a market could get in disorder and would need to be reorganized in a new phase of contraction.[74] The stability of markets probably depended on its type: consolidated markets for generic serial products may have been more stable than markets for fashionable or specialized products. Another question would be whether, in the face of the many periodic markets, markets as social figurations continued or had to be re-established for each market session.

Brokers as Mediators for Making Markets

An important question that deserves more empirical research is how those merchants got together who were finally exchanging goods with each other in a marketplace. Frequent visitors of a marketplace probably knew each other, but merchants and especially representatives of firms seemed to have fluctuated quite frequently. Although sources and detailed research seem to be scarce, in research on commercial centres all kinds of brokers are mentioned.[75] At the present state of research, it can only be suspected that brokers were important mediators for constituting markets. There certainly were cases where the brokers were agents of governmental control, like in the case of the *fondaco dei tedeschi* in Venice, and in many other marketplaces brokers or *sensali* had to be consulted for certain kinds of business.[76] In addition to these official brokers informal brokering seems to have been quite common, especially for servicing inexperienced visitors to the marketplaces. To prevent abuse and fraud, the governance of brokering apparently has been an issue to the authorities in charge of the marketplaces.

Conclusion

Historical markets deserve a more detailed analysis in respect of their social and cultural constitutions to find a more precise comprehension of commercial practices and a historical perspective on repertoires and conventions of economic interaction. Some basic ideas of the sociology of markets could be introduced to inspire further reception and in particular empirical research. The discussion above has shown that markets as a form of social interaction are more complex than considering just the two parties of supply and demand without recognizing the dimension of quality in respect of the actors and the products. It also became clear that the production and distribution of goods are closely linked and should be analysed in their interrelations. Distinguishing different kinds of markets allows for a better understanding of business practices and strategies in relation to different kinds of product qualities. The proposed typologies are not directed to setting up abstract ideal types with which markets may be simply classified; within a framework of pragmatist sociology of interaction, they are intended as possible repertoires of interaction and discourses for a structured interpretation of the empirical findings while analysing markets.

Looking at networks and markets, the introduced approaches mainly draw on the ties that were made up by products that were exchanged between the actors operating along the product line. White's model shows that markets are interfaces either within the networks of production and distribution or at their edges, which do not necessarily constitute social ties between the supply and the demand side. Thus markets offer a form of exchange that allow for connecting different sub-networks along a product line without the necessity of maintaining social ties. This aspect is important for understanding transcultural trade relations, where cultural restraints restricted the emergence of social ties but both sides were interested in exchanging goods.

The stream of goods has to be complemented with the stream of values for which the goods were exchanged. In medieval and early modern business-to-business trade, payments were usually guided by relations of obligations that were caused by the trade with goods but balanced within networks of crediting where liabilities of different transactions could be cumulated. The geographical dimensions in which the transfers of payment took place could be quite different from those for the goods. Thus payments constituted networks and probably markets of their own. White considers his model sufficient to include the analysis of markets for investments in the production and distribution networks,[77] but here further empirical and theoretical research on the modelling of historical financial markets appears to be necessary.[78] While markets for goods allow exchanges without necessarily constituting permanent social ties, it would be important to find out how these exchanges were compensated – immediately, to avoid social ties? Or did some of these transfers constitute ties of credit and obligation beyond the arena of the market?

It is also clear that the actors on markets were tied into other networks of personal relationships like business partners, kinship, religious affiliations, 'nations', local merchant groups, etc., and further research is required to find out how these multiple networks of the actors effected their operations on markets. In recent research it is mainly these networks in the surroundings of markets as arenas of exchange that have been studied, and it seems to be time to take in the markets as a further dimension of analysing commercial networks.

Acknowledgements

This essay is based on research conducted within the project 'Markets – Networks – Spaces. Economic Relations and Migration Processes in Early Modern Europe (1500–1800)', subproject 'New Markets? Economic Relations between Italy and Southern Germany in the Seventeenth Century (1630–1700)', funded by the German Research Association (DFG) from 2009 to 2011.

3 CREATING NETWORKS THROUGH LANGUAGES: ITALIAN MERCHANTS IN LATE MEDIEVAL AND EARLY MODERN EUROPE

Francesco Guidi-Bruscoli

Charles V famously declared that he spoke 'Spanish with God, Italian to women, French to men and German to my horse'.[1] Normally, however, a person would not be expected to be as well learned as the emperor was – or at least declared himself to be.

In the Prologue of the first of his *Satires*, Aulus Persius Flaccus emphasized that parrots and magpies learnt to speak because they were taught by their stomach, i.e. by hunger.[2] In the same way travellers (merchants, pilgrims or others) were often driven to learn foreign languages solely by necessity. In most cases it was enough for them to understand or to be understood: as underlined by Braunmüller and Ferraresi, 'Nobody would ever have expected to know other languages "perfectly" ... the main point was to achieve effective communication e.g. at the workplace and not a "perfect" multilingualism in every respect'.[3]

Introduction

Much has been written on colonies or 'nations' of Italian merchants abroad, on the way they settled, on their activities and on their privileges; but little space has been devoted to the problem of the knowledge of languages. A general feeling of solidarity was obviously connected with the linguistic identity; endogamy could clearly reinforce this identity and be – in turn – reinforced by it. Scholars of various disciplines have written about foreigners in terms of exclusion or inclusion/integration; cultural historians or sociologists have analysed the relation between language and identity or language and community.[4]

Historians and economic historians, on the other hand, have devoted little attention to the use of languages by merchants and in particular to its role in the functioning of markets and the creation of networks. It is difficult to assess to what extent business was influenced by the capability to use foreign languages, but this essay will try to stimulate debate by raising some questions, mainly focused on the case of late medieval and early modern Italian merchants. The first issue that will be addressed is whether they had this capability: in other words, whether their training provided them with the necessary skills, and whether the existing documentary evidence shows these skills. Secondly, we will discuss whether the use of foreign languages was an essential prerequisite for Italian merchants abroad and whether this gave them competitive advantages. Last but not least, we will investigate whether the use of foreign languages was a determinant of network-building or, on the contrary, whether language was a barrier against the formation of a network.

Linguistic Loans

In their investigations on the use of languages by medieval merchants, linguists have dealt extensively with what are known as 'linguistic loans'. About a century ago, Emilio Re stressed the fact that in the thirteenth century there was a 'Christian-European civilization' ('civiltà cristiano-europea') in which language played a very relevant role: merchants were the promoters of this linguistic exchange more than any other category of people. During this period the first anglicisms appeared in the Italian language, e.g. *costuma* for customs, *atornato* for attorney.[5]

In recent years, a number of linguists have drawn attention to the Gallerani books, dating back to the beginning of the fourteenth century (1304–8) and held by the State Archives at Ghent. The Gallerani were a Sienese family, with companies in London and Paris. In early fourteenth-century London, English was spoken in the local community, whereas French was the language of the court: therefore the book belonging to the London branch contains terms deriving both from English and French (anglicisms and gallicisms). These texts show in fact a particular language, which is ruled not by taste, fashion or the prestige of some of the idioms, but rather by the necessity of calling things with their own name in a context characterized by a different language.[6] In other words, according to Trotter, 'as far as they [the accountants] were concerned, these were not "foreign" words (in the sense of "xenisms") but simply ... different technical terms'.[7]

Things could work in the other direction as well: Italian technical terms in the field of finance and banking have entered the vocabulary of German, Flemish and other languages. Moreover, in the sixteenth century, when printed lists of prices began to appear in commercial centres such as Antwerp, Italian was the language in use.[8] This exchange took place in terms of 'borrowing', with the Dutch who continued to speak their own language but used Italian words to define certain things.[9] In other words – in different places and at different times – some sort of 'mixed languages' emerged.[10]

We must be careful, however, to distinguish between the knowledge of a language and the use of specific, technical terms. Merchants were doing business in a clear-cut context and therefore needed to use terms that were precisely related to that context – terms, in other words, that had a very precise meaning and did not have a corresponding Italian word. These linguistic loans can be divided into five categories: (i) units of measurement and quantities; (ii) titles and qualification; (iii) objects and merchandise; (iv) technical, juridical and administrative terms; (v) time and space.[11] What we will be discussing in the rest of this essay, though, is whether merchants actually knew foreign languages.

Merchants and Foreign Languages

As has already been mentioned, historians have devoted very little space to the study of foreign languages by merchants. It seems that their language skills are taken for granted. But what has to be taken for granted: the knowledge of the language by merchants or, on the contrary, the ignorance? According to Braunmüller and Ferraresi,

> They all were (or became) multilingual – but no one would ever have had to emphasize this fact. It was just normal. Therefore there is little evidence to be found in (written) sources which stresses the fact that a certain person was multilingual or that the command of a *lingua franca*, like Latin or any other language for a specific purpose, was mandatory for a certain job. A lack of such linguistic skills would, by contrast, have been worth mentioning.[12]

The evidence, however, seems contradictory and does not always reflect this strong statement. Sometimes the linguistic problem has been underestimated, and conclusions (on the diffusion of certain languages) have been made too light-heartedly and without much supporting evidence. Unfortunately the sources are not very rich in this respect: even letters and *ricordanze* (memoirs) – where one would naturally expect to find some references – only show some rather short and sporadic hints of the problem.

The main commercial towns were melting pots of nationalities and consequently of languages. Port towns like Venice were praised for the fact that so many languages were spoken. Some of the foreigners resided permanently in the town; others stayed for short periods, as for example merchants who arrived on board the galleys or at the seasonal fairs. From the end of the thirteenth century merchants' manuals were used by those merchants who travelled abroad: they provided much information on units of measurement, excise taxes, products, currencies, etc. The most famous of all, the *Pratica di mercatura* by Francesco Balducci Pegolotti, has an opening session called *Dichiaragioni* (declarations) containing commercial terms in various languages (*grechesco, fiammingo, inghilese, ispagnuolo, proenzalesco, francesco*, etc.). Significantly, the last word of the list is 'turcimanno' or 'calamanci', i.e. interpreter.[13] But, in practice, it would have been difficult for merchants to use such documents when they wanted to communicate in foreign languages on a day-to-day basis.

The apprenticeship of young merchants began when they were still children and was mainly devoted to the learning of 'abaco' and accounting skills; practice in a local firm was the following step. Then some of them continued their upbringing through an experience abroad, working for the foreign branch of the family company or for that of some compatriots. By modern standards this relocation took place at an early age, and this made the learning of a foreign language easier. The question is whether Italian merchants exploited this potential; this question is closely related to another issue, that is whether they needed to learn foreign languages.

Some languages were certainly more important or widespread than others in international trade. The *Speculum regale*, a Norwegian text of the mid-thirteenth century, offers a dialogue between father and son: the father tells his son that if he wants to become a good merchant, he has to 'learn all the languages, first of all Latin and French, for these idioms are most widely used'.[14] At the highlight of the Champagne fairs, French was the international language for trade. However, Italian gained increasing importance even though Low German prevailed in the Hanseatic area.[15]

Numerous historians underline the widespread use of certain languages with more or less precise remarks.[16] According to Armando Sapori, an Italian merchant abroad did not need to know a foreign language because the Italian language was known everywhere. More recently, Ugo Tucci wrote that an Italian merchant abroad was mainly surrounded by compatriots and his relations with locals were mainly trade-related: he did not need to learn the language because his own (Italian) 'was known by everyone'. Pierre Jeannin shares the same view: according to the French scholar, during the sixteenth century Italians were in the same situation as the Anglo-Saxons of today because their language was the international language of business, with the exception of the Low German area, between the Low Countries and the Slavic world; second to Italian came French, which benefited from France's geographical centrality.[17] Gurevič, on the other hand, emphasizes that the study of languages was extremely important and that the sons of Italian merchants learnt English and German, whereas the Hansards learnt Russian because it was necessary to trade in Novgorod; but he does agree that Italian was in fact the main language for trade in the Mediterranean, and that German played the same role in the Baltic.[18] It cannot be denied that primacy in the business world found its representation also in the use of languages; conversely, towards the end of the sixteenth century an increasing fragmentation led to multilingualism.

It is also significant that if, during the period of Italian economic primacy, simplified and technical Italian business terms had penetrated many other languages, as centuries progressed and primacy faded, fewer and fewer business terms and more and more artistic terms were borrowed by others.[19]

Even in a context where the use of vernacular languages was widespread, Latin 'often came in handy' ('viene a punto molte volte'), as is remarked in some of the Datini correspondence.[20] In Genoa account books were still kept in Latin in the fifteenth century, and therefore learning that language, though in a simplified form ('gramatica secundum mercatores'), was a very practical skill. In early fifteenth-century Florence, Giannozzo Manetti started work as a child at his father's bank and acquired great accounting skills; at the age of twenty-five, however, he began studying 'letters' and got acquainted with Latin, Greek and Hebrew.[21] In the mid-fifteenth century, Benedetto Cotrugli's ideal merchant was a person who knew Latin; but presumably – as for Manetti – Latin was a skill acquired in order to complete the training of a well-educated man rather than for its use in everyday life.[22] Moreover, though widely used by notaries, lawyers and diplomats, and as the language of justice and administration, when it was spoken by merchants and travellers Latin was just a very simplified pidgin (with verbs reduced to infinitives).[23]

Scattered evidence shows that some merchants were well acquainted with various languages. Already in 1307–8 the Florentine Jacopo da Certaldo, an agent of the Peruzzi and a tax collector on behalf of Philip the Fair, was keeping his accounts in French; in 1315 some partners of the same firm signed declarations in French.[24] The Sienese merchant Beltramo Mignanelli moved to Damascus at the end of the fourteenth century; he knew Latin and Greek and studied Arabic. After his return to Tuscany, in 1439 he was present at the Council of Florence, where he also played a role as an interpreter.[25] Simone Bellandi, Francesco Datini's partner in Barcelona, could write to a Catalan correspondent in Catalan; and Jacopo Rog, a Catalan merchant, wrote to the Datini company of Pisa in Italian.[26] Tuccio di Gennaio was chosen by Datini for the Barcelona branch in 1397 because, having worked for the Tecchini and others in Catalonia, he was well acquainted with the place and 'understood the language well'; on the contrary, someone with no experience would take at least six months before understanding the language.[27]

In the instructions given to Gerozzo de' Pigli, who was about move to London in 1446, Cosimo de' Medici wrote that Alessandro Rinuccini could be trusted as a cashier and – having learnt the language – could be used for errands in the city.[28] The same degree of competence was acquired in the same period in Barcelona by Lorenzo Strozzi, who proudly wrote to his mother that 'I can speak half-Catalan, so that they understand what I say; and I can understand them'.[29] Some fifty years later, just after his arrival to Lisbon in 1509, Giovanni Morelli underwent a very tough apprenticeship, working day and night: in a letter to his friend Giansimone Buonarroti, he wrote that he began 'to understand accounting and to understand the language, and I am working hard'.[30] Carlo Gigli, a Lucchese merchant who made his career in Bruges in the 1430s and 1440s and then moved to England, was ready to teach French to William Worcester, Sir John Fastolf's secretary, who in 1459 was keen to improve his education; presumably Gigli also provided Fastolf with Boccaccio's *De casibus virorum illustrium*.[31]

We know that books in foreign languages – e.g. French or Catalan – were included in the libraries of some of the richest Tuscan merchants. Moreover, among the thousands of letters held by the Datini Archive in Prato there are some written in French, English, Castilian and even Arabic and Hebrew. If they were sent to the headquarters or to some of the other branches, someone must have been able to understand and/or translate them.[32]

Sometimes it was the prestige of a certain merchant that determined the language of communication. At the end of the sixteenth century most of Simon Ruiz's correspondents, even the great Italian bankers of Lyons, wrote to him in Castilian; and when, for the sake of clarity, they were writing in Italian, they felt they needed to justify it.[33]

When they ventured outside the borders of the Old Continent, European merchants showed a certain degree of arrogance, with regard to the use of languages and much else. More often than not they thought that it was up to the Asians to learn their language or to provide translators and/or interpreters.[34] Europeans did not even bother to teach their own language properly. As a consequence, there was the emergence of *lingue franche* which were in fact simplified European languages (both from the lexical and grammatical point of view): in the eyes of the colonizers, this was another demonstration of the intellectual inferiority of the local populations. When they went to Asia, Italian merchants had very rare contacts with the local languages and learnt from these pidgins the only few words that they then reproduced: in other words, they mistakenly identified as local expressions some words which had been exported by the Portuguese and then readapted.[35] Extra-European countries stimulated the imagination to the point that, for example, at the end of the Middle Ages but also in the following centuries, fancy alphabets were developed such as that of the alleged 'kingdom of Prester John'.[36] In relations with Africa and Asia, in other words, myth mixed with reality.

Glossaries and Dictionaries

In order to facilitate conversation in foreign countries, glossaries for the use of merchants began to appear in the Mediterranean in various linguistic combinations, such as Arabic-Latin or Latin-Persian-Cuman. Following a tradition coming from antiquity – e.g. the *Art Minor* by Donato (fourth century), with dialogues in Greek and Latin – *Gesprächsbücher* were increasingly widespread from the fourteenth century. They were not meant to supply an in-depth knowledge of a language, but aimed at providing basic elements for communication during voyages, stays and trading operations; the *Livre des Mestiers de Bruges*, a Franco-Flemish text with a list of around 100 crafts (many of them belonging to the textile industry), appeared in 1349 during the heyday of the Flemish town.[37]

From the first half of the fifteenth century, Italian-German glossaries flourished in Venice. One of the most famous was written in 1424 by Georg of Nuremberg (*Meister Jörg*): this was a real textbook, with a grammar, a list of commercial terms and two long dialogues. The latter are very bright and lively and really recreate the atmosphere of a market, with all the bargaining, the questions and the reassurances on the quality of the product by the seller. Presumably, though, the liveliness of the dialogue is a stronger feature than its practicality.[38]

After the invention of printing, the diffusion of bi- or multilingual handbooks in Europe increased. These manuals collected together useful phrases and some vocabulary and were intended to aid people who travelled abroad by showing practical examples to help them in the daily necessities of face-to-face oral communication.[39] They were mainly written in Italian and German, but other combinations were also taken into account: for example, there is a famous Italian-Flemish handbook of *c*. 1500 aimed at teaching Italian (Venetian) and its use in trade. Written by someone from Brabant, it shows a series of real conversations, including one between an Italian and a Flemish merchant.[40] For the fifteenth century there is even an Italian-Arabic text containing a section on 'measures'.[41] One of the most widely reprinted of such texts, the *Solenissimo Vochabuolista* (first published in Venice in 1477 and presumably written for Italians who travelled to Germany), was initially a bilingual Italian-German handbook, but in time developed so as to include twelve languages.[42]

Doing Business Abroad

When abroad, Italians used their native language for the company's daily management: members of staff (with the exclusion of valets or servants) were all Italians and the internal activities were run in Italian, in the field of both language and business techniques. But then there was the problem of dealing with the local market.

The main international marketplaces were obviously full of interpreters in order to facilitate commercial transactions undertaken by foreigners. 'Nations' abroad could also provide their compatriots with bilingual staff to help them in their business.[43] Moreover Italians could employ locals in order to get their letters translated, but it was always dangerous to disclose some information to third parties. In fact the author of the *Solenissimo Vochabuolista* wrote in his introduction that the knowledge of a foreign language made it possible to avoid the use of interpreters, who could be 'unknown and maybe even an enemy' ('estraneo et forse inimico').[44]

Sometimes not knowing a language could indeed be a handicap. For example, Agnolo Tani, despite his experience in the Medici's Bruges branch, was not chosen as a manager of the bank's London branch when the latter was detached from Bruges in 1446: this was because he knew no English (nor did he know French, the business language in Bruges). The appointed manager was Gerozzo de' Pigli: this was unusual for the Medici, who had normally chosen managers from among their ranks, but Gerozzo had the advantages of knowing English and being an experienced trader in Lombard Street.[45] Some merchants, after many years abroad, underwent a real process of naturalization and it is likely that they learnt the language very well. But this was not always the case. In late sixteenth-century England, Orazio Pallavicino, Genoese by origin, was a financier (but also a diplomatic representative) of Elizabeth I. He was naturalized in 1585 and knighted two years later; but despite being one of the most powerful persons at court, Sir Orazio continued to write his letters in Italian, leaving to his secretary the task of translating them into English. Rarely did he write in French and only once tried English, but was careful to add that 'I beg you to pay no attention to the mistakes but only to the substance'.[46] Indeed, in the mid-sixteenth century Ottaviano Maggi portrayed the perfect ambassador as one who should be fluent in Latin but should also know Greek and – among the modern languages – Italian, French, Spanish, German and Turkish. But he does not mention English because, as Mattingly underlined,

> Nobody in the sixteenth century except an Englishman was expected to speak English, not even the perfect ambassador ... The Italians could usually get along in their own tongue, with Latin for formal occasions. The English, who did not expect foreigners to speak English in England or understand it abroad, made shift with whatever continental languages they happened to know.[47]

There were areas where Italian was in fact the language of business, as for example fifteenth-century Ragusa (Dubrovnik), where even local merchants used it to keep their own accounts or to draw partnership agreements; notarial records were drawn up in Latin or Italian.[48] Clearly Venetian was the first Italian dialect to be used, but from the thirteenth century onwards Tuscan also gained ground, at first among the élites, then among other social classes. The most prominent Ragusan families sent their children to the Italian peninsula, and Italian also became a language used in local literature.[49]

Certain languages have common roots, which makes learning a new language much easier but also makes it, paradoxically, less important, since each party can continue to speak his own language and still be understood. Most of the time the linguistic proximity was also a mirror of cultural proximity. Some of the Italian merchants who moved abroad to areas with a similar language to their own decided to stay, gained citizenship and gradually became more and more related to the local society. This happened in Portugal, Castile and Catalonia, for example, where sources also show clear examples of linguistic interference with 'Portuguesization' or 'Catalanization' of names or other words.

Beyond the borders of Europe the situation was much more complicated. During their long travel to China, the Polos encountered twenty to thirty different languages.[50] Persian had been very useful in the Asian voyages for centuries, and by Marco Polo's time it was a sort of *lingua franca* within the Mongolian Empire: the Venetian merchant had in fact learnt it.[51] Balducci Pegolotti suggested that the journey through Asia should be done with interpreters and servants who knew the Cuman language.[52] But even though these two languages were widespread in the late thirteenth-century Mongolian Empire, they were not spoken in all areas of Asia; and not even a prolonged residence was a guarantee for a deep knowledge of a language. There are not many cases of Westerners who attained a good degree of fluency in a local language after many years spent in Asia. In 1515 the Florentine Andrea Corsali left for his travels in the Indian Ocean: four years later, a compatriot who met him in Cochin, India, could write that Corsali 'knows the Persian and the language of Malabar well'.[53] There were other cases of course, the most famous being another Florentine merchant, Filippo Sassetti, at the end of the sixteenth century. However, these were exceptions and in general Europeans made little effort to get acquainted with the local cultures. In any case, it should be considered that no more than thirty words were perhaps sufficient to meet the needs of daily living (housing, food, etc.).

Business relations were more complicated, and especially when contracts were drawn up, a full understanding of their terms was necessary. Therefore interpreters were often needed. In some places they were appointed arbitrarily by the local authorities, and the risk was that they would act as spies on their behalf; in others they were recruited by foreign merchants and were therefore more faithful to the person who paid them. Moreover, other professional categories could play the same role. Customs officials sometimes included interpreters among their ranks; at times notaries could act as intermediaries between foreign and local merchants, as they had to draw up contracts or other public acts. Sometimes they drew up their deeds in various languages: in 1430 a Pisan notary translated the protestation by a Catalan merchant into Latin and then read it out in the vernacular, so that all parties were well aware of what was going on.[54] A translation might be needed to provide validity to the acts, because it was vital that all the parties had a full understanding of all the proceedings.[55] In sixteenth-century Antwerp notaries could draw up their deeds in Italian, and judicial documents involving foreigners were also at times written in Italian, Spanish or French. Similarly, during trials concerning facts of violence and involving Italians or Spaniards, the sheriff spoke to them in their own language. In their relations with the Antwerp government, Italians mainly had to use the local language, but could at times use their own.[56] This practice was not common in England, however, where some scriveners appear to have been fluent linguists, but only knew Northern languages.[57]

In other words, some places could – language-wise – be more 'foreign-friendly' than others. The following sections will show two opposite examples.

A Difficult Environment: Germany

An area which seems to have created recurring problems to Italian merchants is the German-speaking region. When the Council of Basel settled in the city in the mid-1430s, learning German was not an issue: the clientele of the Italian merchant bankers (among them Tommaso Spinelli) were not locals but rather the representatives of the Roman Curia, including the pope.[58] However, when they moved to other neighbouring regions, the situation became trickier, and life was not easy at all. In their letters some Florentine merchants expressed recurrent criticism of German society and were disgusted by local habits: for example, they held in contempt the German attitude to drinking, in addition to their gluttony, hot tempers and other similar behaviour. The lifestyle was completely different, and therefore many became homesick. Gherardo Bueri, after almost thirty years in Lübeck, had acquired citizenship and a German wife, but he would have been ready (and happy) to return to Florence had he been selected for one of Florence's public posts.[59] Similarly, after spending most of his life between Nuremberg and Frankfurt and marrying a German woman, Lorenzo di Bernardo Villani could not stand it anymore: he wrote to his friends that he did not want to 'die surrounded by these barbarians' ('morire in fra questi barberi'), people 'without faith or goodness, who live worse than beasts' ('né fede né bontà e vivano e fano pegio che le bestie').[60] He did not make it back to Florence, however, and died in Speyer in 1559.[61]

One of the problems was difficulty in learning the German language. It took many years to achieve fluency, and at the beginning progress was slow and the results frustrating. In 1536 Piero Saliti stressed the amount of time needed to learn German: 'even if one spends twenty to twenty-two years [in this place] it is difficult to learn this language and one struggles many years before being able to use it'.[62]

One of Saliti's employees, Alessandro Talani, expressed the same – or even more pessimistic – remarks concerning the possibility of mastering the language: 'You need to know that we cannot do everything because of the language … you should know how little use of the language Bonsi and I can make'.[63] The solution could be the recruitment of young people, who would be readier and faster in learning not only a complicated language but also the German lifestyle:

It is true that we would need a fourteen-year-old boy who could learn the language so that in two or three years' time we would be able to use him as if he was a German ... being young, he would get used to drinking beer as the brother of Bernardo Acciaiuoli did: he is more German than Italian. That is because youngsters adapt to the German habits more readily than the old ones ... Instead of Bonsi you should have sent a young boy because, although we may learn four words, if we had to pray the Saints we would not be able to do it even after ten years here. And this is sure.[64]

In Nuremberg, however, there were many Italians and therefore it was possible to sort things out. But when people moved out of the town, for example to the fairs of Leipzig, things were more difficult. As Talani wrote to Carletti,

Piero [Saliti] left Bonsi in Leipzig ... there may be a possibility for him to learn [German], because here [in Nuremberg] there are so many Italians that it is not possible to learn anything; there he will need to speak German, because there are no Italians.[65]

It must be said that German international merchant bankers often knew the Italian language after periods abroad – especially in Venice – during which they enhanced their all-round education in the business world. Pieter Ugleimer, a merchant and typographic entrepreneur born in Frankfurt but resident in Venice for many years, drew up his testament in Italian before dying in Milan in 1488.[66] Lucas Rem (1481–1541) was fourteen when he moved from Augsburg to Venice: he spent one and a half years there learning accounting and the Italian language, and then he moved to Lyons, where in a year he learnt French. He thus acquired above-average skills which allowed him to begin a career as an agent of the Welsers.[67]

Some Italians believed that not learning a foreign language was a statement of superiority: in other words, they expected others to learn Italian. When the Florentine Tommaso Spinelli received from two of his correspondents (one from Basel and the other from Nuremberg) some documents written in German, he was furious: 'He wrote to us in German!', he exclaimed, because he had been probably used to receiving everything in Italian.[68]

Even in this case it is not possible to generalize, however. There were exceptions, and the behaviour of Ugolotto degli Agli shows that not all of them hated German. In 1360, after many years spent in Germany, the eighty-year-old Ugolotto was so passionate about the language that even in Florence 'he wanted to speak German'.[69] Or at least this is the account given by Sacchetti, who, incidentally, seems to associate the knowledge of a foreign language with some sort of extravagance (this is also the case of Dino di Geri Tigliamochi, who often used Flemish or English expressions).[70] Beyond these literary examples, there are some letters which show an achieved level of integration: as Giovanni Olivieri wrote to Francesco Carletti in 1543, 'I think you have become a good German and you acquired all of their good habits'.[71] In truth Carletti had spent little time in Germany: therefore, either he was particularly gifted, or Olivieri was trying to flatter him with exaggerated praise.

In any case, in order to help trading relations with Germany, where they sent their luxury cloth, in 1472 the Florentine Arte di Por Santa Maria (silk guild) had four interpreters ('interpreti delle lingue') at its service: at least three of them were Germans.[72] It is not merely a coincidence that Antonio di Francesco da Pescia's additions (of 1417) to Saminiato de' Ricci's manual are words written in gothic fonts and in the German language.[73]

Venetians acted somewhat differently from the Florentines and were more inclined to learn German, as demonstrated also by the linguistic manuals produced from the 1420s. Obviously Venice had a tradition of commercial relations with Germany, and from the thirteenth century hosted the Fondaco dei Tedeschi, the location and reference point for the many German merchants and their merchandise in the city. Thus young Lucchese could learn the language in Venice and exploit this capability when acting as *sensali* (brokers).[74] Other merchants from the north of Italy ('Lombards' from Milan, Como and Asti) found it easy to adapt in Northern Europe and gradually stopped using their own language and even modified their names.[75]

In the seventeenth century things had presumably changed. If a merchant wanted to do profitable business during the fairs of Bolzano he needed to be fluent in German, and several merchants sent their sons to Germany to learn the language. In 1611 the Lucchese Vincenzo Burlamacchi left for Nuremberg because he wanted to learn German, whereas others learnt German in Venice.[76]

A Favourable Environment: The Low Countries

From 1384, with the domination of the Burgundian dukes, French was the official language at court and was currently used for business, even by local merchants.[77] This was a godsend for Italians, who could thus avoid learning Flemish, which would certainly be much harder. Despite being no higher than fourth in rank in the management team of the 1466 Bruges branch of the Medici bank, Carlo Cavalcanti was the one in charge of selling silks and brocades at the Burgundian court, due both to his charm and to his fluency in French.[78] The newly appointed manager of the firm, Tommaso Portinari, who was 'very much at home at the Burgundian court', was capable of the same degree of fluency after almost twenty years in Bruges, where he might have picked up the basics of some Flemish as well.[79] Surely some commitment towards the local language was shown by the Lucchese Guinigi, who, in the mid-fifteenth century, owned 'a booklet to learn Flemish'.[80]

In the mid-sixteenth century, despite having lived in Antwerp for some forty years, Giancarlo Affaitati from Cremona did not make use of any other language than Italian.[81] At this time Antwerp was a very cosmopolitan city, which created a very favourable environment for Italian trade and communication. Lodovico Guicciardini made this very clear in his *Descrittione*: it was 'convenient and admirable' that the inhabitants of Antwerp, including many women, were able to speak three or four languages, and some even five, six or seven.[82] Credit had to be given to the schooling system but also to the fact that the Brabantine town allowed proximity between many foreigners and therefore the possibility of practising various languages. Guicciardini was full of admiration for the existence of so many schools where French, Italian and Spanish were taught, so that it seemed that 'this is and must be the common homeland of all the Christian nations' ('questa è, & ha da essere la patria comune di tutte le nationi de Christiani'); and this of course was an advantage for all foreigners, because the native language – Flemish – is very rich but also 'very difficult to learn and even more difficult to pronounce' ('molto difficile ad imparare, & piu difficile ancora a pronuntiare').[83] Moreover, many merchants from Antwerp travelled to Italy to learn the language: knowledge of some Italian allowed them to trade with Spanish merchants as well.

In sixteenth-century Antwerp, members of the illustrious mercantile family Della Faille exchanged letters in Italian not only with their Italian correspondents but also with other Flemings and with some Germans (especially from Augsburg), even though the grammar was often incorrect.[84] Sometimes the use of Italian went beyond the borders of business correspondence; even in some personal letters, words or phrases in Italian could be mixed with sentences in Flemish. The Van der Meulen maintained this attitude even after their transfer to the northern Low Countries at the end of the century. Italian, moreover, was also used in book-keeping, especially in Antwerp, where some words could however be written in Flemish.[85]

Conclusion

Merchants carried out trade with or without knowledge of the local language. Perhaps Florentines hated Germany, but they still sold a lot of luxury cloth there: language was never an insuperable barrier. Language learning was in fact looked at in a very practical way: merchants adapted to the circumstances, made the effort to learn where it was necessary or at least convenient to do so, and were on the contrary less concerned in those areas where they did not really need to know the foreign language. Being fluent in a language was important if it brought advantages: in those places where it was not needed (e.g. because of the similarity of languages), it was not a problem. Where – on the on the other hand – trading was impossible, different solutions had to be found.

Italian, nevertheless, was an important language in business, and therefore Italian merchants could have some expectations of their commercial counterparts knowing it; otherwise they would try to have factors or correspondents able to communicate in the local language. In the last instance they could also resort to the use of interpreters, even though this was also a choice to be carefully analysed, given the danger connected to the disclosure of information to third parties. In addition to professional interpreters, as we have seen, there were other professionals whose linguistic expertise could compensate for the merchants' shortcomings: brokers, notaries, scriveners and others could, in other words, bring different parties together and act as agents in the strengthening of the network-building process.

One of the risks of being (and appearing) a foreigner was the possibility of being cheated, for example by an increase in price.[86] In other instances it could be a matter of safety: in his *Itinerary*, Fynes Morison made several comments on the importance of learning languages for travellers (in the chapter 'Of Precepts for Travellers'). Latin still proved useful in Germany, but his advice was that travellers learnt at least the basics of local languages; he used this trick himself when it came to disguising his nationality in order to avoid dangers.[87]

Generally speaking, it is difficult to comment on the level of linguistic skill attained by Italian merchants. Very few must have become really fluent, especially in Northern Europe: if we look at the surviving ledgers for Bruges and London, for example, we notice that the spelling of all foreign names is heavily mangled. That would not have happened, obviously, had they acquired perfect fluency.

Compatriots abroad were inclined to group together; those coming from the Italian peninsula at times felt 'Italian', while on other occasions they more parochially felt Florentine, Genoese, Venetian, etc. There is no doubt that language is a sign of identity and cultural cohesion. However, it would be hard to consider this solely as the consequence of a linguistic brotherhood, since so many other factors were also involved. If we look at the business world of late medieval and early modern Europe, we certainly find elements of cohesion – features, in other words, that rose above nationality. While it is difficult to consider language as one of them, techniques, nevertheless, could 'transcend linguistic barriers' and constitute a common feature ('facteur d'identification') for the community of international businessmen. Written formalization of certain instruments, such as bills of exchange, was less important than their functionality. They could be understood and used no matter the language in which they were written.[88] In other words, there could be codified formulae that in practice served as 'bridges' for crossing the river of linguistic difference: foreign merchants were often able to write letters in Italian to their Italian counterparts, not necessarily because they knew the language well but because they could base them on some formulaic expressions.

It would certainly be interesting to evaluate whether fluency in a language was a useful weapon in the hands of merchants abroad: that is to say, whether, during commercial relations with local merchants, the knowledge of their language threw a more favourable light on those who possessed it, therefore allowing them better terms of trade and larger profits, although both would be difficult to quantify. One would encounter the same difficulties in trying to establish a correlation between knowledge of languages and volume of trade. Both factual and counterfactual tests would prove unsatisfactory.

On the other hand, it is interesting to note that regulations concerning foreign languages could at times be used as a barrier against the creation of networks. In the 1410s and 1420s the Hansa established that no *butenhansen* (non-Hanseatic traders) in Livonia could learn local languages: clearly this was aimed at preventing them from entering direct trade.[89] In the mid-fourteenth century, the Venetian government prohibited merchants from employing factors or employees who knew German ('scientes linguam teuthonicam') in the Fondaco dei Tedeschi because they often conducted business in private ('faciendo res oculte') and in an illicit way.[90]

Language, obviously, was and is not only a matter of convenience, but also one of the elements by which the desire and capability to integrate in foreign lands can be assessed. The study of a language could thus become a more active choice, not just driven by necessity (doing business) but also by 'pleasure' (the willingness to acquire the habits of the host land). In terms of local networking, this might have a positive effect: dealings with local merchants could become easier and exchange could go beyond a simple business relationship. One might therefore ask whether language was a determinant in creating a network, and whether there was a language-driven attitude to creating a network, or even whether fluency in a foreign language was a prerequisite to penetrate other networks. Was it, in other words, a tool in the hands of foreign merchants? Unfortunately, for the late Middle Ages and the early modern period, evidence is really scant and even letters and memoirs hardly refer to this issue; lack of documentary support is of course even greater with reference to oral communication. Therefore, if it is not possible to give a statement in positive terms (language was a prerequisite to create networks), it is undoubtedly true that the lack of knowledge of foreign languages could hardly undermine the network that each Italian international merchant had carefully developed throughout Europe: a network based on nodal points represented by fellow Italians, but also articulated through smaller local networks where communication did not need to be perfect, but just needed to be effective.

4 NETWORKS AND COMMERCIAL PENETRATION MODELS IN THE LATE MEDIEVAL MEDITERRANEAN: REVISITING THE DATINI

Angela Orlandi

The subject of the presence of foreigners in Europe in the medieval and early modern periods has attracted major scholarly attention since the 1950s with the argument that the expansion of the Mediterranean was based on the circulation of people and goods. Many scholars have accounted for the success of these traders not only by using economic rationales (company organization, business techniques and innovation) but also with reference to shared origin and religion, which ensured close links, mutual support and frequent exchanges of information.[1]

In the wake of these interpretations and giving space to intercultural relations, the issue of economic actors in foreign lands has recently been taken up once again, with work focusing on merchant communities and networks in a range of European and extra-European contexts. Italian, French, English, Spanish, Portuguese and Indian Ocean communities have been analysed in studies that have focused largely on the informal rules underlying the functioning of economic networks scattered over the various areas.[2]

This essay is part of this research trend, and also part of a broader analysis which attempts to reinterpret the organizational choices and commercial penetration strategies used by the Datini group abroad in terms of their effectiveness. My research has essentially focused on at least two fundamental issues: company structure (company form, capital invested, quality of human capital in the various decision-making levels) and the characteristics of the network created by the group. These, as we will see, were networks whose efficiency did not depend simply on size but also on the other two aspects cited above, and thus on the capacity of the merchants to mediate between the need to develop their business and the contexts in which they operated.

For reasons of space and consistency with the contents of this volume, I have decided to leave out the first part of the analysis, which will be published in an alternative form. However, it is preliminary to my network analysis and it would thus seem important to touch here on some of the main themes dealt with in the latter. Lengthy research on accounting documents and other evidence from the Florentine economic environment of the day have convinced me of the need to look afresh at some modern theories on the company expansion mechanisms of these firms. I am not convinced that business success in the fourteenth and fifteenth centuries was simply a matter of large company size and belonging to a powerful family. Such interpretations are merely an uncritical rewriting of the economic histories produced throughout the bulk of the twentieth century, which argued that the Datini holding was inevitably weak because it was of medium size and not linked to a large family. The idea that the international economy of the day was based on the founding action of great capital companies requires wide-ranging re-evaluation. Elsewhere I will attempt to demonstrate this concept from the starting point of analyses of the financial and organizational characteristics of a significant number of companies which had dealings with the Datini group in various parts of Europe. With regard to the assumption that only companies with important families behind them had major competitive advantages, I will demonstrate the extent to which this is unfounded by means of interpretative models which business sciences use to analyse the relationship between family governance and firm performance in my forthcoming essay.

Starting, then, from the assumption that the Datini group was a vibrant system of companies with well-trained human capital, I will attempt to add to analyses of its market penetration capabilities in the various markets by using a network-type analysis.[3] I believe that a strong relationship existed between network characteristics and entrepreneurial success.

The Datini Networks

Economists, sociologists and economic historians have long understood that human action is not always based on rational criteria. Emotional factors also influence behaviour, as do perceptions and influences from events happening around us in the cultural and social context in which our activities take place.[4] There is no need here to cite Karl Paul Polanyi's 1944 contribution to this issue. Polanyi was perhaps the first and best-known scholar to argue that personal relationships are part of social networks based on trust and exchange relationships which are a world away from considerations of economic rationality.[5]

This vision of relationships and the various motives behind economic choices is endorsed by a study of the behaviour of Francesco di Marco Datini, the Merchant of Prato. The recent volume devoted to him on the occasion of the sixth centenary of his death touches on the theme of the influence of secular and religious thought on the choices of Tuscan businessmen on more than one occasion and the ways in which conflict between the strictures of the Church and everyday customs was a fact of life for them.[6] Now convinced of the legitimacy of the wealth earned from trade and prompted by pride in their business success, these businessmen were often successful in their untiring efforts to bring together the various experiences and stimulants which emerged from their complex system of economic and social relationships.

Datini is a case in point. His risk and investment preferences were the result not only of the effectiveness of the Tuscan city 'training' system but also of the influence of the multiplicity of impulses from the context he worked in. The lifestyle models of the urban world of his day made it difficult to separate moral principles from practical action. In the context in which our merchant lived, the economic, social, relationship and religious spheres were indissolubly linked. Small or large, no businessman was free of the effects of these complex influences in his relations with others. Such men interacted incessantly with each other, with economic and social organizations and with the establishment. I would thus argue that it is natural that a better understanding of the actions of such men cannot avoid taking into account Mark Granovetter's thesis according to which economic actions and institutions are influenced by non-economic relationships and the structure of the whole network of which these relationships are part.[7]

The Merchant of Prato's contacts with individuals, companies and public and religious institutions were extensive, and these were relationships which evolved and expanded as Datini's image and turnover increased, taking on characteristics which would appear to be both cause and effect of his entrepreneurial mentality.

For an idea of the geographical size and quantity of these relationships, a partial but significant figure will suffice. For the duration of his forty years of documented activity, Datini and his companies received letters from 4,384 different correspondents in 267 European and Mediterranean trading towns and cities.[8] This one simple figure speaks volumes about the existence of a complex and varied network and its composition and functioning which goes well beyond the actual number of letter writers in itself. It was a wide-ranging network understood as a collection of dyadic bonds based on a range of elements such as business dealings, family ties, acquaintanceship, friendship and other factors.

At least in the first part of this study we will leave the analysis of direct and personal relationships – daily and neighbourhood relationships which are difficult to analyse quantitatively – to one side in order to focus our attention on the volume of links and contacts in the network based on letter exchange, the only means of communication available to the businessmen of the day.

In analysing the commercial correspondence of the day, I have opted to limit my study to a brief period capable of providing important insight into the characteristics of a continually evolving network. My study is thus limited to an analysis of the letters sent and received between 1 January and 31 December 1399, the year in which the system was at its maximum expansion.

The total number of letters dating to 1399 was 6,642,[9] and date, sender, addressee, departure and destination were extrapolated from these.[10] It is important to bear in mind that, in Datini and his correspondents' day, copybooks did not exist and thus the archives do not contain the letters which the group sent to its many external correspondents. The database contains only the letters which were sent to one of the various offices of the group or were preserved there. This allows us to reconstruct the network as whole but prevents us from measuring the intensity of relationships with people and individuals outside the group.

The data gathered was processed using the Netdraw programme.[11] This mathematical model allows us to construct a network formed of threads of variable thickness which link the various entities. I am aware of the limitations of an analysis of the quantitative type. However, at the same time I would argue that it gives us a graphical representation of the structures and subjects that made up the network and thus enables us to identify information on contacts, including interlinked contacts, which would otherwise probably not emerge. Obviously, the visual impact of the summary requires an adequate critical analysis to accompany its quantitative data.

The thickness of the threads is a measure of the intensity of the economic and human relationships, the exchange of information, the forms of partnership, the sharing of commercial choices, the methods used in any mutual support and the degree of trust that was created between the various elements in the network.

In the Datini network, the thickest threads were principally partners, managers and employees occupying various positions in the group's companies. I will call that collection of threads which linked the employees and partners of the companies of our merchant its 'Internal Network'. This was the essential reference nucleus on whose effectiveness the group's economic strategies and potential for success depended. It was based on the Datini companies' wider, fluctuating network of relationships.

The network's efficiency was ensured not only by the expertise of the individuals in it (nodal points) but also by the quality and intensity of the exchanges of news and opinions which took place in various ways between the partners and employees in it. It was sustained by ongoing exchanges between them and between each of them with Datini. The effect of geographical distance was diminished by an intense exchange of letters consisting of official (company) and private (own, as they were called at the time) letters.[12] Even the most superficial glance at the contents of these letters gives an overview of the objectives of these continual exchanges, which contained a great many elements: from the rationality and professionalism of the individuals concerned to their emotions and susceptibility. From the point of view of the business historian, there is interesting information on these men's outlooks and the ways in which they made decisions. Firstly, underlying movements within the Internal Network show stimuli aimed at maintaining a high level of positive tension in relationships between partners and employees and from this emerges a widespread sense of pride at belonging to the group and mutual solidarity, elements which succeeded in reducing the effects of any intense disagreements or opportunistic behaviour. Datini's moral as well as economic stature kept positive feelings to the fore and encouraged good behaviour from the members of the whole Internal Network, which was made up of men who were far apart geographically but brought together by a shared entrepreneurial outlook. Letter exchanges were fundamental in spreading the most important good news of direct or indirect economic relevance.

As has been well known since Federigo Melis wrote his first studies, such commercial correspondence lent itself to a great many analyses. Its highly varied contents provide significant opportunities for interdisciplinary studies. Recent studies have concentrated on specifically linguistic or literary aspects and formal issues underlying writing and reading methods in the letters, on extrapolation and memorization of the contents, and on inventory systems and the places in which the letters themselves were kept,[13] all issues which touch on and enhance analysis from an economic history perspective.

Commercial letters had a structure and framework which we come across in both the Datini group's internal correspondence and their external correspondence. The ritual formula, which began with the date of the letter, was always followed by references to the last letters received and sent. In this way the two correspondents could keep checks on their correspondence. The body of the letter was then laid out in paragraphs of various lengths which usually dealt with open questions and developments regarding them. Apart from such an organized progression, there were no rules which specified that the group's internal issues should be dealt with before other issues. Attacks by corsairs or the confiscation of a shipment of goods were often mentioned before anything else.

The most in-depth questions were dealt with at all times in internal correspondence. Thus, to give an example, an indication of the exchange rates on the most important markets is to be found almost exclusively in the group's letter exchanges.

Essentially, the main subject matters of each letter were negotiations under way, internal corporate issues, assessments of rival economic actors, the economic, political, religious and health situation, transport methods and routes, current prices, exchange rate trends, liquidity conditions on the markets, and customs, weights and measures in the various local contexts.

Whether they were partners, managers or employees, correspondents devoted a significant part of their working day to letter writing. A great deal was at stake because advance news of market trends, reliable information and up-to-date figures on economic and political events were the key to successful decision-making. There is no need to underline here that the frequency of letter exchanges and the wealth of information contained in them was particularly significant within the group. This method of communication, while characteristic of the Tuscans generally – who were merchants with pens in their hands[14] – was not always at the level of Datini's virtual obsession that he expected of himself and his employees.

If correspondents were foreigners, this framework was modified. The Catalans and Castilians, for example, dated the letter at the end and the contents of their letters were more succinct.

Despite the fact that the data gathered refers to a single year, its quantity makes a graphical reconstruction of the whole network made up of the sum of the epistolary contacts of each office within the whole group difficult. Hence this study will be limited to an analysis of certain parts of the Datini network. The first figure in this essay shows the group's internal networks; the second is based on all of the letters sent and received by Francesco Datini and will facilitate an understanding of the intensity of his activity. Finally, in order to examine the group's economic penetration policies in foreign lands, I have chosen to reconstruct the networks based around each of the three Catalan companies (Figures 4.3–5). In the graphs I have distinguished between company correspondence and that of the partners and managers of the individual offices. Such a distinction emerged from the need to portray the intensity of the contacts between the individual partners and between them and Francesco more accurately. Each nodal point represents the subject or company along with the place wherein he/it operated; the legend for the place name codes used in the figures is provided below. Some individuals moved away from the main office, in which case they appear more than once with a note on the place of temporary residence.

Place name legend:

Ai = Aix-en-Provence	Av = Avignon	Ciu = Ciudadela	Ib = Ibiza	Mi = Milan
Al = Alicante	Ba = Barcelona	Co = Collioure	Já = Játiva	Mo = Montpellier
Al = Alicante	Bi = Bibbiena	Cs = Castel-nuovo Scrivia	Lc = Las Cuevas de Vinromá	Mon = Montici (Florence)
Alb = Albocacer	Bm = Barberino di Mugello	De = Denia	Le = Lerida	On = Onteniente
Alc = Alcudia (Majorca)	Bo = Bologna	Fe = Ferrara	Li = Livorno	Ond = Onda
Am = Aigues-Mortes	Bon = Bona	Fil = Filettole (Prato)	Lis = Lisbon	Pa = Paris
An = Ancon	Br = Bruges	Fl = Florence	Lo = London	Pad = Padova
Ar = Arezzo	Ca = Cafaggio	Ge = Genoa	Lu = Lucca	Pal = Palamos
Arl = Arles	Car = Carmignano (Prato)	Gr = Griciglano (Prato)	Ma = Majorca	Pav = Pavia
	Cico = Cico		Mah = Mahon	Pe = Perpignan
			Mar = Marseilles	Peñ = Peñiscolav

Per = Perugia	Pr = Prato	Sf = San Feliu	Sy = Syracuse	Va = Valencia
Pi = Pisa	Pr = Prato	de Guixols	To = Tortosa	Ve = Venice
Pie = Pietrasanta	Ro = Rome	Sm = San Mateu	Tod = Todi	Vf = Vico
Pis = Pistoia	Sg = Santa	So = Solsona	Ul = Località	Fiorentino
	Gonda		sconosciuta	Za = Zaragoza

The Internal Network

The graph of the Internal Network (Figure 4.1) shows the intensity of the letter exchanges between the senior partner, partners, managers and labour masters of the group's companies. The strength of the Florence-based company – as the parent company managed personally by Datini with the vital support of Stoldo di Lorenzo – within the network is immediately apparent. However, in the graph's expanded form the twofold lines of communication which show the direction of the letters between each nodal point would also be fully visible. My descriptive analysis of the network and the table illustrating the exchange of company letters (Table 4.1) overcomes these limitations.

Table 4.1: Correspondence exchanged between the companies of the group, 1 January–31 December 1399.

	Recipient company									
Sending company		Avignon	Barcelona	Florence	Genoa	Majorca	Pisa	Valencia	Dyers guild	Wool guild	Cloth association
	Avignon	0	64	38	32	11	29	6	0	0	0
	Barcelona	0	0	90	92	109	51	142	0	0	0
	Florence	1	37	0	151	32	242	59	0	4	0
	Genoa	0	46	152	0	24	86	23	0	0	0
	Majorca	0	72	29	22	0	32	48	0	0	3
	Pisa	0	41	224	91	12	0	9	7	0	0
	Valencia	0	89	61	35	57	13	0	0	0	0
	Dyers guild	0	0	0	0	0	0	0	0	0	0
	Wool guild	0	0	0	0	0	1	0	0	0	0
	Cloth association	3	21	0	20	35	39	4	0	2	0
	Banking	0	1	0	0	0	1	0	0	0	0

It is, in any case, useful to note two apparent anomalies which emerge from Table 4.1 around the scarcity of links with the Avignon company and that of the Florentine bank.

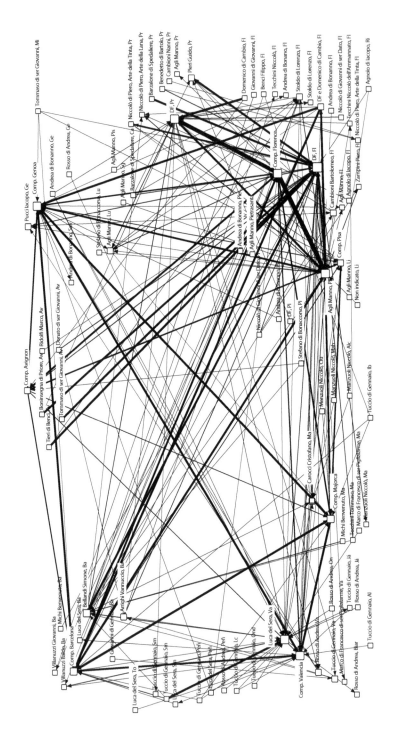

Figure 4.1: The Internal Network, 1 January–31 December 1399.

As far as Avignon is concerned, almost all of the letters received have been lost, with the exception of four letters (one from the Florence company and three invoices sent by the manager of the cloth association). On the other hand, in the correspondence files at other companies, it is clear that Tieri di Benci, the Avignon partner, sent 38 letters to Florence, 64 to Barcelona, 32 to Genoa and 29 to Pisa.

The banking company – which had taken on considerable autonomy from the group almost immediately as a result of its high degree of specialization – was virtually managed personally by Francesco Datini, who, when he was not in Florence, directed its actions by writing to its managing partner, Bartolomeo Cambioni. As Figure 4.1 indicates, this does not mean that it was at the margins of the network. Even a cursory glance at the accounts of each company shows how frequent financial operations and fund transfers with the support of the bank were. We find frequent letter exchanges on the matter between the companies of the group and the Florence company. Rather than with its manager, discussions regarding the bank's functions – which tailed off a few months after it was set up – went through the private and company correspondence between all the partners and managers, showing, in this case too, Datini's strong personal involvement in the fundamental choices and economic trends of the group.

The content and intensity of the letter exchanges in the twelve months analysed show the extent to which all the managing partners and the most important employees took a significant role in decisions relating to the group. This involvement is evident from the immediate visual impact of the graph, which shows a network of contacts linking men and companies, including those that did not go through the intermediation of the Florentine management.

The case of the correspondence exchanged with the Pisa company consisting of 466 letters received and sent by the Florentine parent company is unusual. This almost frenetic correspondence was the result of political difficulties exacerbating a situation of economic crisis which had hit the city several months previously. In February 1399 Gherardo d'Appiano had ceded Pisa to the Conte di Virtù, Gian Galeazzo Visconti, who, as the enemy of the Florentines, was in a position to create considerable difficulties for merchants associated to Datini.[15] The need to receive up-to-date news on developments influenced the correspondence of the other partners too.

Observing the density of the interweaving in Figure 4.1 and the data in Table 4.1 more generally, apart from Florence's obvious role, frequent contacts between the companies relating to their specific roles are apparent. Genoa's importance consisted of its linking role between the north-central Italian and Catalan markets, where the bulk of the group's commercial interests lay.[16] This explains the letter exchanges between Andrea di Bonanno, partner and manager in Genoa, and his colleagues in Catalonia. Links with Barcelona were especially intense because the Genoa offices often sent products for the entire Catalan company there. There was intense correspondence with Pisa too, the natural reference port for the Tuscan hinterland. As well as the usual information on internal affairs, letters dealt with market trends, exchange rates and prices, and all issues concerning navigation, including risks and routes. There were problems with access to the port of Pisa, and the Genoa managers had to carefully assess which ship to entrust each single shipment to and which Tuscan port was best suited for it. All this occurred, clearly, with Datini or Stoldo di Lorenzo's consent. Significant letter exchanges between Andrea di Bonanno and Florence can be explained by the great complexity of the political and economic situation in Genoa. Struggles between the Guelphs and Ghibellines impacted seriously on the economy and city government to such an extent that the group's deputy manager Stoldo argued that it was necessary to dismantle the *fondaco*. It is easy then to imagine the exchange of criticisms, suggestions and opinions between Genoa and the parent company.[17]

With regard to the Catalan companies – the main reference points in the complex Datini group exchange system – they had frequent contacts with everyone and particularly with Florence. It was a network of extremely complex relationships which impacted on all questions of general or specific interest. Internal contacts between the three Catalonia company offices were particularly marked.[18] News, economic and social information and management issues were dealt with in great detail in their letters because of the specific framework of this small holding company within the Datini company system. The shared responsibility which bound together its three managers and the frequent sharing of news and opinions made this network an especially effective management tool. Valencia and Barcelona exchanged 231 letters, Majorca and Barcelona 181, Valencia and Majorca 105. This intense web of correspondence also included the bags which left Florence full of letters for Catalonia. Stoldo sent 37 to Simone Bellandi,[19] 59 to Luca del Sera[20] and 32 to Cristofano Carocci.[21] There was nothing coincidental about this intense correspondence because it was precisely in these twelve months that the decision was taken to promote Simone Bellandi from manager of the Barcelona office to company partner. Until then, next to Datini's name, the Barcelona company name had borne that of Luca del Sera, who had taken a few trips to the Catalan capital in the early months of 1399 to meet its manager in person. Bellandi was made partner at some point between the end of 1399 and early 1400, and thus the desire to make a quick decision and concerns regarding finding the necessary capital prompted him to write as many as 24 letters to Francesco Datini. For his part, Datini replied 14 times and with a detached air urged him simply to 'do well' and told him that, if necessary, he and Stoldo – the Florence company that is – would put up his share of 300 florins![22]

These intense contacts show that the Catalonia partners implemented Datini's strategic projects in general terms. Autonomy and the corresponding responsibility for results obtained were stronger here.

Francesco Datini's Network

Figure 4.2 shows the network which Datini managed personally by means of his 1399 correspondence. Overall he received 957 letters in a single year from 129 individuals, 88 of whom were external to the group, and wrote 298 letters overall. He himself sent 419 letters from Florence, Prato and Pisa[23] to 31 addressees, 11 of whom were external to the company system. These wrote from 31 different places, while Datini sent his letters to 11 different places.

Datini complained that dealing with his correspondence kept him busy day and night. If we consider that 1,376 letters passed through his hands in that year and that we have almost none of those written to individuals external to the group, we can imagine just how well founded this complaint was. In a letter to Luca del Sera, he wrote that he had not been able to reply quickly to his letter 'because it is 8 in the evening, I still have a lot to do and I don't feel well, I'm drowning in all this work'.[24]

The different densities of the network contacts emerge from Figure 4.2. Contacts between the Prato and Florence offices are more frequent, and this was because our merchant moved between his homes in Prato and Florence. When he was in his hometown he wrote a great deal of letters to Stoldo di Lorenzo, whereas when he was in Florence he wrote to those managing his Prato activities. He had two industrial wool cloth manufacturing and dying companies in Prato, where his wife Margherita normally lived,[25] as well as two personal companies – retail workshops – managed by Guido Pieri and Barzalone di Spedaliere.[26]

Of the 1,373 letters, 411 were exchanged with his closest Prato employees and 208 with Stoldo and the Florence company. Overall, from his hometown he wrote to 42 individuals[27] and in Florence to 20.

Datini never missed the chance to make his managerial and supervisory role over the activities and behaviour of his partners and managers felt even in the most distant offices and to encourage their participation in company life. On strictly technical economic issues he shared responsibility with the Florence manager, Stoldo di Lorenzo. The letters exchanged between Florence and the group's offices, as we have seen, had this specific function as well as sharing all relevant economic information with everyone.

Datini's letters were varied in content and meaning. His own words clarify his thoughts better than any consideration of mine. In April 1406 he wrote to Cristofano Carocci to explain how exchanges of information, dialogue, advice and instructions helped staff to perform managerial roles with the constant aim of keeping the system unified and efficient: 'You know that lack of information and insults divide brothers from one another and sons from fathers, nephews from uncles, partners, labour masters and master craftsmen in the same way'.[28]

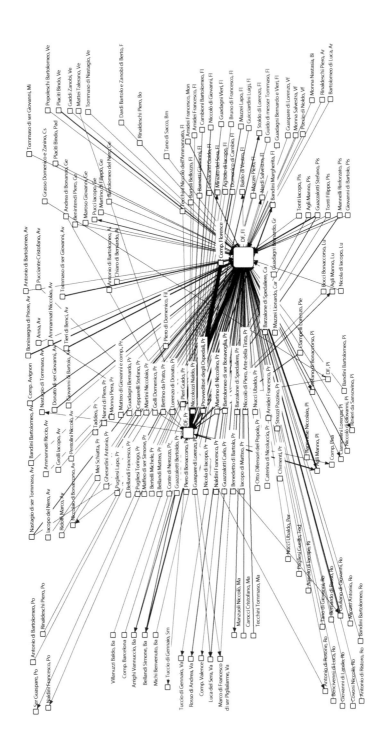

Figure 4.2: Francesco Datini's network in Florence and Prato, 1 January–31 December 1399.

This is the explanation for those long letters that he himself called 'bibles'[29] which were lists and thoughts on all the main issues and principles relating to personal or company relationships on which he continually took his employees to task. Apart from anything else, this allowed him to channel the skills and abilities of his employees in the right direction for the good and honour of both partners and the company.[30] Betraying Datini's and his colleagues' trust meant expulsion from the system. This is what happened to Tuccio di Gennaio, who had to leave Valencia to work for the Albertis. Even Stoldo, Datini's companion for much of his life, was expelled from the group amid great anger and bitterness and replaced with Luca del Sera in 1402.

Datini supervised and intervened to limit internal conflicts and head off opportunistic behaviour. He used his authority to maintain a cohesive spirit and strengthen his role as senior partner. A matter mentioned earlier is a good example of this, the reassuring but peremptory message sent to Simone Bellandi shortly before the latter was made partner. Datini's authority encompassed even the most intimate and personal affairs of his employees; examples of this are his solicitous attention to Cristofano Carocci to look personally after his property in Tuscany, or the determination with which he insisted that Luca del Sera should find a husband for the slave girl who was distracting him from his managerial responsibilities.[31] The partners replied to Datini with respect and devotion but never kept silent if they disagreed with him at any time. Thus Luca del Sera forcefully criticized Datini's decision to open a bank, which he believed would divert funds from the group's companies; and, unable to deny the advantages of an operation which would significantly reduce the unproductivity of such great money reserves, he pleaded the moral issue, adding that at that time those working in exchange were moving towards trade and abandoning money exchange.[32]

A great many nodal points on Figure 4.2 are the group's external contacts (88 subjects) for whom, as I mentioned earlier, we do not have copies of the letters sent to them. For a better understanding of this graph, it is also important to highlight the fact that letter-writing contacts with external companies were mainly dealt with by the individual companies of the group and not by Datini himself. The letters sent directly to Datini, with very few exceptions, were from individuals linked to him in various ways. We thus discover letters which help us to understand the personal contacts and moral care and friendship which had very little to do with business and much more to do with that particular friendship and solidarity value system which was so characteristic of the coterie.[33] It is interesting to note that Datini had as many as 18 contacts in Avignon (in third place after Prato and Florence), a clear sign of the intense and long-lasting relationships which he had built up and maintained in the lands in which his adventures had begun.[34]

There are also letters which show Datini's contacts with town institutions such as the Hospital Superintendents, Antonio Gherardini Prato and San Miniato *podestà* or from the Eight Defenders of the People.[35] We also find letters which speak of pressing economic matters from businessmen to whom Datini had turned for purchases relating to his building work on his Prato *palazzo* and his villa in the hills nearby such as those from the Pistoia companies of Tonti and Guazzalotti with 33 letters. From his bank at the back of a bishop's *palazzo*, Datini's friend and banker Rinforzato Mannelli[36] sent him 12 letters. He sold Datini timber and supplied him with luxury food products from the Pistoia Mountains, particularly game. There were eight different letter writers in Pistoia. Datini also had 9 contacts in Rome (27 letters).

The network set out in Figure 4.2 has been extrapolated from that of the group and takes on a more personal form in order to focus on certain aspects of our merchant's life. To portray the full complexity of the stimuli which influenced his behaviour, to this network of relationships and information we should add the multiplicity of daily contacts and public and private relations which were part of his life in Prato and Florence.

Naturally, family contacts also played a part, particularly those with his wife, Margherita Bandini, and with his closest friend and confidant, Prato notary Lapo Mazzei. As Datini was continually travelling between Prato and Florence, these two fundamentally important ties were also cultivated by means of an intense correspondence. Datini and his wife exchanged 35 letters, while the notary sent 8 letters. The studies carried out on these two groups of letters tell us a great deal about the characters of these three individuals, the strength of Margherita's influence on Datini and the influence of Lapo but also on Datini's liveliness of thought and his formidable business drive.[37]

The Catalonia Company's Extended Network

The vast exchange system that the Datini group was able to establish, as we have seen, was supported by a multitude of traders and companies of varied origin – though the majority were Tuscan and Italian – and guaranteed a direct or indirect presence in all of the largest emporiums in the Mediterranean, the North Sea and Europe. This part of the network varied in size and extended to various degrees according to the number of correspondents. In terms of geographical position, it was located within an irregular polygon with points of maximum extension in Bristol, Safi, Mecca, Tana and Ragusa.

Naturally the strength and role of the various correspondents were not the same. This diversity related to the scope and the continuity of economic relationships, which depended in turn on the economic importance of the area they were based in. We will focus here on the three firms that were subdivisions of the company of Catalonia using data from the letters received from each office and its manager for which each graph presents two different integrated networks (Figures 4.3–5).

For the duration of the twelve months examined, 154 subjects (131 external to the group) wrote 1,641 letters to Barcelona from 36 different towns and cities. 1,107 letters arrived in Majorca from 123 letter writers (109 external) in 28 towns and cities. Finally, Valencia opened 869 letters from 110 writers (92 external) from 29 places.[38]

The distribution of the nodal points and the thickness of the lines present in these three figures give a concrete feeling of the great size and intensity of the relationships with contacts in each location. This considerable density does not allow for an analytical reading of the individual places, but while the significance of internal letter-writing bonds may be obvious, the same is not true of the existence of autonomous and direct relationships with local businessmen present in each of the other two cities of the group. The manager of the Barcelona company could count on 13 contacts in Valencia (171 letters) and 10 in Majorca (100 letters). Cristofani Carocci, the Majorca manager, in turn received news from 27 Barcelona-based (401 letters) and 9 Valencia-based (142 letters) letter writers. In Valencia, Luca del Sera received news from 20 different traders active in Barcelona (301 letters) and 6 in Majorca (51 letters). This took place above all in relation to the most important clients, whose loyalty was encouraged by means of closer contacts which were free of intermediaries. However, the need to strengthen the network as an instrument for evaluating the accuracy of the information which was regularly crosschecked with news from the Internal Network should not be underestimated.

An examination of the intensity and geographical origin of the letters received over the course of 1399 shows the most important economic areas for the Catalonia company. Beginning with the south coast of France, taking in Perpignan, Montpelier, Aigues-Mortes and Arles, in Perpignan the main contact of the three Catalonia partners was Piero Tecchini, a large-scale merchant interested in the famous Perpignan cloth as well as many Iberian and African raw materials. In a single year as many as 20 merchants wrote 341 letters to Barcelona, 55 to Valencia and 40 to Palma de Mallorca from Montpelier. The main letter writer was Deo Ambrogi and Giovanni Franceschi's company which sent 55 letters to Barcelona, 45 to Valencia and 37 to Palma. Other important nodal points on the network were Antonio Saulli and Benedetto Bocci (87 letters), Zanobi Gaddi and Benedetto Ruspi (16 letters) and Piggello Portinari (38 letters). In Arles the contact was Matteo Benini and in Aigues Mortes Giame Consigli.

These intense letter exchanges kept the three managers up to date on movements in the various ports and enabled them to assess the characteristics of those markets, their market potential and the events which might affect them.

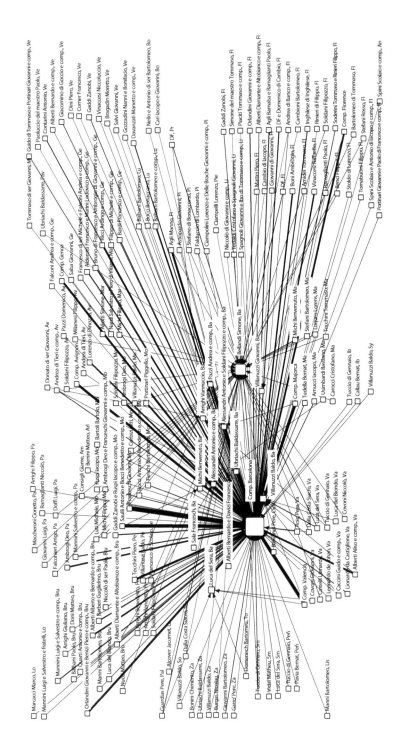

Figure 4.3: The Barcelona network and its manager, 1 January–31 December 1399.

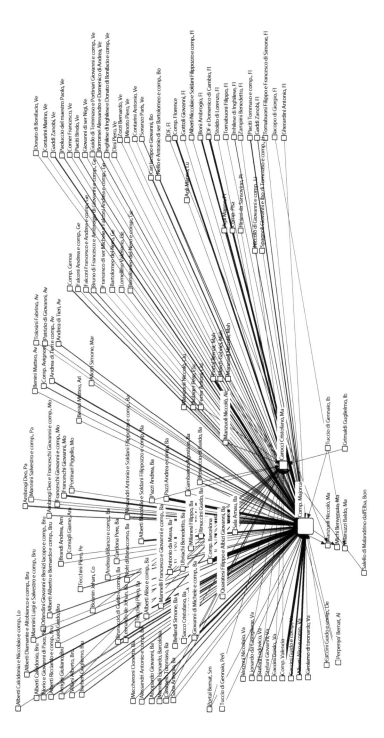

Figure 4.4: The Majorca network and its manager, 1 January–31 December 1399.

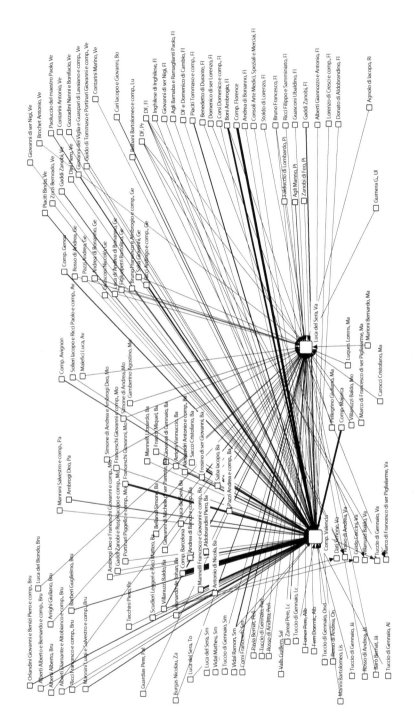

Figure 4.5: The Valencia company network and its manager, 1 January–31 December 1399.

For each type of goods sent to these market places, ranging from kermes to skins, wool, dried fruit and Barbary Coast products, it was important to adjust buying policies according not only to changing economic conditions but also to health, religious, political and social vicissitudes. Thus, for example, when Giovanni Franceschi informed Luca del Sera that the arrival of armed men was expected in the Montpelier area, the Valencia manager got to work speeding up an order for ostrich feathers which likely could be sold to make plumes for crests. In the same way, accurate and detailed information also enabled the company to organize purchases of local goods such as pastel not only for Tuscan dyers but also for those in Barcelona, Valencia and Palma de Mallorca.[39]

The pace of network communication with cities in Northern Europe was significant but less intense. On the Paris marketplace the correspondent of choice was once again Deo Ambrogi and Giovanni Franceschi's company (51 letters), which, with its widespread interests and links, entrusted much of its business in the south-west Mediterranean to the Datini group in Catalonia. Salvestro Mannini was also an important figure for the Datini companies in Catalonia, particularly in Barcelona and Valencia, and 17 letters were sent to him in 1399.

Contacts with London were not particularly strong. The company owned by the Manninis and Marco Marcacci, who each sent a letter, wrote to Barcelona. The Albertis, on the other hand, sent letters to Majorca. Correspondence with Bruges was much more extensive, with 13 letter writers from Barcelona, 11 from Majorca and 9 from Valencia: Alberti, Mannini and Orlandini were the most active. This area was important for the group and the Catalan companies in particular because of the Venetian galleys stopping in Majorca, Ibiza or Alicante. The letters sent from the Northern European markets to the partners of the Catalonia company and the correspondence between the managers show just how much importance was given to the movements of these ships, in which loads were extremely precious not only for the group's trade but also for that of its correspondents. The latter's letters supplied news on prices and demand for Iberian products in Bruges, London and Paris so that the managers of the Catalan companies could send the right quantities of spices, fruit, sugar, wine, oil, rice, almonds, saffron, alum, kermes, cotton, silk cloth and Florentine wool cloth to these markets.

The potential of such information throughout the network was very strong. One example will suffice: once news arrived of the excellent profits to be made selling kermes in Bruges, Guido Caccini, a Florentine merchant in Valencia, ordered several hundredweights, leading to an immediate price hike which prompted Luca del Sera to write: 'he has damaged himself and others and put money in the pockets of these Moors'.[40]

In October 1399 Giovanni Orlandini and Piero Benizi's company sent a letter from Bruges to Luca del Sera to inform him that recently crowned Henry IV had eliminated the 12 *denari* per *lira* tax on goods. This was news that prompted an immediate reaction, and Orlandini's letter to the effect that it would be a good idea to invest in English wool and cloth was almost superfluous.[41] The London correspondents sent shipments of tin and lead on the Venetian galleys as well as precious madder.

The transit of Venetian galleys in Catalan waters was the element that the three Datini companies had in common with Venice: 15 letter writers from Majorca, 13 from Barcelona and 12 from Valencia scattered along the canals of the Serenissima. Undoubtedly the most important was Zanobi di Taddeo Gaddi and his commission agent who sent 18 letters to Cristofano Carocci, 12 to Simone Bellandi and 10 to Luca del Sera in 1399. Other important contacts were the Contarinis and the Corners, excellent clients for the Barcelona companies and, above all, for Valencia, which supplied them with Maestrazgo wool.

If these were the elements which the three Catalan companies had in common, a reading of Figures 4.3, 4.4 and 4.5 brings out a number of peculiarities. Firstly, their different roles emerge. Barcelona, the leading company, had an intense correspondence with the Datini companies. This was prevalent also in the intense contacts with many of the Catalonia company's main reference areas such as London, Bruges, Paris, Montpellier, Perpignan and Venice. Its specific commercial activities extended well beyond the region between the Ebre river and the Pyrenees, yet it was in this latter area that they made themselves most intensely felt. Figure 4.3 shows that control of this trade was ensured by contacts with local economic actors in some of the most important hinterland marketplaces such as Lerida and, above all, Saragozza. A comparison of this figure with the following Figures 4.4 and 4.5 relating to Majorca and Valencia respectively shows that with very few exceptions, their links to the European cities were weaker, and their territorial specializations emerge.

With regard to Majorca, the network shows strong links with the Majorca merchants who lived and worked in these flourishing Balearic towns and with merchants of Maghreb origin who traded with the Barbary Coast. It was thanks to contacts with similar individuals that Cristofani gained his expertise in the many aspects of these markets and the characteristic features of each island such as Minorca, for example, about which he wrote: 'The island is small and when a bird arrives here everyone knows about it'.[42]

The Valencia offices specialized in trading Maestrazgo wool. It is well known that Tuccio di Gennaio moved to San Mateo in 1397 specifically to get directly involved in this trade. There is nothing coincidental about the fact that he wrote 28 letters to Luca in 1399, while the manager helped by keeping up correspondence with a number of local traders and large-scale breeders such as Pere Zareal di Cuevas de Vinromá and Ramon and Matheu Vidal in San Mateo.

It is well known that the specialized and joint functions of the three offices of the Catalonia company produced remarkable economic results. However, in the initial phase of its activity, above all in 1398 when his dearest partner Boninsegna di Matteo died,[43] Datini seemed to lose his enthusiasm for his plan to expand in the Iberian peninsula and turned his attention instead to reinforcing relations between Venice, Pisa and Florence. It was the relationships within the Internal Network and the widespread participation of all its managers that led to a different outcome. Luca del Sera, the Valencia manager, on the strength of the formidable system of information which he exchanged with both internal and external correspondents, held that the Catalan companies would be sufficiently successful if they gave priority to Montpelier, Bruges, Paris and Venice. Sustained also by other partners, he quickly garnered support for his vision of expansion.

On the Subject of the Capacity for Expansion: Catalonia and the Barbary Coast, Penetration and Means of Dealing with Different Cultural and Ethnic Groups

One of the reasons for the striking success of the Catalonia group was its marked ability to carve out a niche for itself – either directly or indirectly – among the nodal points of the trading system. We have seen that Luca del Sera maintained that direct links with the merchants present in certain European cities were important to strengthen the Catalonia group's trade on commission. This would have been easier for him if he had been able to keep up with competition from other companies which took large quantities of strategic raw materials in the Iberian Peninsula such as wool, dye substances and Iberian and North African leathers. Following the same line of reasoning, the Majorca company had also been set up with the intention of using it as a bridge to the Barbary Coast.

An analysis of the Catalan network and the contents of its correspondence shows the way that every peripheral structure and every manager at its head created its own network of relations, some of which were not related to dealings with traders and institutions in its own area of activity. This network of contacts swelled the group's wider network.

In a geographical – though not a commercial – sense these contacts were more limited, and we can imagine a network which was more detailed and complex in which letter exchanges were as important as direct personal relationships. This time the network in question was made up of daily contacts which were motivated as much by work and money as by human relationships based on trust and friendship. This additional element of organization of the movement of ideas, goods and money both allowed for and determined the methods used for penetration into the area concerned. Our merchants came up against situations determined by contexts which were very different from their own, and in

addition to skill and economic strength they also had to prove themselves able to
adapt to such new contexts and get to know the customs and formal and informal rules of these markets.

What happened to the Datini group in Maestrazgo and the North African
countries – particularly interesting areas from a trading point of view but equally
complex from the social as well as political and religious points of view – is a case
in point.

We have looked at the Datini's group's interest in the wool of the sheep reared
in the vast, rugged region to the north-east of Valencia. To make purchases of
this raw material more efficient, the company used the services of Prato-born
Tuccio di Gennaio, a great expert on these lands, at least for a few years. He
knew how complex the organization of this market was, how numerous the
merchants working in it were, and also how numerous the customs which regulated exchange and how strong the conflict between markets were. He knew
what cards to play and established direct contacts with breeders, nearly all of
whom he visited in their enclosures in the rugged hills of the region. The sums
of money at his disposal allowed him to reserve the wool before shearing and
ensure rapid payment in gold coins, the most popular coin. This was especially
effective behaviour because it put Tuccio in a privileged position compared with
both foreign and local companies.[44] Indeed, between February and December
1398 he bought wool from at least 118 different individuals. These included
great merchant-breeders like Piero Zareale, who sold him large quantities of
Albocásser wool, and Piero Moserrato, who controlled some of the Catí, 'Terici'
and 'Las Coves' production.

Along the routes which linked Tuccio to the nodal points on this particular
network moved convoys of mules loaded up with wool as well as bags full of
gold florins which were the measure and guarantee of the intensity and solid-
ity of these relationships. Tuccio expertly added his own personal touch to the
money issue. He thus had a pair of glasses picked up in Valencia for Piero Zarre-
ale di Cuevas de Vinromá's brother and asked Luca del Sera to put up Arnao di
Giardino, the nephew of Peñiscola's 'comandatore maggiore', who was travelling
to Valencia. These were relationships and contacts which were useful to him in
times of difficulty too, such as in 1398 when rumours of Florentine expulsion
were circulating in Valencia. Tuccio's friend Ramon Moraghes immediately
interceded with the Grand Master of Montesa in order to extend Tuccio's stay
in San Mateo.[45]

With regard to market penetration in the North African markets, Datini's
partners were well aware that the bulk of the trade with the Barbary Coast went
through Valencia and Palma de Mallorca.[46] Groups of Muslim merchants were
active in the city of Grao with strong links or offices in the Maghreb. These
included many distinguished names such as Xupió and the Abenxarnit family,

who were in close contact with Luca del Sera. In Majorca, which played a more important role than Valencia, our merchants had close relationships with the Salomó and Xibillí companies which were part of the sizeable Jewish component of Maghreb origin in the city. There is no need to underline here that both Luca del Sera in Valencia and Ambrogio and Cristofano in Majorca had positive relations with all religious groups as Christian, Muslim and Jewish.

After looking into the potential for opening new offices in these parts of the world, they decided not to do so. Barbary Coast products were certainly fundamentally important in the group's trade exchanges. The chance to buy and sell, including for third parties, kermes, leathers and other African products in demand on the European markets was certainly indispensable. This decision was based on efficiency considerations but even more on considerations of risk reduction and transaction costs. Such outcomes could not always be achieved by merchants establishing themselves directly in the areas in which raw materials originated. This latter option was chosen, as we have seen, for purchases of Iberian wool but was not for the Barbary Coast.

It seemed more useful to take account of the strong influence of Majorca traders who were attempting to defend their role as privileged intermediaries with the African coast. Antagonizing such groups would have created difficulties for the Majorca merchants, and Luca and Cristofani could not underestimate the risks of navigation, which was very dangerous in these seas because of political instability that had significantly increased Corsair raids.

They decided to extend and make use of their network of trading and personal relationships with the most important local merchants.[47] This meant that the various Catalan and Majorca merchants, whether Christian, Jewish or Muslim, acted in the name and on behalf of the Datini group, which had earned their trust thanks to the continuity of their relationship and rapid, precise payments. The active proximity of these particular friends reduced the difficulties inherent in a market which was under-regulated, and allowed the group to obtain regular supplies of Barbary Coast products at competitive prices and also to sell significant quantities of Florentine and European products such as cloth, precious spices, pearls and semi-worked gold on these markets.

On 4 July 1402, for example, Magaluff ben Atllon, a Jewish trader who travelled to Majorca, advised Carocci to send 20 roves of copper to Honaine where he himself was headed and offered to deal personally with the sale of it. In order to facilitate sending the metal, Magaluff recommended that Carrocci follow the indications with which another Jewish trader called Naxon den Lamia would supply him.[48] The letter was written in Catalan just like those sent by other local operators, but it is likely that the managers of the three Datini companies had rapidly learnt the local language. The choice of Tuccio di Gennaio was made on the basis of the fact that as well as being a good accountant, he also knew the language.[49]

This positive relationship also worked in reverse. The bond between Luca del Sera and Ali Abenxarnit, one of the most important families in Valencia's Moorish community, was a strong one. At the beginning of 1403, Ali sent his nephew Fillel to Algiers and agreed with del Sera that shiploads of goods should be sent to the Datini company in Majorca which would have dealt with transferring it, by means of a specific exemption certificate, to the city of Grao.

A cursory glance at the ledgers of the Majorca branch suffices for an understanding of the way that the group obtained its supplies of Barbary Coast products. An examination of these shows that between 1395 and 1411, the Majorca managers had trade relations with 954 merchants who were external to the Datini group. Of these, 751 were local (Minorca and Ibiza are included in this figure). Many of them were Jewish or recently converted Christians often of Maghreb origin who supplied the group with almost all of its African goods. The most frequently used included the members of the Xibilli family, Maghreb Jew Samuel Fatueri, originally from Oran, and newly converted Christian Ughet Gilibert. These were the three most important – although not the only – suppliers of leathers, kermes and other products.

On the basis of an analysis of the activities of the Valencia and Palma de Mallorca companies taken together, we can conclude that they managed to incorporate into their network a large and efficient fabric of contacts, which mitigated the complexities and operational limitations of the Maestrazgo and the Barbary Coast.

Conclusion

While it is true that the reason for the group's success is to be sought in its highly motivated staff, I would argue that its market incisiveness and consequent economic success[50] were principally the result of highly organized management of the skill levels required to take decisions, which, while hierarchical in style, was the fruit of widespread participation, a sort of 'collegiate' approach that reinforced mechanisms of loyalty and pride in belonging. The group's companies were scattered over a range of market contexts, often with little regulation and different norms and customs. This obliged its partners/managers to develop skills and abilities which were appropriate to the marketplaces they worked in and to the widest trading contexts.

All this rested on an efficient network of economic and personal contacts which they built up themselves. For an understanding of the value of this network, I have tried to examine the network in its entirety together with the complexity of its fabric, both in terms of the links which bound the partners and companies of the group together and those less substantial but no less important links which bound each partner and company with the variegated outside world.

The elements which enabled the network to function well were manifold. Firstly, it stimulated the exchange of information and the capacity to create and maintain solid relationships at every level. It was for this reason that the correspondence within the group's Internal Network was especially intense, although it was always and at all times combined with an adequate correspondence with traders outside the group. This was not only because news was a precious commodity but also because this meticulous correspondence showed the hard work and reliability of individuals' behaviour at all times.

It could be said that the network, which played a part in every decision, had an educational role which helped its employees to gain an understanding of the many aspects of daily and local life. It was for this reason that acquaintanceship, personal friendship and physical proximity were important. These relationships grew and developed through solidarity and mutual help mechanisms which were stronger the closer the customs. These developed not only among the Tuscans, though this was more likely, but also with traders from other countries.

There was nothing coincidental about networks founded on letter exchanges and every other type of personal relationship. They were based on economic plans and prospects. The training of Datini's men took account of the role of strategic products for each of the group's companies and its place in international trade. This is particularly in evidence for the Majorca and Valencia companies which, even more than Barcelona, took advantage of the opportunities offered by the local economy and its geographical position to incorporate local goods into international trade and, as Federigo Melis noted on several occasions, assign the two companies a centralizing and sorting role for goods from all over the Mediterranean and the North Sea. The network and the choice of its main players were a consequence of this vision.[51]

This particular network of relations was shot through with trust, the powerful but fleeting life force which made these relationships more effective and workable. It was precisely this trust which enabled Tuccio in 1397–8 to brush the competition in wool purchases to one side, including that of a certain Subiraza, a representative of the Soldanis, future partners of the Albertis in Barcelona. It was trust which enabled the Majorca company to benefit from Barbary Coast trade without needing to venture to these places itself. It was trust and personal relationships with local notables and establishment figures which enabled the group to resolve or get around limitations on trading activities or excessive taxation.[52]

This specific type of network, all of the main aspects of which I have attempted to set out, obviously interacted with the whole system of economic relations of the day, and its positive effects were felt on other levels too. The Datini network took part in – although it did not initiate – important processes of innovation in mercantile techniques. It was the Florentines, who represented a city which was a maritime power without being a naval power, with their ability to influence the choices and routes taken by ship owners, who used the network to introduce the process of freight diversification. It was thanks to its network that the Datini group was able to gradually introduce contracts of maritime insurance that were referred to as *alla fiorentina* into Palma de Mallorca and Valencia.

5 NETWORKS AND MERCHANT DIASPORAS: FLORENTINE BANKERS IN LYON AND ANTWERP IN THE SIXTEENTH CENTURY

Heinrich Lang

Networks and Markets

In his recently published *Economy of Renaissance Florence*, Richard Goldthwaite describes how the Florentine economy and its position in later medieval and early modern or pre-capitalist Europe were developed by the Florentine network outside Florence:

> In short, many more Florentines must have taken their chances in foreign trade, and numbers alone can explain greater geographical diffusion and growth of a more extensive, denser trade network abroad than merchants from small places could possibly have formed among themselves ... By their sheer numbers, not to mention the density of the network they built up among themselves, Florentines eventually shoved the other Tuscans out of the markets where they did business.[1]

Goldthwaite refers to expanding social and commercial relations, which he calls without any further definition a 'network'. This 'network' came into existence from the thirteenth century onwards and reached its greatest extent during the 1330s in England, and again in fifteenth-century Bruges and early sixteenth-century Lyon. With regard to any of these Florentine communities, we observe a varying situation in terms of numbers of merchants from Florence and a significantly changing density of network indicators. In the later sixteenth century it tended towards a gradual constriction which marks a slow decline in the performance of the Florentine trans-regional economy.

The dimensions of Goldthwaite's network are to be understood geographically. The network's substance consisted in the activities – particularly the economic fields of commerce, banking and government finance – which could be potentially realized within this network: Florentine merchant bankers themselves employed said network as a tool of their business, or as a resource in their economic activities, because it comprised the circle of trustworthy – mainly Florentine – merchant bankers. Hence, the spatial range of the Florentine merchant bankers 'network' is used as a parameter for economically defined periods and as a quantitatively perceived expression for the evolution of the 'economy of Renaissance Florence'.[2]

However, at this point the question arises: which specific qualities made up the ties of networks, and what were the specific qualities of 'mercantile' networks? In general, the term used, the 'network', is an etiquette-based category which is apparently open to some varying contents. Though the impression of the evident existence of mercantile networks derives from various types of sources left by merchant bankers – account books, letters, privileges, diaries and laws – and based on this evidence seems to be convincing, its historical relevance is an interpolation of things we do not really know. In the historian's understanding, networks link social action to social systems.[3] To a certain extent we simply suppose that mercantile networks represent the social embeddedness of historical markets.[4] Mere statistical evidence of contacts may describe the extension of networks, but it neither reveals how networks were constructed nor what resources they had recourse to and what practices made them work effectively. The mere counting of vertices does not explain what made networks 'networks'. Some economists describe networks as an institution which reduces transaction costs and makes the economic system operate.[5]

According to a general definition offered by historians, a social network is a system of social relations which, in some senses, determines potential action.[6] An economic network may be delineated by counting commercial and financial transactions, and so be interpreted as an indication of economic growth or decay. Even in that case it could be seen as a geographical system such as trade routes or globalization. Moreover, it could be considered as a 'commercial network', defined by Maria Fusaro as 'a group of people who are in contact consistently over a sustained time period through commercial interests and actions, having as a common goal the desire to profit economically from commercial activities'.[7] Stated categorically, networks aim to reduce the uncertainty inherent in the position of the agents on markets and are built up by transactions of goods or services between social – and in some cases even culturally defined – strangers. Network practices based on interaction between individuals or organizations and their resources shall be focused on in an analysis of market-based mercantile relationships.[8] According to this notion of networks, they are one of the 'social forces' which provide resources for reducing the risks inherent in market-based transactions and shaping action in markets as institutions and cognitions do.[9] An actor- and process-oriented perspective on networks tends to examine their social and economic practices and their embedding contexts. It seeks to interpret historical markets as subfields of the economic field and their conditioning resources through social relations between the market agents. Hence, quantitatively oriented methodological approaches assume less importance.[10] Furthermore, networks are seen as a medium for the exchange of information or knowledge between merchant bankers about developments in markets or technological aspects, and therefore as networks of communication. This network of communication is interlinked with other forms of network practices and intersects with other social forces such as the aforementioned cognitions and institutions. Networks should be viewed as multilayered webs of social, economic and cultural relations or ties.[11]

Anthropologically speaking, networks belong to the set of frameworks which gives scene to a market. In a market, personal interaction and transfer of goods or services take place as 'acts of exchange'.[12] The point of reference is the praxeological perspective on markets and trade. Hence, networks are qualitatively interpreted because they are formed by social interaction and, hence, represent a resource outside markets which is deeply entangled with transactions on markets.[13]

Markets and Diasporas

With regard to historical markets, this means that we focus upon 'real communities', which entails that a specific form of data has to be taken in consideration. The Florentine communities outside Florence are generally referred to as the *natio fiorentina*. The spatial and social agglomerations of artisans, merchants and other professionals residing in gateway towns such as Bruges, London, Ragusa, Barcelona, Geneva, Naples, Constantinople (Pera) and Lyon from the thirteenth century onwards formed communities which usually came together as an institutionalized entity (*natio*) with its statutes, administration and representatives.[14] They preserved their identity by juridical markers, cultural symbols and particularly religious rituals. The *natio* was the formalized representative of local and territorial authorities and thus constituted a legal framework of reference for Florentines living abroad. The self-explanatory expression used to refer to non-Florentines as 'foreign to us' articulates Florentine identity within the *natio*. But it does not give any further explanation regarding the criteria which determined what constituted a 'Florentine'.[15]

However, this degree of formal organization was not achieved everywhere and, furthermore, was not necessary to those Florentines who were referred to as a *natio*. In the case of Barcelona, the Florentines who lived there grouped together but were never allowed to establish a formal *natio* with a consulate. Still, Catalan authorities and authors used the terms *nació* or *comu* to identify Florentines, Pisans and other groups.[16]

The term 'merchant diaspora' recurs in Robin Cohen's 'trade diaspora' as a peculiar phenomenon of 'diasporas' in general.[17] The debate on 'merchant diaspora' reveals at least the precondition of being forced to leave home for those who gather together within emigrant communities. The Florentine merchant diasporas were formed by a large number of traders and agents who left of their own accord to seek their economic fortunes, but also by a large number of exiled merchants and their families. In exile they continued their mercantile activities and pursued their business. The statutes of the 'nations' claimed the exiles as being outsiders to the Florentine communities and as such prohibited contact between exiled and non-exiled merchants. However, since Florentine merchant bankers had based their mercantile networks on mutual trust and ongoing business practices, they nevertheless maintained business relationships among each other – although naturally there were revealing exceptions to this rule. All of them had a strong sense of their relations to Florence as their place of origin.[18]

Particularly in the fifteenth and sixteenth centuries, southern France and the Duchy of Savoy were important areas for Florentine merchant bankers who were either exiled or opposed to the ruling regime at home. In addition to the famous Florentine exiles of the Guadagni family who moved first to Geneva and then to Lyon, the first director of the Salviati company, Francesco Naldini, had to leave Florence in a dramatic escape in 1497 and settled down in Lyon.[19] However, the social behaviour of Tuscans who moved to southern France was by no means uniform. While the Lucchese Bonvisi who had been settled on the banks of the Rhône since 1466 refused to integrate,[20] the merchant Antonio Gondi, who left Florence of his own accord and who set up a *compagnia* in Lyon in 1505, soon married Marie-Catherine Pierrevive, who came from a family that was well established in the French king's service. But like other Florentines he did not set out specifically to become a naturalized citizen. Between 1567 and 1578, when some of the Florentine merchants operating in Lyon received citizenship, it is not possible to make out any uniform social behaviour. In general, exiles tended to acquire local houses and lands at an earlier time as their fellow Florentines.[21]

Viewed from an analytical perspective, a mercantile diaspora was characterized by the treatment of foreign merchants as diaspora emigrants. The exclusion from activities such as economic transactions on their own behalf or political careers was symptomatic for non-citizens. The reluctantly conceded privilege of citizenship – naturalization, denization, etc. – shows the local elites' consciousness of their own advantageous position. Notably, there were 'diaspora moments' such as the question of Florentine origin in 1521, when goods possessed by Florentine merchants resident in Lyon were seized by the French king for political reasons, or the question of Catholic confession in 1561, when Lyon was captured by the Protestant party during the outbreak of the Religious Wars.[22]

The significance of the concept here is due to the fact that merchants' diasporas were a resource outside the markets but also belonged to the framework of the trade fairs held in Lyon four times a year. The Florentine diaspora upon the river Rhône formed part of the mercantile networks and institutions which provided Tuscan merchant bankers active in France with a more advantageous position compared with merchants from elsewhere.

The Salviati Family and its Companies Abroad

In the following, the case of the Salviati family of Florentine merchant bankers who set up a company in Lyon in 1508 and later in Antwerp in 1540 will be analysed. This expansion of the Salviati business is documented in the family's archives at the *Scuola Normale Superiore* in Pisa, which show that they were one of the biggest players on European markets at the time. The Lyon series of account books is virtually complete for the decades in which the branch existed in the Salviati's hands (1508–61).[23] Iacopo Salviati (1461–1533), who founded the *compagnia* on the Rhône, was a Florentine patrician with extensive political connections and the main investor in a highly profitable agglomerate of business partnerships. As his daughter Maria married Giovanni de' Medici *dalle Bande Nere* in 1516, and Iacopo was to be grandfather to Cosimo, first Grand Duke of Tuscany, he was a curial banker and held the position of treasurer of the province of Romagna from 1514 onwards.[24] His cousins Averardo and Piero sought further expansion when they attempted to establish an affiliate company of the Lyon branch in Antwerp.

Though the Antwerp enterprise was supported by highly effective business contacts and formed part of a highly consolidated network, it failed after just four years. In 1544 the company had to withdraw from the Schelde river, apparently as a result of a lack of economic success. The expansion of the Salviati company to Antwerp cannot be simplistically identified with the expansion of the Florentine merchant bankers' network to the Schelde in general.[25]

Apart from an article by Agnès Pallini-Martin[26] and a *tesi di laurea* (dissertation) submitted by Valeria Pinchera,[27] no in-depth study of any of the Florentine companies established in Lyon and in Antwerp exists.[28] Thus the opening up of a branch of the Salviati company on the Rhône in 1508 and on the Schelde in 1540 exemplifies what Goldthwaite refers to when he adopts the model of a Florentine network and its impact on economic opportunities.

Indeed, a certain dynamic can be observed within the Florentine networks and, in particular, the attempt of a major Florentine agent in Lyon to gain a more advantageous position among their fellow Florentines through a combination of cooperation and competition. In addition to insights into economic history on the basis of account books and correspondence, the case study sheds new light on practices within networks in the mercantile and diaspora context in the middle of the sixteenth century. It reinterprets economic transactions in terms of the cultural behaviour which formed part of consumption patterns and strategies of social distinction at the same time.

This case study on mercantile networks is in three sections. The first introduces the *compagnia* established by the Salviati in Lyon. The second discusses its expansion and ultimate failure thereof through its affiliate company in Antwerp. The third focuses on the influence of networks on markets.

The Salviati *Compagnia* in Lyon

After the transfer of the Geneva fairs to Lyon, which was brought about in particular by Louis XI's invitations during the 1460s, the metropolis on the Rhône had not only become the gateway to the markets of the French kingdom and offered attractive opportunities for commerce and banking but also was a favourite place for Florentine exiles under the protection of the French king.[29] When Iacopo Salviati as the main partner in half a dozen Florentine companies charged Francesco Naldini with the establishment of a new branch of his expanding business in 1508, he was able to recur to an effective web of economic, social and political relationships with other Florentine firms, partners and friends. Among them were Lionardo Bartolini (b. 1464) and Lanfredino Lanfredini (1456–1520), both from the Florentine elite, who were the de facto heirs of the Medici bank because they had been partners of Lorenzo *il Magnifico* and Piero di Lorenzo de' Medici before the apparently shrinking bank was liquidated in 1494, when Piero was exiled.[30]

Francesco Naldini had been working for the Medici bank in the early 1490s. He moved to southern France and became director of the Salviati company there until his demise in 1519. Giving 5,000 *scudi di marchi*[31] as primary capital to the Lyon company, Iacopo Salviati and his cousin Alamanno, who was a few years older than him, held a one-third share, like Francesco Naldini, the operating partner who contributed 5,000 *scudi di marchi*, and the aforementioned Lanfredino Lanfredini, who joined as a third partner with a share of 5,000 *scudi di marchi*. Alamanno and Iacopo were the main investors in a banking enterprise in Florence at the same time, while Lanfredino Lanfredini ran a bank in Florence as well.[32] The strong ties between the Salviati, Lanfredini and Bartolini were multiply structured by intermarriage, economic bonds created by capital entanglement and shareholder aggregation, and substituted by a variously organized set of connections such as jointly arranged political interest such as office-holding connections, neighbourhood alliances, shared habitual patterns such as patronizing arts, and friendship. In this case there certainly was a sensitive understanding which allowed the Bartolini-Lanfredini-Salviati aggregation's network to expand to Lyon, making use of all of its relationships with the French aristocracy and the king's household on the one hand and the curial milieu on the other. It should be remembered that the establishment of the Bartolini company in Lyon in 1499, like that of the Salviati company in 1508, took place during the exile of the Medici and their friends. In political terms, the economic presence of the Bartolini-Lanfredini-Salviati companies in France reflected the Florentine setting abroad.[33]

When Iacopo Salviati's relative, Giovanni de' Medici, became pope and took the name of Leo X in 1513, the Salviati company in Lyon became involved in government finance, in addition to its main commercial and banking activities. The transfer of money from the Kingdom of France to the Apostolic Camera, which administered the pope's income, at the time constituted one of the main businesses of the new *compagnia* which bears the name Iacopo e redi d'Alamanno Salviati & co. Thus it invested 1,500 *ducati di camera* in an *accomandita* shared with the Florentine partners Bernardo da Verrazano and Buonacorso Rucellai & co di Roma in 1513 and invested a further 1,000 *ducati di camera* in another *accomandita* with the royal banker Giovannozzo Salviati. The model of the French court–Lyon–Rome axis was evidently successful, as it continued for several years. Indeed, Iacopo Salviati and the former Medici bank director Giambattista Bracci were the key investors who backed the *accomandite* and the Salviati company in Lyon.[34] The short-term or limited-liability contract (*accomandita*) represented an increasingly important instrument for Florentine bankers to invest their capital in specific businesses without participating actively in them and to reduce risk.[35] The growing use of such a form of investment also indicates the growing amount of capital transferred by Florentine merchant bankers in commerce, banking and government finance abroad.[36]

The account books Naldini kept in Lyon clearly show that the longest-standing accounts and the accounts with the highest frequency and amounts of exchange belonged to other Salviati companies such as the one which they owned together with Bernardo Davanzati in Naples, to cooperating firms like the aforementioned Bernardo da Verrazano e Buonacorso Rucellai & co di Roma, or to a number of other Florentine companies. Thus it may be concluded that kinship, common origin, friendship and capital shares constituted the basic relations within a business network. In other words, the internal history of such business partnership agglomerates (*storia interna*) and the history of the families concerned were essentially entangled. This primary constitution of a Florentine enterprise depended largely on the political position of the shareholders and their familial relations.

Even when there is no direct evidence about the reasons Iacopo and Alamanno Salviati had for expanding their companies to the flourishing fairs upon the Rhône and whether there were any new markets that remained to be discovered by the Salviati, the account books may reveal some probable answers. One aspect was silk trade: Lyon was a centre of redistribution of raw silk and silk cloth from Florence. The accounts of some of the major Spanish companies like Francisco de Salamanca and Rodrigo de Carrión held with the Salviati show a large quantity of raw silk imported from Spain. Moreover, there were a growing number of contacts with French merchants who bought Florentine silk cloth from the Salviati and sold it at the court and to the nobility.[37] Another aspect was the specialized government finance, the transfer of *servitia* and annates from the territory of the French Crown to the Apostolic Camera, the financial service to the court aristocracy and, later on, the enormous loans managed on the French Crown's behalf.[38]

The *libro segreto* kept by Francesco Naldini underlines the economic causes for expansion: the Salviati branch in Lyon was achieving profits of about 3,000 *scudi di marchi* a year from 1508 till 1538.[39] The main reason for establishing a partnership in Lyon was the effectiveness of an underlying web of economic relations. The latter consisted of the practices of transferring goods and payments along the trade routes through the gateway of Lyon which made up the geographical dimension of mercantile networks hidden behind the merchant's motives but still detectable from the account books displaying the development of interrelations between companies at various places.

Other important instruments of economic transactions consisted of the various forms of cooperation which were employed in a variety of contexts. The *accomandita*, for example, was a short-term contract of business cooperation and, moreover, was embedded in a web of social relations. Indeed, the forerunner of the Salviati *compagnia* in Lyon was an *accomandita* in Toulouse shared between Francesco Naldini and his cousin Domenico on the one side, and Johann Vöhlin and the Welser-Vöhlin branch in Lyon on the other. The company *Anton Welser und Mitverwandte* was an amalgamation by intermarriage and business partnership of members of the merchant family Vöhlin from Memmingen and the Welser from Augsburg. Anton Welser (d. 1518) was also a member of the upper echelons of South German merchant bankers.[40] Though this rather unique formalized business cooperation between Florentine merchant bankers and *Kaufleuten* from South Germany lasted just one year, it exemplifies the multiplex relationship the Salviati group and the Welser *Handelsgesellschaft* maintained during a period lasting for some decades. The abovementioned *accomandita* in Toulouse continued its business operations under the conduct of the Naldini: in 1508 it was renewed by the recently founded Salviati company in Lyon with a primary capital of 3,900 *scudi di marchi*.[41]

The convergence of business interests explains the reasons for the particular relationship. On the one hand the Welser from Augsburg were seeking access to the Mediterranean and Levantine markets, and the Salviati provided the necessary connections and developed the requisite means of transactions. On the other hand the Salviati required credit for their involvement in government finance and were keen to obtain a stake in the Antwerp commercial network. The Welser contact provided them with the means to obtain both, and thus enabled the Salviati to became involved in financing Francis I's wars. However, this was quite a precarious situation, as Anton Welser's firm was second besides the famous Jakob Fugger in providing opponents of Francis, the emperors Maximilian and Charles V, with loans.

Both merchant banker agglomerates opted for various means of cooperation. The account books document a large number of apparently straightforward transactions such as the sale of German silver and mercury to the Salviati or of Florentine silk cloth to the Welser. Yet all these commercial and banking transactions happened to be embedded in well-established patterns of cooperation. Some of them formed part of a series of single-venture arrangements. In the long run, the relationship between the Welser and the Salviati families diversified. Anton Welser, for instance, sent his son Hans to Lanfredino Lanfredini in Florence for an apprenticeship. Francesco Naldini explained in a letter to the headquarters of the Welser company how to keep accounts in particular cases. In their correspondence the Welsers and the Salviatis would inform each other about economic developments and exchange rates. Consequently, the Salviati group and the Welser *Handelsgesellschaft* shared a common stock of information and knowledge.[42]

The analyses of the complex relationships between the Welsers and the Salviatis offer substantial insights into merchant's networks. The interest in profit motivated merchants all together to the search for new markets. They sought to build up their social aggregations, which extended far beyond mere commercial transactions. Gradually they aimed to consolidate their business relations by patterns of obligation and cooperation. Especially for transactions of a certain importance, they chose single-venture arrangements or even founded an *accomandita* as a formalized way of collaboration and controlling competition. However, the contractual aspect of strongly linked mercantile networks was accompanied by the constitution of a less formal network of weaker ties: a web of mercantile knowledge. In particular, the apprenticeship of fellow merchants' sons from other 'nations' created a transcultural milieu, such as Hans Welser, who was sent by his father Anton to Lanfredino Lanfredini in Florence in 1509, or Georg Rem, nephew of the Welser shareholder and manager Endres Rem, who held the *cassa* of the Salviati company in Lyon in 1513–14.[43]

The examples just cited in particular represent a widening range of types of interaction between merchants which were the driving forces of their networks. The case of Iacopo Salviati's founding of an affiliate company in southern France prepared the narrative of a success story. The increasing volume of economic transactions and the array of business partners with a growing variety of forms of interaction can be seen with the eyes of the accountants who were keeping the Salviati books as a mercantile network in the context of trade diasporas.

The Salviati *Compagnia* in Antwerp

The expansion of Salviati enterprise to Antwerp might be considered a story of failure, as it ended in failure after only a few years. Although the reasons for the end might be multifactorial, the decline was mainly economically motivated. The company's capital was withdrawn and its volume of business collapsed. Was the failure of Salviati-Antwerp a purely economic disaster? Such an economic breakdown questions the correlation of a well-established network and business prosperity. Why were the Salviati's networks not able to counterbalance economic decrease? Was the failure due to exclusive networks of competing companies? Or was it rather the breakdown of the network itself?

In around 1539–40 the Salviati enterprise reached one of its hubs: in Lyon the *compagnia* experienced a period of booming commerce and equalled the performance of its highly profitable forerunners during the late 1520s. The account books of the company, which now operated under the direction of Averardo and Piero Salviati, reveal major investments in the Levantine trade and a growing volume of business with South German and Spanish merchants. In January 1540 Averardo and Piero settled the claims of their cousins – the sons and grandsons of Iacopo, who had passed away in 1533 – by paying off the profits which had derived from the enterprises in Florence, Pisa and Lyon.[44] Consequently, in 1542 the bank in Florence was renewed and completely handed over to Alamanno's heirs, his sons Averardo and Piero.[45] In the same year the ledger of Averardo e Piero Salviati & Co di Lione shows the bookings of transfers from Lyon to Florence for the investor's share.[46]

Perhaps it was these events of 1540 which spurred Averardo and Piero Salviati to set up an affiliate *compagnia* on the banks of the Schelde – incorporating the edge of the corresponding network into a formalized structure being present at the Antwerp markets without intermediation of commissioned agents. Ever since its early years, the Salviati company in Lyon conducted its commercial and banking activities via Flanders on the basis of agents by cooperating with partners such as the Welser affiliate in Antwerp or the Florentine merchant bankers Frescobaldi and Guicciardini who were active in Bruges and on the Schelde.[47]

On 24 January 1540 Averardo and Piero Salviati were ready to found the company in Antwerp: beside the major partners Averardo e Piero Salviati propri di Firenze, who invested 2,400 *libre di grossi* in the firm's *corpo*, or capital stock, its minor partners came exclusively from the Salviati affiliate in Lyon: Lionardo Spina, the director of the Lyon branch and shareholder with 1,200 *libre di grossi*,

Lorenzo Pasquali, shareholder of the Lyon branch and shareholder with 1,200 *libre di grossi* in the Antwerp enterprise, and Tommaso Corbinelli. The latter held a share of just 600 *libre di grossi* and was due to become director of the new firm. All three had learnt business in Lyon, and half of the primary capital for the Antwerp affiliate was transferred from Lyon.[48]

Averardo and Piero Salviati travelled to Lyon and Antwerp several times and, hence, took an active part in the business in France and Flanders. Lionardo Spina, who was a social climber within the context of the Medici heirs and lived in Lyon, played a key role for the Salviati enterprises in the French kingdom.[49] He fostered close relations with influential representatives of King Francis's court and the royal administration. His brother Piero was installed as *Hoffaktor* on the behalf of the Salviati and supplied members of the French elite with banking and commercial services.[50]

Virtually at the same time Averardo e Piero Salviati propri di Firenze held the major share in the *compagnia* in Lyon with 15,000 *scudi di marchi*, while the aforementioned Lionardo Spina and Lorenzo Pasquali had contributed 2,700 *scudi di marchi* each. So the primary capital of Averardo e Piero Salviati & Co di Lione comprised the reasonable sum of 20,400 *scudi di marchi* and performed quite well in the following years.[51] While the Salviati company was a major player at the fairs of Lyon, its affiliate *compagnia* upon the Schelde river was only of medium size. Moreover, Averardo e Piero Salviati & Co in Anversa appeared essentially dependent on the intervention from its parent company in France.[52]

In January 1540 Corbinelli and his staff moved to Antwerp into a house in which business partners of the Salviati lived, Giambattista Nasi and Giambattista Gondi – both well-situated Florentine merchant bankers who had been active in Flanders for years. To start banking in letters of exchange, the new firm invested the considerable rate of 19,000 *libre di grossi* at the fairs of Castile. The factors of Lesmes d'Astudillo, Bartholomäus Welser, Diego de Medina Macuolo and Francesco Corsini – all of them well established and, hence, trustworthy partners in exchange operations – agreed to pay.[53] The Salviati affiliate in Antwerp was one of the major export firms. The Salviati intended to connect the trade routes from England to Italy and to get access to the spice markets. In either case they were interested in the opportunities booming Antwerp offered.[54]

Nevertheless, the Salviati branch of Antwerp had to close down in summer 1544. The accounts of the most important depositors such as Erasmus Schetz, Bonvisi and Diodati, Guaspare Ducci, Bartholomäus Welser, Giambattista Nasi, Giambattista Gondi and the Burlamacchi from Lucca had already run dry in 1542.[55] The withdrawal of these investors shows the loss of confidence in the success of the Salviati enterprise in Antwerp. The emperor's regulation of the exchange market in 1541 and the renewed outbreak of the Habsburg–Valois Wars in 1542, particularly in Brabant and Ghelders, blocking trade routes, caused severe crises in Antwerp.[56] In January 1542 Tommaso Corbinelli complained bitterly to the headquarters of the Salviati in Florence about the mandate promulgated by Charles V the month before. The emperor planned to back each contract on exchange transactions and deposits with two-thirds of gold – a measure which was difficult to put into effect because of the lack of gold upon the Schelde, as Corbinelli concluded in his letter.[57] Thus the Salviati branch did not survive. But others did. Tommaso Corbinelli remained in Antwerp, and so did some of the former cooperating partners of the Salviati.[58]

The tight commerce and banking situation on the river Schelde in the early 1540s may have dealt the decisive blow to the Salviati affiliate there. The most profitable deal with which Averardo e Piero Salviati & Co in Anversa became involved was the lease of alum of Tolfa and, hence, the privilege for selling 12,000 *cantara* of alum at Antwerp markets each year. Because of the disappearance of the Salviati *compagnia* on the Antwerp markets, the contract was only effective from 1542 to 1545.[59] Although the Salviati managed to gain from the exchanges rates, for transfers of money between Antwerp and Lyon, and although they were able to transfer what were apparently substantial quantities of silver from the Schelde to Florence via Lyon, they were not able to counterbalance the suffocating effects of the blockage caused by the Habsburg–Valois Wars and the regulations which Charles V had put in place on the exchange trade.[60]

They were even less able to compensate for the lack of cooperation shown by the South German, Spanish and Italian merchant bankers like Bartholomäus Welser, Diego de Medina Macuolo and Guaspare Ducci who had previously been vital partners on Antwerp markets. In times of crises the established major players perceived the expansion of the Salviati on the Schelde as a strategy that would increase competition. Thus the withdrawal of the Welser, De Medina, Erasmus Schetz, Gaspare Ducci and other influential companies and agents from investment in the Salviati commerce and banking signals not only a lack of confidence in the success of the Salviati *compagnia*, but also a striking degree of reservation in respect of an expected increase of competition.

This last point may be proved by the ceasing development of the cooperation between the Salviati company and the *Handelsgesellschaft* of Bartholomäus Welser in the 1540s: After a series of extremely fruitful joint ventures around the years from 1539 to 1441, the volume of mutual transactions was shrinking to an unremarkable dimension. The deposits of a wide-ranging group of merchant bankers the Salviati *compagnia* had at its disposal for providing enormous sums as loans to the French king no longer primarily consisted of deposits by Bartholomäus Welser like it had been before.[61]

Networks on Markets

Having made the case for cooperation as an indicator of networks, the inter-dependence of operational instruments and relationships between business partners will be exemplified by two aspects. Firstly, a significant innovation reflects the merchant bankers' awareness for complex and differentiated business relations. In 1534 the Salviati company in Lyon introduced a short-term credit system on its own: the *libro de' committenti*, the client's book, documents the loans received for financing commerce. The aforementioned Lionardo Spina used the loans for any sector of commerce. Accordingly, he did not depend just on letters of exchange for short-term credits, or on deposits, but by employing capital of the lenders he was able to augment the quantity of outside capital from fair to fair. Hence, the accounts of the *libro de' committenti* show the specific credit network which was mainly based on current business relations. The vast majority of the lenders who provided short-term credits were Florentine partners.[62] None of these instruments, whether the previously described instrument of obtaining investors' capital, the *accomandita*, or the short-term loans, proved to be transferrable to the Antwerp enterprise, as the Salviati's network there lacked coherence and did not sustain the same variety of commercial and banking affairs as it did in the French context. The Salviati network on the Antwerp markets was based on already established business relations. It depended on the motivations the Salviati company in Lyon could give to partners upon the Schelde. It was not multilayered as the Salviati network in Lyon was. Lacking any additional socially aggregated impact, the Salviati network on the Antwerp markets remained purely on an economic level and finally unravelled.

A second example, another instrument for raising outside capital, the *dipositi*, corresponds with the resuming of considerable credits to the French Crown in the early 1540s.[63] Lionardo Spina was able to back government finance by a cumulative quantity of invested capital from business partners. In 1553, when the Salviati contributed large sums to the king's loans, the amounts in the accounts in the books which registered the *dipositi* had grown in the same dimension as those of the king's loans. Among the financiers of the Salviati's loans to the king were many of the South German merchant bankers, like Andreas Imhof from Nuremberg and Hans Welser who was from Nuremberg as well, and also a relative of Bartholomäus Welser: Michael Sailer, who was the Welser agent in Lyon in these days, contributed to the loan to Francis I on his own behalf, but not so much to the share the Salviati raised for their part.[64] In general, confidence in financial and banking operations between the Salviati and the Welser remained, albeit on a lesser scale, and obviously their common interest had faded away.

Networks as market resources are not simply to be identified with business relations. Moreover, the characteristic of mercantile networks is their multiple and synergetic structure: commercial and financial transactions are complemented by relationships deriving from 'standard' transactions on various levels such as exchange operations, single-venture arrangements, short- and medium-term loans and limited-liability contracts. Distinct layers of networks – commercial, banking, knowledge – are entangled with relationships of special qualities such as kinship, business partnerships, common origin, political partisanship and shared economic interests. The success of the enterprise depended greatly on the density and profundity of these networks – in some cases networks as a resource outside markets were sufficient to counterbalance economic difficulties. However, we need to describe any degree of coordinating action on markets and cooperation, and hence, to interpret the quality and range of instruments employed for transactions in order to understand mercantile networks.

The dynamics and practices of social interactions indicate how the networks operated. The mere existence of social or commercial interaction does not constitute a mercantile network; frequent interaction to reach some common goal is necessary. Thus the reference to resources outside markets does explain the way networks were set up and what effect they could potentially have on markets. The particular situation of merchant bankers abroad organized in diaspora-like aggregations highlights the characteristics of mercantile networks and transcultural transactions. The case of the two Salviati enterprises presented here shows the entanglement of economic and social interaction and thus illustrates the cooperative and the competing performances of mercantile networks in long-distance trade.

Acknowledgements

This essay initially derives from the project 'Markets – Networks – Spaces. Economic Relations and Migration Processes in Early Modern Europe (1500–1800)' sponsored by the German Research Foundation (DFG) in the years 2009–11; I am grateful to the Gerda Henkel Foundation, which awarded a research grant in December 2012. This essay is dedicated to Sven Thorsten Schmidt (†26 November 2012), who was a dear friend of mine and a passionate colleague to my work.

6 THE ASTUDILLO PARTNERSHIP AND THE SPANISH 'NATION' IN SIXTEENTH-CENTURY FLORENCE

Francesco Ammannati and Blanca González Talavera

Introduction

In the history of trade, very few words have engaged historians in search of a definition, or the precise identification of a phenomenon, as much as the term 'nation'. Economic as well as social, political and legal historiography has had to deal with this elusive, multifaceted word, ultimately emphasizing its multitude of meanings and the impossibility of reducing it to a single significance.[1] A great many studies have now been written on 'nations' conceived of as communities of people settled abroad: the topic has been approached both from the point of view of a particular 'national' colony active on many foreign marketplaces[2] and from that of a host city with several nations living within it.[3] While pioneering studies were often limited to quantitative or descriptive surveys, recent studies have aimed at obtaining a comprehensive framework of the relationship between foreigners and the political, economic and social environments in which they integrated and also the links between their places of origin and settlement.[4]

Moreover, other studies have focused on the nature of the networks that merchants created, or into which they integrated.[5] Particular attention has been paid not just to the existence of formal or legal institutions, but rather to aspects such as reputation, trust, the ability of these groups to learn about the commercial practices and habits of the place they settled in and their capability to integrate into already established/existing networks. Such a network-based approach does not rely on mathematical analysis of the social network and uses the concept of network to structure qualitative analyses of social interaction. On the basis of this approach, this chapter will show how the Spanish nation in Florence emerged from commercial networks and its repercussions on commerce and urban society. The idea of networks is used as an approach with which to analyse complex forms of social interaction in a qualitative way, or a specific set of connections existing within defined groups of people, with the added value that the characteristics of these connections as a whole can be used to interpret the social interaction patterns of the actors involved and take it beyond relationships within a single national community-based approach.[6]

Taking into account all of the above, in approaching the study of a community of traders operating far away from its homeland, some preliminary questions must be posed: what was the attitude of this group towards local society, economy and institutions? Were the individuals within it aware of belonging to it, and did they aspire to external visibility? Whose was the greatest advantage in this relationship, the host society or the guest community? And, in general, what influence did the foreign nation have on established economic structures?[7]

Our contribution will attempt to answer these questions by analysing the Astudillo company in the context of the Spanish nation in Florence from the end of the fifteenth century to the seventeenth century. The section which follows will, therefore, present the main economic activities of the Spanish merchants in Florence during the sixteenth century in order to show the context in which they were operating. The second section will analyse the Astudillo company, the family which ran it and its relationship with the Spanish nation in Florence. This evidence will be related to the general system of Spanish *consulados* across Europe. In the third section we will show its activities on the marketplace and the links it created with the main business and financial centres of Europe which will be analysed on the basis of their accounting books and business correspondence. The fourth section will focus on the relations between companies and urban society as well, showing the interactions between the Astudillo and the other Spanish merchants and Florentine society. While the large quantity of business letters belonging to the Astudillo kept in the Naldini Archives in Florence allows us, in principle, to draw up a detailed picture of the dynamics of the commercial networks operating on a European scale, here it will be mainly used to complement the study of ledgers which is the main source used for the following analysis. Covering, in particular, the early years of the last decade of the sixteenth century, this dense and rich source still offers a unique overview and a precise insight into the company's business. Rather than focusing on the links which existed between the many Spanish partnerships based in Florence, the study of a single company, taken as a paradigm, enables us to analyse all the networks (urban, regional and supranational) in which it was involved.[8]

Spanish Merchants in Florence

The relationship between Castilians and Florence was mainly motivated by the need for a steady flow of raw materials to support the town's major industry at that time. An understanding of the importance of Spanish wool in the Florentine economy of the sixteenth century requires a look at certain aspects of the textile industry. By the first half of the fifteenth century Florentine companies were differentiating between two types of manufacture. High-quality cloths were woven by workshops in the area of the city of San Martino, which had a monopoly over the use of the best and richest raw material: English wool. The remaining workshops, generically identified as Garbo, produced lower-quality cloths using Italian and Spanish wool. The latter, in particular, was a great success in Levantine markets. After decades of widespread use of good-quality Italian wool from the Abruzzi region, the Garbo workshops started buying large stocks of Castilian Merino wool as relations with Iberian merchants improved.[9] The use of Spanish wool in the production of cloth was not a novelty in the late fifteenth century. As early as the end of the fourteenth century, Florentine wool makers were accustomed to using large quantities of raw material from the Balearic or Maestrazgo areas for medium-quality production.[10] A change in the place of origin and type of Spanish wool took place: from the second half of the fifteenth century onwards, not only did Merino equal imports of other kinds of Iberian wool but it even began to overtake, at least until the end of the sixteenth century, the Abruzzo wools which had dominated in the production of Garbo cloths since the mid-fifteenth century.

The names of some Spaniards were occasionally to be found as suppliers of wool in the account books of many clothiers from the 1480s. Their presence increased rapidly, as the accounts opened for dealing with Spanish merchants became more numerous and frequent.[11]

The system of trade relations between Spanish and Florentine merchants developed significantly in the course of the century.[12] On one hand, the second half of the sixteenth century saw a more peaceful Italian political scene after sixty turbulent years of war and, on the other, a difficult situation had developed in the Spanish Low Countries, the most important market for Iberian wool, which were now in revolt.[13] These facts had profound repercussions on the realignment of Spanish exports. Another aspect to consider is the process of product innovation that the Florentine wool industry had undergone since the 1540s. Garbo cloth had been improved and refined perhaps even as a result of the higher quality of Merino wool. Tuscan textiles began to be exported beyond the Alps, the leading product being *rascia*, a lightweight but very thick fabric, with a combed warp and a carded weft.[14] Together with other cloths of slightly lower quality, *rascie* was increasingly in massive demand in the main European textile markets such as Lyon, Antwerp and Medina del Campo.

Even the absolute value of exports of Spanish wool from Seville, but especially from Alicante and Cartagena, to Italy, and thus via the port of Livorno to Florence, evolved. Series are not complete and do not cover the whole century. The data is affected by the presence of tax documentation and, for the period before 1558, statistics have, at least until now, not been available. After 1558 a new form of taxation makes an estimate of the number of sacks of wool that passed through Castilian customs possible and shows clear and sustained growth from the 1550s onwards which reached its apex towards the end of the 1570s.[15]

Manuel Basas has provided a set of data obtained from the Burgos Consulado documentation, which allows us to identify both the types and quantities of wool sent to Italy by Burgalese merchants.[16] When, in 1562, merchant Balthasar Suárez arrived in Florence, he noted 'havevano negotio aperto da 18 a 20 nobilissime famiglie spagnuole' ('eighteen or twenty aristocratic Spanish families had opened shops').[17]

What was the impact of these companies on the Florentine economy and in particular on local wool manufacture? There is nothing accidental about the fact that this period is called the 'Indian summer' of the Florentine wool industry and of the Italian economy in general. It should be noted that some of the Castilian wool that reached Florence was sold in Venice, where the manufacturing industry experienced its maximum expansion during this period.[18] Without the support of a constant flow of a good-quality raw material, the improvements in quality which took place in Florentine manufacturing with non-English wool could not have taken place. Certainly, though, the sale of wool on the Florentine marketplace was not a Spanish monopoly.[19] Prices and import volumes were strongly influenced by local demand, and the Castilian mercantile community continued to be up against competition from Italians who, even in Spain, controlled most of the wool trade to Italy.[20]

The strength of the Castilian merchants at home was their ability to organize the various steps of acquiring, preparing and transporting the wool,[21] but its final distribution usually took place through the networks of the 'grand capitalisme cosmopolite' which was in charge of exports to Flanders, France or Italy.[22] Henri Lapeyre has identified the continued overwhelming dominance of the Genoese over the Spaniards in the wool business in the 1560s. The latter were direct exporters to Italy only 15–20 per cent of the time.[23] These conclusions also apply to cochineal, which, from the second half of the century onwards, began to be sold by the Castilian merchants involved in trade with the New World.[24]

When their active part in this trade began to decline by the late 1560s,[25] many Spanish merchants decided to try the adventure of emigration in order to get involved in direct trade in what was considered the economically most promising and politically less risky market of that period: Italy and Tuscany, in particular. This was, in fact, the Spanish nation's most prosperous period in Florence.[26]

Florentine wool makers certainly saw this increasing presence as an advantage, while the Spanish merchants found in this industrial revival a good opportunity – especially after the downsizing of the Flemish market – to extend their business network to a place which offered them excellent political ties with their homeland and solid and well-structured commercial and financial networks as well as the chance to obtain textiles which were in great demand in Spain in exchange.

An analysis of the activity of the Astudillo company is a good example of the success of these merchants, even in a scenario of competition between fellow countrymen and other local operators, in creating a business space which made use of direct links with their corresponding 'headquarters' in Spain.

The Astudillo and the Spanish Nation

The Astudillo are typical of the Burgalese merchants who, during the age of the greatest development of Castilian trade, managed to build an extensive commercial network – based on kinship – connecting the most important economic centres of the time. In fact, Astudillo interests involved an area spanning the New World and Northern Europe with a fulcrum between Burgos and Florence.[27]

Here we will focus exclusively on the Tuscan branch of the Astudillo kin network. Around the years 1558–9 Melchor de Astudillo resided in Florence, where he founded a merchant company.[28] His stay was not short-term, as is shown by surviving company documents. The Naldini Archives in Florence preserve part of the documentation of his firm,[29] and the partnership remained in his name at least until the late 1560s.[30] The company also included Antonio Salazar, Francisco de Castro Mugica and Gabriel de Castro, all of whom lived in Burgos[31] and organized the company's business from Spain.[32] The name Melchor Astudillo (often distorted to 'Melchiorre d'Astudiglio') also appears in some Florentine wool workshop account books at that time.[33] In addition, the correspondence of merchant Simon Ruiz of Medina del Campo, who remained on good terms with the Tuscan city, shows that young merchant Baltasar Suárez was put up by Melchor de Astudillo when he arrived in Florence in 1562.[34] Probably Melchor acted in some way as a guide and introduced him to the business world of the Tuscan city. This attitude was prevalent in foreign trade communities, and the Astudillo themselves often housed Spanish colleagues or friends in Florence. A son of the important '*cargadors*' of Seville, the Jorges, lived at their home around 1565, for example.[35]

Lesmes de Astudillo subsequently followed his older brother to Florence, and it was perhaps due to the inexperience of the former that Melchor remained for some years in Florence. In 1562 the old partnership Melchor Astudillo–Gabriel de Castro came to an end, but its business continued under the name of 'Melchor, Lesmes and Gaspar Astudillo' (the latter was living in Seville).[36] Around the mid-1560s Melchor returned to his native city, where he married his cousin Beatriz de Astudillo Mazuelo in 1568 and received important positions both in the Consulado (1572–3) and in city government, becoming regidor.[37]

Once he settled in Florence, Lesmes set up a branch of the dynasty that would remain in Italy, integrate with Tuscan society and follow a path of social advancement which was typical of the family strategies of the Castilian merchants of the day. He married for a second time in 1578 to Costanza Arrighi from an aristocratic Florentine family, who was already three times married. This union enabled, or at least reinforced, a process which involved building a family property in Tuscany that included possession of land and buildings and consolidation of mercantile activities.[38] His previous marriage to his first wife, Lisabetta (although it is not clear whether an official marriage ceremony took place or even whether she was the natural mother),[39] had produced Baldassarre in 1572, the first of Lesmes's sons, who successfully took over the family business after his death in 1594.[40] The important role that Lesmes attained within the Florentine Spanish nation is clear in the Spanish Grand Chapel of Santa Maria Novella,[41] where a number of memorial plaques bear witness to his role as Consul of the Nation in 1577 and the fact that his son followed in his footsteps in the late 1590s. The wealth he accumulated enabled him to commission architectural work such as the access door leading from the chapter hall of Santa Maria Novella to its Great Cloister (an architrave there still bears the merchant's name) and artistic work such as the decoration on the lunette that crowns the same door and some of the frescoes in the cloister.[42]

An analysis of the words used in the Florentine Castilian community documentation shows that both 'consulate' and 'nation' are used. The creation of a 'consulate' in Florence was expressly stated in the process establishing the Consulate of Burgos promulgated by the Catholic monarchs in 1494,[43] and the use of the term 'Nazione Spagnuola' in numerous sources confirms that a nation actually existed.

The affiliation of each person to the nation involved receiving and enjoying a number of privileges granted by the host society. This practice ascribed a socio-cultural, ethnic, linguistic and religious identity to the nation or community.[44] In line with the guidelines provided by Hilario Casado in his studies of the Castilian communities around Europe, the Spanish nation in Florence enjoyed a series of political, judicial and religious privileges. Politically, the colony was under the tutelage of the consul, a magistrate chosen by the community itself in total independence from the King of Castile, the Consulado de Burgos and the Dukes of Tuscany. Alongside the consul, the management and administration of the Florentine Nazione Spagnuola depended on its deputies, high-ranking assistants whose role was to advise him. In Florence, there were four deputies of the nation, as is well documented in the public Instrumento signed by the Nazione Spagnola, the Operai and the Prior of Santa Maria Novella in September 1566, when the community definitely took 'per se, et eorum successores' the chapter room of the Dominican convent of Santa Maria Novella.[45] As well as a commercial court, the Nazione Spagnuola had its own notary, which in Florence was Lorenzo di Camillo Muzzi, 'civis ac Notarij publici florentini, et inclite Nationis Hispane in hac civitate Floren' cancillarij', 'escribano público y del número de Florencia' and 'Chanciller de la nación española de Florencia' between 1569 and 1608 and possibly longer.[46]

Commercial Activity

Information about Lesmes and co.'s economic activities can be found in the registers of many Florentine wool workshops in the second half of the sixteenth century. The company was one of the most important suppliers of Spanish wool and Mexican cochineal in Florence, and these were often exchanged with the much in demand *rascie* that the company put into circulation through its network of correspondents living in the major European commercial and financial cities. A special section of the Astudillo company's accounting system was also dedicated to financial operations carried out in Lyon and, later, at the fairs of Besançon, then also called di Bisenzone, when they were moved to Piacenza.

Figure 6.1: Map of the locations of the main correspondents of the Astudillo partnership, 1591–4.

The Astudillo company's commercial activity was on a European, if not an Atlantic, scale, and deeply rooted in the Florentine market, around which all company business revolved. The economic influence of the company was structured in concentric areas gradually moving away from Florence where its headquarters were based. On Figure 6.1 the location of the main Astudillo correspondents on the basis of ledger entries are shown covering the years 1591–4.[47] As well as the most important cities of the grand duchy – Siena, Pisa and, by extension, Livorno, the main port of the state which, from the end of the sixteenth century, became the key hub for Mediterranean trade[48] – the affairs of the company led it to make contacts with the Republic of Lucca, the port of Ancona, and of course Rome and the capital of the Kingdom of Naples. The Italian area also included primary economic locations such as Venice, Milan, Genoa and Piacenza. Looking outside the Peninsula, the Astudillo obviously had strong ties with many Spanish cities, but also with international marketplaces such as Lyon, Nuremberg, Antwerp and London. This is the general framework, and it is important to note that nothing in the business correspondence and account books leads to the conclusion that a broad system of 'sister partnerships' existed or at least those in which the Astudillo supplied part of the capital, in contrast to the large Florentine, Lucca or Genoese banking and trading companies operating on the same marketplaces. Another feature of the business of the company, which was common to all the big commercial firms working in an international environment at that time, was a fully developed system of sales on commission. Buying as well as selling goods in their own name or in partnership with other companies, the Astudillo were commissioners on behalf of other, non-Florence-based firms and became a nodal point in a network capable of moving goods from Italy to the rest of Europe and vice versa, of reaching the New World via Seville.[49]

The existence of a system of nations (colonies of Spanish merchants living in the main European marketplaces)[50] responded to the functioning logic of commercial networks formed by several individuals grouped by virtue of their status as subjects of the same king or political authority. This was mainly motivated by the need to rely on partners, relatives or friends living in foreign parts in which business was to be done. These networks were characterized by mutual interdependence between individual merchants and/or small partners who were economically, socially, culturally and politically embedded in their respective localities and regions but working with large commercial groups of companies. In this way they could diversify their business onto a larger scale.[51]

In Florence the Astudillo were conducting business relationships with at least sixty-eight wool workshops, to which they supplied Spanish wool and bought textiles in exchange. This activity, documented since the 1560s,[52] involved the greater part – almost two-thirds – of the city's wool industry.[53] The wool was purchased from Spain directly by the Astudillo on their own behalf or, more often, along with other Castilian merchants who resided in Burgos but had company branches in Florence (Diego de Salamanca, Juan de Ramos, Luis Alonso Maluenda, the Castro, etc.).[54] The company also acted as agent for some major Genoese merchants (Paolo Doria, Filippo Spinola) who sent Merino wool from Genoa or directly from Spain through the port of Livorno to be distributed on the Florentine market. In this case, too, it sometimes happened that the Astudillo did not limit themselves to sales on behalf of others and had their own share in those transactions.[55] A considerable part of the wool did not remain in Tuscany but made its way to Venice. Here the Paolo Donati[56] and Lorenzo, Roberto and Alessandro Strozzi[57] companies acted as sales agents for the Astudillo, to whom they assured supplies of Levantine textiles called *ciambellotti* which would have been sold by our company in Spain later on.[58] Spanish wool was also in demand in Siena, and the Libro Mayor identifies at least a dozen Sienese operators involved in this trade.[59]

These lucrative transactions were seldom paid for by Florentine wool workshops in cash (indeed, the delay could be very long, in some cases more than a year) but rather debts were often made good by means of the sale of textiles, mostly *rascie*, but also cloths of lower quality such as *perpignani*. At this point the other nodes of the Astudillo network of business contacts came into play: *rascie* were sent to Spain[60] by correspondent Juan Bautista Gallo di San Romani and Hernando Bretavillo, who took care of sales at the fairs of Medina del Campo[61] – in the Kingdom of Naples, traditionally a thriving market for Florentine cloths, although progressively declining[62] – and especially in Antwerp. It would appear that the Flemish city was still absorbing a considerable part of the high-quality wool production of the Tuscan city in the last decade of the sixteenth century. The shipments of bales of *rascie* that the Astudillo sent off to Giuseppe, Bernardo, Bonaventura Arnolfini and Ottavio Micheli, a large commercial company from Lucca with a permanent branch in Antwerp, confirms this.[63] A significant amount of *rascie* and *perpignani* was then destined to Ancona, where, through correspondent Gioacchino Berardi, it was probably distributed in the Balkan and Levantine markets.[64]

A similar trade mechanism as that for wool products was set up for silk. Through their distribution network, the Astudillo connected the suppliers of raw silk in southern Italy with redistribution markets on the Iberian Peninsula, once again through the fairs of Medina del Campo and marketplaces of central Europe such as Nuremberg. There are forty-three Florentine silk makers named in the Libro Mayor. These accounted for the bulk of the silk coming from Naples, via Cosimo Orsucci[65] and Antonio Romano,[66] who ran the supply chain in Monteleone (now Vibo Valentia, Calabria) where the raw silk was actually produced. Additional amounts of raw silk came from Venice, delivered by Donati as mentioned above.[67] The silks of the Florentine manufacturers who had redirected their production to a less sophisticated and cheaper product by the second half of the sixteenth century [68] were both sold on the local market and shipped to Nuremberg, to the Bottini and Buti companies.[69] These latter provided the Astudillo with German linen or cotton-linen fabrics, fustians, that were then sent to Seville.[70] Small amounts of highly priced *drappi auroserici* (these were textiles made with metalized thread, spinning gold and silver together with silk) were sold through Castilian correspondents to the social elites of Burgos and Madrid.[71]

Finally, Astudillo traded three other major products: cochineal, pepper and sugar. There is no need to underline the importance of Mexican cochineal to textile dyeing from the second half of the sixteenth century onwards or, as a direct consequence, its prominent role in Atlantic trade.[72] As far as trade in this product is concerned, the sources do not show direct links between the Florentine company and the Astudillo family members living in the New World and Seville in this period. All the cochineal which appears in the Astudillo accounting books was purchased from Francesco Maluenda of Seville, a partner of the powerful family company of Burgalese origin which distributed large quantities of this dyestuff all over Europe.[73] In some cases, our company did not act on its own behalf, but only as an agent for sale on commission. Buyers were not only dyers and wool workshops: cochineal was, in fact, sent to Naples, Ancona, Lucca, Rome, Perugia and Venice too.[74]

Commerce with pepper and sugar appears to have been organized in a different way because these goods were primarily sold to the many Florentine *speziali* (apothecaries) who had dealings with Astudillo (there were twenty-three in this period) and other local merchants. Suppliers of pepper, for which our company acted as a sales agent, were Francesco Ximenes and the heirs of Rui Nunes of Anversa, of evident Portuguese origin.[75] Sugar, which mainly originated from 'de Barberia' and Brazil, was sent by three Iberian firms based in Pisa: Fernando Cardoso, Domingo Rodriguez Pardo and Diego de Marchena.[76]

The purely commercial activities that we have described so far were accompanied, if not closely interconnected, by financial transactions with other major merchant companies of the time. While the fundamental structures of the international markets and their business techniques had undergone their first 'commercial revolution' in the late Middle Ages, they had remained essentially unchanged except for a few details. The sixteenth century saw the expansion of European economic horizons and a consequent development of traffic and increase in product quantity and quality and especially in means of payment.[77]

The Astudillo company was fully embedded in the European credit market. Figure 6.1 shows how the firm was linked to the most important financial centres of its age, both fair locations (Medina del Campo, Lyon and Piacenza) and large international emporiums where activity was intense throughout the year (like Antwerp or Venice). It is not possible here to analyse the cash flows that linked Florence to these places in detail. Certainly, the transactions described above, except those carried out in city markets, which were subject to the almost exclusive action of the largest local bank of the heirs of Federigo de' Ricci,[78] were settled by a continuous circuit of bills of exchange. The vectors in this traffic put the foreign financial or commercial centres in contact with Florence parallel to merchandise trade by land and sea according to the scheme illustrated by Felipe Ruiz Martín in his study of the business letters exchanged between Medina del Campo and the Tuscan city during the decade of 1570–80.[79]

The Astudillo was one of a large number of firms which acted as intermediaries for these merchants, not only contributing, as commission agents, to the allocation of goods in accordance with market demand, but also providing for the transfer of large volumes of payments through the circulation of bills of exchange and entries in the current accounts opened for their various correspondents. These cash flows originated both in commercial transactions and in the need to transfer money between different markets. Astudillo's international contacts and the presence of several branches of large firms of merchant bankers in Italian and other European cities gave a triangular shape to these flows. Some examples which illustrate this scenario can be found by looking at the various 'sister' companies of the Arnolfini, present alone or in partnership with other merchants in Antwerp, Lyon and Ancona and in constant touch with the parent company in Lucca, and of the Bonvisi or the Balbani, whose business branches encompassed Lucca, Lyon and Genoa (the former) and Milan and Antwerp (the latter).[80]

Other Italian cities were also involved in this movement of large funds, especially Rome with traditional close ties with the Tuscan city. The Astudillo corresponded with the Capponi in Rome, as well as the Capponi in Venice.[81] In the markets for certain goods such as pepper or sugar,[82] moreover, Rome was home to a large colony of Spanish operators[83] who, through our company, moved money between Florence and Spain (Madrid and Burgos in particular).

A synthesis was finally found during the great financial fairs of Lyon and Piacenza, where the lion's share of the business operations and financial speculations carried out by the Astudillo on their own and on behalf of their customers was settled. The accounts – impressive in number and amount – that they opened at the 'Dinero y sacado remitido' for Bisenzone and Lyon in their Libro Mayor, describing the operations carried out during those periodic fairs, are characteristic in this respect. These operations fuelled the accounts of 'Encomiendas', or commercial and financial commissions, through which the Astudillo credited their clients. The great international bankers active in Piacenza who corresponded with the firm were large Florentine and Genoese partnerships such as the Galilei, Del Bene, Spinola, Negroni, Centurione, Paravicino and others.[84] This, in short, is an illustration of the economic activity of the Astudillo firm and the connections it maintained with the international business community of the time.

Urban Society

Now that we have outlined the commercial relations of the Astudillo company, we will look at the ties of its members with the urban society of Florence. Unfortunately, the company did not survive into the third generation, not so much or not only because of Lesmes's son's and grandson's lack of entrepreneurial ability (a full judgement would require a much more in-depth analysis), but because of the progressive withdrawal of Florentine merchants from European big business.[85]

From the early seventeenth century onwards, the Astudillo firm entered a phase of depression. Firstly, just like the great merchant families of the Tuscan city, they seemed to be losing interest in direct involvement in economic activity and to be searching for a role which was more appropriate to their new social rank, and they began to gravitate around the Medici court. Lesmes's son Baldassarre's marriage to Lavinia of Francesco Del Nero Bourbon del Monte should be seen in this light. In 1605, when he was still very young, their son Francesco was made partner in a company with Florentine Francesco Naldini. The reasons for this are still unclear – perhaps Baldassare, whose business was not doing well, took advantage of the new member by passing his debts onto him – but the company went bankrupt shortly thereafter and with it the Astudillo merchant dynasty.[86] Nevertheless the family continued to enjoy prestige and public office in Florence: Francesco himself held the post of Cavalry Captain of the Grand Duke of Tuscany. He married Camilla Petruccini, who gave birth to a son, Leonardo, a future Senator of the Grand Duchy, General Auditor of the State of Siena and of the Pratica Segreta and Commissioner in Pontremoli. Finally, Leonardo was granted Florentine citizenship in 1678.[87] The dynasty died out less than a century later with its last member, Baldassarre Astudillo.

The strategies that led the Astudillo to integrate into Florentine society while keeping, at first, certain traits of cultural difference was a common pattern.[88] The integration strategies of the members of the Nazione Spagnuola consisted mainly in obtaining citizenship (naturalization), marriage settlements, taking public office and gaining entry to the aristocracy through the Order of St Stephen. The case of the Castilian merchants who settled in Florence is unique in that they managed to put down roots in the city without giving up their national identity.

Intermarriage between Spanish men and Florentine 'dames' is a clear sign of the path they took to integrate into Tuscan society. Even if they themselves were never naturalized, their descendants, who were born in Florence, were. The Suárez de la Concha family, merchants from Segovia who settled in Florence in the second half of the sixteenth century, is one of the most significant examples. Baltasar was the first of the Suárez de la Concha family to arrive in Florence in 1574. Following the advice of Antonio Ramirez de Montalvo, he achieved what 'no Spaniard was able to get over there': he married Cosimo I de' Medici's sister-in-law, Maria Martelli, 'a woman who would deserve a king for a husband'.[89] Years later, when Maria died, Baltasar strengthened his ties with the Medici family even further by remarrying to Caterina de' Medici.[90]

Holding public office was another form of integration into Florentine society. The political career of Sebastián Ximénez de Aragón (originating from a family of merchants) is significant in this regard. As a relative of the Medici dynasty by his marriage to Caterina de' Medici, Sebastián was granted the title of Lord of Saturnia in 1593 by Grand Duke Ferdinand I, a recognition that paved the way for a brilliant future. He was admitted to the Consiglio dei Duegento in 1615 and ordained Senator and a member of the Otto di Guardia e Balia in 1625. Between 1629 and 1631 he also served as Counsellor to the Grand Duke, in 1629 he joined the board of the Magistrato dei Pupilli and in 1633 the board of the Monte Comune, and he was also chosen as Commissioner of Pisa, the last position he held before his death in 1633.[91]

The culmination of this process of integration was obtaining a title. Noble rank was the highest aspiration of Castilian merchants both abroad and in Spain itself, as it involved attaining the highest social status in the cities they lived in. In this case the key was access to the Order of St Stephen. Founded in 1561 by Cosimo I de' Medici after the conquest of Siena to confirm the regional integrity of the Principate and supply it with a navy, the Order became a vehicle for the promotion of social mobility. Becoming a member was a way of facilitating the process of ennoblement by supporting its legitimization.[92]

However, this integration did not involve the loss of a specific identity which distinguished these Spanish merchants from the surrounding population. The community of merchants faced a complex balancing act between mixing with the new society and moving away from its Hispanic origins while still maintaining strong ties with relatives left behind in Castile. Thus the merchants of the Spanish nation developed a cultural identity by means of stratagems such as these. They kept a Spanish anthroponomy: names like Baltasar, Alonso, Santiago, Diego and Lesmes were used frequently as children's names by Spaniards born in Florence. The Spanish language was generally retained because all the members of the nation used Castilian primarily for business, as can be seen in their letters, account books, wills, bills of exchange and so on. The use of their native language did not keep the Spaniards, however, from learning the Tuscan language, which is 'so easily learn[ed] that language'.[93] Spanish taste shaped their home furnishings, as the description of the furniture of the Ximénez de Aragón palace in Borgo Pinti shows, where numerous references can be found. For example, the room attached to the 'salotto da mangiare' was decorated with a painting depicting 'two little figures dressed in the Spanish fashion'.[94]

Finally, they kept their national devotion; as for the religious privileges of the Spanish nation in Florence other common traits of the Castilian presence in Europe should be considered,[95] since they always had their own chapels within the churches of the host cities. The whole community gathered there on national religious festivities, for processions and other ceremonies, and even to talk about business. In the current case, Castilian merchants used the chapter house of the convent of Santa Maria Novella, now known as the 'Spanish Chapel' and a meeting place, where they celebrated Mass and performed their annual processions in honour of St James the Apostle. The chapter was also the burial place for the most important members of the community. This feature indicates that integration into Florentine society was accompanied by an intense religious life, expressed through festivals and ceremonies which were celebrated in this place of worship.

The Spanish nation developed corporate practices of settlement and integration into Florentine society, including the important strategies of patronage, and the establishment of confraternities gave the group solidarity and internal cohesion and created a fund of money aimed at alleviating the potential problems of its members. The existence of a brotherhood of the Spanish nation in Florence is a topic which still needs to be explored, as the sources that seem to point to the existence of a company of St James are quite contradictory.[96] Probably it was a secular organization managed by the consul and deputies whose primary concern was 'to maintain and celebrate a main chapel of great authority for the nation, which is in the Monastery of Saint Dominic called Santa Maria Novella, and to give alms to the Spanish priests and soldiers and to the many other poor of the nation as well as to the almost infinite number of pilgrims in need'.[97]

Conclusion

The system of trading nations formalized by the Spanish kingdom by the end of the fifteenth century was based on the presence of Iberian colonies of merchants already operating in various European cities. Taking advantage of family ties and common citizenship, they created a network of correspondents which spread from the city of origin to the most important economic urban centres of the time. In some cases these kin-based commercial networks even went beyond the Mediterranean, crossing the Atlantic Ocean. If the approach of the Spanish merchants was often to permanently integrate into the host society,[98] the case of the Florentine Spanish nation showed the extent to which community members felt the need to maintain a distinct identity and represent it to the outside. Only a few of those who moved to Tuscany decided to make Florence their city of choice by integrating, through well-planned marriages, into local society. Many members of commercial companies returned home or moved elsewhere when business began to decline. We must not forget, after all, that the very creation of such a big Spanish community was largely due to the mutual advantage that the Iberian merchants trading raw wool and the Florentine clothiers enjoyed in a privileged relationship.

By the end of the sixteenth century, a period of fierce competition and profound change throughout the international economic landscape, the Florentine textile industry and the woollen industry in particular revealed its fragility.[99] It was the largest manufacturing sector in the city, and the crisis in the wool industry impacted on the entire Florentine economy. In the seventeenth century, other Spanish families remained in Florence alongside the Astudillo: the Aldanas, the Ramírez de Montalvos, the Suárez de la Conchas and the Ximénez de Aragon. Other families arrived at the beginning of the seventeenth century, such as Narvaez Saavedra.[100] Living an aristocratic life was their foremost ambition, and this meant having a wealthy agricultural base, being identified as landowners and following a military career, or if this failed, entering public office. The trend for ennobling Spanish families was aimed at financial security and social status.[101] It has been said that the Spaniards who settled in Florence 'rage by and die by the cavalry'.[102] To be recognized as members of the Tuscan nobility, the Spanish families who lived in Florence during the seventeenth century had to meet a number of requirements: they had to document all their assets in the records of the Decima Granducale, acquire Florentine citizenship and Tuscan naturalization, commission a personal chapel and register in the Florentine patriarchy.

The traditional view of the political and social life of Florence after the creation of the grand duchy – according to which the economic basis of the main families gradually changed, shifting from commercial and industrial investments to less risky purchases of land – has been revised in recent decades, if not strongly challenged.[103] The dynamism of those families who became rich through business survived at least until the mid-seventeenth century, thanks to the development of new institutions such as the *accomandita* intended to direct investments into trade and industry.[104] Nevertheless, there is no doubt that the trend followed by the Castilian families who settled in Florence during the sixteenth century follows the trajectory of the new aristocracy of the city in the modern age fairly closely: the withdrawal of their capital from commercial or manufacturing activities, the desire for social advancement through the recognition of full citizenship and entry into the ranks of the nobility of the Court. Few followed this path, however. Most Spanish companies decided to leave Florence at the first signs of the economic crisis in the city, considering it too risky or unprofitable for their businesses. This bleak scenario was vividly described by Baltasar Suárez, who around 1607 asked the grand duke to be appointed consul for life of the Natione Spagnuola, as in Florence 'there had always been a consul

appointed by the merchants resident there, but given that the number of companies of Spaniards are much decreased, at present there are two, no one is running
for this office'.[105]

Acknowledgements

Although the present work is the result of close collaboration between the two
authors, sections 1 and 3 can be attributed to Francesco Ammannati, paragraphs
2 and 4 to Blanca González Talavera. The introduction and conclusion are the
outcome of joint work. However, both accept full responsibility for the whole
of the essay.

7 MERCHANT NETWORKS IN THE CITIES OF THE CROWN OF CASTILE

David Carvajal de la Vega

Introduction

The social and economic structure of the Crown of Castile underwent significant changes in the transition from the Middle Ages to the modern era, partly due to the strong pace of urbanization, a process which had been going on for some time, as was also the case in the rest of Europe.[1] The expansion of regional trade and the incorporation of Castilian products within Europe's trading networks were some of the most remarkable consequences of this process. These changes inevitably led to the emergence of collaborative efforts and collective actions that, as was usual in other territories, supplemented the individual activities of great merchants.[2] By means of these occasional relationships, there came about an organized system based on regular commercial, social and political contacts through the participation of the most important merchant families, who generally shared the same neighbourhood. To live in the same city, in the same neighbourhood, even in the same street meant to share the daily life and favoured the creation of kinship relations or business in common. The example of Castilian merchants at the end of the fifteenth century and the beginning of the sixteenth century is very instructive as we try to understand how small local agents became large companies, corporations who had a strong familiar component and who were able to join the urban elite groups of the kingdom.

Some historians have considered the advisability of using diverse methodological points of view to study merchant communities.[3] One of the best theoretical approaches during the last decades has been 'social network analysis' (SNA). A large number of historians have shown its virtues as a useful tool to study social groups and particularly merchant communities.[4] Nonetheless, we do not give up understanding networks using case studies and other methodologies focused, for example, on the importance of kinship and credit relations or on the role played by a multi-layered institutional framework. The application of new methodological approaches allows us to get acquainted with the functioning of great companies and with the influence of family structures on socio-economic relationships. The use of 'relational analysis' implies the incorporation of a paradigm that has already made significant contributions to the knowledge of history; in our case, in fact, it involves a better understanding of the development of family relationships, trading connections, etc., in an attempt to promote both individual and group interests.[5] The graphical expression of these relations and of merchant networks by means of SNA confirms the possibilities of a tool widely used in studies with a strong relational ingredient, both in the medieval and the modern periods.[6]

In the present essay we aim at using this paradigm to analyse the advancement of some merchant families as the new urban elites, paying attention to the creation and institutionalization of a social network through the consolidation of merchant associations. Therefore we try to prove how important it was to be part of a merchant network and how it exerted a powerful influence on the growth of business, as well as on the ability to climb up the social ladder. With this purpose, we begin with a case study based on some of the most relevant social and economic relations forged among the members of the most powerful Burgalese merchant families during two generations from 1480 to 1520. They were members of one of the most active merchant communities with Toledan and Sevillian merchants. Historians like Hilario Casado, Betsabé Caunedo, Manuel Basas or Yolanda Guerrero have studied the community and the most prominent families.[7] Their works have provided us with information about the social and economic dynamics on the creation of companies or marriage ties between members of different families. We have added complementary data taken out of the Court Seal's Registry in the Archivo General de Simancas and legal sources, above all civil lawsuits – about all kind of debts, companies, dowries, etc. – from the Archivo de la Real Chancillería de Valladolid. Debt lawsuits litigated in the Royal Chancellery in Valladolid are a documentary source underexploited by historians of Castile's economy. The qualitative information contained in testimonies and all kinds of documents allows us to understand some relevant aspects that might break or strengthen the relations among merchants.[8] In addition to the application of SNA on the bibliography and the available data, the compiled sources provide us with a rich discourse about the quality and intensity of relations between merchants that allows us to know more about their objectives and the motivation behind their decisions and cooperation.

Castilian Cities and their Networks

The process of urbanization in Castile promoted a significant increase in the commercial relationships among cities and agents throughout the whole territory. As we advance into the fifteenth century, it becomes easier to notice the emergence of dense networks of trade and financial relationships that contributed to fostering the economic integration of the territory, despite the marked differences between the North and the South.[9] This proliferation of networks reveals how important these financial groups were and how necessary it was to be part of them as a business strategy.[10] In the South economic relationships revolved around the cities of Seville and Cordoba, while in the North financial networks tended to be included in great urban centres such as Toledo, Segovia, Valladolid, Burgos and Vitoria. This urban network was further favoured by the links created by the development of a cycle of trade fairs in Castile, where the celebration of the fairs of Villalón, Medina de Rioseco and especially Medina del Campo constituted its climax. Medina del Campo became the most important meeting point for Castilian and foreign merchants, for it combined commercial and financial businesses in the same place at the same time. These urban centres were key nodes in the Castilian commercial-financial network as well as the places of origin of the leading merchants in the kingdom.

In turn, the inner dynamics of each city have revealed how some groups interested in gaining control of economic and political resources – a key aspect of urban life, the supply of all kinds of goods, is a perfect example of this trend – developed a series of relational structures at a local level. The creation of a network linking the families who occupied or wished to occupy the top positions in the political life of the city was essential to obtaining or keeping a higher degree of power. This can be seen in a place like Valladolid, where these kinds of associative and collaborative strategies to control the most important urban spheres – commerce, taxation, politics, etc. – were proved useful to those such as the Verdesoto family.[11] This type of behaviour was also emulated by more modest groups in their attempts to gain control over a smaller area of power, as was the case with tax farming systems. Merchants and urban elites, who shared their goals and the means to achieve them, took advantage of the emergence of institutional frameworks that helped them to regulate and control the proper functioning of relationships. For example, in Valladolid the Cofradía de la Misericordia – the local merchants' and moneychangers' guild – was the institutional framework that ordered social and economic relations because it had the privilege to judge all lawsuits between its members.[12] This phenomenon manifests itself in other Castilian cities such as Bilbao and Vitoria where merchants began to develop complex systems of relations, most of them related to the future creation of

guilds and consulates, which were intended to defend their economic privileges
and to obtain political gains at a local level.

Merchant Networks in Burgos

Among the urban and merchant structures in Castile, the city of Burgos is a privileged field of study. The city, known *Caput Castellae* ('Head of Castile'), was the
base of operations of some of the leading merchant families and companies of the
time, although no market or trade fair was held in its surroundings. The privileged
geographic location of the city accounts for its progress as a gateway between the
commercial activities of the inner areas of the Peninsula – especially the wool
trade in centres such as Medina del Campo – and the harbours located along the
northern coast. It was a route that ran through the Iberian Peninsula from South
to North and that contributed to the ascent of numerous groups of merchants.[13]

Two institutions owned the resorts of power in Burgos throughout the Middle Ages: the cathedral chapter and the town council, the latter of which, despite
the control exerted by the traditional oligarchy in its composition, was the more
permeable institution.[14] However, the ever rising commercial significance of Burgalese merchants brought changes to the political structure inherited from the
past, as little by little new families were included in the local government. The
widening of trade frontiers and the inclusion of Burgalese merchants within the
Castilian international trade was a complex process that took place throughout
the fifteenth century. This expansion process involved the creation of new networks in different locations in Castile and the main international harbours and
markets in an effort to consolidate their businesses and manage them accordingly. In order to achieve that goal, the inner structure of Castilian companies
was reorganized by introducing some management innovations and by implementing commercial tools and techniques that had their origins in Italy or the
Low Countries, the two chief destinations of Castilian merchants.[15]

Burgalese merchant companies soon applied all these novelties, thus definitely promoting their presence in the greatest international markets and
establishing merchant colonies in different locations throughout Europe. Some
instances of this kind of institution/corporation are to be found in major cities
such as Bruges, Rouen, Nantes and Florence – where they founded consulates –
or Antwerp, London, La Rochelle, Bordeaux, Lisbon, Valencia, Barcelona, Pisa
and Rome – where there were important merchant colonies. The commercial
network was based on the weak ties created from the contact with foreign merchants in foreign centres and within Castile, above all in fairs like Medina del
Campo. By virtue of this international trading network, Burgalese merchants
could rely on a relationship system that improved the efficiency and the efficacy
of their activities and secure the success and durability of their business.[16] It was

a model of internationally oriented business, rooted in the existence of a 'university of merchants' in the city of Burgos. The positive experience derived from the cooperation among merchants, who shared common objectives like the control of wool commerce and trade relations with the northern European seaports, promoted and intensified new relationships among different groups of merchants, thus avoiding the predominance of particular families, a similar strategy to that found among Hanseatic merchants, who opted for this model rather than for the system of the great Italian companies or the one developed in southern Germany at the end of the Middle Ages.[17]

Strong Ties: Families and Companies

The reinforcement of the Burgalese merchant network, based on its expansion throughout Europe and its consolidation in Castile's inner markets,[18] led those families involved in the trade business to obtain a high level of economic power and social prestige. This in turn led them to pursue new goals. As they belonged to the social elite, they necessarily had to be active participants in the institution commissioned to govern the city and to regulate the life of Burgos citizens: the town council. However, this goal was not automatically fulfilled; rather, several generations were needed in order for the new merchant families to establish a new power structure. These families, the true leading characters in the social, economic and political development of Burgos – like in other cities[19] – were the true foundations of the strategies promoted by merchant groups as they made great inroads into the local structures of power in the course of two or three generations.[20] Nonetheless, analysis of the families is still problematic with regards to the adscription or not of some merchants, for it was usual that some members of well-known families changed their family name. Moreover, others gave up their origins and were quickly integrated in the society and the city where they moved, thus preventing us from following their trajectories.[21] In any case, we cannot renounce the family as a prime subject of study.

The foundation of companies or the joint participation in them, as well as the commercial representation of Burgalese merchants in Castile's major fairs and business centres, constitute clear evidence of the significance of families in the process of expansion of the Burgalese merchant network. In Burgalese businesses a clear geographic diversification is manifest. It derived from the establishment of family members and company agents in other cities. For instance, agents of the Pardo, Soria, Salamanca or Castro families developed this system, as they carried out important operations from the cities where they resided, such as Seville or Cordoba.[22] Both in Castile and abroad, the members of the families who stayed in Burgos were interested in keeping contact with their brothers, sons, cousins or other relatives, strengthening their ties and sustaining the commercial network by way of agents (*factores*). These *factores*, who could be members of the same family or of close ones, played an essential role as economic and financial intermediaries in many locations such as Bilbao, San Sebastián, Toledo, Alcalá de Henares, Guadalajara, Cuenca and Écija using weak ties with other merchants based on singular transactions. They also carried out minor businesses in smaller towns, where they stocked up on raw materials or basic products such as meat and wine. But the relationships with the providers were a priority; this explains, for example, the strong ties between Burgalese merchants and the suppliers of some regions, such as Soria, famous for its wool.[23]

Another symptom of the maturity of the Burgalese merchants was their ability to carry out business and to sign contracts with merchants from other locations. Foremost among these were the relations with families in places where they had previous ties and where there was an active former presence, as was the case in Seville, Cordoba, Toledo, Medina del Campo and Valladolid, centres where it was easy to share interests with other merchants and where they had the opportunity to engage in new businesses or to obtain credit to undertake greater endeavours.

Among the multiple relationships that Burgalese families established, we can observe at least two basic ties that contributed to the development and consolidation of the merchant network. Family relations based on marriages and trade relationships founded on the creation of companies are two examples of relations whose voluntary nature[24] was meant to support each other in order to climb up the social ladder and to strengthen one's own position within the Burgalese elite. To these two relationships, we must add a third one previously mentioned: the commercial representation of different families, usually carried out under a hierarchical relation.[25] These three relations emerge was the foundations of the Burgalese merchant network, and they give us some insight into topics such as the inner organization and hierarchical structure of the network. Some groups were able to acquire greater power and influence within the network, something that was further favoured by the desire of minor families to establish ties with the more influential ones. The most powerful merchants – according to their participation in the local council government or their election as officials in the consulate – were members of families like the Sorias, Pardos, Castros, Burgos or Maluendas and used their social position and relations to expand their business towards Flanders, France, England and Italy. The relation between power and family hierarchy dominated the network in the beginning of the sixteenth century, as we can see by the way minor families were dependent on major ones, for example in their work as sales representatives.

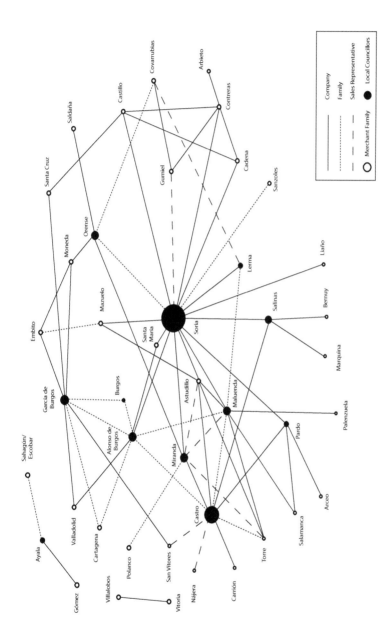

Figure 7.1: Burgalese merchant network: companies, families and sales representatives, *c*. 1480–1520. The network lines represent the existence of a relation (to establish a company, a marriage between family members, a sales representative–merchant relation or a contract). The data have been collected from works by H. Casado, B. Caunedo, M. Basas and Y. Guerrero (see n. 7 to this essay, p. 274) and from AGS registries and ARChV lawsuits.

Beyond its graphic representation, the network reveals the central position of some families in the city of Burgos, especially those who gradually took over the local city government (Figure 7.1). By the middle of the fifteenth century the leading families in the city, according to their social status, were the Cartagenas, the Villegas and the Bocanegras, representatives of the local nobility who would keep their position in local government throughout the sixteenth century; the Lermas, the Covarrubias, the Arceos, the Castros and the Burgos,[26] as representatives of the new merchants; and some others of minor significance, such as the Maluendas or the Ayalas.[27] At the end of the fifteenth century and the beginning of the sixteenth, the situation had changed notably, since some families, for example the Castros, driven by a solid relational structure, were able to obtain an important degree of power within the town council and within the 'university of merchants', where they acted as *cónsules* together with another relatively new family, the Pardos. Noble families kept their political position as town councillors, and they tried to carry out marriage negotiations with new merchant groups such as the Covarrrubias and the Burgos. New families began to stand out among the Burgalese elite, above all the Lermas, the Maluendas, the Salinas, the Orenses, the Bernuys and the Mirandas. Trade company relations seemed to predominate among them, except in the case of the Burgos, who focused on marrying their children with the leading families of the city, and the Castros, who established family ties with three different families of councillors: the Burgos, the Torres and the Maluendas.

The good results of financial cooperation and marriage unions among families cast little doubt on their effectiveness. New families took over the political life and the town council in Burgos, as they occupied ever more important positions in the municipal finances and the local administration of justice. However, at the end of the fifteenth century there was a change in this trend, derived from the emergence of Diego de Soria in the city of Burgos. Since he was an outsider, we are not acquainted with his previous family ties; it is amazing how an external agent, whose origin was far from the social dynamics of the city, ended up occupying the central position in the highly rigid Burgalese society and in the merchants' network. Before his appointment as a town councillor in 1480, the merchant had established a name for himself on account of his trade business of weapons and wool. His economic power led him to be close to the Catholic monarchs, to whom he lent money and provided with different goods. To assume the risks associated with credit operations in favour of the kings, such as delayed payments, was rewarded with their support. For example, the kings granted Diego de Soria the constitution of a *mayorazgo*, a privileged economic institution based on the juncture of their patrimony under a special regulation that, in theory, impeded the fragmentation of immovable property. His role in Burgos was settled in barely two decades, the time it took him from being an outsider to becoming the man with whom all leading families wanted to establish marriage ties or found trade companies. As proof of his influence, it was Diego de Soria who obtained from the Catholic monarchs the privilege to found the 'consulate' of Burgalese merchants in 1494.[28] This fact, together with the accumulated social and relational capital of the family, placed the Sorias as a model in the aspirations of the new merchant elite.

The cooperation among families that we can discern in our network, however, did not always favour the relationships among them. The Soria family is a prime example of this. Despite their marriage strategies with the Maluenda, Pardo and Lerma families, the result of their unions proved to be disastrous for the interests of the Sorias, whose wealth dwindled on account of several factors. Financial problems with Diego de Soria's defiant son-in-law, Alonso de Lerma, who acted as an associate in Florence and other locations,[29] as well as the disintegration of Diego de Soria's huge patrimony – *mayorazgo* – between his grandchildren,[30] entailed that the Sorias were no longer the most influential family among the Burgalese merchants. This fact must lead us to suspect that the network's own dynamics tended to avoid the proliferation of people who might occupy such a lofty position.

After the large merchant group took control over the local government, the final years of the fifteenth century bore witness to a new triumph at the institutional level. In this case, it was prompted by the recognition of the 'university of merchants' – whose members took part in the local guild, Cofradía del Espíritu Santo – as a 'consulate' in 1494. Up to that point, European expansion had given birth to a small and local institution, the 'university', whose power in Castile was very limited. The petition raised by Diego de Soria to constitute a consulate in the name of his companions was received favourably by the Catholic monarchs, who, among other things, granted the consulate the capacity of judging its members in business-related lawsuits both in the first place and after an appeal – something that worked against the process of expansion of royal justice above all other particular jurisdictions. This fact concurred with a process of institutional consolidation boosted by the Catholic monarchs. In that case, they granted the privilege to judge to one of the most powerful merchant communities, alongside Toledo and Seville, in exchange for their financial and political support. This was further evidence of the power of some Burgalese merchants and of their strong cohesion as a community, something needed in order to face the tough competition posed by the merchants and shipowners of Bilbao, who were established as a 'university' in 1489 and who, like their Burgalese counterparts, were able to create their own consulate in 1511.[31]

Although the Burgalese merchant network – an open structure – surpassed the limits of the consulate, both maintained analogies in respect of their participants, their influence and the interaction of certain families. The new consulate was organized from new ordinances and developed a formal structure headed by the *prior* and two *cónsules*, both selected each year among the members. The internal organization in the consulate was a faithful reproduction of the relationship structure among the most important merchant families. All families were represented in the consulate government, above all the Orenses, the Pardos, the Pesqueras and the Covarrubias.[32]

Financial Relationships: Families and Credit Networks

At the end of the Middle Ages, credit, along with other methods of payment, played an essential role among European merchants.[33] We can document this type of social and financial relation in Castile from earlier times in places like Seville, where the large Genovese merchant community remained socially united and was economically integrated by means of financial operations among its members.[34] Castilian merchants, and especially Burgalese merchants, resorted to credit for many purposes: instalment payments, inversions and a fast supply of necessary money.[35] Therefore the flow of credit and debt among Burgalese merchants is an excellent indicator of the level of integration of the trade network, for it reveals the existing trust among all the parts in monetary terms.[36] Moreover, towards the end of the fifteenth century the rise of credits made clear the close connection between the commercial and institutional spheres in Burgos, like the Catholic Church and the local council, where merchants were clergymen and facilitated the conditions of access to credit to councillors, a perfect example of the dynamics of local government institutions in an ever greater need of financing.[37] Most times the moneylender was a member of the local council; for example, Diego de Soria lent to the council two million maravedis (5,480 ducats) in 1495, a perfect illustration of the strong relations between merchants and local politics.

The development of a favourable legal and economic environment and the consolidation of the institutional framework explain the expansion of credit;[38] but beyond these ideas, we must take into account the impact of the involvement in relational structures in order to have better access to credit. Within an increasingly connected society, especially among merchants,[39] the enormous influence of commercial and family ties was clear when developing financial networks among Burgalese merchants. The comparison between Figure 7.2 and the documented credit relations derived from commercial sources such contracts, accounting books and, above all, debt lawsuits shows that the flow of credit and debt reproduced previous relationships, while at the same time reinforcing and supplementing them. However, credit was also a powerful tool to create new relations among families without former kinship or commercial ties, as we can notice in the case of the Sahagún-Escobar family, discussed below.

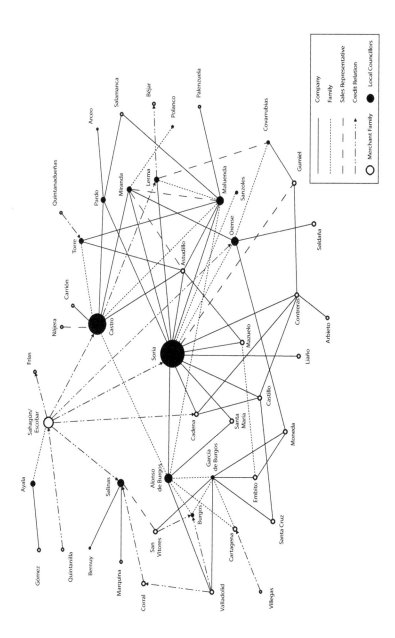

Figure 7.2: Burgalese merchant network: companies, families, sales representatives and credit relations, c. 1480–1520.

Company
Family
Sales Representative
Credit Relation
Local Councillors
Merchant Family

We know about the importance of families as large structures able to provide a solid base to do business and to reinforce long-distance trade, as Francesca Trivellato argues.[40] In Burgos, family ties played a decisive role when offering loans in times of need: the merchant Juan de Ayala lent his brother Pedro Rodríguez de Ayala 50,000 maravedis. Trusting a family member seems to be logical, as we understand social relationships, although there are some cases where family ties became a problem when the debt was not satisfied. When Pedro Rodríguez de Ayala died, his widow refused to pay the outstanding debt to her brother-in-law, who eventually took her to court, accepting the economic and social consequences derived from the lawsuit.[41] Nevertheless, debt was a problem somehow regulated by the Burgalese merchant community, for not all defaults of payment ended up in the royal court of justice. The existence of family ties between creditors and debtors was a significant factor in reducing conflicts by renegotiating the debt or renewing the contracts. In addition, we must consider the administration of justice by the members of the consulate of Burgos in those cases where merchants were involved, as they resorted to customary law to solve financial and social problems.

One of the best examples of the financial potential of family ties is the one of the aforementioned Diego de Soria and his son-in-law, Alonso de Lerma, members of the Burgalese political and commercial elite. Alonso de Lerma married Beatriz de Soria, Diego de Soria's eldest daughter, and became part of the company his father-in-law had in Italy, where he was appointed as an agent. In 1494 Alonso de Lerma began to undergo financial hardships, and the merchant asked Diego de Soria a loan of 1,000 ducats because he did a bad business, a considerable amount he spent to pay his own creditors.

Alonso de Lerma had enough capacity and contacts to obtain 1,000 ducats by other means. He engaged in different businesses with another Burgalese merchant, Pedro Castro, who in 1491 owed him 21,000 maravedis on account of a bond.[42] As a sign of the intense and varied activity of Alonso de Lerma, in 1491 the merchant had to answer to a lawsuit by Valencian merchants Gaspar Roel and Jaime Marja, who requested from him 36,208 maravedis for the credit sale of 803 quintals of raisins, 100 quintals of figs and 10 wineskins sent from the harbour of Alicante to Rouen, where an agent of the Burgalese merchant should have sold them.[43] There is no doubt that Alonso de Lerma was a merchant with financing possibilities to cover his needs and cancel his debts. Why did he ask his father-in-law for such a considerable loan? It is possible that Alonso de Lerma fell back on Diego de Soria on account of their family ties, thinking about the many economic advantages of his decision. Diego de Soria had two daughters, so after his death Alonso de Lerma was planning to control half his wealth, and thus Lerma could take the 1,000 ducats as a part of his future inheritance. Moreover, the requirements of guarantees and deposits were lower, and the whole process was therefore simpler. Besides, Lerma was in Florence operating Diego de Soria's business, and the financing costs abroad were higher; acting as he did, he only needed the approval of his father-in-law. The loan was given by Diego de Soria's agent in Florence, Alonso de Santo Domingo; however, it eventually became just one of the many problems that, on account of their commercial dealings, arose between Lerma and Diego de Soria towards the end of the 1490s. Despite attempts by both merchants to solve their differences, and after the mediation of the consulate, the intensity of the conflict led to a lawsuit, with fatal consequences for the future of the Sorias.[44]

There are more examples showing how credit relations reproduced and supplemented the previous ties among the most powerful families. Family groups such as the Pardos and the Castros also reinforced their economic dealings by means of credit relations. Along with the trade company created by both families, we know that their members signed several credit contracts, as the 22,500-maravedis bond between Diego de Castro and Juan Pardo witnesses. This bond was the result of some debts derived from a copper sale of the company and from the transfer of some company rights. After the company broke up, the only economic tie between both merchants was this debt. Diego de Castro, however, did not cancel it, leading to a lawsuit between both families. As members of the same community, the 'university of merchants', they decided to resort first to the consulate's arbitration. The case was finally tried before the royal justice, as usually happened when the sentence did not satisfy any of the parties.[45]

The new network, where credit relations were included and which was far more cohesive and dense than the previous one, accounts for the development of credit operations among the leading families, such as the Burgos (Alonso de Burgos and García de Burgos), and other minor ones, such as the Santa Cruz, the San Vítores or the Valladolid. In addition, these families contributed to the network with new financial ties, and therefore we can find nodes that did not previously exist or whose inclusion was occasional and marginal, like the Corral family. This family, absent in our first sample, is now well attested in the Burgalese merchant network thanks to the activities of Alonso del Corral, creditor of Rodrigo de Valladolid and Juan de Salinas, who owed him 500 ducats.[46]

The Importance of Belonging to a Network

As we have seen, there was an intense reciprocity and cohesion in the Burgalese kinship and trade network, and important ties were based on credit relationships. Eventually some families were not included in the merchant network, and they were forced to establish their own network in different locations of the kingdom. The Sahagún-Escobar family is a perfect example for studying the negative impact of not counting on the support of the merchants of their hometown,

Burgos. It seems that the family did not take part in the relational structure of the city; that is, they maintained few kinship and trade relations with Burgalese merchants. The Sahagún-Escobar members did not participate in the council or consulate government, and they hardly took part in company with their neighbours or did business with them, except in the case of some credit operations, where they mostly appear as debtors. The Sahagún family bet on creating companies among their own members, as in the case of Tristán de Sahagún, a move that involved keeping all their resources within the family structure.[47]

Outside Burgos, the Sahagún-Escobar family carried out numerous businesses,[48] alien to the relationships we can observe in Burgos's leading families. Their interests were far from their hometown, and they made an effort to establish ties with important investors, like Alonso de Quintanilla, Comptroller of the Kingdom, and some merchants from other significant locations (Medina del Campo and Valladolid). Andrés de Escobar's relations revealed a marked distance with the Burgalese merchant community, and therefore his companions and neighbours did not support him when the family business experienced its most critical moments. This is in contrast to what happened to the powerful Diego de Soria, who in his time of need found the support of the most prominent men in the city, giving us an example of the network's cohesion.[49] In 1499 Andrés de Escobar was alone when he had to face a lawsuit brought by twenty-seven creditors, among them the Burgalese Diego de Soria, Francisco de Orense and Alonso de Castro. The 'university of merchants' stayed away from the case and transferred the lawsuit to the Royal Council, a special court under the direct control of the king and his counsellors. Since he was defenceless in facing his creditors' demands, he looked for the protection of the Royal Council. They gave him several insurance letters in order to collect his debts throughout the kingdom without being constantly threatened by his creditors.[50]

Many creditors were aware of Andrés de Escobar's financial ties and knew that he was capable of paying the debts they claimed. Therefore some of them agreed to offer him more time to get their money back; but others did not accept it and succeeded in placing him in jail. Once imprisoned, the debtor appealed to his friendship with Fernán López de Calatayud, a well-known merchant from Valladolid, who acted as his guarantor and was able to free him in 1502.[51] This in turn raised new complaints of creditors from Valladolid and some other places, up to a total of fifty-four creditors, mostly merchants and investors from Soria, Bilbao, Toledo, Cuenca and Seville, as well as foreign agents such as Bernabé and Agustín Nigro, from Geneve. In addition, new merchants from Burgos, like Rodrigo de Frías, got involved in the lawsuit.[52]

We have no further information regarding the lawsuit, and no data have been preserved concerning how it ended; yet by 1515 Andrés de Escobar was collecting some rights in Medina del Campo, and that means that he was able to continue with his activities. That he was able to reorganize his finances, or at least a part of them, is confirmed by his businesses with several moneychangers, especially with those who lived far from Burgos.[53]

Another example of an important merchant family who had sparse ties with the Burgalese leading families was the Quintanadueñas. The documents that have come down to us do not clearly link them to the merchant community, except in the case of some indirect news regarding their relationship to the Torres.[54] Some members of the Quintanadueñas family (Pedro, Fernando and Juan) signed contracts with Castilian merchants from places like Alcalá de Henares,[55] Córdoba or Guadalajara. The seeming openness of this family was manifest when they established their businesses in places far from Burgos, their hometown,[56] and their supposedly convert origins were not a problem at all for their activities.[57]

Conclusion: A Merchant Network as the Base of a New Oligarchy

At the end of the Middle Ages, Castilian merchants were aware of the benefits derived from cooperating in an environment characterized by the favourable economic situation and the consolidation of the urbanization process in Castile. It was a fitting context where trade networks experienced a hugely successful expansion throughout the Castilian territory and reinforced their position in Europe's main trading places.

Most networks were born out of the neighbourhood ties among merchants, a fact that in turn led to significant changes in the social and economic structure of Castile's major cities, such as Burgos and Valladolid. In that sense, marriages established permanent unions between families, which were further consolidated by the birth of children. Families reinforced their status as the basic units in articulating this type of relation; they were at the base of all strategies used by merchants in their attempt to consolidate their position among the top elite. Therefore economic interests paved the way to higher political goals.

Burgos was not a key commercial node – there were no significant markets or trade fairs. Yet its geographic location contributed to the emergence of one of the most powerful and best organized merchant communities in the Crown of Castile. This community (that included old convert families), built around a well-connected trade network, was able to position its members at the town council, replacing some families of the traditional oligarchy. This in turn brought about new relationships with other established groups –the clergy and the nobility – and bolstered the relationships of some Burgalese merchants with the Catholic monarchs, whom they served sometimes as creditors.

The strengthening of the Burgalese merchant network derived from the recognition of the consulate of merchants in 1494, the final step in the consolidation of the merchant web within an institutional framework. Participation in the merchant network and in the consulate meant the ability to count on the support of others when doing business or looking for a quick and safe loan. The way in which merchants participated in the commercial activities depended on their positions within the urban institutions, their economic capacity, and the social capital developed from multiple relations inside and outside the network. Problems were solved according to the mercantile law and custom of the consulate of Burgos. Hence Burgos's merchants who were outside the network – Andrés de Escobar, for instance – could not rely on the help of Burgalese merchants.

At the beginning of the sixteenth century, the great merchant families, such as the Sorias, the Castros, the Pardos, the Lermas, the Maluendas, the Orenses or the Burgos, controlled the political life of the city, owned companies integrated into the regional and international trade circles, and tried to make their businesses prevail as they competed with some other merchant corporations, like the consulate of Bilbao. Their political, social and economic dominion marked the evolution of their strategies, focused on the formation of large patrimonies. The foundation of the right of primogeniture, the acquisition of estates, and tax farming characterized the progressive aristocratization of the great Burgalese merchants, who decided to leave aside their involvement in the trading business and focus instead on the management of their estate and rents, forgetting the ties that took them to the top of the urban society.[58] This strategy, along with the decline of the wool trade, the main commercial activity in Burgos, gave way to a complicated future as the sixteenth century unfolded.

Acknowledgements

This work has been supported by the project 'Poder, sociedad y fiscalidad en la Meseta norte castellana en el tránsito del medievo a la modernidad' (HAR2011-27016-C02-02). I want to express my gratitude to Cinzia Lorandini for her useful comments.

8 GALLEY ROUTES AND MERCHANT NETWORKS BETWEEN VENICE AND THE NORTH SEA IN THE FIFTEENTH CENTURY

Stefania Montemezzo

Introduction

The success of Venetian merchants in the trade between Asia and Europe made Venice one of the main gateways between East and West during the medieval age and the early modern period. Venetians were involved in the long-distance trade that allowed oriental spices and goods to arrive in European ports to be sold to the richest part of the population, and equally for European manufactured goods to be exported to the Middle East ports, from where they were transported to continental Asia. This system, based on private and public navies, reached its apogee during the fifteenth century.[1] However, towards the end of that century, although the galley system, the system of laws and the organization of the *arsenale* seemed to be running correctly, certain flaws began to surface and became increasingly evident. The same elements that had made Venice one of the most important and richest cities of the 'Old World'[2] started to decline and show their weaknesses. The decline of the public *mude* (convoys), changes within the noble mercantile class and the latent status of war with the Ottoman Empire, later followed by the ascent of the Atlantic powers, seem to have been the antecedents of the slowing down of the Venetian economy.[3]

Despite the gradual fall of the *mude* during the sixteenth century, it is interesting to examine the public system of navigation to gain an understanding of the kind of structure it gave to the markets of Bruges and London and how this structure was able to allow 'mobile' Venetian merchants to trade. What kinds of networks could be established during a galley voyage? How were they organized, and what support did they afford travelling merchants?

Through the study of two accounting ledgers, written by Giovanni Foscari in the 1460s during two voyages to Bruges and London on a state galley,[4] in this essay I aim to analyse how a merchant was able to operate and trade in foreign ports thanks to an established structure of guarantees and protections (such as privileges and the consulate),[5] granted in part by the Venetian state, which supported compatriots and local links. The structure of trade offered by the galley system was not merely linked to the advantages brought by the privileges conceded to the public navy (such as special terms on duties or the semi-monopoly within the Venetian commercial system)[6] in markets established for the merchants investing in the *mude*; it concerned, above all, the formal and informal support offered to the individual merchant once he arrived in a foreign market. As a reward for the risks and the expense sustained by the investors, the Senate was ready to offer tangible assistance to Venetian traders,[7] laying the basis of a network of links and nodes ready to be used by the seasonally mobile merchants.

Accounting documentation, especially in the Venetian case,[8] has not been used as widely or as often in research on social and mercantile networks as have correspondence or notarial records.[9] The reason for this is that the scarcity of available sources results in limited information. In studying accounting documentation, I adopt a network approach rather than network analysis, as the characteristics of the sources do not completely fulfil the definition of a social (or merchant) network given by scholars.[10] However, the network approach will be helpful in studying the data furnished by the ledgers. The accounting books kept by Foscari, in spite of some problematic characteristics, have several interesting features: they are satisfactorily complete with regard to the information provided on partners in different places, the kinds and characteristics of merchandise, prices, types of payment, financial transactions, transportation and transaction costs. However, the ledgers do not furnish specific details on the relations between actors, offering only a unilateral perspective, or the frequency of relational exchanges, which would provide the basis for reconstructing networks. In addition, the ledgers cast light on only two relatively short periods – three to five months in a single market – over a period of four years. Thus the source documentation cannot provide a general frame for the study of social networks. However, the richness of information on goods and financial flows can provide some nodes for the ties in which Giovanni Foscari, as a mobile merchant, was involved. Furthermore, it can help in understanding how the Bruges and London markets were organized and used by seasonal Venetian merchants.

Venice and the Public Navigation System

One of the main peculiarities that characterized the Republic of Venice was the strict relation of the city with seaborne trade and the presence and influence of the noble class (the *patrizi*) in and on it. The Venetian Senate, which was the most important authority of the state and was composed of patricians, was not only one of the most important powers in the government of the Republic, but also acted as a lobbyist for merchants, promoting policies that favoured commerce. It was positioned at the centre of the commercial system, the city and its merchant community.[11] One of the most useful and powerful tools used by the Senate to control and regulate the flow of goods through the city and the regularity of mercantile contacts was the public galley system, the so-called *mude*.

Until the end of the thirteenth century, Venetian sea commerce was in the hands of private shipowners. However, in 1294 the Senate decided to take control of the management of merchant galleys, stabilizing this practice during the fourteenth century. From this time, for over a century sea trade was balanced between the public and private sectors.[12]

Public navigation relied on the use of merchant galleys, owned by the state, armed and crewed by 200 men or more (predominantly oarsmen), and powered by oars and sails.[13] The galleys were rented (*appaltate*) only to Venetian noblemen, who had the responsibility for arming and freighting them for the whole trip.[14] The types of merchandise allowed on galleys were of a wide range, but priority was given to the valuable products (such as spices, silks, jewels and oriental goods) typical of Venetian commerce.[15] The private sector was left to independent shipowners: their boats, 'cogs', were normally unarmed and powered entirely by sails, and their capacity was three times greater than that of the merchant galleys.[16] Private sector trade represented the largest share of the traffic passing through Venice as it took care of supplying the city.

Despite the importance and capability of the private sector, the Venetian government decided as early as the thirteenth century to enter the competition and intervene in the regulation of seaborne trade, especially that regarding spices and goods with a high added value. Why? The Venetian mercantile class, which governed the city, saw in the coordination of commercial flows through the *mude* organization the opportunity to favour the economic development of the *Serenissima*. In particular, this control could intensify the centrality of the Rialto market with respect to Asian-European trade. Thanks to the extended legislation and control of galley routes, Venice was able to guarantee the regularity of naval flows, favour the fair periods (especially those related to currency exchange), and procure stable labour for the *arsenale* in times of both peace and conflict; besides, they ensured the safety of the majority of vessels during the travels, thanks to the obligation to voyage in convoy.[17]

In the fifteenth century, the central moment in the development of the system, there were eight active lines covering the whole Mediterranean basin and the Atlantic coasts from Spain to Flanders and Great Britain.[18] These lines were fundamental to Venetian commerce and an important step for the city in maintaining their position as the central market of the Mediterranean.[19] The ever stronger alliance between Genoa and Florence and the political problems that made use of the continental passages increasingly difficult pushed the *Serenis-*

sima to create some sea routes that covered the Western and African markets. However, these lines (directed to North Africa, Spain and France) were not always stable; they were often suspended due to political problems and eventually anti-Venetian policies (such as those adopted by French kings).[20]

The only public ocean route to reach Northern Europe was that for Flanders (*muda de Fiandra*). Established between 1315 and 1322 (the first sailing was in 1298, immediately after the Genoese passage), it became the alternative to the continental routes to Bruges. The creation of this route was consistent with the Venetian aim to cover all the main Mediterranean and European markets with its network of commercial flows. This system allowed the control (together with Genoa) of the exchange of oriental products and ensured regular connections and exchange, the rapid development of commercial affairs and the stable and faster re-entry of invested capital.[21] In addition, trading in Bruges with the merchants from the Hansa, among others, assured the redistribution of oriental products throughout Northern Europe.[22] All these advantages were important to the Venetian merchants, certainly, but also to their foreign partners. Knowing that Venetian ships, laden with oriental products, would arrive in their ports within fixed periods aided cooperation and the establishment of new connections and the creation of new merchant networks that favoured not only trade but also the spread of common knowledge and tools.[23] The galley system was, then, a vehicle for the creation of trust and thus networks.

All over the Mediterranean and Europe, Venice was able to establish agreements, in no small part due to consuls who protected Venetians as well as their relations. In Bruges, besides the presence of the consulate, Venetians were protected by local power: their presence and their trades were regulated and favoured.[24] From our point of view, one of the most interesting measures was exemption from payment of the regular taxes for merchandise arriving in Bruges on a state galley if the goods were sold within forty-five days following arrival in port.[25] This dispensation was combined with a prohibition on private ships leaving for Northern Europe in the month following the departure of the *muda*, which was enforced by the Venetian government. This privilege guaranteed Venetians using the state line for their commerce a strong advantage over their competitors.[26] In London, however, the atmosphere during the first years of the second half of the fifteenth century was not as amicable as that in Bruges. Ever since the end of the thirteenth century, the English Parliament, at the request of the merchant class, had tried to regulate more strictly the presence of strangers. In particular, there were attempts to force alien traders to live with an English householder who was responsible for their behaviour. Moreover, new impositions (such as requesting special permissions to stay in England and taxes) made Italian trade in the country more difficult. The rapid rise of the foreign presence (Italians, Hanseatic and Flemish) and the traders' success in international commerce caused discontent among English traders, who on several occasions used, or tried to use, violence against the continental merchants present in the capital. The Peasants' Revolt in 1381 and subsequent anti-alien riots (in 1456, 1457, 1493 and 1517) almost caused the abandonment of London by Italian merchants and might be seen as the response of the English mercantile class to the lack of law enforcement from the state on foreign traders, as well as a symptom of resentment towards the business methods introduced in England by the Lombards.[27]

Venetians between the Mediterranean, Bruges and London in the 1460s

The example used in this essay to analyse the status of Venetian relations in Bruges and London is strictly connected with the advantages and issues arising from the public navigation system. Giovanni Foscari was a member of one of the best known, most important and richest families of the Venetian *patriziato*. He was the descendant of Marco Foscari, the brother of Francesco, *doge* between 1423 and 1456.[28] Renouncing a political career very early on, he devoted his life to trade together with his brother Alvise. The firm he built was the typical *fraterna*: a family business, with no branches abroad, managed by kin living under the same roof and relying for the most part on agents for international affairs.

The two ledgers were written during two different voyages to Flanders on a state galley and report the affairs of Foscari, both as a merchant (and agent) and as *patrono* (responsible, then, for the single ship, named *Foscara* after him). The accounts presented in the books, gathered in a single manuscript, relate to merchandise charged on board the *Foscara* (and for which Foscari was responsible in the majority of cases) and merchandise loaded on one of the other ships of the *muda*[29] by resident merchants, as well as all the accounts related to the salaries of the crew and payments for the support of the ship.

The two *mastri*, named *quaderni* in Venice, are written following the rules of double-entry book-keeping according to the Venetian tradition. The *dare* (debit) and *avere* (credit) columns are on two adjacent pages (the debit column on the left-hand side and the credit column on the right-hand side) which occupy the two opposite sides of the *quaderno*.[30] Each record has its own heading, followed by all the economic variations concerning the subject (which might be an actor, merchandise, or a category of expenses or income). Each annotation has a reference (*contropartita*) on the opposite side of the ledger, but not necessarily in the opposite entry. Fundamental to double-entry book-keeping is the equating of every account with its counterpart. This is particularly important for the aim of this kind of accounting, namely detecting errors and discrepancies. For this reason, when a transaction was over and no other variations were expected, the whole account was barred diagonally. In the Foscari ledgers, some entries make reference to other books: that of the galley,[31] in which all the necessary expenses for the ship were noted; the book of the *sescalco*, the officer responsible for the distribution of the mess (*mesa de galia*) and control of the food stocks; or the company books, which contained all the accounts related to debtors and creditors.[32] Unfortunately, none of these books survived.

All the most important partners and bankers are noted in the Foscari ledgers (as well as intermediaries). This tended to be the case for Northern Europe in particular, whereas in the Mediterranean ports most buyers and sellers remained unidentified (with the exception of the Genoese and some Spanish-Arab merchants).[33] As the ledgers were considered semi-public documents (Foscari was an officer on a public galley and the books could be used as evidence in the case of a trial),[34] the records are in most cases rich in detail, especially in relation to expenses concerning the galley, bank transactions and transportation costs. Bankers, as well as business partners, are mentioned and have their own account for all the exchanges and operations in which they were involved.

Although the ledgers offer a wide range of information (salaries, crew conditions, mediation costs, rates of exchange, etc.), I focus my analysis especially on goods and capital flows, business partners and intermediaries. The study of merchandise and capital flows enables a structural picture of relationships to be drawn, showing those aspects on which most attention was focused and where the most important investments were made. Partnerships shed light on how investments were carried out, with whom and through which intermediaries. When analysing all these factors, it should be borne in mind that the series of exchanges and contacts were made during short intervals (five months for Flanders and three months for England) and with limited freedom in the choice of partners. A mobile Venetian merchant, usually quite young and travelling on a state galley to an unknown city, as Bruges and London were for Foscari (at least during his first trips in 1463 and 1464), could not possibly have had an established web of correspondents, ready to trade as soon as he arrived in their city. Young merchants, who probably had a limited knowledge of the local language, were then forced to rely on a network of operators – often of Venetian origin – who would be willing to help by sharing their resources and local contacts;[35] as we shall see in particular clarity during Foscari's first voyage, in Bruges his main intermediary was the Venetian consul.

The ledgers list a high number of contacts during both trips. Taking into account only the people mentioned specifically by name, in 1463–4 Foscari lists 148 different contacts, while in 1467–8 the number increases to 255.[36] The kinds and numbers of relations and exchanges differ considerably from place to place, with a clear differentiation between Mediterranean ports, Bruges and English cities.

Table 8.1: Kinds of transaction based on place, 1463–4.

Place	Total number of contacts*	Purchases	Deliveries	Sales	Total value (Venetian ducats)
Tunis	4	4,110	400	4,385	8,895
London	4	2,381		4,797	7,178
Bruges	24	1,052		4,232	5,284
Southampton	3	3,397		43	3,440
Malaga	2	897		1,012	1,909
Siracusa	1	213		808	1,021
Cadiz		27		787	814
Honain				474	474
Almeria	1	143		143	286
Majorca				101	101
Palermo				82	82
Messina		71		10	81
Oran	1	38		32	70
Muros				24	24
Total value		**12,329**	**400**	**16,930**	**29,659**

* This includes only exchanges of merchandise and not those involved in financial operations.

Table 8.2: Kinds of transaction based on place, 1467–8.

Place	Total number of contacts*	Purchases	Deliveries	Sales	Total value (Venetian ducats)
Bruges	40	1,555		13,141	14,696
Tunis	3	2,845		2,247	6,699
Southampton	8	3,870	1,028	631	5,529
London	8	2,085		1,207	3,292
Parenzo	1	386	209	171	766
Siracusa	1	104		313	417
Cadiz		255		139	394
Sandwich		5		379	384
Oran	1	123		53	176
Pola	1			100	100
Malaga				23	23
Capo San Vincenzo		3			3
Majorca		4			4
Palermo		4			4
Sluis		2			2
Total value		**10,861**	**1,237**	**18,419**	**32,489**

* This includes only exchanges of merchandise and not those involved in financial operations.

As can be seen from Tables 8.1 and 8.2, the differentiation is clearly marked in both cases. From the point of view of the exchanges linked merely to merchandise, there is a great difference in the weighting of northern markets. Although the total value of trade is similar for the two trips, there is a great divergence in the localization. In 1463–4 (Table 8.1) the Flemish market shows a lower number of transactions, especially when compared with the second trip (Table 8.2). In 1463–4 trade in Bruges only amounted to 18 per cent of the total value, and the Flemish market was eclipsed by Tunis (where 30 per cent of the total value was traded) and England (London and Southampton saw 35 per cent of the total exchanges).[37] In contrast, in 1467–8 Bruges was highest in relation to the sum of sales and deliveries, with 45 per cent (14,696 ducats) of the total value exchanged there; the Flemish market was therefore the most important in Northern Europe, followed by the English market (27 per cent of the total transactions value) and Tunis (20 per cent). Other transactions of importance were made in the Mediterranean in Malaga and Syracuse. However, the importance of other Mediterranean ports appears to have diminished during the second voyage compared with the first.[38] Apart from purchases regarding the galley and two small transactions in Messina (1463–4) and Pola (1467–8), no further exchanges are recorded during the outward voyage. All trades started in Bruges. The reason was the habit (and imposition) of bringing all merchandise to Northern Europe. The obligation to sell only after arrival in Flanders was usually established in the *appalto* contract and aimed to maintain regularity in the number of oriental products on the market in Bruges and London, moreover avoiding excessive speculation in prices.[39]

Considering the number of Foscari's contacts in each city, always taking in account only those known by name, a considerable difference is clearly visible between the Flemish and English cities, as well as between these and the Mediterranean ports. Whereas Foscari was able to take advantage of a broad web of local and Venetian merchants, brokers and bankers in Bruges (54 in 1463–4 and 114 in 1467–8, of whom 26 and 61 respectively were Flemish natives), in London the situation was slightly different. In 1463–4, he was in contact with only 15 people (of whom 5 were native English), whereas in 1467–8 the number increased to 22 (of the 13 native traders, 7 were new contacts in Southampton). The Mediterranean markets were characterized by a distinctly lower number of partners and a concentration of exchanges, from both a geographical and a merchant point of view. In 1463–4, even though Tunis appears to be the most important market for the amount of merchandise exchanged, there were only four contacts, two of whom were companies composed by almost the same partners.[40] The same pattern applies to other ports: the Berber and Spanish markets might be defined as specialized, particularly from a mercantile point of view; only a few deals were carried out with a very small number of traders and for specific goods (leather and gold).

Table 8.3: Most important commercial partners in 1463–4.

Place of contact	Merchant or company	Nationality	Amount
Bruges	Francesco Zorzi	Venetian	723
	Iacopo Devett	Flemish	673
	Iacopo Bules	Flemish	483
	Filippo Donde Clocon	Flemish	435
	Andrea and Francesco Bragadin	Venetian	381
	Colart	Flemish	242
	Ruzier	Flemish	225
	Gervaso Corner	Venetian	218
London	Thomas Stalbruc	English	2,051
	Thomas Belleter	English	786
	Rizardo drapier	English	298
Southampton	Marco da Pesaro	Venetian	1,104
	Tommaso Stalbruc	English	569
Malaga	Amet el Brentillo	Spanish Arab	1,794
Almeria	Baco Moro	Spanish Arab	286
Tunis	Chierico Cattaneo and Benedetto Imperiale	Genoese	1,863
	Chierico Cattaneo, Benedetto Imperiale and Giovanni Pinello	Genoese	1,785
	Piero Contarini (agent of Dandolos)	Venetian	400
	Lionello Spinola	Genoese	287

Table 8.4: Most important commercial partners in 1467–8.

Place of contact	Merchant or company	Nationality	Amount
Bruges	Donazio de Mor	Flemish	6,189
	Antonio Ruzier	Flemish	842
	Ambrogio Rubuis	Flemish	726
	Zuan Loscardo	Flemish	576
	Michiel Hottino	Flemish	498
	Zuan Dunt Gross	Flemish	495
	Rigo Bus	Flemish	493
	Paolo Rubin from Antwerp	Flemish	420
	Piero Soranzo	Venetian	382
	Iacopo Rat	Flemish	355
	Marco Vandeveler	Flemish	294
	Nicolao Labie	Flemish	250
London	Rizardo Lalton	English	851
	Tommaso Mocenigo and Bernardo Giustinian	Venetian	739
	Zuan Vand	English	346
	Zuan Stanbi	English	305
	Filippo Pini	English	240
	Antonio Licanelli	English	220

Place of contact	Merchant or company	Nationality	Amount
Southampton	Filippo Lomellin	English	1,326
	Marco da Pesaro	Venetian	960
	Donazio de Mor	Flemish	450
	Piero Vattazi	English	340
Tunis	Giovanni Battista Grimaldi, Ilario Grimaldi and Benedetto Giovanni Pinello	Genoese	3,470

The composition of the group of contacts in Foscari's trade network was quite heterogeneous from both a quantitative and a qualitative point of view. In Bruges and London, the traders were quite numerous and (especially for Bruges) mostly native. In particular, focusing on the amount of money invested, it becomes clearer that the more profitable exchanges were made directly with Flemish or English merchants. Going beyond the quantitative aspect and looking at the type of expenses in connection with the names of intermediaries, a few figures appear to be linked to the essential services necessary for newly arrived traders. The services consisted in getting the merchandise on the market and finding a place to stay, an office and a warehouse to store the goods waiting to be sold.

From a comparison between the payments for these expenses and personal accounts, the important involvement of Bartolomeo Zorzi becomes clear. In the early 1460s Zorzi was the Venetian consul to Bruges; his job consisted of collecting taxes (*cottimo*), and providing assistance to Venetian merchants and introducing them to the city. He acted as a guarantor for Venetian travelling merchants, obtaining housing for them and storage for their merchandise, and acting as an agent after the departure of the ships when necessary. Foscari noted that many postponed payments were collected by Zorzi once the *muda* left Bruges, and some merchandise was left behind and entrusted to him. His position becomes still clearer when considering the financial transactions. Zorzi acted as intermediary (recipient or payer) for several payments by letter of exchange to a total value of 1,686 ducats. He also figures as the payee of a draft from Giovanni Foscari, who was repaying him for the several advance payments Zorzi made for him. As consul, Zorzi was not allowed to trade on his own account, and laws strongly contraindicated the consul's involvement in affairs as a broker: it was considered that a neutral position with respect to other traders was important for the functions a consul had to carry out. However, in the first ledger, Foscari mentions Zorzi, together with Girolamo Michiel, as a mediator in the affairs of Marino and Francesco Dandolo (resident in London; see Table 8.5). In the accounts, however, Foscari is careful never to define him as a *fattore* or broker of any type. He simply asserts that some affairs were undertaken in the name of Zorzi and Michiel; however, the profit would have been recorded in the Dandolo *fraterna* account.

Thus, in Bruges, certain traders acted as key figures and played an important role in mediating the affairs carried out by the travelling merchants. In Foscari's case, during the first voyage his hosts were Marino and Francesco Dandolo. Their *fraterna* appears to be important and to have had a strong international vocation as they are mentioned as *fattori* in Bruges in 1470–6 by Alvise Michiel (see Table 8.5). In England the situation was rather different as the travelling traders were required to be hosted by a Venetian merchant resident in the city who was thus responsible for their actions, rather than being hosted on a voluntary or informal basis.

Financial Tools and Methods of Payment

During the first voyage, a key role was also played by Domenico Trevisan, one of the other *patroni* of the convoy. Trevisan, who appears to be an expert merchant, acted as mediator in several transactions, namely the selling of cotton, spices and bows. The value of the goods sold with his help between Bruges and Southampton was more than 4,000 ducats. Records of the financial operations also confirm the importance of Trevisan's role: he acted as intermediary (recipient or payer) for several drafts amounting to 1,511 ducats.

In 1467–8 the situation was very similar in both Bruges and London. However, in the case of Bruges, some specific aspects should be noted. Probably because of the experience gained in the first voyage, in Bruges it becomes more difficult to distinguish a key figure or figures. The pattern of exchanges and investments is quite different from the first voyage. Besides highly specialized and sizeable transactions (such as that with Donazio de Mor, who purchased cotton for more than 6,000 ducats), there are myriad exchanges which might be defined as of a medium-high level (between 300 and 850 ducats in value). Taking into consideration financial operations, it is possible to discern some important figures. In addition to some actors mentioned as bankers (such as Colinet de Mai and Giovanni Rolando), several other people are involved in payments and currency exchanges amounting to a remarkable sum of money. Focusing on brokers for the purchase of certain services, such as procuring an office, or paying crew members and native citizens (for services rendered), sheds some light on the identities of these people. In Bruges, Piero Soranzo acted as mediator in renting an office and some exchanges of goods,[41] but also as drawee for several bills of exchange (1,392 ducats). In London, the place of Marino and Francesco Dandolo in 1463–4[42] was taken by Tommaso Mocenigo and Bernardo Giustinian. They offered Foscari board and lodging and were involved in several drafts, as drawee, deliverer and payee (for 1,299, 973 and 928 ducats respectively). Mocenigo and Giustinian specialized in the cloth trade, acting as brokers for the sale of Mediterranean fabrics (such as cotton) and the purchase of English cloth. They were also present in Southampton, although here Foscari's main contact was Marco da Pesaro. On both occasions he was an important contact for the trade of English cloth (a total of 1,145 ducats in 1463–4 and 960 ducats in 1467–8), an agent for the sale of *panni bastardi* (low-quality cloth, totalling 1,028 ducats), and involved in several drafts as payee, in particular in 1463–4 (2,267 ducats).

Table 8.5: Italian traders abroad in 1464, 1468 and 1470–6.

Name	City	Year	Kind of relation	Comparison with the Michiel ledger*
Piero Contarini	Tunis	1464	*Fattore* for the Dandolos in Tunis	
Marino and Francesco Dandolo	London	1464	Board and lodging; appear to have had a close relationship with Bartolomeo Zorzi and Girolamo Michiel	In 1470–6, *fattori* for Alvise Michiel in Bruges
Bernardo Giustinian	Southampton	1464	*Fattore* for Piero and Antonio di Priuli	In 1476, *fattore* for Alvise Michiel in Alessandria
Marco Pesaro	Southampton	1464	Trader in English cloth; broker	
Francesco Priuli	Southampton	1464	*Fattore* for Piero and Antonio Priuli	In 1476, involved in the commerce of tin
Paolo Priuli	London	1464	Mediator for drafts directed to London	In 1476, involved in the commerce of tin
Giacomo Salviati	London	1464	Banker	
Griguolo Spinola	Malaga	1464	Broker	
Bartolomeo Zorzi	Bruges	1464	Consul of the city and broker for the Dandolo *fraterna*	
Alberto Contarini	Bruges	1467	*Fattore* for Antonio Giustinian	
Leonardo Bondumier	Bruges	1468	Priuli's agent	
Bernardo Giustinian	London, Southampton	1468	Board and lodging; advance payments	In 1476, *fattore* for Alvise Michiel in Alessandria
Marco Giustinian	London	1468	Advance payment	In 1470, involved in the commerce of tin
Alberto Grimani	Bruges	1468	Selling bows for Foscari	
Tommaso Lippamano	Bruges	1468	Pewter trade	
Andrea Malipiero	All English markets	1468	Mediation on payments; arrived in England on the Foscara	

Name	City	Year	Kind of relation	Comparison with the Michiel ledger*
Tommaso Mocenigo	London	1468	Board and lodging; advance payments	In 1476, *fattore* for Alvise Michiel in Alessandria
Pesaro Marco	Southampton	1468	Delivery and sales of various goods	
Ulisses Salvador	London	1468	Clerk to Marco Giustinian	
Piero Soranzo	Bruges	1468	Broker (rent of an office in Bruges, several exchanges and payments)	In 1476, *fattore* for Alvise Michiel in Bruges

* The ledger of Alvise Michiel is an unpublished company accounts book, written in the 1470s. Source: State Archive of Venice, *Miscellanea Gregolin*, b. 15.

An important role was also played by bankers, widely used in Bruges.[43] The amount of value, both for payment and currency exchange, is remarkable and increased during the second voyage. In 1463–4 the bankers used in Bruges for the payments were Zuane Grisel, Zuane Rolando and Girardo Febre, whereas in 1467–8 the bankers were Collinet de Mai and Zuane Rolando (Table 8.6). There is no evidence of bankers, or at least named as such, in London. In England, those acting as recipients or payers were usually Venetians or of other Italian origin (such as Ambrogio and Giorgio Spinola, acting in currency exchanges to the value of 1,413 ducats in 1467–8).

Table 8.6: Local bankers in Bruges, 1463–4 and 1467–8.

Name*	Year	City	Kinds of transactions	Transaction amount (Venetian ducats)
Girardo Febre	1463–4	Bruges	Bills of exchange, withdrawal	1,638
Zuane Grisel	1463–4	Bruges	Bills of exchange, deposit	1,412
Zuane Rolando	1463–4	Bruges	Bills of exchange, withdrawal	994
Zuane Rolando	1467–8	Bruges	Bills of exchange, deposit	9,997
Collinet de Mai	1467–8	Bruges	Bills of exchange	4,650

* These actors are only marked as bankers in the two ledgers. All the financial operations were undertaken from Bruges on both occasions.

Bills of exchange were the main operations for which banking services were requested. The bills could be used as a tool for the payment of merchandise and services (as brokerage), or as remittance, or transfer, of funds to another city in a different currency to make a profit playing on the rate of exchange. In the case of Foscari, the two currencies used were usually the Flemish pounds groot and English pounds sterling.

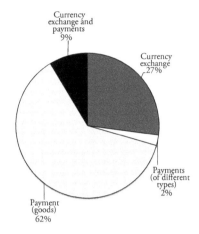

Figure 8.1: Use of bills of exchange, 1463–4.

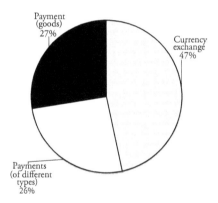

Figure 8.2: Use of bills of exchange, 1467–8.

During the two voyages there was very different use of bills of exchanges. In 1463–4, the majority of drafts were used to pay for merchandise and services (3,612 and 137 ducats respectively), whereas only a third of such bills were used to invest in exchanges between Flemish and English currencies. In 1467–8, in which period there was a considerable increase in the total number of exchanges, the situation was considerably different. More than half of the drafts were employed for currency exchange (totalling 9,595 ducats). Also payments by bills of exchange increased for merchandise (5,293 ducats) and services (4,046 ducats), although payments for merchandise using this method diminished in terms of percentage share. The increase in the total value of transactions relating to goods in 1467–8 was followed by an increase in capital invested between Bruges and London. These investments involved the participation of Venetian traders for the most part, but also other Italian traders (from Genoa and Tuscany), and both traders and bankers from Bruges. However, in the letters concerning currency exchanges, no English parties are involved. This lack of English traders might be related to the issues in the relations between native English and alien merchants. The capitalist approach to funding investment employed by Italian merchants could well be considered one of the causes of the anti-alien movement that periodically shook the stability of the London market.

Financial operations using bills of exchange involving bankers or financial mediators were not employed in the Mediterranean ports, where all payments were made by cash or barter. The main importance of these markets appears to be the links they could offer with traders of other nations, especially Italians. In the case of Foscari, these places were particularly important because of the presence of the Genoese, who were involved in coral trading and predominantly dealt in cash.[44] The Spanish and Northern African markets and the Sicilian cities were used primarily for the trading of Flemish and English cloths. Barter was normally used with native traders (the identities of whom unfortunately remain unknown in the majority of cases) and involved wax, leather, slaves, tropical merchandise (such as monkeys, porcupines and Berber horses) and gold. As the stop in Spanish and Berber ports tended to last no more than a week and exchanges were limited to a few products, the structure and functioning of the markets are difficult to identify.

Table 8.7: Exchanges in the main Mediterranean ports in 1463–4.

Place	Merchandise	Purchase	Delivery	Sale
Cadiz	One black boy*	25		
	Damask fabric			37
	English wool cloth			723
	Pepper			27
	Porcupines	2		
Siracusa	Berets			35
	Dates (⅓ of the society)	166		230
	Frisetti (wool and cotton cloths from Holland)			25
	Capes and naps from Reims			24
	English wool cloth			378
	Scarlet cloth	23		
	Satin			80
	Silk	24		
	English wool cloth from Sussex			36
Tunis	Four monkeys	10		
	Lamb leather	90		
	Berber horses	35		
	Wax	567		
	Leather	326		
	Grana† cloth		400	
	English wool cloth			4,269
	Satin			11
	Holland cloth			13
	Berber gold	2,891		

* Probably a slave.
† A red dye extracted from an insect, the *Coccus Ilicis*.

Table 8.8: Exchanges in the main Mediterranean ports in 1467–8.

Place	Merchandise	Purchase	Delivery	Sale
Cadiz	Red satin cloth	73		
	Scammony			70
	Slaves (two males and two females)	182		
	Sex larghi (English wool cloth)			60
	Sex stretti (English wool cloth)			9
Oran	Silver carved in the form of a cup	71		
	Dates	52		
	Sex stretti (English wool cloth)			53
Siracusa	Bow wires			78
	Salted cheeses	25		
	Cloth (several types)			102
	Cloth 'bresvatter'	51		
	Satin	26		
	Sex stretti (English wool cloth)			133
Tunis	Berets			65
	Berber wax	349		
	Furry leather	1,258		
	Panni larghi (English wool cloth)			2,179
	Sex stretti (English wool cloth)			3
	Ox leather		120	
	Berber gold	1,238		

Conclusion

Drawing on the accounts of a Venetian merchant, this essay shows that there were considerable differences between trading in Northern European ports and those in the Mediterranean in the fifteenth century, both in terms of the actors involved and the scope of their activities. The markets in Bruges and London had a similar system of trade for a travelling merchant: they were well organized, with a strong institutional presence, and visiting merchants could rely on the presence of more expert compatriots who hosted and guided them in their contacts with native traders. In Bruges local merchants and bankers especially can be discerned as fundamental sources of support in the network of a seasonally mobile merchant. Together with the institutional Venetian representative (the *console*), these actors, in some cases appointed by the Bruges authorities, were the starting point for the creation of a temporary web that allowed traders travelling on the *mude* to undertake business of considerable value.[45] The local authorities favoured Italian merchants with privileges and relative freedom and safety in their exchanges. Moreover, the increasingly precarious situation of Bruges, which was losing its leading position in favour of Antwerp, probably made the local authorities even more ready to accept the conditions requested by Venetian merchants.[46]

In London, the situation was different as the Italian merchants were subject to much stricter control and regulation. This attitude might explain the lack of English actors in financial operations. The English markets, moreover, did not benefit from the increase in exchanges in 1467–8 (in comparison with the previous voyage), the value of transactions remaining very stable, especially when compared to the 'liquid' situation of Bruges.

Whereas Bruges and London, besides their differences, share the common characteristic of having the key figures necessary for the introduction of the mobile traders to the market, the Mediterranean ports appear simply to be in a different world. The most important market here is Tunis, above all due to the presence of Genoese traders. Apart from the exception represented by Tunis, from Cadiz to Siracusa we can identify a similar kind of market: highly specialized. The specialization is linked to the qualities of products exchanged, a relatively small number, as well as to the total number of partners: apart from other Italian merchants, only a few local traders were involved, most of whom are not identified. This lack of information makes it difficult to analyse the functioning of the North African markets with regard to a Venetian travelling merchant, even if we know that the *Barberia* was a very important partner for the Serenissima's commercial system. The fact that the ledgers here analysed are relative to the Flemish *mude* must also be kept in consideration.

The mercantile web of a seasonally mobile merchant could work due to the integration of a number of elements. The first is a strong institutional presence in the foreign markets and formal security governing exchanges; where these are present, the number of exchanges tends to be high, quite diversified, and enriched by the investment of capital in financial operations. The second element is the existence of an established web of compatriots who, with their local contacts, could manage the business of the newly arrived traders. Last but not least were personal capabilities and skills. In a market in which formal institutions were not perfectly organized, or necessarily present, the ability to count on personal and pre-existing contacts could enhance opportunities to undertake major trades and profit completely from the possibilities afforded by the public system of galleys.

Acknowledgements

I am grateful to the editors and also particularly to Maria Fusaro, Francesco Guidi-Bruscoli, Cinzia Lorandini, Claudio Marsilio, Amélia Polónia and Francesco Vianello for their valuable advice.

9 NETWORK TAKERS OR NETWORK MAKERS? THE PORTUGUESE TRADERS IN THE MEDIEVAL WEST

Flávio Miranda

The question of whether traders were network takers or network makers is relevant for the understanding of commercial relations, business dynamics, group attitudes towards a common purpose, and socio-economic relationships over time; but the existence of those dynamic patterns among the Portuguese is rather hard to identify for the late Middle Ages. Nevertheless, this question is important for several reasons.

Portugal held a very modest rank as a commercial player in Europe's medieval economy, and one might not immediately consider its merchants and seafarers as protagonists of noteworthy socio-economic networks. The bulk of Portuguese medieval trade was mostly of traditional Iberian commodities, such as figs, raisins, wine, olive oil, oranges and cork, and sugar from Madeira, wood from the Azores and ivory from Guinea in the second half of the fifteenth century. And we know little of the existence of any remarkable Portuguese merchant families or groups of merchants that could have intertwined traders from Portugal with the ones from other European regions, establishing trade meshes and efficient multifarious business webs. So, to a certain extent, there is a gap in our knowledge about what one knows about what was bought and sold, how merchants interacted with each other to make the system work, and how those socio-economic relations shifted over time.

However, some evidence suggests that there was voluntary participation of traders in groups pursuing the same common goal, and complementary resource transfer, in the long-distance trade in the medieval Atlantic that interconnected the port cities of Portugal with those of England, the German Hanse, Zeeland, Flanders, Normandy, Brittany, Spain and other parts of Europe. After the commencement of Portugal's commercial expansion by the end of the thirteenth century, its seafarers began to establish colonies abroad in Harfleur and Bruges and to develop frequent commercial contacts with Bristol, Southampton, London and Middelburg, whether as merchants or as freighters. In the second half of the fourteenth century, the movement of ships between Portugal and other parts of Europe increased significantly, in a commercial relation that included hundreds of different merchants. In Southampton, for example, many Portuguese ships arrived laden with commodities that belonged to merchants of Portugal, but also to traders from Italy and England. And in the mid-fifteenth century, with the beginning of overseas expansion, Portugal's Atlantic commercial system was thus amplified with the inclusion of the islands of Madeira and Azores and multiple port towns in western Africa; the consequence of this fifteenth-century maritime enterprise was the redefinition of European commercial exchange, bringing trade at a larger scale than ever before, and the formation of new economic structures, new trade routes with new commodities to negotiate, and new partnerships, linkages and networks.

The problem is that to answer the question as to whether the Portuguese were network takers or network makers, one needs to know exactly how those linkages or networks were created, who the actors were, how they interacted with each other, their individual functions, their common goal, their expectations, how long those connections lasted, how other people joined a pre-existing network, how that affected their business performance, the collective and individual advantages of being part of that system, why someone would abandon it, and how and why a network would cease to exist. Moreover, one needs to consider all the external variables that have conditioned the political and socioeconomic environment of the late Middle Ages, in particular commercial diplomacy, economic policies, institutional development, competition between traders and warfare. Only then will one be able to know if they were network makers – creating *ex novo* trade routes, establishing new partnerships, presenting alternative forms of cooperation, and enabling business relationships far beyond their core of operations – or network takers – using pre-existing trading webs, joining organized groups of traders, and enjoying existing forms of cooperation without contributing much to the 'infrastructure and mechanisms of trade'.[1]

This essay is divided in six sections. The first two sections are devoted to discussing the problems posed by the historical sources and relating them to the concepts used throughout the text. They will also explain the evolution of the geographical contours of Portugal's commercial interactions in the late Middle Ages. The third and fourth sections aim at examining how the commercial system was created, and how this stimulated the formation of trading networks. Since we lack specific sources to analyse the birth of socio-economic networks in Portugal, and how merchants took advantage of them, this overview of trade relations and commercial contacts is necessary to observe patterns in overseas trade. The fifth section is on the relationship between networks and cities, and it will demonstrate how networks intermingled Portuguese with European and Euro-African marketplaces. The final section will conclude this essay.

Problems and Concepts

The task of finding archival records to analyse the Portuguese traders' role in a network is quite intricate. How is it possible to understand network dynamics without notarized records?[2] How to interpret the meaning of connections and the quality of ties, when sources are scarce and the information is not entirely clear? Is it really possible to talk about networks, or do the connections between merchants represent some different pattern?

The sources used for this essay comprise about 900 documents from Portugal, Spain, France, Belgium and England.[3] These sources go from the twelfth century until the end of the fifteenth, but most of the records only cover the period between 1300 and 1500. These 900 documents record hundreds of merchants, shipmasters and seamen from several different parts of Europe, but their names do not repeat very often; when they do repeat, it is not possible to say if they are talking about the same person or someone completely different. This obviously causes some problems in the analysis of merchant networks, as will be discussed below.

The major hindrance has to do with the type of available sources. There is a lack of empirical data for consistently scrutinizing the functioning of Portuguese merchant networks for the late Middle Ages, regardless of the macro or micro level of analysis applied to the research. Portuguese archives hold no notarized contracts made between merchants for the entire medieval period. Nor do they have merchant families' records, correspondence, business ledgers or port custom accounts.[4]

The archives outside Portugal keep very important collections of sources for the study of Portuguese medieval trade, especially the port custom accounts at the National Archives (Kew, UK) and the judicial records at the Staadsarchief Brugge (Bruges, Belgium). But despite the useful data contained in both archives, there are at least two major obstacles. Firstly, the typology of those records is completely different. In England, aside from the petitions submitted to the king and Parliament, most of the records list the name of the ship, shipmaster, merchant and commodities; yet one is not entirely able to recognize the existence of network connections within these documents. In Flanders, a great deal of records were produced by the town court, and they usually suggest the presence of links between traders; but they refer to specific cases and not to continuous commercial activities between those men involved in the business contract. Secondly, evidence suggests that many merchants had commercial interests in more than one Atlantic region, importing and exporting goods from Middelburg, Bruges, Harfleur, London or Southampton; alas, most of the records were produced in different decades, and it is nearly impossible to cross-reference merchant names of those that eventually did business in Portugal, and on both sides of the English Channel.

Another important aspect to consider is the fact that merchant companies, such as the ones that existed in Italy throughout the Middle Ages, apparently have never been created in Portugal, and there were no merchant guilds organizing traders and business as there were in other parts of Europe. But there was, in some occasions, the appropriation of urban institutions by merchants, some insurance and freight contracts (known especially through judicial cases), a considerably high number of petitions, court minutes and sentences, and references to partnerships in certain privileges.

Not all problems are related to the sources but to what they tell us. Hundreds of names of Portuguese, English, Flemish, French, Spanish and Hanseatic merchants were identified in the sources. However, two immediate problems emerge from the examination of the records. Firstly, names such as 'Afonso Eanes', 'João Afonso', 'João Gonçalves', 'João Martins' and 'Pedro Eanes' were very common, making it hard to recognize who's who in the records. Secondly, for those who have been positively identified as being the same person, the number of references is usually low, creating problems for examining the duration and quality of the commercial contact and the characteristics of the trade network. For example, in 1403 João Afonso, Gonçalo Martins, Vasco Rodrigues and João de Leiria exported wine, honey and ox hides to England.[5] The first two paired together on another occasion, the third appeared just this once, and the last continued in England alone.[6] How is it possible to understand the socio-economic interplay between those men? How to understand that same interplay when they interact with alien merchants?

Since it is difficult to characterize some network connections with the available sources, I have decided to divide the type of processes into three categories in the scale of ties: interactions, partnerships and socio-economic networks. The first refers to commercial actions between individuals or groups, which can be further differentiated into regular, repeated or infrequent. Interactions are rather commonly found throughout this essay: since a commercial contact does not make a network, what one observes, most of the time, is a socio-economic interaction that has happened sporadically between traders. The second is an association of traders while performing business operations, and it usually existed as a formal relationship. Alas, the facets of those partnerships are only visible in a few records on Portuguese traders. The final category is broader and generally applied to cases where two or more (Portuguese and foreign) merchants interact, thus forming or using pre-existing commercial networks. As we shall see, socio-economic networks were easier to find in urban areas in Portugal and in the most important marketplaces of Europe, especially Bruges.

Geography of a Network

The dimension of the network varied according to the type of business, the necessities of the traders, the partnerships created, and the markets that merchants were exploring with their commodities. But Portugal's commercial areas suffered several mutations in shape, size and geography in the late Middle Ages, and one can divide them into at least three different phases. The first phase begins in the twelfth century and goes until the end of the fourteenth century, and it can be characterized as the period of Portugal's maritime commercial expansion. The second phase begins in 1415 with the conquest of Ceuta, followed by the discovery of the islands of Madeira (1418), Azores (1427) and Cape Verde (1456); the exploration of the western African coast, and first contact with the island of São Tomé (1471); the establishment of the *feitoria*-fortress of São Jorge da Mina (1482); the crossing of the Cape of Good Hope (1488); Vasco da Gama's journey to India (1498); and the discovery of Brazil (1500). Finally, the third phase is the period beyond the threshold of the late Middle Ages that was characterized by the economic transactions performed by merchants between Europe and Africa, Asia and the Americas in the sixteenth century.

It was during the first phase when the movement of men and vessels to England, Normandy and Flanders increased significantly, and the Portuguese established 'nations' in foreign regions and performed business with native traders from those port towns. At the same time, merchants from Italy, the Hanse, Flanders, England and Brittany were settling their communities in Lisbon. What was occurring was the formation of a wide Atlantic commercial structure that unified a vast array of port cities and complementary markets into an urban network. But how were those links developed? How did traders organize their commercial activities between their hometowns and foreign markets? Were they creating any economic networks or establishing informal bi-directional business activities between origin and destination? Were they cooperating with merchants from other Portuguese cities? Were they partnering up with traders from other parts of Europe? Is it possible to evaluate the strength of those connections? Is it possible to know if those connections were indeed useful for merchants to achieve their economic goal? How did those links evolve through time?

Building the Commercial System

Portuguese merchant companies are not known for the medieval period, nor are merchant families whose commercial activities were pursued for several generations. In a certain way, this invalidates any attempts to detect kinship among the Portuguese commercial networks; indeed, only a couple of records show that merchants' relatives were also active traders, not specifically as another node in a network, but complementing the business transaction. This was, for example, the case of João Ramalho's wife, for she frequently replaced her husband, a late fourteenth-century merchant from Porto, in the commercial activities that they both had in Atlantic and Mediterranean markets.[7]

The unfeasibility of tracking kin relationships among merchants does not mean it is impossible to detect geo-commercial, urban and market-type relations in other sources. In the early twelfth century, while Portugal was still experiencing the commencement of its commercial expansion, a group of merchants decided, apparently, to work together for a common goal – to trade in England.

In 1226 the king of England issued two safe-conducts to traders from Portugal: the first was granted to forty-three merchants, and the second to sixty-three.[8] This means that 106 Portuguese traders were awarded the right and privilege to negotiate in England. The uniqueness of this document lies in the fact that it was given to so many different merchants at the same time. Violet M. Shillington and A. H. de Oliveira Marques have argued that at the origin of those safe-conducts was an incident in England with a Portuguese ship in 1225, and that the event was enough to cause panic among traders.[9] But we know that medieval merchants faced graver dangers throughout the centuries, and rarely did they react in a similar way – by requesting charters of protection and safe-conducts – unless they felt that their business relations could be at stake; and there is no other evidence that such was the case. Instead, this document may be one of the oldest proofs of the existence of formal linkages between merchants in medieval Portugal.

Portugal's overseas trade was rather frequent by the end of the twelfth century, whether in Atlantic or Mediterranean markets, and its merchants travelled as far as Dublin, Bristol, Bruges, Marseille and Thessaloniki.[10] References to Anglo-Portuguese trade in the first decades of the thirteenth centuries are scant, but it is likely that those contacts were much stronger than sources show.[11] The licence to trade in England obtained by the Portuguese in 1226 can thus have several meanings and indicate more than it seems.

Many of the merchants are referred to in the safe-conducts by their names and places of origin, and most of them were from Porto, Guimarães, Bouças (now called Matosinhos), Maia and Coimbra. This means that the majority were from or lived within a 10 km radius (Bouças, Maia), a 40 km radius (Guimarães) and a 100 km radius (Coimbra) from Porto. Chances are that those men represented the merchant elite in northern Portugal combined with other minor traders, possibly involved in other occupations, and had a set of commodities worth exporting to England. For this to happen, they had to be organized and integrated into a communication network that was able to inform on what the English market and consumers wanted, and the necessary institutional requirements to get there. It is likely that these 106 men shared the same goal, which was to profit from overseas trade, and that Porto was their operations centre – the core of their commercial and urban network. Unfortunately, there is no way to know what happened to those men, or if they were successful in their commercial transactions, due to the lack of archival information for the months following the issue date of the safe-conducts.

A Portuguese law of 1253 (*lei de almotaçaria*), created by King Afonso III (r. 1248–79) to set the resale prices throughout the realm, contains thirty-eight different types of expensive cloths that were being brought to Portugal from England, Flanders, Brittany and Castile, and which were frequently negotiated in local fairs.[12] This commercial exchange was obviously executed by Portuguese and foreign merchants, but Portugal's commercial system was enlarging significantly.

In 1309 King Philippe IV of France (r. 1285–1314) granted special privileges to the 'marchands de Lisbonne establis à Harfleur'.[13] A few decades later (1341) the same type of privilege was renewed and given to the merchants of Lisbon and Portugal.[14] And in 1352 Afonso Martins Alho headed a merchant embassy to negotiate a treaty with Edward III (r. 1327–77), which resulted in a fifty-year Anglo-Portuguese commercial statute granted to the merchants and maritime communities of Lisbon, Porto and the rest of the kingdom.[15] I will not discuss why these charters were given to the Portuguese; but they have points in common that suggest the existence of linkages between merchants.

As mentioned at the beginning of this essay, there were no merchant companies or guilds in medieval Portugal that might have served, as in other parts of Europe, as 'privileged, corporate associations of wholesale traders', acting as efficient administrative bodies for overseas operations.[16] The non-existence of guilds and other corporations does not invalidate the existence of cooperation between traders or the presence of some institutional arrangements to organize commercial activities locally and in overseas territories. But building a network, even if extremely informal, implies the existence of a set of tools and mechanisms to make possible the management of interdependent relations, actions and decisions for a common goal.

The Portuguese merchants' commercial interest in the medieval West could not be achieved if the common goal was the only thing they shared with each other. Partnerships implied that members aimed to help other members of the network, but it is obvious that some nodes stood in strategic positions with their resources, which they usually shared for a price. But in order for this to work, they had to communicate with each other, organize their commercial approaches and protect their interests.

Late medieval Portugal did not have merchant guilds, but these corporations were also not used in Italy, for example; yet the Italian urban institutions provided similar functions on behalf of their resident merchants.[17] And the same happened in Portugal. One cannot prove without a shadow of a doubt that the 1226 safe-conducts were made by merchants supported by the town hall of Porto, but the previous charters of privilege for them to trade in Normandy and England, granted by the French and English rulers, were addressed to the merchants of Lisbon and Porto; and the merchant who negotiated the 1353 Anglo-Portuguese commercial treaty was also the *procurador* (town attorney) of Porto. Indeed, traders were so entrenched in Portuguese maritime cities' political life that in Lisbon, in the beginning of the fifteenth century, up to 96 per cent of the municipal positions were occupied by merchants.[18] In a way, these examples reinforce the perspective that cities were representing merchants and merchants were representing their cities in foreign affairs, for in both situations the main addressees of such privileges were the merchant communities from Lisbon and Porto.

Other evidence indicates that we are undeniably in presence of a strong merchant–city institutional binary, given that it organized, coordinated and participated in important negotiations that favoured the pursuit of merchants' collective goals. Following the dire consequences brought by the Hundred Years' War to trade, and the animosity that Portuguese merchants faced in Atlantic markets after Portugal joined England in a perpetual political alliance sealed by the Treaty of Windsor in 1386, commercial exchange dropped to a minimum and piratical attacks increased drastically.[19] But notwithstanding Portugal's alliance with England, the Englishmen represented a serious menace to Portuguese navigation, for many Portuguese ships travelling to English, Norman and Flemish markets were constantly under attack. Aware of the dangers that pirates and privateers posed to navigation in Euro-Atlantic waters, the merchants of Porto sought a way to collectively shield their interests. So, in 1397, the city of Porto commanded Diogo Afonso to travel to England to submit a request to the Parliament in order to obtain a copy of the commercial treaty of 1353, and to bring it back home so that Porto's merchants could use it as protection while crossing English waters. The expenses of this expedition to England were paid for by a special levy that the aldermen of Porto created, which would charge a predetermined value to each shipment of commodities leaving the city.[20] Not only were traders looking for a solution to protect their commercial interests, but they were also using urban institutions and privileges for the collective goal of the merchant network, and for the common good of the city (*por prol Cumunal da Çidade*).

This merchant–city osmosis reached other important levels in the protection of traders' shared objectives. Since merchants were in office in Portugal's largest cities (Lisbon and Porto), they were summoned by the king to appear as urban representatives in the Portuguese Parliament (Cortes), where they submitted all sorts of complaints and requests related to their hometowns. They were, as Armindo de Sousa called, 'municipal aristocrats'.[21] It is true that they reported to the king many of the issues that affected their cities; but most of the petitions were clearly written by merchants who wanted to protect their mercantile interests, for they were related to taxation, ways to stimulate trade, and requests to reduce the hindrances caused by the competition of alien merchants in Portugal. The problem is that it is impossible to know for sure if everyone's interests (i.e. every merchants' commercial ambitions) were being defended in the same proportion, and if every trader's opinion or suggestion was heard inside their socio-economic community. But perhaps the non-existence within the sources of harsh criticism against those socio-economic elites may indicate that mercantile association was open to everyone who intended to work for the larger common good, which was to generate profit, and to complement other merchants' business enterprises, enabling them wider, riskier and possibly more profitable commercial undertakings.[22] This does not mean that merchants did not move away from their fellow 'nationals', or that they did not decide to run their business outside certain institutions. In 1516 Lopo de Calvos of Porto decided that the Portuguese 'nation' in Antwerp was no longer useful for him, so he stopped making his contribution for that institution.

For those who lived and negotiated outside Portugal, the existence of a socio-economic network was even more important. It was in Normandy and Flanders that the Portuguese established their two major resident merchant communities in the late Middle Ages, even though there were also some traders living in England. In Normandy, Harfleur had become their base of operations; in Flanders there was a 'Portuguese Street' at least as of 1308, which might indicate the presence of a significant community of traders.[23] For England there are some indirect references to Portuguese who might have been settled there. In 1416 Bonaverus of Bologna filed a legal action for debt in London against Pedro Afonso for £13.10; Afonso's goods were then collected and handed to Bonaverus in partial payment of the debt.[24] The valuables confiscated from Pedro Afonso included items such as drinking pots, candlesticks, a backgammon or chess set, an image of a Pietà of alabaster, one green crupper for a horse, packing chests, some bags, a dagger blade, a blanket and a sheet, two hoods, an old doublet, three pairs of hose and three curtains. Most of these items were personal, suggesting that Pedro Afonso was living in England.

In the fifteenth century Portuguese commercial relations became more complex, and the economic system grew significantly thanks to the inclusion of the Atlantic islands and western African trading posts. This was perhaps the moment that the linkages between merchants turned into something more than an informal association, to become a mercantile network that interlinked five axes of international trade structured around the inland trade with Castile and overseas exchange with the European Atlantic, the Atlantic islands, the Mediterranean and Africa.

Building the Network

The Flemish Civiele Sentëntien contain a very interesting case regarding a Portuguese merchant, his clients and presumably his commercial partners, and members of his socio-economic network. Not much is known about Luís Martins: he was born in Portugal, in an unknown date and place, traded for thirteen years in Flanders, was married most probably with a Flemish woman, and died in Bruges in March 1470. His line of business included the negotiation of dragon's blood (a red resin used by medieval textile industries to dye clothes) and sugar, which he sold preferably to Italian merchants. Martins's death must have come unexpectedly, for he left no will and some business transactions and debts were yet to conclude. In order to solve Martins's pending matters, the aldermen of Bruges created a commission formed by three Flemings and two Portuguese, leaded by the consul João de Santarém, to go through his ledger and pay any debts, and to collect any money people owed him.[25]

By looking carefully at Luís Martins's commercial activity in Bruges during his lifetime, those with whom he was doing business, and where and how he was getting the commodities, one realizes that this brief example contains all the necessary ingredients to depict the interplay between traders, shippers, partnerships, commercial routes, commodities, institutions, the socio-legal environment and conflict resolution mechanisms faced by merchants in European trade. Furthermore, it displays the multiple variables of an international network.

Places like Middelburg, Bruges, Harfleur, London and Lisbon were 'tangles of human networks', embracing socio-economic groups from several different origins that were organized within systems and institutions.[26] They were the central nodes connecting other significant and peripheral ones by the gravitational equilibrium generated by the trade, and they were the privileged stage for cross-cultural commercial exchange.[27] Cities were the place where merchant companies, individual buyers and sellers, brokers, moneychangers, hostellers and craftsmen gathered and interacted through monetary transactions. We know, of course, that each of them pursued their own personal interests and that conflict sometimes emerged between them. Thus they formed an equation that combined places and people, markets and occupations, and institutions and laws in order to establish the most favourable conditions for long-distance commercial exchange. In other words, those socio-economic groups and institutions created 'stable expectations of the behaviour of others', which promoted international trade.[28]

The first step in determining the type of connection and the hypothetical transformation from network taker to network maker is to identify with whom merchants were establishing linkages, and how those partnerships evolved over time. Portuguese commercial interests focused particularly in the area around the English Channel, particularly in Flemish (52.2 per cent), English (35.3 per cent), Zeelander (8.2 per cent) and Norman (4.3 per cent) marketplaces.[29] The percentage of links with foreign merchants is actually not too high, representing less than a quarter of the total, a number that one might consider as within the average value. Indeed, this fact is not entirely unexpected or extraordinary, for it is identical to what happened in other European regions. Janet T. Landa's study of institutional economics and ethnic trading networks has demonstrated that smaller merchant communities had little to gain by including in their commercial network members of other origins.[30] The Portuguese case seems to fit this theory well.

Considering the commercial exchange with foreign merchants for the period from 1300 to 1500, the network included especially the Flemish (36 per cent), the English (25 per cent) and the Italians (22 per cent); Hanseatic, French and Castilian merchants represented less significant ties in overseas trade. But if one focuses only in the period from 1400 to 1500, the percentages change slightly, with more Fleming-Portuguese interactions (45 per cent), followed by Italian-Portuguese (24 per cent) and Anglo-Portuguese (17 per cent).

Table 9.1: Commercial exchange with foreign merchants, 1300–1500.

	Fourteenth century	Fifteenth century	1300–500
Castilian	3%	7%	6%
English	56%	17%	25%
Flemings	3%	45%	36%
French	23%	4%	8%
Hanseatic	–	3%	3%
Italians	15%	24%	22%

Source: F. Miranda, 'Portugal and the Medieval Atlantic. Commercial Diplomacy, Merchants, and Trade, 1143–1488' (PhD dissertation, University of Porto, 2012), p. 204.

Table 9.1 shows four significant changes.[31] Firstly, the number of connections with Flemings grew significantly in the fifteenth century, contrary to what happened in the previous hundred years; however, this situation can be related to the scarcity of sources on Flemish-Portuguese trade. Flemish merchants, hostellers and others appeared frequently in fifteenth-century documents, but their names are only mentioned in the Civiele Sententiën, which means that this type of record was made to answer some specific problem and not to define the nature of their relationship. The lack of identical records for fourteenth-century Flanders makes it hard to trust entirely in these variations. Notwithstanding these limitations, it is necessary to stress that the commercial relations between Portugal and Flanders grew exponentially after the wedding of Isabel with Philip the Good in 1430, and with the institutional development of the 'nation' of Portugal in Bruges in 1438. Portuguese resident merchants in Bruges and their ties with local businessmen were indeed responsible for the lion's share of these commercial partnerships and associations.

Secondly, partnerships with the English dropped significantly in the fifteenth century, especially after the Treaty of Windsor (1386) and the subsequent truce with Castile in 1388, which led to the recovery of Anglo-Castilian trade and to Portugal's immediate loss of importance for English traders. The type of interaction between the Portuguese and the English was less intense than the one with the Flemish, suggesting that business was limited to occasional partnerships. In the fifteenth century, only a few cases indicate the existence of partnerships between the Portuguese and the English. Afonso de Almada, for example, established a commercial relationship with Henry Weldon and John Gonell, both English, and Vicent de Plagnevent from Normandy to promote trade between England, Normandy and Brittany in the 1430s.[32]

Thirdly, liaisons with French merchants were significant to some extent in the fourteenth century, but this situation changed radically in the next hundred years. Only 4 per cent of commercial contacts suggest the existence of partnerships or any other type of association between the Portuguese and people from French regions in the fifteenth century. Nonetheless, to understand this percentage one must take into consideration the fact that the Portuguese were no longer actively exploring Brittany or Normandy; instead, the Bretons and the Normans were travelling to Portugal to exchange grain and other commodities, as were Bristolians after the Hundred Years' War in search of wine that could replace the ones from Bordeaux.

Fourthly, Mediterranean traders progressively became more important and more active in Portugal and in Euro-Atlantic trade. The Italians based in Lisbon and those partnering with the Portuguese in Bruges had a keen interest in the cork, dyestuff, silk, alum, sugar and other commodities they could find in Portugal. Especially for the Genoese merchants, Portugal was far from being a peripheral kingdom; it was undoubtedly an important platform between the Mediterranean and the Atlantic.[33] The direct intervention of Italians on Portugal's productive system, their monopolies over certain commodities and their financial power made them valuable commercial partners for the Portuguese.[34]

Commercial Networks and Cities

Although the Portuguese had thriving communities in Normandy and Flanders, trade with England grew exponentially as of the 1370s, and it allowed the formation of small (in size and number) commercial networks. Bi-directional trade between Portugal (Porto or Lisbon) and England (Bristol, Southampton and London) was very frequent, interlinking the Portuguese with English and Italian traders. Those linkages were established at many different levels.

The 1226 safe-conducts are an example of how merchants might have cooperated to facilitate overseas commercial exchange, but there are other similar
cases of domestic networks. The merchants of the small town of Viana, in the
north of Portugal, seem to have specialized their overseas commercial activity in
Anglo-Portuguese trade. It is therefore easy to find that the same merchants, and
sometimes the same ships, were the ones travelling to Bristol (1380s) to sell their
commodities. Their modus operandi remained unaltered in the fifteenth century: the domestic network of Viana's merchants never included members from
outside their community.[35] Unfortunately, one cannot say if this was a voluntary
choice, nor it is possible to measure how advantageous it might have been for
them to have lingered in relative isolation from merchants coming from other
cities or European regions.

Due to the characteristics of certain sources, it is sometimes hard to distinguish whether merchants were forming a dense commercial network or a
wide-ranging commercial service. In 1352 the Portuguese were shipping commodities in several vessels to Harfleur, where João de Rates and Nicolau Mouro
acted as agents in order to sell the merchandise to Robert de Hommet, the vis-
count of Montivilliers.[36] A few decades later, Lourenço de Sousa seems to have
established a small socio-economic network with some Englishmen with the
intention of negotiating between Portugal, England and Normandy, at least
until he faced some obstacles in Rouen due to the political animosity generated
by the Hundred Years' War.[37] Other cases reveal identical multilateral commercial linkages. In 1407 Nicolau Eanes managed to interconnect Portugal, Ireland
and England by selling wine in a ship called *Katerine* of Gdansk.[38] At the same
time, João Pinhel became quite active in England partnering up with English
and Italian merchants, and he also might have had contacts in the Mediterranean.[39] And some merchants from Portugal were forming societies to interlink
Lisbon with Barcelona.[40]

In 1443 the Portuguese factor in Bruges issued a letter of quittance concerning the business transactions between Portugal and Flanders. From that letter
one can see that mercantile agents were representing more than one hundred
people in Portugal, meaning that those middlemen were controlling 57.6 per
cent of all Portuguese commercial exchange to Flanders.[41] Those men were from
Valença, Ponte de Lima, Barcelos, Braga, Guimarães, Monção, Bragança, Vila
Pouca, Vila Real, Mesão Frio, Porto, Leiria, Lisbon, Loulé, Faro and Tavira.
Once again, it is nearly impossible to determine how this group of people, of
diverse socio-economic origins, constituted by sailors, shipmasters, shoemakers,
coopers, clerks of counts and dukes, goldsmiths and knights, came together. But
there is no doubt that these non-specialized traders managed to create a professional network capable of favouring their overseas commercial interests, thus
improving communication, sharing resources and reducing costs.

With the inclusion of the Atlantic islands and African markets, Portuguese traders enlarged their commercial framework, and the kingdom witnessed its steady take-off towards a modern economy.[42] Favoured by successive royal decrees, Lisbon was transformed into a central place for merchants from all over the realm and abroad, and a pivotal port in Euro-African trade. Lisbon had become, said one observer, 'as large as London'.[43] This urban growth in Portugal, the inclusion of Atlantic and African markets, and the development of Portuguese merchant communities in Flanders were of the utmost importance for the creation of wider commercial networks that interconnected traders, cities and commodities. In the 1480s Wouter Despars spent seven years in Lisbon buying sugar and shipping it to his brother and commercial partner Jacob in Bruges, whereas the Portuguese used to buy from them tapestries, woollens and fustians from Flanders.[44] In 1493 the Despars brothers were already connecting Lisbon to Antwerp.[45] But the best way to observe how these different variables intertwined is to relate them all.

By comparing the origin of merchants, the type of commodities exported and the markets to which they were being exported, one finds that there was indeed a correlation between those different variables. Lisbon's merchants were frequently interacting with English (46 per cent), Flemish (20 per cent) and Italian (20 per cent) traders, and travelling especially to Bristol, Southampton, Bruges and Middelburg. From Lisbon they would export wine, figs and raisins, three commodities that had high demand in England. A similar correlation between origin–partner–product–destination is identifiable in medieval Porto: its merchants were often in business with English (34 per cent), Italian (33 per cent), French (20 per cent) and Flemish (13 per cent) merchants, and those relations can be explained by looking at the preferred destination ports, located in England and Flanders, and the type of commodities negotiated by Porto's merchants, which included hides (especially sought by the Italians), oil, figs, raisins and salt (which were being sold in the aforementioned towns).

Bruges was possibly 'the first "network" city in European economic history', and its characteristics fostered the formation of commercial partnerships.[46] Other cities in Europe gained similar features, allowing traders to thrive thanks to the opportunities offered by merchant companies and 'nations' in a single space, where they could interact, engage in partnership, and access the necessary services provided by transporters and seafarers, hostellers, moneychangers, insurers, proctors, attorneys and many other people and professionals. Álvaro Dinis was one of the Portuguese merchants that benefited from this network city model. Dinis was born in 1441 and lived in Bruges for many years, trading with merchants from Italy, Castile, England, Flanders and the German Hanse. His trade partners were the Italian Lomellini, six other Portuguese merchants with whom he frequently did business, some Flemings and Castilians, but he also privileged the commercial interactions with the duke of Burgundy and the king of Portugal. It is likely that Dinis's social and economic reputation allowed him to take the office of consul of the Portuguese factory, being one of the men responsible for verifying if his subjects in Flanders respected the king's monopoly over African commodities.[47] And it is also likely that Dinis managed to enjoy the advantages of being a network maker (creating new partnerships and commercial linkages) and a network taker (by using pre-existing socio-economic webs of traders in Flanders for his own benefit).

Conclusion

Were the Portuguese traders network takers or network makers? It all depended on the level and range of business. From the examples seen above, one might argue that most Portuguese merchants were subordinated to larger economic and commercial circuits, dominated by businessmen and traders of other European origins. Yet there were some active and entrepreneurial groups of traders in Portugal that sought commercial privileges, developed trade routes and established institutions to manage their activities in overseas commerce.

The Portuguese were network *takers* while they were conducting bi-directional trade and cooperating in shipping services to markets in England, Zeeland, Flanders, Normandy and other parts of Europe, for they were not necessarily forming new mechanisms of commerce. They were, indeed, taking advantage of pre-existing trade routes, markets and institutions, by adopting short-term commercial linkages and trading contacts that involved, most of the time, agents and other middlemen. This does not mean that commercial contacts were void of new socio-economic networks, for it has been seen that even small traders, usually operating at a local and regional scale, generated their own web aimed at a common goal. The individuals within their smaller network were, therefore, taking advantage of the benefits of a wider world of commercial contacts.

The Portuguese were also network *makers*, especially from the moment they began connecting Europe with Africa, and later with Asia and the Americas, making partnerships and networks larger and considerably more complex. Their importance for trade and traders grew exponentially, for they now had to deal with strong rival networks and challenge monopolies and politico-economic empires.[48] But if this is true for the late fifteenth century on, one must consider the relevance that some traders and markets had for a few Portuguese commodities. Portuguese wine, olive oil and cork are, still today, of recognized quality, and the truth is that those products have been exported overseas since the twelfth century. They had the markets, the clients and the opportunity to succeed with their small, stable commercial network.

The fact that most merchants lived on the 'Rua dos Mercadores' in Lisbon and Porto and on Portuguese Street in Bruges, close to the *alfândega* (custom house) and the *bolsa* (bourse), facilitated network contacts, whether to form new connections or to use pre-existing ones. Self-organized merchant communities in Portugal, empowered by urban institutions, formed regular trade routes and linkages that allowed a regular flow of trading vessels to several parts of Europe, thus feeding the marketplaces and, consequently, the households of noblemen, clergymen and rich merchants. It seems, therefore, that Lisbon and Porto were the homes of socio-economic groups, which often ensued collaborative work, collectively defending their common mercantile interests in domestic and international affairs and promoting overseas trade. Outside Portugal, the colonies of merchants in Harfleur and Bruges were equally paramount in organizing trade and commercial routes and linkages with foreign traders. Unfortunately, the available sources are not sufficient to understand the strength of network linkages and the impact that these networks had on Portuguese overseas trade in the fourteenth and fifteenth centuries.

10 PEPPER AND SILVER BETWEEN MILAN AND LISBON IN THE SECOND HALF OF THE SIXTEENTH CENTURY

Benedetta Crivelli

Introduction

This essay considers the definition of a social network model by focusing on commercial companies established by Milanese merchants on the Iberian Peninsula from the second half of the sixteenth century onwards, with particular attention of their settlement in Lisbon.[1] In defining the purpose of the study, we examine the merchants' socio-economic profile and the group to which they belonged, studying their origin, their economic rise within their community, their investment strategies and their cooperation through different types of relationships.

In subsequent paragraphs, we analyse how the Milanese merchants' activities developed and how they were structured and progressively integrated within a commercial network which transcended regional and national boundaries. We then provide a descriptive analysis of the commercial and financial activities developed by merchant groups in order to understand better the mechanisms through which they became integrated in different market areas, and also how they adapted to the economic and political changes which characterized the regions in which they established their companies. The analysis focuses on the pepper trade, which represents the main business through which Milanese merchants attained a position of status in the economy of the Iberian Empire and strengthened their ties to the Crown.

Attempts to define an image that might represent social networks have so far usually produced a general 'sociometric' concept of network which does not adequately 'problematize' social actors, in other words the individual, or agents, who were connected within social networks.[2] The image of a 'root' (or rhizome)[3] offers an alternative explanation which gives an appropriate 'weight' to the multidimensionality of the rationales which motivated agents and also to the multiplicity and fluidity of the network relationships themselves. This alternative analysis focuses on the spatial and temporal elements[4] of networks,[5] the structures of which come together and are taken apart in response to multiples factors, without a real constant centre.

However – as Owens has pointed out[6] – despite the fact that with the 'rhizome' metaphor the focus of analysis turned to the dynamic elements of networks, an understanding of the complexity of social networks and multiform relations between human communities was still lacking.

Taking these complexities into consideration, it can be said that 'the polymorphous context of social relations flows from the capacity of actors to manoeuvre across multiple social contexts by coupling and decoupling, that is tightening and loosening, ties'.[7] The studies by Harrison C. White[8] suggest that social actors, linked in multiple social networks that intersect irregularly at different nodes, embody multiple identities and capacities which enable them to pass from one type of tie to another, playing different roles at the same time.

The fluidity of the relations which make up social networks can be studied through a 'micro' analysis, the purpose of which is to describe how mutual implications and collective obligations evolve in daily social practices. This approach makes it possible to make a comprehensive study of the merchants and families that are the objects of the analysis, and it provides useful information about personal circumstances, and individual choices made, which in turn facilitates the understanding of macro phenomena connected with a complex kind of business which involves commercial and financial aspects such as the pepper trade.

The micro-analysis approach is in part dictated by the nature of the sources available to us. The attempt to clarify the position of the famous Milanese merchant Giovanni Battista Rovellasca as a major actor in overseas trade has led us to trace the path that took him from Milan to settle in Lisbon. The absence of direct sources relating to the Rovellasca family in the archives of Milan, and the amount of information on the presence of Giovanni Battista in the Portuguese capital between 1560 and the early years of the seventeenth century, convinced us to follow the 'trails' that he left by reconstructing the relationship paths that his many activities had created and that had allowed his enterprises to intersect with those of major bankers and merchants who were active in the Iberian world.

Accordingly, both in the corpus of letters of Simón Ruiz, one of the main sources of our study, as well as in judicial and notarial documents found in Milanese and Spanish archives, it is evident that Rovellasca's actions were always mediated by other agents, who became important nodes of the network examined in this study.

The activities of the *hombres de negocios*, key figures in the economic history of the modern age, have attracted great interest since the 1950s on the basis of a historiography which aimed to look at the consolidation of the fortunes of the great families of German, Spanish and Italian bankers of the sixteenth century not as a result of individual effort, but as a result of economic cooperation between different figures in various commercial and financial spheres.[9] One of the sources used over the years for such studies, which despite the large number of works dedicated to it[10] has not yet been exhausted, is the private correspondence of Simón Ruiz, a merchant from Medina del Campo. Through the Spanish merchant's letters, it is possible to identify the trajectories of action of many of the economic agents who moved within the imperial space and who found their point of connection in Medina del Campo, which was home to Ruiz's company.

The letters contain a great deal of information not just of an economic but also of a political, military and diplomatic nature. Through the letters, decisions on how, where and when to invest were communicated, and direct or indirect information regarding the credibility and solvency of specific economic agents was exchanged.[11] Reciprocity became one of the most powerful weapons used by business people of the time to extend their business networks. The flow of information exchanged allowed solidarity to form and contracts to strengthen. The risk of fraud was minimized so long as there was the necessary trust to develop sincere business cooperation between the parties who exchanged the letters.[12]

The Political and Economic Context

When we talk about of the broad area of the Iberian Empire during the modern age, we must consider its specific political and institutional structure, which inevitably demands an examination of the combination of 'local', 'global' and 'transnational'. The concept of 'polycentric monarchy'[13] implies 'an emphasis on the local political conditions, on the institutional and social diversity of the different realms, on the different traditions that define them, and on their informal constitutions, but also on the nexuses of articulation between these territories'.[14]

During the sixteenth century, the Iberian monarchs imposed their political prerogatives on an economy which had expanded under colonialism. The political project elaborated in Europe, centre of the Hispanic Empire, led to models of integration and centralization that expressed themselves with the creation of institutional structures designed to control overseas trade.

Portugal, in particular, controlled the Asian sea and supported a maritime form of Crown capitalism with monopoly on oceanic trade, introduced by Manuel I in 1506. The Crown used the Estado da Índia to establish an Asian commercial network of trading posts. These territorial institutions gathered pepper, along with other products, which were then transported to Portugal via a convoy of ships known as the Carreira da Índia. The goods were then sold to wholesalers by the Casa da Índia's officials in Lisbon.[15]

Portugal's Asian trade resembled a state enterprise insofar as it involved little private capital and reserved the most profitable opportunities to the king and a few nobles. Nevertheless, private participation in oceanic trade increased and merchants became very successful in Asia and elsewhere overseas. From the 1570s onwards the Crown granted private merchants the right to exploit commercial routes in return for payments of the *fazenda*'s rights (kingdom's custom duties). After customs duties, pepper allotments, other mandatory contributions and the interest and principal on borrowed funds had been paid, a significant amount of funds was still available for reinvestment in subsequent Asian voyages. On top of profits from Asian trade, merchants generated further profits from their investments in the African slave trade and trade with Spanish America, which was particularly important for the import of silver and precious metals.[16]

Pepper was a non-replaceable commodity which commanded high internal returns with elevated profit margins. Monopoly practices provided favourable conditions for profiting from this kind of trade.[17] The spice trade produced higher profits than those obtained from the import of gold and those from the other activities of the kingdom, especially when competition from other European traders was limited. However, from the end of the century onwards, merchants faced declining returns and profits over the long term, as more European competitors entered the trade in the seventeenth century.

Furthermore, participation in trades of private entrepreneurs reduced the rent produced by the process of monopolization and developed a complex system of relationships between the monarchy and the contractors. The king sought to extract additional funds from the private merchants on more favourable terms, while the contractors took advantage of the needs of the Crown and tried to extend the terms of their contracts.[18]

The Iberian Union and the designation of Philip II as king of Portugal in 1580 paved the way to new opportunities for private merchants and became a decisive factor in the perpetuation of multiple identities in the Spanish monarchy, whose actions and intentions were generated from different areas not only in Europe but all over the known world at that time.

Despite the fact that the new political course would have had to ensure the conservation of particularism and the safeguarding of the political and administrative monopolies associated with the exploration of respective overseas possessions, unification under one ruler came to be reflected in the suspension of the actual frontiers imposed by the Treaty of Tordesillas, strengthening Portugal's integration in the stream of transatlantic routes. The infiltration of Portuguese merchants in the trade network of the kingdom and the nearby empire escalated after 1580, opening up new opportunities both in Spanish America and on the peninsula itself.[19]

If 1580 represented a turning point in the political history of the Hispanic monarchy, the years between 1575 and 1596 were no less important for world finance. The two bankruptcies that happened within twenty years led to significant changes in the financial system of the Hispanic monarchy, which also affected the movement of goods and money within the imperial sphere.

Historiography has emphasized the challenges which Philip II, as head of the world's first 'superpower', had to face in managing public finances: the lack of a centralized capital market and his inability to exercise direct control over the administration of taxes, which had to be negotiated with the Cortes. Moreover, a large share of state revenues was subject to independent shocks due to the mining and transfer of silver from the Americas. In addition, the majority of Crown's expenditures were abroad.[20]

Despite an attempt to reorganize the state finances after the bankruptcy of 1575, historians agree that Philip II could not avoid using *asientos* when the needs of war forced him to do so. Moreover, his inability to increase taxes forced him to recover rents through the consolidation of floating debt.

The years that followed the *medio general* saw a change in the financial circuit with the decline of Medina del Campo, preceded by Lyon and Antwerp, and the rise of Piacenza. In addition, new forms of payment emerged: silver in coins, which came from India, were collected in Castile and sent to Italy from the ports of Barcelona and Alicante, as well as bills of exchange, the circulation of which centred on the fairs of Piacenza.[21]

At the end of sixteenth century, Piacenza became the complex centre of a 'credit system', since the small Italian city had quarterly meetings for exchange fairs and also because most European financial transactions passed through there.[22]

Even though Genoese merchants dominated the exchange fairs of Piacenza, the most famous merchant bankers from Milan began to take part in the exchange fair negotiations, demonstrating a certain cohesion in particular when, on two occasions in 1581 and 1584, they appealed directly to Philip II about the need to establish new rules to avoid payment delays which would have compromised credit with several 'nations' and caused the loss of their trustworthiness.[23] The higher echelons of the Milanese economic system were made up of bankers, foreign exchange dealers and international merchants whose business interests often overlapped. Indeed, the traders who had business dealings with international markets commonly conducted exchange operations and regularly provided loans.[24]

The Milanese Merchants in Lisbon

Between 1565 and 1582 the Milanese merchants Giovanni Battista and Agostino Litta set up four mercantile companies to develop their commercial and financial activities in the major exchange fairs of the Iberian Peninsula – Medina del Campo, Madrid and Seville – as well as in the major port of Lisbon.[25] They continued the business activities that their father Geronimo had begun in Spain and Portugal.

Before arriving in Lisbon, since the end of the fifteenth century the Litta family had been engaged in intense commercial activity with Spain, from Valencia and Valladolid, where one of their representatives resided permanently. Almost a century later, the Iberian peninsula was still the favoured location for the family's commercial activities, although it continued to invest in property in the Milan area.[26] Giovanni Battista and Agostino Litta were members of the Universitas Mercatorum, where Giovanni Battista's presence was documented in 1577. Agostino, who bought Gambolò and Valle's feuds to assure his descendants of a noble title, maintained a political role and sat among the sixty *decurioni* of the General Council.[27]

Litta's business partners were members of Milan's financial elite, which included Domenico Chiariti, Ludovico Visconti, Cesare Negrolo and Giovanni Battista Rovellasca and his brother Francesco, who actively participated in the setting up of commercial companies with substantial capital shares.[28]

One of them, Cesare Negrolo, was an important node linking the companies' activities to the Bisenzone fairs. He was educated first in Lyon and then Paris and sold 'arcchibusi, corsaletti et morioni'[29] on behalf his uncle's company and, on returning to Italy, became 'publico campsore et mercatore mediolani civitati' and one of the wealthiest bankers in Milan.[30] He was admitted to the chamber of merchants of the Universitas Mercatorum of Milan on 26 October 1575[31] and was the university's dean six times between 1576 and 1584.[32] Although Cesare Negrolo was not on the decurional council, he was one of the representatives of the Milanese 'nation' in the Piacenza exchange fairs. This position gave him a political edge and bound him to the king in a valuable financial relationship.

An important role, among Litta's partners, was also played by Giovanni Battista Rovellasca, attorney of Litta's companies in 1577 and 1579. Giovanni Battista Rovellasca moved to the Iberian Peninsula in the 1570s, where he also acted as Cesare Negrolo's agent, while his brother Francesco, partner of Litta's company in 1575 with Cesare Negrolo and Domenico Chiariti, settled in Milan and became Cesare Negrolo's attorney specifically in relation to activities of financial intermediation.[33]

It is not possible to affirm the constant presence of Giovanni Battista in Spain and Portugal, but it is known that he regularly travelled to Lisbon for his business affairs. Agostino Litta died in Lisbon in January 1583, where he had arrived after a trip to the Iberian Peninsula to accompany the Empress Maria of Spain.[34] At his side was Giovanni Battista Rovellasca, who remained in Lisbon and became the executor of Litta's will.

As was customary in Genoese and Italian companies, where each member signed in the name of the company and not with their own signature, the Littas, too, preferred to set up non-hierarchical companies which worked by virtue of their degree of cohesion. They were set up with the specific scope of transmitting and concealing information within the networks and did not exhibit a high degree of stability.[35] Cohesion inside the network was guaranteed by the sharing of risk, for in all of the companies each partner was committed *in solidum*, i.e. each member of the company was responsible for the other members. However, this strategy to maintain the business as secured and financially sound had not avoided illicit behaviours that could seldom be sanctioned with the exclusion of a partner due to the vastness of the interests held by each partner. In the event of disputes between partners, the company was broken up and the profits shared among its members.

Normally the Littas took on the name of the companies in which they participated and reserved the right to negotiate on their own. Notwithstanding the fact that this privilege was usually not conferred upon other partners, it was granted to Rovellasca in 1571, allowing him to continue to negotiate his affairs in Seville, where he was involved in the other important business of the slave trade.[36]

Although they were essential to guarantee success in commercial activities, family or friendship ties were not essential factors in determining long-term commercial partnerships. Rather, they seem to have been more a means of strengthening bonds of trust and to showing strong integration, both in real terms and in the perception that the rest of society might have had.[37]

The Construction of a Network

When the Littas reached Lisbon, they found Ippolito Affaitati from Cremona to be a reliable partner. Affaitati was familiar with the Portuguese market as he had worked for years in Lisbon in association with Niccolò Giraldi and Giacomo de Bardi,[38] who were both Florentine bankers. Their company had been established in the city of Lisbon since 1471. Bardi had a close business relationship with the Affaitatis, as the Spanish document, in which he is referred to as 'milanes', states.[39] The main branch of the Affaitati business was in Antwerp, an important node in the Portuguese spice market, in which the Affaitatis had several interests. However, in 1570 the accounts of the Antwerp companies recorded substantial losses in the Iberian Peninsula due to debts accumulated with the king of Portugal.[40]

Giacomo de Bardi, in addition to the spice contract that he owned in association with the German Nataniel Jung, obtained the contract for the San Jorge de Mina gold mines from the king of Portugal in December of 1576. The deal was worth almost 200 contos de reis.

In the same year, the contract for administration of the collection of the kingdom's custom duties was split between the Genoese businessman Stefano Lercaro and Bardi, who kept his participation secret. This concession, which was granted without respecting the requirements for this type of business affair, was guaranteed by Cristoforo de Tavora, who was a member of an important Portuguese family and also the son-in-law of the Genoese Antonio Calvo. However, it was contended by Simón Ruiz and his agent in Lisbon, who likewise would have wanted to control one of the peninsula's most profitable businesses.[41]

Giovanni Battista Rovellasca also obtained concessions granting him the authority to administer the kingdom's customs affairs in 1586,[42] and he subsequently enjoyed the fixed income resulting from the Mina contract.[43]

The Litta brothers began importing and redistributing pepper from the capital towards Europe, in particular to Italy and Flanders, thanks to the competitive advantage that the Italian community had gained in the Portuguese market. In 1560 the Littas advanced 35,000 ducats in credit to the king of Portugal, D. Sebastião I, which was to be recollected in Lisbon and Antwerp. However, they were unable to recover the full amount, which was only partially repaid in pepper valued at 5,300 ducats. Nevertheless, by leveraging his network of acquaintances, which is believed to have extended from Milan to Lisbon, Giovanni Battista Rovellasca was able to increase the amount of credit up to 58,000 ducats and was rewarded by the king with various batches of pepper, sent to Livorno and Venice, where they were sold at a profit of 10 per cent. One of those who showed the greatest commitment to raising the capital needed to finance this speculative operation was the Milanese Geronimo Tavola, a partner of the Littas in the company established in 1567 and of Rovellasca in the company established in 1571. Tavola, who resided in Spain, where he had several interests in Medina del Campo, Toledo and Seville, managed to obtain from D. Sebastião I the privilege, only enjoyed by few merchants, of gaining interest on loans to the king.[44] It was agreed that the interest to be collected was that which had accrued on the money that Giacomo de Bardi lent on behalf of the Litta company. By the conclusion of the operation, it had been possible to collect 65,000 ducats.[45]

This speculative practice was often used by Rovellasca and demonstrates how pepper, with the high profits that could be obtained from its sale, was used as a bargaining commodity in negotiations of loans to the Crown, which was a profitable business for the Milanese companies operating in the Iberian Peninsula.

The bargaining power that Giovanni Battista Rovellasca was able to obtain both within and outside his own community guaranteed the economic position that he maintained thanks to his relationship with the Italian group that settled in Lisbon. Rovellasca and Giacomo de Bardi were able to negotiate directly with the Crown, and this in turn gave them a privileged position. In 1577 the Bardis granted a loan to the king at a very attractive rate. This was unknown to Rovellasca, who had intervened to take on the Crown's debt. As the debt negotiation did not have a positive outcome, the king paid the 40,000 ducats back plus interest to Giacomo de Bardi in the form of the rights over Casa di Índia. In the same year, Giovanni Battista Rovellasca signed an asiento with the king, who owed 47,000 ducats in principal and interest. As collateral, he demanded that the king concede 6,000 quintals of pepper to be sold in Italy. The Litta company, for which Rovellasca worked, was able to sell the pepper gradually, thus ensuring its liquidity.[46]

It is probable that eventually Giovanni Battista Rovellasca's ambition led him to clash with his more conservative partners, such as Giacomo de Bardi and Niccolò Girardi. Indeed, in accounting records dated February 1584 written by Giovanni Battista Litta, reference is made to a loan with the king of Portugal granted by Giovanni Pietro Visconti, one of Girolamo Litta's partners, to Giacomo de Bardi and Niccolò Girardi in 1577. Florentine bankers wanted to suspend the loan, while Rovellasca wanted to enter into a new contract with the king by providing another 80,000 ducats, which were rewarded with 4,050 tonnes of pepper at 34 ducats per quintal, subsequently sold in Lisbon (625 tonnes), Venice (2,108 quintals), Genoa (607 tonnes) and Livorno (768 tonnes).[47]

It appears that of the 80,000 ducats lent to the king, the Litta company had put up 6,000 ducats while the rest had been advanced through letters of exchange with various creditors, which would have been collected under protest. The Milanese Deifebo Rocchi and Cristoforo Riva, attorney of the Affaitatis company, which had reached Lisbon in 1577,[48] also supported this operation. Deifebo Rocchi operated as an intermediary for the payment of bills of exchange on behalf of the Portuguese bankers of Antwerp, and his name was often associated with that of another Milanese, Ottavio Paravicini. Rocchi had also had a key role in guaranteeing a number of loans made by Geronimo Resta, Litta's agent, on behalf of Rovellasca.[49] The presence of Cristoforo Riva was due to the growing indebtedness of the Affaitati company, which was trying to secure new credit.

With the aim of extracting maximum profit from this business, which needed large amounts of capital, in 1579 Giovanni Battista Litta, Giovanni Battista Rovellasca and Cesare Negrolo set up a company with the outstanding amount of capital of 200,000 ecus. The headquarters of the company were in Madrid and Lisbon, where the pepper that came from East India was stored.[50] When Giovanni Battista and Agostino Litta died in 1583, Giovanni Battista Rovellasca moved to Lisbon permanently.[51]

Relying on the support of a network characterized by strong bonds of kinship and business partnerships, Giovanni Battista Rovellasca extended his business within the boundaries of the largest network of interests which was constituted by the pepper trade, largely dominated by important *cristãos novos* families.[52] In 1583 Rovellasca, with the Portuguese *contratadores da pimenta* (pepper traders) Antonio Fernandes Delvas, Luis Gomes Delvas and Tomas Ximenes, assigned a commitment to pay 3,000 cruzados (in the Malacca currency)[53] to the shipowners Antonio Brandão and Luis Gomes de Acosta, who had been granted the right to rig the Malacca ships. Payment was made through the medium of bills of exchange by the *feitores* of pepper traders who settled in India.[54] Giovanni

Battista Rovellasca's business interests intersected with those of Conrad Rott, a merchant from Augsburg, and his agent Giraldo Paris, who sought to obtain from the king two pepper trading contracts, one to import merchandise from India and another to sell the goods on European markets.[55] In the 1580s Conrad Rott failed in this plan and had to give up the pepper trading contract that was granted by Consejo de Hacienda to Rovellasca.

In 1582, when Giovanni Battista Litta purchased the pepper trading contract shares from Conrad Rott, the company owned by Marco Fugger and his brothers in Augsburg intervened in the negotiation to redeem the bills of exchange thanks to Cesare Negrolo's intermediation.[56] The Milanese banker often acted as drawee of bills of exchange in the name of Fugger's company, which redeemed bills of exchange on behalf of merchants operating in the Lisbon market.[57]

The German bankers did not limit themselves to financial deals, and they entered the spice trade themselves directly following Rott's failure. In around 1590 the company set up by Filippo Edoardo and Ottaviano Fugger became part of the consortium of merchants that bought the rights, in 1591, to import pepper from Malacca from King Philip II.[58] The composition of this consortium was the result of long negotiations in which the interest of the king and of his creditors played an important role, as is explained below.

In the 1590s Giovanni Battista Rovellasca was a member of the *contratadores da pimenta*, a group of merchants made up mostly of Portuguese and Germans. In correspondence between Fernando de Morales and Simón Ruiz, the expression 'Rovelasca y alemanes' (Rovellasca and the German merchants)[59] appears, indicating a close commercial relationship between the Milanese and the German community agents. However, during the same years, Giovanni Battista Rovellasca and his brother Francesco, on different occasions, were appointed administrators of Igreja de Nossa Senhora de Loreto, a parish which represented the Italians who resided in the capital city of Lisbon.[60]

The Commercial Network and the Financial Network

From the 1580s onwards, Lisbon grew as an excellent trading centre where the availability of goods and precious metals meant an abundance of capital. Portuguese merchants knew how to exploit this situation by integrating into the European financial system and using the exchange fairs of Medina del Campo and Piacenza for their business.[61]

The Portuguese merchants managed their businesses by exploiting family ties and friendships through a horizontal structure that guaranteed a reduction in risk. In this way they could maintain a high level of exchange and secure profits. The Portuguese Jewish merchant Marcos Nuñez Perez maintained an extensive network of influence on European merchants thanks to the presence of his agents on the principal marketplaces, some of whom were linked to him by family ties. Luis Perez, Marcos Nuñez Perez's brother-in-law, resided in Cologne, and Martin Perez de Varròn, Luis Perez's son-in-law, received payment from the exchange fair of Antwerp. Pedro de Tolosa was a correspondent in Seville.

From the 1580s onwards, Marcos Nuñez Perez, thanks to Florentine banker Luigi Francesco Capponi's brokerage, was involved in financial activities in the Piacenza exchange fairs. Marcos Nuñez Perez's payments in those fairs were addressed to Cologne on behalf of Luis Perez.[62] Moreover, the Portuguese bankers maintained contact with the marketplace in Antwerp and Lyon, where the Italian firm of Bonvisi acted as their agent. Cesare Negrolo and Giovanni Battista Rovellasca were Luis Perez's intermediaries of payment in Piacenza.[63]

Marcos Nuñez Perez became a fundamental node in Giovanni Battista Rovellasca's networks, as he supported his business by issuing credit. Through his actions Marcos Nuñez Perez attempted to draw the boundaries of the pepper trade network in an attempt to minimize losses and increase profits.

In 1590 Marcos Nuñez Perez decided to enter the pepper trade, along with his brother-in-law, Luis Perez, to attempt to recover a credit that they had with *contratadores da pimenta* amounting to between 65,000 and 70,000 ducats of principal and additional interest accrued over ten years. The *contratadores* wanted to use *devitos viejos* (market-traded public debt securities) to buy pepper, which at that time was in the royal warehouses, and the amount of pepper that would arrive over the next three or four years. Nuñez Perez tried to use the pepper as currency to pay off debt he had contracted with *contratadores da pimenta*. Perez required 1,500 tonnes of pepper every year, which was enough to repay the debt with contractors.[64]

Because of the importance of the commerce and of the lack of security implicit in this type of business – the success of which depended on several variables, not excluding the possibility of losing the goods as a result of shipwrecks or looting – Marcos Nuñez Perez always affirmed up front in order to have access to fair negotiations in Bisenzone, Lyon and Antwerp, with the certainty that the Bonvisi business and that of the Milanese Ottaviano Cassina and Giovanni Battista Canobio were available to pay bills of exchange in the fairs of Piacenza for the amounts demanded by the Portuguese.

The frequency of correspondence between Cassina and Canobio and Nuñez Perez indicates a stable relationship that was justified by the Milanese by the kinship with Luis Perez and Martin Perez de Varron.[65] Collaboration between the two companies went beyond exchange fair negotiations; it extended to the transport of goods and other deals, as Cassina and Canobio stated in a letter.[66] In addition to banking activities, Ottaviano Cassina and Giovanni Battista Canobio's company was one of the largest exporters of trimmings and gold and silver yarn, which were the most sought-after goods on European markets from Flanders to Spain.[67]

As we have seen, financial networks had a horizontal structure with little hierarchy; stability was provided by the high degree of cohesion among its members. Management of information flows was fundamental to guarantee success.[68]

Action strategies were based on information. Marcos Nuñez Perez decided to enter the pepper trade because he believed that he knew enough about the Lisbon market in order to gain from trading, in contrast to some of the other *cristãos novos* families (Evora, Urtado, Mendez, Caldeira) who had refused to enter the pepper trade, presumably because the demands of the Crown were excessive. Ultimately the ones who were genuinely interested in the pepper trading contract were the merchants who had accumulated large debts with the king, as they hoped to have the debts repaid using the goods from the East as a means of payment.

The contract for the pepper was supposed to be agreed in the name of Giovanni Battista Rovellasca and the German merchants, who would buy goods from the king for 42 cruzados per quintal. A quarter of the total cost could have been paid using debts that the merchants had accumulated in previous negotiations. When faced with Rovellasca's uncertainty in concluding the trade, Marcos Nuñez Perez intervened to support Giovanni Battista Rovellasca by offering to advance 40,000 of the 50,000 ducats that had to be paid in Seville or Madrid. The opportunity to enter into the pepper contract depended on the availability of goods to sell to the king, and consequently on the availability of resources to purchase silver and other precious goods (such as *caudal*) to send to India.[69]

Marcos Nuñez Perez, operating in Lisbon, was in possession of useful information about the arrival and departures of vessels to and from India, upon which the availability or scarcity of money on the market depended. This privileged position enabled him to infer which businesses were optimal to avoid the need to contract excess debt, given that the default of a trading firm could prevent the access to credit on the part of others linked to it.

The uncertainty of overseas trade was liable to damage the position of agents such as Giovanni Battista Rovellasca, who were trading on credit. In March 1591 Marcos Nuñez Perez informed Simón Ruiz of the dishonest behaviour of Rovellasca, who claimed to have delivered a shipment of pepper in Madrid, whereas the goods had not arrived at the port of Lisbon. The information that Marcos Nuñez Perez possessed proved to be of great importance in protecting the trades undertaken by Simón Ruiz, who, having learned from the Portuguese that 'no me contentan nada su negocios como per mis cartas lo e significado' ('I do not like his [Rovellasca's] business, as I have said in my letters'), took the decision to insure 6,000 ducats that he had lent to the Milanese. With the money received, Rovellasca had managed to assure his partners that he had sufficient credit to carry on his trading activities, which, however, were not concluded successfully, while Marcos Nuñez Perez' comment was that those partners were people who did not know Rovellasca well enough.[70]

This information reached Simón Ruiz thanks to correspondence sent by the Milanese Geronimo Resta, who was also interested in the result of Rovellasca's trading activities as he was awaiting repayment of a loan that he had extended to Rovellasca. Rovellasca had accumulated a debt of 160,000 *cruzados* with the Spanish bank Vittoria y Isunza. However, under pressure from his creditors, he appeared to be ready to repay all his outstanding bills of exchange, including a bill of 2,000 ducats that got bounced by Marcos Nuñez Perez in Antwerp.[71]

A default on Rovellasca's part would have created a profound crisis in the financial system, followed by a chain of subsequent defaults, as actually happened in Lisbon in 1594.[72] The financial bailout of Rovellasca was in the interest of King Phillip II, who, in a letter sent on 10 March 1591 to Cardinal Albert VII, governor of Portugal from 1585 to 1595, claimed that in order to preserve his hacienda it was important to maintain secrecy regarding Rovellasca's reputation and to continue trading with him. At the same time, it was important to evaluate whether it would be better to subcontract the pepper trading contract to the Portuguese merchants, who offered greater security.[73] For this reason the consortium that obtained the pepper trading contract in 1591 had been extended to include the Portuguese merchants Tomàs and Andrè Ximenes and Luis Gomes Angel. The consortium was also extended to the Germans Matteo and Marco Welser, to Giraldo Paris from Aachen, who acted as Giovanni Battista Rovellasca's partner, and to the Spanish merchants Pedro and Francisco Maluenda, who shared the thirty-two quotas of the contract.[74]

Faced with such a complex situation, Marco Nuñez Perez, although while of the opinion that the pepper trading contract had to be subcontracted to Portuguese merchants operating with their own funds,[75] had to admit that Rovellasca's business was not safe, but it was necessary to grant his will to avoid greater damage to the creditors.[76]

Conclusion

What can be observed by analysing the dynamics involving the various social networks described above is that high levels of cooperation developed between their members that were independent of their origin or ethnic identity.[77] Although the agents involved in financial and trading activities structured their networks around family ties and ties based on their origin and friendships, their modus operandi exhibited a desire to broaden such ties so that they could react by implementing new solutions to the weaknesses which could have brought about the downfall of the complex system in which they acted.

Rovellasca's strategy was to favour passable borders in the commercial and financial networks which allowed the creation of different and heterogeneous relations, and to access specialized markets in which high profits attracted the interest of several groups of merchants, as witnessed by his involvement in the multiple social networks that shaped his multiple social identities in relation to the changing context of his interactions with others.

In the last years of his life, Rovellasca settled in Lisbon and became *vecino de Lisboa*. He married a Portuguese *cristã nova* woman, Elena Bezzera, and he died in the Portuguese capital,[78] far from Milan, the city in which he began doing business and one which had been an important node for the conduct of his business. From Milan came the funds with which Rovellasca had begun his activities in the Iberian Peninsula. Indeed, Milan at the time was beginning to acquire a degree of financial specialization that stemmed from the growing importance of Milanese operators on the circuit *asientos* negotiated with the king of Spain.

However, from the 1580s onwards colonial trade underwent a transformation, as it was threatened by the emergence of new competition in Europe – which turned into clashes between old maritime trade management models and new and more competitive maritime powers – leading to the inclusion of the Carreira da Índia within the network of imperial Spain, thereby subjecting it to a greater tax burden.

The need for new financial resources forced the Milanese merchants to expand the network of credit by joining forces with other agents who, through the pepper trade, intended to join the broader financial network that provided the Crown with money and precious metals. Nevertheless, such financial support as was required to limit losses within an increasingly weak and heterogeneous commercial network came from Milanese companies, which, through Giovanni Battista Rovellasca, still retained interests in the colonial trade.

To ensure the efficiency of the network, cooperation between the partners was essential in order to meet diverse needs with a view to a shared goal. Specifically, the high level of cohesion and trust that developed within the network dominated by companies controlled by the Littas, which ensured the necessary cooperation, prevented Rovellasca's bankruptcy in 1591. During the liquidity crisis that the Milanese suffered in 1590 due to the loss of ships on which he had interests in the form of pepper and other goods, Ludovico Visconte intervened with a loan of 38,761:18:3 ducats paid at the June exchange fair in Medina del Campo. Visconte, a partner of the Litta company of 1577, also retained interests in the company in 1579, as it was customary for the Littas to reinvest the capital of earlier companies in those that were established subsequently.

The use of credit allowed the Milanese merchant to restore his reputation within the financial community, who had already taken his bankruptcy for granted. Trust and reputation became fundamental concepts in defining the boundaries of social networks. Individual intentions that aimed to establish and maintain confidence acquired an even more important role. Three 'levels' of reputation were available to merchants in order to determine trustworthiness: individual, family and collective. Thus the reputation enjoyed by each merchant in the community in which he operated depended on the interaction between these three levels.

11 THE WOOL TRADE, VENICE AND THE MEDITERRANEAN CITIES AT THE END OF THE SIXTEENTH CENTURY

Andrea Caracausi

In recent decades the circulation of people and goods has become the subject of renewed interest in the fields of social and economic history.[1] This attention has stimulated new studies in the ways in which products have been transferred, appropriated and consumed. 'Trading diasporas' have been largely reconsidered and revaluated. As informal institutions, these groups ensured transactions and economic success across spaces, as well as sustaining exchanges beyond religious, cultural and social borders.[2] The concept or research strategy of the 'network' allows researchers to focus on boundaries rather than on the homogeneity and structures of those groups.[3] Moreover, it shows how modern institutions (normally conceived as legal) were not antithetical to 'pre-modern' ones (based on trust, reputation and reciprocity) and state commercial powers did not replace stateless merchant groups in dominating trade.[4] Impersonal exchanges, which were placed on the market, were not automatically more efficient than personal exchanges, which were based on values such as kinship, friendship or communitarian membership. Thanks to these studies, the evolution of commercial institutions as a teleological process has been deeply criticized.[5]

This essay aims to enrich this field of research by focusing on the role of a raw material – wool – and the social and economic interactions it created across the Mediterranean cities at the end of the sixteenth century. With respect to the most common approaches in recent studies of trade history, I will shift the focus from traders to products.[6] My first goal is indeed to link commercial strategies in long-distance trade to regional contexts, showing how those circulations affected productive areas, especially manufacturing ones.[7] The second goal is to show how commercial networks influenced domestic politics and governmental bodies, stimulating economic policies designed in order to favour the circulation of technologies, capitals and people.[8] The last goal, which is partially the subject of a research study I am currently undertaking, is to reconsider some of the dynamics concerning labour migration and craft circulation across the early

202 Commercial Networks and European Cities

modern Mediterranean, avoiding 'national' approaches (i.e. focused on early modern states) or the classical division between East and West.

A focus on the wool trade during the late sixteenth century is not unjustified. First, as several commercial treatises and mercantile manuals also suggest, products were generally the main element in attracting merchants to certain cities. The search for and knowledge of products that were traded in specific places represents one of the most important reasons for the displacement of merchants and the creation of merchant networks.[9] Moreover, the study of products allows us to avoid the analysis of commercial routes which were linked excessively to a single or distinctive merchant group (a 'diaspora' or a 'network'), whereas it invites us to follow their impact on the various segments of distribution, production and, sometimes, consumption.[10] Secondly, the focus on a commodity (and in particular on the industrial sector activated by that commodity) allow us to discuss more deeply the ways in which innovation, knowledge and technological skills were transferred across spaces and boundaries.[11] This last aspect invites us to investigate the existing link between the circulation and typology of goods and the necessary craft migration in order to develop and sustain certain manufacturing activities.

Finally, the wool trade is interesting because of the role that this specific raw material played within the woollen cloth manufacturing industry of early modern Italian cities. The sector was one of the most important economic urban and rural activities during the Renaissance. Some scholars have argued that in the late sixteenth and early seventeenth centuries, competition from the most advanced commercial institutions such as the (British) Levant Company affected the commercial and manufacturing costs of the Italian woollen industry, causing a decline in productivity.[12] Therefore the focus on the wool trade during the late sixteenth century allows us to investigate the 'marginalization' of the Mediterranean during the 'early modern globalization', although this process has been recently debated and reconsidered.[13] The study of this commercial system during one of the key moments between the 'apogee' and its suddenly 'decline' allows us to discuss some mechanisms concerning economic development or crisis in general.

This perspective requires a circumscription of the object under investigation. From the geographical point of view, I will focus on the city of Venice as the nodal point between the arrival of the wool from Iberia (especially from the ports of Alicante and Cartagena) and the Eastern Mediterranean markets, in particular Aleppo and Alexandria. From the chronological point of view I will focus on the last three decades of the sixteenth century. This choice depends, on the one hand, on the need to study in depth the actors of the wool trade and, on the other, on the role of the Venetian woollen industry in the context of European manufacturing at the end of the sixteenth century.

The essay is organized as follows. The next section introduces the woollen cloth industry in Venice at the end of the sixteenth century. The aim is to explain the importance of Spanish wool and to describe the general context in which economic actors interacted. The third section shows the functioning of the wool trade from the Western Mediterranean ports to Venice. I examine the social and economic basis of the traders, the forms of linkages and networks they created, the structure of companies and the type of transactions, as well as the mechanisms the merchants used in order to safeguard their investments. The fourth section shows the exchanges that the wool generated in Venice and their impact on financial markets and technological changes, as well as on urban politics and the social dynamics of foreign traders. I also discuss the consequences of the circulation of these goods for the regional economy and labour movements. In the fifth section I investigate the distribution of the final products (woollen cloth) in the Eastern Mediterranean (mainly in Aleppo and Alexandria), underlining also the 'returns' that these exchanges generated from the East to the West (southern Italy, Iberia and South America) and highlighting some cases of reciprocity among the economic agents. The final section offers some general remarks about the particular commercial route generated by the wool trade at the end of the sixteenth century.

The Venetian Woollen Industry at the End of the Sixteenth Century

Several studies have underlined the persisting dynamism of Venice as a port at the end of the sixteenth century, showing how the city maintained an important function in connecting Eastern markets with Western ones. This role was possible thanks to several factors: the relative political stability in international relations after the Cyprus war (1570–3), the reopening of maritime trade, growing exchanges with the Dalmatian coast, Greek islands and southern Italy, and the still unchallenged supremacy of Venetian merchants in Aleppo and Alexandria.[14]

The quality and quantity of merchandise that the Venetian port could offer these markets played an important role to ensure its function as an international hub.[15] At the end of the sixteenth century the growth of the maritime trade relied also on the increasing supply of local manufactures, especially in glass, printing, silk and woollen cloths. The woollen cloth industry experienced the most important growth, especially in comparison with the general decline of production in other Italian areas. During the second half of the sixteenth century, the Venetian woollen cloth industry registered a real boom, producing from 10,000 to 24,000 cloths annually. The growth is relevant especially in comparison with the rest of the Italian peninsula, where the silk industry replaced woollen cloth production in several urban economies and rural areas. The war of Cyprus did not stop this trend. After the peace, the recovery was so fast that production reached a peak in 1602 (28,728 pieces, an average of 23,573 over five years) and then declined over the following decades.[16] The quality of the cloth included fine heavy broadcloths (the so-called *panni alti*), with considerable weight and double width (the *panni da 60*), and lighter cloths of lower quality, such as *saglie*. The latter represented a true process of imitation and innovation that allowed the local cloth manufacturers to curb the rising competition from the draperies of north-western Europe. *Saglie* was at the basis of a large expansion that started in the sixteenth century and ended by the 1620s. This 'double' strategy (high- and low-quality production), however, was based on the uncontested role played by Spanish wool, whose quality was sometimes excellent, and access to the raw materials for red colour dyes (as grain, kermes and cochineal).[17]

Research on the woollen cloth industry has shown several aspects concerning the sectorial evolution in Venice and the Venetian mainland, highlighting the processes of reconversion that allowed merchant-manufacturers to compete with other European manufactures during the worst decades.[18] These studies have largely reconsidered the role of Venetian craft guilds during the Renaissance and the early modern period.[19] On the other hand, some scholars have argued that the loss of competitiveness was largely due to diplomatic and institutional aspects. In particular, because of the Levant Company, the superiority of the naval technologies of other European states, uncertainty due to the growth of piracy and poor protection, Venetian merchants faced higher transaction costs and lost competitiveness in the Levantine markets.[20] Recent studies on the Mediterranean trade in general, including the English and Dutch merchants, have questioned these assumptions and raised more than one question.[21] Moreover, with respect to the early modern woollen cloth industry, we need to consider carefully another factor. The wool itself represented the main cost of production, sometimes representing 50 per cent of the final product and being the greatest part of the circulating capital that was necessary to start the production.[22] The analysis of the ways in which the wool arrived in Venice is then fundamental to understand the functioning of this industry. With the exception of the wool locally produced on the mainland, the Venetian merchant-manufacturers depended on productive markets that were beyond their control and their domestic borders.[23] It is thus necessary to analyse the functioning of this trade and its social and economic foundations.

From Iberia to Venice

From Alicante to Genoa (or Livorno)

Exports of wool from Castile were subjected to rigid fiscal and duty controls.[24] At the end of the 1570s, as a consequence of the increasing troubles in Flanders (especially the plunder of Antwerp), the Italian peninsula became the largest market for Spanish wool.[25] With respect to the trade with Italy, the cities around Cuenca, Toledo and Granada were the main centres for buying wool in Castile and Andalusia. The Genoese merchants controlled this trade. In Cuenca it was the Cattano, Interiano, Imperiale and Natarello families (as well as the Añon e Dada, from Milan); in Toledo, the Gentile, Doria, Imperiale, Pinello, Cernucalo and Fornaro; in Granada, the Spinola, Quartenone, Ferrari, Usodimare, Doria, Cattaneo, De Franchi and Grimaldi.[26] From these cities the Genoese merchants sent the wool to the ports of Cartagena and especially Alicante, where other Genoese, Venetian and Milanese merchants exported it to Italian ports (especially to Genoa, Livorno or Venice). From the 1560s the woollen exports from Spain to Italy increased significantly, from an annual average of about 12,000 to 20,000 tonnes.[27] The second route always started in Andalusia and ended at the frontiers of Yecla and Murcia. From there the wool was shipped directly to Livorno and thence transported to Florence. This trade was normally, but not exclusively, in the hands of Spanish merchants who controlled the wool exports thanks to a complex network of agents and communities.[28]

With respect to the first route, in the Spanish ports several agents participated in this trade, sending the wool to Genoa. From the point of view of business organization, a hierarchical structure was preferred to market or networks, and several branches were established in the Spanish ports. The Balbi, one of the most important Genoese families, were associated with another Genoese family, the Maggiolo, who had a permanent base in Granada. This association was fundamental for the importation of wool from Spain. The company had several partners in Granada, Alicante and Genoa. Pellegro Maggiolo, the brother-in-law of Genesio Balbi, represented them in Granada, being also the attorney who was entitled to settle the purchase of wool and the payments at fairs. The partnership of Vincenzo, Niccolò and Pellegro Maggiolo was one of the most important importers of wool in Genoa. The Maggiolo were also in partnership with the Veneroso, buying with three-year contracts, which were more competitive than the one-year contracts offered by other merchants.[29] After the purchase of the wool in Spain, the Genoese merchants sent it to Alicante and Cartagena, where it was loaded on ships to Genoa and Livorno. This trade was regulated by a specific duty, the *derecho de las lanas*.[30]

The Genoese merchants exported between around 5,000 and 15,000 *sacchi* (sacks) of wool annually from Spain to Genoa (and partially Livorno). The greatest amount of the wool was thence re-exported to other Italian cities, while the production of the Genoese woollen cloth industry was declining. This trading intermediation, as well as that managed by the Spanish merchants, sustained most of the Italian wool industry.[31] Understanding the functioning of this trading system and the typology of the links that the product created from Genoa to Venice, one of the most important centres for woollen cloth, became crucial.

From Genoa to Venice

From Genoa, wool was sent to Venice by two routes. The first was by sea, circumnavigating the Italian peninsula and stopping over at some Adriatic ports. From 1575 Venice became one of the main destinations for Genoese wool, against the declining trend in other Italian industrial centres, particularly Milan. The wool was exported using ships from Venice, France, England or Ragusa (Dubrovnik). In particular, during the 1570s the Genoese merchants encountered a series of troubles with the captains from Ragusa.[32] The ships indeed stopped in Ragusa, where the wool was sometimes discharged and sold in order to sustain the local production.[33] For this reason, and perhaps also due to the rising costs of piracy in the Mediterranean, wool was also transferred from Genoa to Venice overland. From Genoa the wool was carried to Cremona or Piacenza and then to Venice, using both local and Genoese agents.[34]

What was the basis of the wool transfers from Genoa and Venice? What type of links did the exchange of these products establish? The configuration of the network of the wool trade can be shown using the registration (*fides*) that the Genoese merchants made periodically in Venice in front of their consulate when the wool arrived. These sources do not represent all of the transactions, but their number (about 400 *fides* are recorded) allows us to highlight some peculiarities.

The *fides* records the name of the Genoese merchant who received the wool in Venice (and, eventually, the name of the partnership), the owner of the wool in Genoa and, sometimes, the name of the broker or merchant from Genoa who sent the wool. Thanks to network analysis, the contacts and types of these links can be analysed for the period 1580–95.[35]

The graphs allow us to highlight some points (see Figures 11.1–3). The main nodal points in Venice are in black and they included some Genoese merchants and partnerships in Venice: Agostino di Franchi, Gerolamo, Francesco and Giovanni Antonio Marini, Niccolò and Giacomo Berti, Silvestro Millegosio, Gerolamo and Paolo Cavana, Franco Borsotto and Gio.Batta Sauli. Over fifteen years, the disaggregated analysis of three periods (1580–4, 1585–9, 1590–4) shows how during the first and second period the different nodes were more interlinked, while in the third period just four almost isolated groups polarized and controlled the wool market in Venice. This fact meant that during the first two periods the merchants in Genoa were able to choose more intermediaries in order to sell their wool, while in the last one the exchanges were more linked to one single agent. (During the 1590–4 period the only merchant in Genoa who sent the wool to two different merchants in Venice was Bernardo Soprani, while during 1580–9 more merchants were able to shift from one group to another group.) With respect to the wool trade, only small networks appeared, while the configuration of the exchanges was more segmented in several linkages among merchants. However, we can argue that after the boom of the first 1580s, the wool trade evolved from a more 'open' to a more 'closed' market with the dissolution of the previous networks.

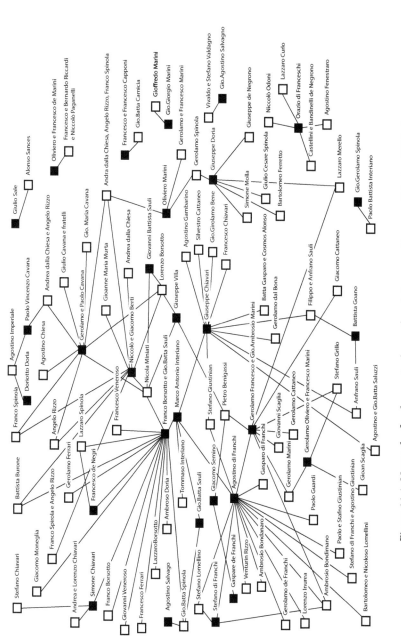

Figure 11.1: Network of exchanges in the wool trade between Genoa and Venice, 1580–4.

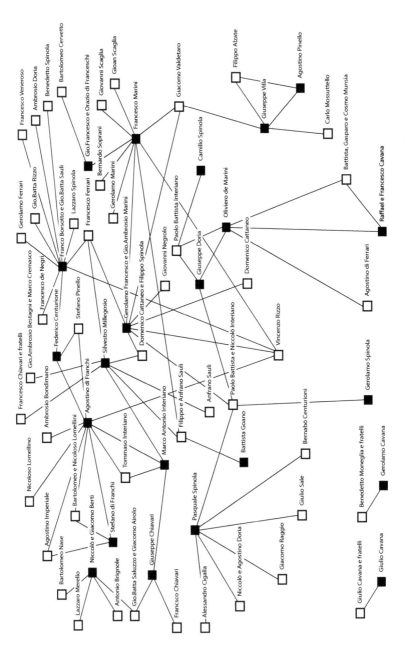

Figure 11.2: Network of exchanges in the wool trade between Genoa and Venice, 1585–9.

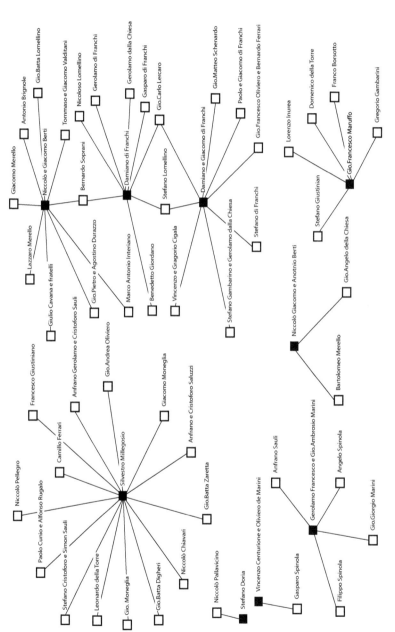

Figure 11.3: Network of exchanges in the wool trade between Genoa and Venice, 1590–4.

Some points of interest emerge if we analyse the internal coherence of these groups and the economic and social basis of these linkages. The first is the predominance of kinship, at least for the nobles. When they sent their wool from Genoa to Venice, the members of the di Franco family (Gerolamo, Gasparo, Paolo and Giacomo di Franchi) chose Agostino, Damiano or Giacomo di Franchi as their agents. The Chiavari and Spinola families, especially in the first period, followed this pattern, as did the Cavana and Marini. In Venice, the members of these families also received wool from other merchants in Genoa who did not change their partners, but belonged to the same group. These linkages remained stable over the decades, but several merchants became more important in the Venetian market. During the first period, for instance, Silvestro Millegosio had fewer contacts, and they were mainly with three families (Interiano, Sauli and Spinola). Over the following decade, he became the main agent of a group of Genoese merchants, including the Sauli, Interiano, Moneglia and Pellegro. The brothers Silvestro and Pompeo Millegosio decided to stay permanently in Venice at the end of the 1580s, continuing the partnership they had already formed, sharing profits and losses.

In general, the wool trade between Genoa and Venice confirms the general idea concerning this 'diaspora'. As argued by the Genoese scholar Edoardo Grendi, this group of merchants operated closely thanks to kinship ties and membership of the same communitarian institution, the Genoese 'nation'. However, there were some exceptions. The Florentine partnership of Niccolò and Giacomo Berti was one of the main nodes in the 'Genoese' wool trade, acting also as the main broker, particularly in the 1590s, for the Genoese noblemen and families such as the Cavana, Durazzo, Lomellino and Interiano.

The role of the Berti (as well as the Milanese firm 'Dada & Villa') in the context of the Genoese wool trade is interesting for two reasons. First, they represent an anomaly in a model strictly based on kinship or communitarian origins and institutions. The second point is that the Berti were also present in the other route by which the wool arrived in Venice overland, though Florence and the Appenine mountains. Moreover, the Berti operated there in tandem with other Florentine and Spanish merchants, who were sometimes in competition with the Genoese.

From Livorno to Venice

From Livorno the wool was sent to Florence and then, across the Apennine passes, to Ferrara and finally to Venice. The amount of wool that arrived by land was greater than by sea.[36]

Unfortunately, we have less quantitative evidence for the Florentine merchants compared with the Genoese. However, from a qualitative point of view we can argue there were different patterns in the 'Florentine' wool trade. The

Florentine merchants adopted two different strategies. The first involved the direct acquisition of wool in Spain, and the transfer by sea (or land); the second was to rely upon the intermediation of Spanish (and even Genoese) merchants in Florence or Genoa. The most active Florentine partnerships were the Allegri, Strozzi and Capponi, in addition to the Berti.[37] The trade from Spain to Venice carried out by the Florentines also depended on the link between the latter and the Spanish merchants, most of whom were located in Florence.[38] Moreover, as a large part of the Spanish wool arrived thanks to Florentine intermediation, the Spanish partnerships in Venice were less numerous than in Florence. The configuration of this linkage between Spanish and Florentine merchants depended on the particular structure of the Spanish wool trade that had its main nodal point in Florence.

The Spanish (and Florentine) merchants sent wool to Venice with respect to the cloths to be produced. In general the highest quality wool remained in Florence, while the second- or third-grade wool was sold largely in the Venetian lagoon.[39] When the wool was not sold in the Florentine local market, it was turned over to Venice. The situation in the Rialto also could affect the arrivals; prices in the Venetian market could influence the decisions of Spanish and Florentine merchants in Florence.[40] The business correspondence between Simon Ruiz and his agent in Florence, Baldassarre Suarez, illustrates this clearly. The destination of the Spanish wool depended on the quality of the product: wool for the production of *rascie*, a particular kind of Florentine cloth, was sold in Florence; otherwise it was sent to Venice and sold there for the production of the Venetian *panni alti*. According to calculations made by Martin Ruiz, more than 50 per cent of the Spanish wool that arrived in Florence at the end of the sixteenth century was therefore re-exported, and Venice was the biggest market.[41] The same Baldassarre Suarez sent some quantities of low-grade and second-grade wool to the Strozzi in Venice, the only market that would take that wool.[42]

As mentioned above, in the Venetian market the Genoese and the Spanish-Florentine merchants were in competition and speculated in order to make profits from the wool prices. As Baldassarre Suarez wrote in a letter, the Genoese were less careful about these kinds of speculations, trying to sell their merchandise rapidly.[43] However, the same Genoese merchants tried to speculate, waiting until the Venetian woollen cloth manufacturers finished all the 'Florentine' (i.e. sold by Florentine merchants) wool before selling them the 'Genoese' wool. From Milan, Giovanni Francesco Pallavicini wrote to his agent Stefano Doria, in Venice, recommending how to profit extensively on the wool he sent to him. Doria had to wait until the Venetian drapers had consumed the wool that arrived from Florence before selling them the wool that arrived from Genoa.[44]

Genoese, Florentine and Spanish merchants speculated on wool prices in order to raise the possibility of profits. In this game, the expectation and confidence that the principal had in the agent became crucial, explaining why some merchants preferred to use one habitual correspondent. Moreover, knowledge of the particular product became a key aspect, as it was necessary to recognize the various types of wool and to know which type could be sold in a particular place and at a specific time.[45] The most important consequence, however, was the effect that these commercial networks had on the other node of the wool trade: the Venetian market.

In Venice

Credit and Manufacture

In Venice, the imported wool generated a series of effects on the urban economy. The first point concerns the selling of the raw material in the local market. The transactions were carried out using credit: the payments would be settled after one, two or even three years. The wool trade therefore became a means to finance business activities. The balance of payments would take place in different forms at the end of the manufacturing cycle, taking into account the profit from sales of the cloth.

Examples of this kind of transaction are numerous and testify how the Genoese and Florentine merchants played a crucial role as intermediaries between Spain and Venice. During the 1580s the Genoese merchant Agostino di Franchi sold several quantities (*balle*) of wool to Giovanni and Lorenzo di Gotti, Giovanni Pietro Rizzo and Battista Rolla on credit.[46] The price was around 34–44 ducats per 100 lbs, with payment due in twelve months. Moreover, Pasquale Spinola was a creditor of the Venetian wool merchant-manufacturer Angelo Manzoni for 11 *balle* of Spanish wool, whose value was 727 ducats and 22 *grossi*. In order to secure the loan, the contract included a mortgage over the house of Domenico Busini, Manzoni's dyer and partner.[47] Sometimes the wool merchant-manufacturers were in financial difficulty and delayed the payments. Giovanni Battista Sauli sold 16 *balle* of wool for 1,308 ducats and 23 *grossi* to the Venetian wool merchant Domenico Fornaretto on credit. After three years Domenico still had not settled the debt.[48]

The wool trade became then a system to finance the woollen-cloth manufacturing firms, linking the Genoese and Venetian merchants as well as the woollen-cloth manufacturers for several years. The length of the partnerships varied widely, from one to five years. During the 1580s Alvise Poccobello from Lugano (Switzerland) owed 1,600 ducats to Giuseppe Chiavari for some wool, which was totally and exclusively sold in order to pursue the partnership that Alvise started some years earlier.[49] The partnership agreement was signed by Alvise Poccobello and the Venetian patrician Giovanni Lippamano, who was in charge of receiving the wool that was sold by Giuseppe Chiavari.[50]

Even in the case of Florentines the debts were significant, around 1,000–2,000 ducats, but in exceptional cases of 13,000 ducats for a single firm.[51] From 1572 to 1574 Francesco Allegri, a Florentine merchant in Venice acting as agent of several Florentine merchants (Antonio Berti, Francesco Comparini and Baldassarre Ficardi), sold more than 70 *balle* of Spanish wool to several Venetian merchants and drapers (Giacomo Ragazzoni, Giacomo di Agostini, Paolo di Marco Pencino and Giovanni Antonio Castoro).[52]

In order to reduce the circulation of money, the sale of raw materials could be balanced with the purchase of manufactured goods, linking even more closely the suppliers of raw materials to the Venetian merchant-manufacturers. In the case of the Florentine merchants in Venice, these forms of credit were used to generate several interactions between the two cities from the point of view of the manufacturing systems. The Venetian draper Piero Antonio Lupini agreed to produce fifty-one Venetian cloths for the merchant-manufacturer Giulio d'Alessandro, once Giulio had delivered the wool from the merchant Piero de Silvan in Florence.[53]

Actually the Venetian market lacked a real system for financing the firms, limiting the operations of several producers (especially those with less capital) and weakening the whole manufacturing system. The Spanish merchants Simon Ruiz and Baldassarre Suarez complained about the absence of a structured channel for financing the wool trade: indeed the purchases served to start the production, and the payment would come only later, after one year at least. The Genoese relied upon these small and medium-sized firms, but frequently the cloth producers were unable to pay, declaring themselves bankrupt. Moreover, the same Venetian cloth-manufacturers often sold the debts they held from other cloth producers in order to balance the cost of wool purchased from Florentine and Genoese merchants.[54] These loans were not strictly linked to the wool trade, but they were sometimes connected to the foreign exchange market in the fairs in Bisenzone, again managed by the Genoese and Florentines.[55]

The second effect that the wool trade had on the Venetian economy was on the manufacturing itself. As underlined in the previous section, the total volume of Venetian woollen cloth production increased during the period 1570–1600. It is important now to understand the main actors involved in the manufacturing, focusing on the types of partnership and the organization of production. The first point is the various social backgrounds of people who invested in the woollen cloth production. An important contribution came from Venetian nobility (the Donado, Trevisan, Gradenigo and Sanudo families) but also from merchants from the mainland (the Zois) and several foreigners (the Poccobello).[56] The second point is that the wool trade stimulated the mingling of Venetian and non-Venetian investments in terms of capitalization. Even without comprehensive and detailed data about the capitalization of woollen cloth producers, as for other cities, we can argue some general aspects concerning the Venetian woollen cloth industry.[57] In general, the partnerships were in the form of limited liability companies, and the amount of capital varied from 2,000 to 10,000 and even reached around 25,000 ducats.[58] Sometimes the production was linked to the commercialization of products. At the beginning of the seventeenth century, a partnership agreement for the Levantine trade was signed between Tommaso Contarini, Antonio Querini and Giovanni Rusca. Rusca was to use the capital, 24,000 ducats, 'with his own industriousness, good faith, and with all diligence and care to produce woollen cloths'.[59] Other investors included merchants and inventors, like the entrepreneur Giulio d'Alessandro from Modena, who was well known for his machines in the recycling of liquid oils (*ogliazzi*).[60] Finally, in the woollen industry several small and medium-sized enterprises of craftsmen and drapers operated, as the cases of the debtors of the Florentine and Genoese merchants show.[61]

The wool trade had several consequences not only in Venice but also in the regional economy, and especially in the nearest districts of Padua and Treviso. The presence of the Florentines and Genoese, and their links with the financial markets, stimulated in these cities investments in the woollen industry and fairs. In Padua, Tommaso Bartoli, the agent of Lorenzo, Roberto and Alfonso Strozzi, was a creditor of the woollen merchant Lorenzo Verdabio for payments in the Bisenzone fairs.[62] Other Florentine merchants sold Spanish wool in the Venetian mainland, purchased clothes and bonnets from the local producers, and then sent them abroad. The range of the investments of the Florentine merchants in the wool industry went beyond the Venetian environment, embracing other cities of the Venetian state. The Florentine Vincenzo Bardi had a partnership with Battista Barilli importing woollen socks and other items from Padua, dyeing them in Venice and then sending them to Ancona, where their agent Giovanni Antonio Nicolini would receive them.[63] The woollen-cloth production of several cities in the mainland attracted foreign merchants from Venice: even during the 1580s, several woollen cloths from Vicenza, Padua and Feltre, a small centre near Belluno, were acquired by Genoese and Florentine merchants and exported abroad.[64] Finally, the overland trade in wool also stimulated the diffusion of the raw material across the Po Valley, especially in Bergamo and Ferrara, where the Florentine merchants, like the Strozzi, had several agents to receive wool from Florence.[65]

Concerning the impact of the wool trade on manufacturing, the last important consequence was on the links that this commercial network generated between Venice and the mainland. In particular, some patrician families had in their rural properties large flocks of sheep (more than 300–600 sheep), which produced fine wool very similar to the Spanish wool.[66] Moreover, the patrician firms were characterized by two elements. First, the volume of production was very high for the times, with the production of individual manufacturers exceeding more than 140–60 cloths per annum.[67] Second, the cloths produced were of high quality (*panni alti*) and they were normally sold in the Levantine trade (through Venice).[68] These investments had relevant consequences on the productive territories (as in terms of agricultural production), and this feature was common to other merchants (e.g. the Zambelli, Mersi, Manzoni and Verdabio) that had several links in the woollen industry in Padua and Venice.[69] The same Florentine merchants who imported wool from Spain acted directly as merchant-entrepreneurs in the Italian mainland. Giovanni Paolo Belfante, a wool merchant-manufacturer in Padua during the 1570s, was one of the bigger producers (211 cloths made in 1577) and was actually the agent of Andrea dell'Oste, an important Tuscan merchant in Venice.[70]

Privileges and Circulation

The wool trade and the intertwined connections across the Mediterranean cities and between the local and foreign mercantile class necessarily influenced Venetian politics. The first effect concerned the grant of exemptions or discounts on duties in order to favour the arrival of wool by sea, using Venetian ships and reducing the overland trade. The exemption on the wool that was traded by sea was therefore conceived as a means to balance the maritime/overland trade rather than favouring some foreign communities. Trading the wool overland, the Genoese and Florentine merchants were more able to speculate and raise prices, whereas the maritime trade could avoid these fluctuations. In particular, the wool traded through Livorno and Florence caused great inconveniences. As claimed by the Cinque Savi alla Mercanzia (the Venetian Board of Trade), the Florentine merchants, 'in an industrious manner, are able to benefit from all the merchandise and in particular wool and *cremesi* [dyeing material]', holding them in Florence 'with damage' to the Venetians.[71]

Apart from the fiscal trade policy, the second effect of the wool trade on Venetian institutions was on the granting of privileges in order to favour the circulation of technologies. For instance, at the beginning of the 1580s the Florentine Giovanni Antonio Manzini received a privilege in order to produce '*rasse*, that is *sagie*, in this city [Venice] following the Florentine style', with a twenty-year monopoly.[72] Four years later, on 7 July 1588, Cesare Pucci, son of Giacomo, Francesco, son of Niccolò del Benvenuto, and Antonio Manucci, son of Leone, all Florentine citizens, testified that the Florentine Francesco, son of Nicolò Pagliuzzi, had worked for at least five years in several workshops and that during the last year he had stayed in the workshop of the patrician Mocenigo. They also affirmed that for the past four years Mocenigo had produced *saglie alla fiorentina* ('in the Florentine style') thanks to the privilege granted to Giovanni Antonio Manzini, who was their director (*ministro*).[73]

The privilege itself also had important effects on craft circulations. It gave Manzini the freedom to bring to Venice 'foreign workers' who were not obliged to enter the Venetian guilds or brotherhoods, but who had to pay all taxes and contributions. However, they could not work other typologies of clothes, but only those included in the privilege.[74] At the beginning of the seventeenth century, the Venetian Senate received petitions (*suppliche*) from other Florentine merchants who asked to import or introduce to Venice other types of Florentine cloths.[75]

The flow of capital (in terms of the wool trade in order to finance woollen cloth production) thus influenced the circulation of technologies and labour migration. In the Mocenigo workshops, many Florentine workers were employed in various stages of production under the direction of the Florentine craftsman Giovanni Antonio Manzini. This circulation did not depend exclusively on the origin of the merchants or the artisans who imported the technologies because these productions stimulated temporary migration flows. Since the productive volumes fluctuated hugely from one year to the next, seasonal migration between neighbouring districts was a distinctive feature of the woollen cloth industry. Most of the labour force in the first stages of production in Venice came from the other territories of the Venetian mainland and the Po Valley.[76] In the Padua workshop of the wool merchant Giovanni Paolo Belfante, the artisans came mainly from the nearby cities of Bassano, Verona and Treviso.[77] The merchant-manufacturers stimulated these migratory flows, attracting workers and artisans from abroad, paying wages in advance, and ensuring financial aid in case of the cessation of production.

The circulation of people also concerned the foreign merchants who tried to start strategic productions for long-distance trade, such as the woollen industry. The granting of citizenship shows the relationship between the state and the foreign merchants.

Venetian citizenship was a complex institution.[78] With respect to trade and manufactures, the Senate granted foreign merchants two kinds of citizenship, *de intus* (in Venice) and *de intus et extra* (in and outside Venice). The first kind of citizenship was granted to people who had been in Venice for at least fifteen years and who paid local taxes; it gave the right to trade in Venice with the same rights as the Venetian merchants. Citizenship *de intus et extra* included more rights. Although twenty-five years of residence were required, it allowed the holder to trade in the Levantine ports with the same fiscal exemptions as the Venetian merchants even if the use of the 'Venetian' name was necessary. In the sixteenth and the seventeenth centuries, several Florentine and Genoese merchants who were particularly dynamic in the wool trade received citizenship of Venice *de intus* or *de intus et extra*, such as Pasquale Spinola, Simone Chiavari, and the brothers Francesco, Giovanni and Ambrogio Marini. When they were asked to advise about the granting of citizenship *de intus* to Simone Chiavari, the

Cinque Savi alla Mercanzia recognized him as worthy of the title and mentioned that he imported 'great quantities of Spanish wool' and other merchandise for 'thousands of ducats'.[79] Simone Chiavari gave an important contribution to the local economy, sustaining not only the indirect taxes but also the manufacturers and the workers of the wool industry. Between the late sixteenth and the early seventeenth centuries, other Genoese and Florentine merchants as well as several foreign woollen manufacturers were granted Venetian citizenship.[80]

The granting of citizenship, and in particular citizenship *de intus et extra*, was an important institution because it allowed merchants to trade both in Venice and in the Levantine ports. There the last connection of the wool trade occurred.

From Venice to the East (and Back)

The third segment of the wool trade in the late sixteenth-century Mediterranean was the connections that the product encouraged in the form of trade in manufactured goods with the Levantine cities, and especially with Aleppo and Alexandria. As mentioned earlier, thanks to the revival of the caravan trade and the slow affirmation of the northern empires, the commerce between Venice and the Levant still prospered at the end of the sixteenth century. Within this trade, the growth of the wool industry was a key element because the *panni alti* were exchanged for various Levantine goods such as raw silk, *zambellotti* (clothes), cotton and spices.[81] This aspect stimulated the efforts to ensure the supply of raw materials: wool and dying materials (e.g. alum).[82] The woollen cloths substituted perfectly for silver in the payments; in 1592 10,000–12,000 Venetian woollen cloths were sold in Aleppo, 4,000 in Alexandria, 5,000 in the Balkans and 3,000 in Constantinople. The total amount, 22,000 cloths, was around the 90 per cent of the total Venetian production.[83]

The 'currency' Venice needed in order to pay for purchases from the East relied largely upon the export of woollen cloths and other manufactured items (such as window glass, mirrors and glass beads).[84] The Venetian Board of Trade was always aware of the role of manufactures in the balance of trade.[85] As Baldassarre Suarez wrote to Simon Ruiz, Venetian woollen cloths (*pannina veneziana*) were manufactured for Levantine customers.[86] With respect to product quality, the same manufacturing choices depended on the markets where the cloths were sold. For instance, in the mainland those merchants who traded with Venice and the Levant (e.g the Zambelli, Sanudo, Bombardino and Mersi) produced only high-quality cloths (*panni alti*), while others manufactured only low-quality cloths (*panni bassi*).[87]

The Levantine trade affected the wool trade itself. On 28 February 1585 Baldassarre Suarez wrote to Simon Ruiz that he could not send wool to Venice because of the trouble between the Venetian Republic and the Ottoman

Empire.[88] One Venetian ship was retained and the captain was beheaded. The wool market was stationary and he was not able to conclude an agreement with a Venetian partnership. The cochineal trade also depended on the expectation concerning the local consumption of 'Levantine' products.[89] After all, the Spanish merchants re-exported most Venetian products (like *rasce* or damask) to the Western ports using Venetian ships.[90]

However, with respect to the woollen cloth industry, what was the basis and the structure of the Levantine trade? Which cities did these exchanges connect? At the end of the sixteenth century, the commerce in woollen cloth still relied upon the traditional public galley system, while the use of private ships was minor. The historiography has largely underlined the general change of the Venetian patriciate during the late Renaissance, with a gradual shift from trading activities to investments in real estate, especially on the mainland.[91] However, several patricians still participated in the Levantine trade, whereas the role of new social groups, such as citizens from the mainland and foreigners, became more relevant.[92]

Some examples can best illustrate this point. Some partnerships were signed exclusively for the commerce in woollen cloths. In this case (e.g. the specialization in trading in a single product), the partners were less frequently members of the same family. Francesco Gradenigo and Piero Morosini, both patricians and wool merchants, had a partnership with the patrician Alvise Donado, son of Matteo, in Alexandria.[93] The 'corporate' identity was not an exclusive value, and commission agents were also Venetian citizens, merchants from the mainland or strangers such as Jews or other minorities. In terms of capitalization, the wool trade participated in the encounter between noble and non-noble capital. Giovanni Renier, Marco Antonio Foscarini and Benedetto Ragazzoni signed a partnership with the Jewish merchant Beniamino Lappada, who was entitled to sell their woollen cloths in Izmir.[94] Salamon Rivola, Antonio and Gerolamo de Zuanne Ca' Bianca and Costantino Gervato signed a partnership ('Antonio & Gerolamo Ca' Bianca & Co.') over 9,000 ducats which were constituted by ninety-nine Venetian and foreign woollen cloths. Costantino Gervato was entitled to go in Syria to sell all their cloths and merchandise, sharing the profits and losses.[95]

During the 1580s and 1590s in Aleppo and Alexandria, a closed group of Venetian merchants (Paolo d'Avanzo, Servolo di Berto, Niccolò Crivelli, Alessandro di Fondi, Pietro Michiel, Ettore Mondini, Francesco di Schietti, Zuanne Torre and Zuanne Ventramin and Zaccaria di Zuanne, among others) were entitled to recover the merchandise in case of damages, failures, etc.[96] As an institution, the Venetian consulate played an important role, considering also the role of familiar and personal ties. The patrician Francesco di Priuli, son of Zuanne, and the Venetian Stefano, son of Giacomo Peroto, carried on their business in Alexandria, but only during the time of the consulate of the patrician Domenico Dolfin.[97]

The trade that the wool activated was not exclusively limited to the selling of woollen cloths in the Levant. Several products, among them many woollen cloths, came back to the Western markets. Genoese merchants such as Pasquale Spinola purchased the woollen cloths of the Venetian mainland in Venice and then they sold them in southern Italy or in Livorno, before re-exporting to Iberian markets.[98] Florentine merchants, as the Strozzi, Guadagni or Baglioni, purchased Venetian cloths from Feltre, near Belluno, and re-exported them to Iberia with other Levantine goods.[99] Other merchants balanced their credits in the wool trade by purchasing Levantine goods for the Western markets.

From the point of view of the 'returns' to Western ports, the merchants (Florentines and Genoese, but also Spanish, Sephardic and Dutch) who supplied wool to the Venetian port acquired several kinds of goods (wine, oil and other manufactures) to be sold in Palermo, Livorno, Alicante, Cadiz (where they also acquired wool and dyeing materials) or Lisbon. In these places the Florentine and Genoese merchants chose to rely upon Venetian (e.g. Giovanni Andrea Ullio in Alicante), Florentine (e.g. Giovanni Filippo Bartoli in Cadiz) or 'Italian' agents (e.g. Raffaello Fantoni, Giovanni Battista Rovellasca, Alvise Vezzato and Francesco dalla Pigna in Lisbon). In the case of the trip organized by Francesco da Ponte, Roberto Strozzi and Donato Ullio, the business correspondence was sent though the Venetian channels of information (Ambrogio Soranzo, ambassador in Madrid, or Giovanni Andrea, consul in Alicante), but financial remittances were managed following the financial channels of the Strozzi, showing an interesting phenomenon of reciprocity in the circulating channels.[100]

Conclusion

As John Munro recently stated,

> The apparently sudden rise and very rapid expansion of the Venetian woollen cloth industry during the early and mid sixteenth century, and then its equally rapid decline in the seventeenth century, is certainly one of the very most fascinating events in the history of the early-modern Mediterranean trade, and especially the trade with the Levant and the Ottoman Empire.[101]

The commercial network organized around 'wool' as a product (as raw material, dyeing materials, semi-finished goods, cloth and capital) contains indeed more than one intriguing aspect. The frequency and the volume of the trade in these objects were decisive in influencing the location of investments and productions as well as the kind of linkages that were at the basis of these transactions.

For instance, with respect to the wool trade through Genoa, the internal coherence and social profile of those groups who controlled the raw material influenced the configuration of networks and linkages. On the one hand, the 'hierarchy' dominated in terms of the opening of new branches or commission agents in Venice (and Spain); on the other hand, kinships and communitarian ties (at least for noble families) prevailed, apart from some exceptions, as the case of Berti and Dada & Villa shows. This fact depended on several elements. First, the specific merchandise (the wool) had more relevance within the spectrum of 'Genoese' merchandise rather than Florentine. Secondly, with some exceptions, the Genoese merchants sold the wool directly in Venice, while the decision of the Florentine and Spanish merchants depended also on the local condition of Florence and its industry. In the case of the Florentines, the social basis of those groups was different, with less hierarchy and more intra-communitarian contacts between Spanish and Florentine merchants. Once again, the strategy (the type of linkages) depended by the structure of the trade (the predominance of the Florentine woollen market).

A first interface between commercial markets and productive markets appeared in Venice. This encounter generated several forms of exchanges that cannot be simply identified as 'pure' market. Instead the wool market represented a form to finance the woollen industry, where hierarchical relations (in terms of dependence) governed economic relations more than networks. On the other hand, in the case of the 'returns' from Venice to Iberia and of the trade between Venice and the East, the Genoese, Florentine and Venetian merchants reciprocally exchanged their commercial and diplomatic agents.[102]

The commercial network of the wool trade affected the urban economy. First it activated a channel of investments that engaged various social strata, patricians, citizens and foreigners. Secondly, the regional economy was widely involved in this trade, from the collecting of capital and merchandise for export up to direct production in several districts of the mainland. These processes again generated hierarchical structures of business forms, based on the foundation of partnerships and branches, following the lower or higher volume of exchange and product quality.

Urban and state politics were also influenced by these exchanges. Privileges, grants and exemptions from duty aimed to attract the flow of goods (in particular raw materials) and sustain their transformation into finished products. Moreover, this commercial network stimulated technological innovations (in terms of new products) on the one hand, and the labour migrations (in terms of both seasonal and permanent migration of skilled and non-skilled workforces) on the other. Normally these movements fluctuated across the existing borders, and merchants and manufacturers were able to create independent areas for migrations.[103]

Studies on the Venetian manufactures have shown how several factors sustained the growth of the woollen cloth industry, such as technological innovations and market strategies in the East. Moreover, the analysis of the wool trade demonstrates how this trend relied largely on decisions made in terms of capital flows (in the form of the raw material) by those merchants who controlled the commercial routes and production areas. On the other hand, these choices depended on the access to the Levantine markets that the Venetian manufacturers and merchants enjoyed on the other side of the Mediterranean,[104] but also on the subsidies and grants (in term of privileges, commercial exemptions, citizenships) that the Venetian state offered to these international traders and groups. Commercial networks then affected productive areas (in terms of technological circulations and labour migrations), showing the predominance of the commercial capital on production and how innovation came though trade as well as craft migration and technological transfers.[105]

With respect to the manufacturing activities, most studies have emphasized the competition among regional states in the Italian peninsula, with the decline of one centre (Milan or Florence) and the sudden growth of other cities and smaller centres (Venice). In particular, the woollen industry of Venice and Florence experienced processes of imitation and import-substitution over the sixteenth and seventeenth centuries.[106] However, a research-based approach that looks at commercial networks allows us to understand how the manufacturing dynamics of productive areas were more complex, depending on the particular contexts and merchant groups. With respect to the Venetian woollen industry, the productive choices depended on a long productive chain that started in Spain and ended in the Levant, which had its nodal point in Venice. In this context, a closed group of merchant-capitalists controlled the most part of the financial flows (in terms of wool) and influenced the productive choices of the territories following the opportunities they looked for in order to limit the circulation of money and to profit from the sale of wool on credit, disseminating the production where labour costs were low (as in Venice, Padua or Treviso), and selling the raw material according to the trends in the markets (as in the case of the Levantine trade). Most of them were Genoese and even Florentines: they decided where it was more convenient to finance the production in order to have more gains in terms of competitive advantages and making more profits on price-differentials. This fact also explains the fluctuations in the annual volume of production.[107]

The case of Niccolò and Giacomo Berti, a Florentine firm in Venice, is exemplary of this interconnected system across political borders. Having acquired the wool in Spain, they sold it in Venice on credit; then they bought the cloths (sometimes from the same debtors), and they finally sold them to other merchants for the Levantine trade or for export to the Western European markets.[108] Other Tuscan merchants, such as the Oste or Guadagni, applied the same strategy, as did some Genoese merchants.

As this essay has shown, the textile industry of early modern Italy, as well as of other areas, should be seen as interwoven webs of investors, traders and small, medium and large producers, crossing the borders of territories and beyond the Italian peninsula. For woollen cloth manufacturing, the supply of the raw material was the most important aspect, representing a form of investment *ante litteram*. But the supply depended most on the merchants who controlled the importation of wool and supplied the manufacturing centres. This aspect can explain the difficult periods of the woollen cloth industry of the city of Venice in the seventeenth century. From the first decades the routes of the Spanish woollen exports to the Italian peninsula changed radically, and ports such as Livorno received less than 15 per cent of the wool previously imported in 1573–93.[109] Moreover, during the 1630s the higher manufacturing costs of the industry resulted from the poor supply of Spanish wool, which was in the hands of a few speculators.[110] Finally, the diplomatic relations with the Levantine markets changed dramatically during the war of Candia (1645–69). On the other hand, woollen cloth production emerged contemporaneously in several areas of the Venetian mainland (Padua, Bassano, Treviso, Bergamo), while southern Italy and central-eastern Europe became the main markets.[111] Instead of a general decline of the whole industry, preliminary evidence suggests the beginning of a general restructuration of the whole web with respect to Levantine ports that appeared during the mid-seventeenth century.

The evolution of the Venetian woollen cloth industry during the seventeenth century is then certainly another chapter in the history of the early modern Mediterranean that requires further investigation. Working with network-based approaches allows a better understanding of what happened in terms of economic crisis and development, where transnational flows affected local changes, technological primacy and labour migrations.

Acknowledgements

This essay has been published within the framework of the projects 'Forms of Statehood between the Middle Ages and Early Modern Times: The Mediterranean Dimension and the Dominion of the Mainland in the Venetian Model' (PRIN2009W4PHLJ_003) and 'Maritime Borders in the Mediterranean: How Permeable Are They? Exchange, Control and Denial of Access' (FIRB2012RB-FR12GBQZ_002), financed by the Italian Ministry of Instruction, University and Research. I would like to thank Daniele Andreozzi, Edoardo Demo, Christof Jeggle, Claudio Marsilio, Elisabetta Traniello and Francesco Vianello for their useful comments. Moreover, I am extremely grateful to Cristina Munno, who kindly introduced me to network analysis and the use of Netdraw.

12 THE SCERIMANS AND CROSS-CULTURAL TRADE IN GEMS: THE ARMENIAN DIASPORA IN VENICE AND ITS TRADING NETWORKS IN THE FIRST HALF OF THE EIGHTEENTH CENTURY

Evelyn Korsch

The Armenian diaspora in Venice, its activities in the Eurasian gem trade and its trading networks are at the centre of this analysis. As a case study, the commercial activities of the Sceriman family in the first half of the eighteenth century will be shown. These Armenian merchants settled in Venice and Livorno, which were the strategically most important business locations in Italy. Venice served as a significant turnover hub for trading and processing diamonds and other gems. Moreover, it functioned as a gateway connecting markets in Italy to those in the Levant, Persia and India. Livorno, meanwhile, was the most important centre for trading coral and manufacturing coral products. Furthermore, the Tuscan port linked Italy with the Atlantic markets, the West Indies, Africa and India. Both cities had commercial relations with markets in the German territories, in Vienna, Poland and Russia. Hence the diamond trade run by Armenian merchants was based on global networks that provided them with capital, information, infrastructure and specialized personnel.

Introduction

The trade and transfer of diamonds and other precious stones were based on economic, financial, social and ethnic networks that constituted and influenced specialized markets. In general the actors in these networks were private traders, as opposed to the Dutch and English East India Companies, which were mostly involved as carriers by shipping diamonds to Europe. These trading practices evolved from the rules established by the Mughal emperors who had monopolized the mines of Golconda and preferred to collaborate with private merchants. Diamonds were usually paid for with coral, emeralds and gold or silver bullion.

These luxury goods had to be acquired in international markets, and their prices could vary greatly. The East India Companies had little ready money at their disposal, and thus were constrained to paying for part of their acquisitions in kind, mostly with cloth. This prevented the Dutch and English merchants from entering the diamond trade on a large scale. Therefore they were involved mainly in shipping.[1] When the English East India Company legalized private imports of diamonds at the beginning of the 1660s, English merchants travelling to India combined this private trade with their commission business. As the private English diamond trade was organized in a similar manner to a diaspora structure, it lent further confidence in the potential of such an organizational form for mercantile endeavours.[2] Consequently, the diamond trade was mainly in the hands of the Armenian and Sephardic diasporas. Indian precious stones were exchanged for intensely coloured emeralds that had been found along the African coasts of the Red Sea and in Peru. These were highly appreciated in India due to their rarity, and had to be imported.[3] Venice-based merchants acquired emeralds in Antwerp, where they arrived via Seville from Peru. Mediterranean coral was fished mostly off the coasts of Genoa and Naples and sent to Livorno. In the mid-seventeenth century, the Tuscan city emerged as the most important centre of coral trading and manufacturing. Venetians, however, extracted coral along the Dalmatian coast. It was then processed in workshops in Venice in order to be shipped to India via the Levant. In Europe and Asia, coral was at the bottom of the hierarchy of precious stones. In Asia, however, it had a symbolic value that stimulated its trade.[4] From the seventeenth century onwards, the demand for coral increased and consequently raised the price. As a result the Mediterranean states competed for coral fishing for most of the eighteenth century.[5]

Armenian agents operated within different networks in order to strengthen their activities. Their networks were an example of successful business policies because of their cooperation with both the East India Companies as well as with other trading networks, e.g. the Sephardic and Huguenot diasporas. Until the middle of the eighteenth century, the trade of luxury goods was firmly in the hands of Armenian merchants.[6] They brought silk from Persia and gems from India to their main turnover emporium, Aleppo. From there, the goods were transported to the Mediterranean coast by caravans in order to be shipped elsewhere. The most important markets in Italy were the ports – and gateways – Livorno and Venice. The latter's position as the location of a mint carried additional significance.[7] Livorno, however, was an important centre for the export of coins, which themselves were considered goods.[8] The success of the Armenians derived from a relatively strict organized clan system, flexible trade practices, payment mainly in specie and silver or gold bullions, and specialized legal forms ensuring the continuity of their trade activities. Their operations were founded on trust and shared ethical norms whereby costs could be saved.[9] Long-distance trade with diamonds and precious stones, for example, was connected with high investments and therefore risks. In order to ensure the greatest degree of trust, Armenian merchants assigned only agents working within the same network. In the gem trade with India they did not use the services of Hindu agents, as occurred in the diamond trade run by Sephardic merchants.[10]

New Julfa, a suburb of Isfahan (in present-day Iran) and an important centre of the silk trade, served as headquarters to the Persian Armenians. Around 1600, 86 per cent of the European demand for raw silk was supplied via merchants residing there.[11] The Safavid shahs granted the Armenian merchants several privileges for this lucrative trade, elevating them to a special position. Therefore the East India Companies had to deploy the Armenian agents as middlemen.[12] The Armenians could even strengthen their position of power by acquiring public offices within the Persian state. Some of them were entrusted with the supervision of currency, gold and silver resources, and other banking functions. Moreover, they had direct access to the Safavid court. Often the shahs granted the rights of royal merchants as well as diplomatic assignments in political or economic dealings with Europe and Russia to Armenian businessmen. In regard to the gem trade, the Armenian agents cooperated with the most famous jewellers at that time: Jean-Baptiste Tavernier and Jean Chardin. The two Huguenots supplied courts in Europe and Asia.[13] In 1688, for instance, a trade agreement was reached between the English East India Company and Armenian merchants that had been arranged by Jean Chardin. New Julfa emerged as the centre of complex diaspora and network structures.[14] In order to establish an information network, agents and correspondents were placed in strategic locations in Asia and Europe. Constantly updated information made extremely high profits possible. An effective trade practice represented the Armenian custom of offering valuable gifts to rulers in order to achieve political and economic privileges. As a result, the Armenian merchants were allowed to trade from New Julfa through the Ottoman territory even during numerous military conflicts with Persia.

Venice and Livorno were the most important headquarters of the Armenian trading networks in Italy. While Venice served as a particular link to the Levant, the Ottoman Empire, Persia and India, Livorno connected the Italian markets with Vienna, Hungary, Poland and Russia, as well as Africa, the West Indies and India. In Venice, for instance, the Armenians were not allowed to process diamonds but only to trade them. The grand dukes of Tuscany, however, granted privileges to promote trade in Pisa and Livorno.[15] Already in 1551, Cosimo I had invited Levantine merchants to settle in Livorno. The trade privileges were extended with the so-called *Livornine* by Ferdinando I in 1591 and 1593.[16] Therefore the port of Livorno attracted many Armenian and Persian merchants. The Venetian Senate responded to the increasing migration of Armenians to Livorno only in 1650 by reducing customs relating to the silk trade.[17] In 1603

Ferdinando I had granted the Pisa-based Broccardi family the monopoly for trading and processing coral. This privilege was valid for the whole grand duchy and also included the periods of fairs, thus excluding all other merchants. At the end of the 1650s, in order to launch new potential earnings and aware of their strong economic position, Armenian merchants requested the privilege to trade coral abroad, especially in India. Their request was granted, and a commercial basis for the lucrative exchange of Mediterranean coral and Indian diamonds was established and culminated in the eighteenth century.[18]

The Scerimans: An Armenian Family of Merchant Bankers

The Scerimans were an Armenian merchant family with origins in Old Julfa. Aga Murat, the patriarch of the family, was among the Armenians deported by Shah Abbas I in 1604 and settled in New Julfa. The Scerimans represented the wealthiest and most influential family among Catholic Armenians in New Julfa. They held high-ranking state, military and religious offices.[19] In the mid-seventeenth century they made every effort to expand the family's wealth and influence. Zaccaria, a son of Sarat, served, for example, as a royal merchant for Shah Suleiman I. In 1659 Zaccaria travelled to Moscow for negotiations and offered to Tsar Alexei I a gold-plated silver throne that was decorated with thousands of diamonds and precious stones; it was worth about 80,000 ducats. By means of this gift, the Scerimans presented themselves as exclusive gem merchants. As intended, Zaccaria obtained several exemptions and trade privileges from the tsar.[20] Among these, Julfan merchants were granted the right to export silk to Europe via Russia.

The Sceriman family in New Julfa played a significant role in the domestic and international commerce of Persia by taking advantage of their contacts within and outside the country. They had business branches in Venice, Livorno, Rome, Amsterdam, Cadiz, Paris, Vienna, Moscow, Constantinople, Basra, Bagdad, Madras and Pegu (present-day Bago in Myanmar).[21] Their family venture was organized in the traditional Armenian way, and therefore as a trade company. It was headed by the father or, in his absence, by his eldest son, and each male member of the family owned a specific share of the company. As long as the company existed, the profits were accumulated in the capital, and all family members received an annual pension in order to cover their living expenses. Although individual family members were allowed to invest parts of their own savings independently, their complete separation from the family business was not accepted.[22] Junior members were sent to all-important emporia in order to gain trade experiences. Moreover, this practice served to permanently update the headquarters with information about market developments abroad. Consequently, trading activities could be adapted to any changes in demand or supply. In this fashion, profits of up to 500 and 600 per cent could be achieved.[23]

The success of their trade activities was based upon a large network of factors working for the company. It was a centralized network with New Julfa as coordinating headquarters, which cooperated closely with Venice after part of the family had moved to the lagoon. The Scerimans in New Julfa managed imports from India and exports to Europe as well as general accounting until the division of the company in 1717.[24] Unlike most Armenian merchants from Julfa who specialized in the silk trade with Europe, the Scerimans operated mainly as diamond and gem merchants. Their branches were located strategically at the most important centres for trading diamonds and jewels: Pegu for rubies, and Madras as well as Surat for diamonds. In addition, their headquarters in New Julfa provided pearls acquired in the Persian Gulf.

Venice and the Gem Trade

As early as the eighth century Venice was famous for its gem trade, and from the thirteenth century onwards it also became an important centre for trading and processing diamonds. The basic techniques of diamond finishing were developed in India and then transferred to Venice, from where they spread to Paris, Augsburg and Flanders.[25] During the sixteenth century Venice lost its leadership in the diamond trade to Antwerp, from where it shifted to Amsterdam in the seventeenth century. Nonetheless, it maintained its important position in the processing of diamonds.[26] In 1680 the Venetian diamond cutter Vincenzo Peruzzi invented the brilliant 58-facet cut. This new design was immediately very successful and increased the demand for diamonds.[27] In the following decades Venice became the most important European centre for processing precious stones.[28] For a long time the lagoon metropolis enjoyed a favourable strategic position by linking Europe with the markets in Persia and India via its Levantine trade. Until 1728, when the first consignment of Brazilian diamonds reached Lisbon, the mines of Golconda in India were the only suppliers of these precious stones.[29] As the Venetian diamond trade with India used the routes via Ormus and Aleppo, the exploitation of the Atlantic sea routes by the Portuguese had no negative impact on this particular business. On the contrary, Venice was the European centre for the goldsmith's art, and rough diamonds were in such high demand that the city's artisans were compelled to buy more of them from Antwerp and Lisbon.[30] The Scerimans responded to this development by intensifying their commercial relations with Venice, and of course this fact strengthened their decision to migrate. Similarly, when the Venetian market for diamonds began to decline the family transferred part of their activities to Amsterdam and Paris.[31]

The Venetian Sceriman Branch and its Trading Activities

Since the 1650s the Scerimans had intensified their trade relations with Europe, in particular with Italy. Gasparo, a son of Sarat, travelled twice throughout France, Holland and Italy, where he spent long periods in Venice, Livorno and Rome.[32] Already by 1646, his father, Sarat, had converted to the Roman Catholic faith. During his travels in Italy, Gasparo had been instructed in Roman Catholicism, and after his return to New Julfa he exerted a strong religious influence on his relatives. By 1685 as many as eleven members of the family had converted. Basilio, one of Gasparo's sons, was even sent to the Urban College in Rome in 1692 and became a priest in 1707.[33] The family's conversion was crucial to its success in Europe. In 1696 Pope Innocent XII granted the whole Sceriman family full citizenship of Rome as well as trading privileges for the ports of Civitavecchia and Ancona in order to promote the commercial activities in the Papal States.[34] The papal bull paved the way to access to the courts and ruling classes in Europe. Thus the Scerimans strengthened their commerce in luxury goods. As a result of their personal relations and financial support, they also received privileges, citizenships and noble titles in other territories.[35] As early as 1613, the Scerimans owned a house in Venice that was located in Corte dei Pignoli. This was near St Mark's Square and the Frezzaria, which represented one of the main business thoroughfares. In addition, it was close to the political centre and its offices. The Scerimans used the building in Corte dei Pignoli as a warehouse as well as a temporary residence for their agents and family members. In 1693, for instance, Nazar, a son of Murat, lived there.[36] Until the beginning of the Afghan invasions in 1722, however, New Julfa remained the family's headquarters.

As a result of increasing pressure on the part of Shah Sultan Hosayn in the 1690s, the three brothers Gasparo, Marcara and Murat decided to migrate to Venice. There they settled with their families between 1694 and 1699. The Scerimans tried to facilitate their integration into the host society by means of financial investments. Between 1692 and 1698 the brothers Nazar and Seriman offered substantial loans to the Venetian Republic in order to finance the war against the Ottomans: 200,000 ducats in 1692, 150,000 ducats in 1697 and 170,000 ducats in 1698.[37] A further 110,000 and 90,000 ducats were given to the Republic for grain provisions. Their investments amounted to a total of 720,000 ducats and showed their extraordinary financial power.[38] In addition, Marcara strengthened his standing in Venice by making a personal loan of 200,000 ducats, also destined for the war against the Turks.[39] Marcara had two sons, one of whom, Diodato, migrated to Venice shortly after 1701 and married into a wealthy Venetian citizen family, the Tornimbens, in 1705.[40] On settling in Venice, he possessed a respectable capital of 134,000 ducats, while his wife Elisabetta added a dowry of 107,201 ducats.[41] Diodato's brother Emanuel remained in New Julfa, where he pursued a career as an ambassador. He was sent first to the Russian court and then in 1725 to the Porte.[42]

Gasparo invested 100,000 ducats in loans to the Venetian Republic at an interest rate of 4.75 per cent. The sum was divided up into several public deposits relating to meat, salt, wine and tobacco.[43] In 1698 two of Gasparo's sons, Giacomo and Stefano, were also present in Venice.[44] However, shortly after the turn of the century, the elder of the two brothers, Giacomo, was sent to Amsterdam in order to manage the family's diamond trade there. He operated with a power of attorney and the seed capital given to him by his father. In 1707 Gasparo divided his wealth, which amounted to 401,000 ducats: Giacomo, residing in Amsterdam, received a quarter of this sum at his disposal, while the other three-quarters remained in Gasparo's hands.[45] In the accounting records for the year 1707, Giacomo noted that he had available 98,813 ducats as well as additional cash and bills of exchange.[46] Moreover, he possessed coins such as *cechini, filippi, genovine* and *lirete* that served for his international trade activities and were worth 28,450 ducats.[47] Giacomo's commercial and banking activities relied on a Eurasian family network. He operated together with his cousins Sarat, Pietro and Giacomo, sons of Murat, as well as Diodato, son of Marcara, who all lived in Venice. Furthermore, he collaborated with his cousin Veligian, son of Michele, and Veligian's brother-in-law, Arutun Acravenz, who both resided in Livorno. Giacomo added the debts accumulated by Arutun to Veligian's account, and so a cross-holding related to commercial activities run by more distant relatives is becoming apparent.[48] Though Giacomo's brother Basilio had become a priest in Rome, he was still involved in the family business.[49] Sarat, son of Murat, acted as a guarantor for Venetian noblemen. Alberto Romiero, for example, borrowed 900 ducats from Giacomo. Romiero's guarantor Sarat consigned 500 ducats as well as a yellow brilliant to his cousin.[50] Sometimes a pledge was also given for small loans, for example of 60 ducats.[51] Giacomo bought diamonds, emeralds and pearls from his cousin Acop (Giacomo), another son of Murat, who travelled between Isfahan and Venice. Evidence of regular gem supplies by the family members residing in New Julfa is found in the fact that the brothers Marcara, Murat and Michele made high payments to the headquarters.[52] In a balance of accounts prepared by Giacomo's brother Stefano in 1712, 11,000 ducats are recorded as the profit from pearl sales.[53] Furthermore, the Scerimans collaborated with Armenian merchants who were not their immediate kin, such as Caciattur di Menazachan and Arapiet Darvissenz. The latter was indebted to Giacomo and repaid his debts in part with wax and *corami* (Venetian dialect for *cuoi d'oro*, a wall decoration made of gilded leather), which Giacomo sold.[54] Caciattur, however, operated as an agent as well as in partnership with Gasparo. Together they owned a stock of merchandise at the Rio Barbaro in Venice. When Gasparo sold the building, he kept three-quarters of the goods and the remaining quarter was given to Caciattur.[55] In contrast to the numerous Armenian connections, in the 1707 account records only one Jewish contact is specified: a certain Lunel who was charged as agent.[56] In 1713 Giacomo sold a diamond to a Jew called Valenzin.[57] Only in 1717 did he mention another one: a banker named Levi.[58] Therefore it seems that contrary to the family branch in Livorno, in Venice the Scerimans did not cooperate often with Jews. Outside of Venice, customers in Verona, Bergamo, Florence and Rome were specified.[59] Presumably the Scerimans had clients either in India or with an Oriental taste, since they offered jewels backed with foil to enhance the glittering effect.[60]

Among the Venetian business partners, there were bankers such as Betti & Antonetti and Antonio del Teglia as well as numerous members of noble families.[61] The records show examples not only of commercial ties but also of kinship between these families. The lawyer Bernardo Nave, for instance, belonged to a wealthy, ennobled family of spice traders. He wedded Cornelia Corner, and his niece Elena was married to Tomaso Querini.[62] The Sceriman family's account books list not only Bernardo but also his brothers-in-law Giovanni Battista and Cornelio Corner.[63] There is evidence in Alberto Gozzi's last will that Bernardo was his close friend and distant relative. Gozzi himself was a wealthy silk merchant and succeeded in joining the Venetian patriciate.[64] He reconstructed the Palazzo Dolce at Santi Apostoli, which Stefano Sceriman bought from Gozzi's widow in 1727.[65] Until this acquisition, the whole family resided in the Palazzo Dolfin Bollani at the Campo Santa Marina, which was near both of the city's commercial areas, St Mark's Square and the Rialto. Gasparo had bought this residence and left it to his nephews Diodato and Emanuel while Stefano moved to the Palazzo Dolce.[66] After Stefano's marriage to Lucrezia Malatesta in 1715, the accounts for 1717 also show business relations with the Malatesta family.[67] Two noblemen and business partners served as witness to the marriage: Sebastiano Venier and Gian Piero Pasqualigo. Stefano and Lucrezia had four sons and two daughters. Among the godfathers of their children were also business partners who belonged to the Venetian patriciate: Carlo Contarini and Giandomenico Ruzzini.[68] One son and both daughters joined noble families by marriage: Basilio wedded Marquess Marianna Dalla Torre, and Eleonora was married to Silvestro Valier; in 1733 their sister Maria Aspasia wedded Giorgio Corner.[69] Giorgio was a nephew of Pietro Capello, from whom the Scerimans had rented an apartment at San Giovanni in Laterano.[70] Diodato, too, succeeded in arranging marriages into noble families for both of his daughters: Elena wedded Francesco Minotto but shortly after died in childbed;[71] her sister Regina married Giorgio Bembo in 1725.[72] As Giorgio's grandfather Paolo Sarotti was a sugar trader, who temporarily resided as Venetian envoy (*residente*) in London, a preceding mercantile relationship with the Sceriman family seems most likely.[73] Thus it can be stated that kinship created commercial ties, and the latter in turn could result in family links. Finally, both types of connections reconfirmed each other.

In Amsterdam, Giacomo commissioned cutters and polishers to process the rough diamonds he had acquired. He focused on large, high-quality stones with a high purity grade. In 1707 his stock comprised jewels and gems worth 24,190 ducats. Apart from very exclusive jewels such as, for example, a pearl necklace for 3,600 ducats or diamond earrings for 2,200 ducats, Giacomo also offered an extraordinary diamond with a weight of 51 *grani* worth 9,000 ducats.[74] However, he did not succeed in selling it. Therefore the diamond was still listed in the 1718 inventory and its value had fallen to 7,500 ducats.[75] A comparison with the price of the Palazzo Dolce at Santi Apostoli, which Stefano bought for 11,000 ducats, shows the high value of these jewels.[76] In 1714 Giacomo proudly wrote to his father that he had commissioned the cut of two brilliants, each weighing 41 *grani*. These stones seemed so perfect to him that he desired to offer them to the emperor in Vienna for 14,000 *ongari*.[77] The Scerimans were on good terms with the Habsburg court, since Leopold I had granted them the title of counts of Hungary in 1699.[78] However, due to the tense situation in Vienna regarding the succession in Spain, Giacomo did not present the gems to Charles VI. He could not find another purchaser either, since this pair of brilliants is still listed in the inventory of his jewels that was made in 1717.[79] As Gasparo preferred more solid transactions, he did not agree with his son's ambitions. Besides, as a result of local differences in taste, large gems could be sold at a much higher price in Indian markets. Consequently, other diamond dealers acquired stones in India, had them finished in Europe and then sent them back in order to sell them to Indian customers.[80] A dispute between father and son began, which ten years later resulted in another division of Gasparo's wealth as well as a separation from Giacomo's business activities. In 1718 Gasparo appointed his second eldest son, Stefano, chief representative.[81] On this occasion, he asked Giacomo to consign inventories and accounts of the family's commercial affairs since 1707.[82]

As requested, Giacomo provided several inventories of his father's stock as well as accounts for the period between 1707 and 1717.[83] The related account books give evidence of sales and acquisitions for a period that was generally said to show the first signs of a recession in the diamond market.[84] Gasparo's customers in Venice mainly belonged to the most influential and noble families, including the Barbaro, Barbarigo, Giustinian, Corner, Venier, Morosini, Soranzo, Malipiero, Trevisan, Contarini and Ruzzini families. They did not only buy or lease jewels but also took out loans. Beside diamonds, emeralds and pearls, other luxury goods were sold, such as Ardassa silk, damask, black velvet, *corami* and silverware from Augsburg.[85] Gasparo was assisted in his transactions not only by agents but also by noblemen or jewellers. These middlemen received an average commission of about 150 ducats.[86] Between 1707 and 1717 Gasparo sold diamonds and diamond jewellery for 50,000 ducats as well as pearl jewellery for 14,000 ducats. Jewels worth 25,000 ducats remained in his possession. On the acquisition side, he bought diamonds for 12,600 ducats and had to pay commissions amounting to 5,300 ducats. Of receipts, which totalled 64,000 ducats, 16,000 ducats were related to goods acquired within the aforementioned period. The rest of the jewels were already in stock in 1707.[87]

The large stock of jewels held at the beginning of the eighteenth century and the following diminution of purchases until 1717 confirmed the generally observed development of the diamond trade. There was less demand in Venice because of the expanding diamond trade in other markets such as Amsterdam.[88] The balance, however, was positive. Moreover, the incipient decline of the Venetian diamond trade had no negative effects on the family's individual economic situation. The Scerimans had extraordinary capital resources at their disposal. In addition to the large loans mentioned above and Gasparo's great fortune, his brother Murat's cash holdings alone amounted to 254,500 ducats.[89] Thus the Scerimans were able to adapt the commercial strategies of their activities to changing markets. Giacomo, for example, moved to Amsterdam in order to strengthen the family's diamond trade. His cousin David succeeded in this business in Livorno. The Venetian family branch, however, did not completely abandon gem trading. Giovanni Stefano, son of Salvatore and nephew of David, continued to deal in diamonds and rubies but was not particularly successful. Evidence of his deals can be found in the documents related to legal proceedings from the 1730s to the 1750s.[90] The more successful and wealthy family members in Venice invested their capital in real estate by purchasing large areas of land around Chioggia, Verona, Padua and Este.[91] Moreover, the Scerimans focused on the banking business, which guaranteed high profits.[92]

The Sceriman Family's Commercial Activities in Livorno

While settling in Venice, the Sceriman family also established intense commercial relations with Livorno.[93] As mentioned above, the port city belonged to the most important markets in Italy and granted financial privileges for trading and insuring goods. Moreover, it offered a rather liberal climate for religious minorities. Thus the numerous foreigners also included an Armenian diaspora from the beginning of the seventeenth century onwards.[94]

In 1700 Stefano, son of Gasparo, explored the possibilities for trading in Livorno. After his return to Venice, he recommended that some family members should reside there in order to strengthen the family's commercial activities. Three of his cousins were therefore sent to Livorno. Nazar, son of Murat, and Veligian, son of Michele, acquired a representative palace with three floors that was situated close to the port as well as the city centre.[95] In August 1702 they established a trading firm there. In the same year Diodato, son of Marcara, opened another trading house in the neighbourhood.[96] This strategically favourable area between the Fortezza Nuova and the Piazza Grande was preferred by Armenian merchants. Thus the wealthy Mirman family also settled there.[97] This immediate proximity strengthened cooperation within the Armenian network.

The members of the Sceriman family residing in Livorno operated in agreement with their fathers who conducted the business in Venice. All commercial activities were based on a clan system, which was typical for Armenian families. In this way, the family branches living in Europe were in permanent contact with the headquarters in New Julfa. Through these headquarters each office was linked with all other locations, including caravan centres such as Aleppo. As a result, the Scerimans were able to create a worldwide trading network that facilitated import and export transactions between Europe and Asia. The diamond trade in particular benefited from this mercantile system. It connected Madras with Amsterdam via Venice, and Surat with Lisbon and London via Livorno. After the family settled in Livorno, the Adriatic route, usually departing from Smyrna and ending in Venice,[98] was extended by connecting their trade firms with Atlantic locations such as Lisbon and the West Indies. New shipping routes to India could be used if they were considered more profitable. David Sceriman, for example, travelled after his move to Livorno often via Lisbon to Goa in order to purchase diamonds. For a few years the Scerimans in Livorno had been shareholders of ships together with other Armenian merchants. But then, in around 1710, they sold their interests in order to be more flexible in trading.[99] By chartering ships they could avoid obligations towards partners and commissioners. Thus during their travels they were able to respond immediately to market developments abroad by changing their routes. This practice corresponded to the legal basis of the contracts stipulated with their agents who accompanied the goods. The so-called *jughier*, which means 'partner' in Armenian, was based on trust and flexibility. The travelling partner received a certain amount of capital in order to buy goods. He decided the route and was authorized to sell goods during his journey if market developments promised a high profit. At the end of journey he had to draw up a detailed account of all purchases and sales. Out of the returns, he received one-third as remuneration.[100] It was also common practice for the merchants themselves to travel, as David often did.

In 1706 Murat and Michele wound up their company and split their jointly owned properties in Venice and Livorno. Nonetheless, they continued their commercial activities in both cities. This was convenient since they dealt in the same commodities, and both cities were supplied from the same locations in Asia. In order to give other family members the opportunity to gain mercantile experience, Nazar and Veligian returned to Venice and were each replaced by their respective brothers, Pietro and David. Pietro traded mainly in luxury textiles. He bought raw silk in Persia, which he consigned to Florentine weaving mills. He then commissioned satin draperies of specific qualities and colours. In doing so, Pietro was able to obtain a discount of 48 per cent on the final products, which served to cover his expenditures and provide him with an asset. He reduced transport costs by a special agreement with the shipowners, consisting of a kind of 'standing order' for chartering vessels that enabled him to ship the goods at any time at a fixed price.[101] The main business of the Scerimans, however, remained the gem trade. David managed the trading firm in Livorno and became an extraordinarily successful merchant and financier. First, he operated with a full power of attorney. From 1719 onwards, after the death of both his elder brother Veligian and his father Michele, he conducted his business independently.[102] As Venice was the most important centre for processing gems, David maintained strong ties with the family residing there, even when he became head of the company in Livorno. He also established cooperation with gem finishing specialists in Livorno in order to respond to fashion trends.[103] Apart from merchandising diamonds and other precious stones, David focused on the coral trade, which was connected in various ways to the gem trade. He benefited from the fact that Livorno was the centre for trading and processing coral. Hence David set up a workshop where coral was decorated with gems and *pietre dure*, thus making coral an exclusive luxury object and allowing him to meet the high demand for these goods. David increased his profit by buying raw coral from Tuscan fishermen in the port and using precious stones from his own gem trading activities. In 1723 his was one of the most important coral workshops in Livorno.[104] The commerce of raw coral was very lucrative too. The items purchased from the coral fishers were sold as individual pieces and sent not only within Europe but also to the Levant as well as to India.[105] As only specialists were able to value the qualities of gems and coral with precision, this market was risky for merchants and customers. David was an expert in the matter, yet his knowledge did not prevent him from having lawsuits taken out against him. Sometimes the quality of the consignment did not match the quality of the sample on which the order was based.[106] David also at times delivered goods of a more minor quality than that of the sample, or took advantage of customers' lack of expertise by demanding prices that were too high.[107] In 1741 an agent of the Scerimans even visited the French court in order to sell an inferior diamond to Louis XV with fraudulent intent.[108]

Like the family branch in Venice, David established a banking business. He lent money with rates of up to 26 per cent and also drew ordinary bills of exchange as well as a special type used by Armenians.[109] The latter were paid out by his relatives in New Julfa.[110] David also made loans by accepting diamonds in pledge. This practice was first introduced by his cousin Giacomo residing in Amsterdam. It had resulted in a serious conflict between Giacomo and his father

Gasparo, who did not agree with this kind of credit. When Giacomo disobeyed Gasparo's order to return to Venice, he was excluded from the family firm in 1717. Nevertheless he remained in Amsterdam and continued to trade gems on his own account.[111] Since David was the head of the Livorno company, he could operate independently and took his own decisions concerning commercial practices. He was also able to deal in gold coins and foreign currencies, which were needed for international trade activities. For gold coins, a commission of 7 per cent had to be paid. The exchange business provided a variable profit that was based on the difference between the exchange rate and the actual weight of the coins.[112] David always had large sums of cash at his disposal. Trade in luxury goods required payments in cash or in exchange for other exclusive products. He purchased coral, for instance, in exchange for diamonds, silk and cash.[113] In general he preferred to use cash payments for his transactions, thereby obtaining a discount of 2 per cent.[114]

Of the Armenian merchants in Livorno, David was the wealthiest.[115] Until the decline of the diamond market around 1730, which was caused by initiating consignments from Brazilian mines, he made a fortune by dealing in diamonds from India. The privilege for trading diamonds that was granted to the Armenians by the Mughals in 1688 was no longer respected by the Dutch and English East India Companies. Thus David had no qualms about smuggling. In addition to his 'official' gem trading activities, he also purchased contraband stones on which he could make profits of up to 600 per cent.[116] In 1725, for example, he charged agents with joining his confidants who resided in Surat and Madras. In these two cities the trade of diamonds supplied by the Golconda mines took place. Obviously, the true intention of such an enterprise had to be disguised.[117] Therefore the agents' journey to India was detoured. It took them from Livorno via Marseilles, Lyon, Paris and Calais to London, where they embarked for Surat.

David stipulated a *jughier* contract with three Armenians. He knew one of them, Giovan Battista Giamal, from Livorno.[118] The other two agents, Pietro di Saffar Nuri and Menazacham di Ahan, were business partners of the Venetian family branch.[119] Though Giamal had failed in his own commercial activities, David appointed him head of the mission to India. He provided Giamal with capital amounting to 8,000 *pezze*, which was to be paid out at Basra. Illegal transactions required cash. The English and Dutch East Indian Companies had forbidden travelling with cash within their territories in order to control the whole trade and to tax goods. Thus all legal transactions had to be paid by bills of exchange.

Unfortunately, David's trust was abused. In Lyon Giamal bought silk and other textiles, which he intended to sell on his own account in London. As Giamal had no personal capital at his disposal, he paid for it with a draft drawn on David in Livorno without the latter's consent. Therefore David deprived Giamal of the mission after the agent's arrival in London. While Giamal remained there, the other two agents continued their journey to India. In London, they were assisted by two Sephardic correspondents who belonged to the Franco family. The Francos were Livorno-based merchants on very good terms with the English East India Company. They owned a large number of ships in Livorno as well as in Venice. One of the main routes operated by their vessels ran from Livorno via Lisbon to Surat.[120] Jacob and Abraham Franco, both residing in London, shipped coral and diamonds on David's account to and from India.[121] They provided from the English East India Company an authorization to ship a cargo of coral and to bring two Indians back home. The captain and crew of the vessel were paid for accepting the two Armenian agents as the pretended Indians. Thus Pietro and Menazacham arrived in Surat where they met the factors of the Sceriman family, who supplied them with rough diamonds purchased on the black market. Following the acquisition, the agents could decide on which way they would return to Livorno. Along each route, the Scerimans had placed confidants who managed free passage at customs by corrupting the officials.[122] If the agents did not pass through Basra, where the family had a distribution centre for precious stones, or did not lucratively sell a part of the goods during their journey, they consigned the whole quantity of diamonds in Livorno. There David commissioned their finishing. After a number of negative experiences with diamond cutters who spoiled the stones, he stipulated special contracts. The diamonds were sold to the cutters with the obligation to repurchase them after they had been successfully processed.[123] A part of the gems were then sent to Venice or any other market that might have promised higher profits. Due to the Scerimans' global network of correspondents, the family was kept continuously up to date with market developments and current prices and thus enabled to take instantaneous decisions regarding transactions. In addition, a share of the diamonds was used for jewellery, which was sold to customers in Livorno and the surrounding area. Occasionally David leased jewellery. This practice was risky if the client failed to pay.[124] Another business fraught with risks was represented by the illegal purchase of diamonds, since it was not guaranteed that they would reach the commissioner. Nevertheless, if the stones arrived safely, the profit was so high that it offset any eventual losses. Legally conducted deals based on *jughier* contracts already resulted in extraordinary profits. Once, for example, David's agent Pietro di Saffar Nuri set out on his journey with a sum of 600 *tumani* and returned with 3,500 – a profit of almost 600 per cent.[125] From the journey that Pietro undertook together with Menazacham, a profit of 500 per cent was expected.[126] On the other hand, financial losses could also result from the irregular business conduct of relatives. In 1709 David, together with his cousin Pietro, ordered goods – probably diamonds – from the Indian merchant Zorab di Alucan, who sent them via Goa to Livorno. As Pietro never paid his share, Zorab allowed some of David's bills of exchange to be confiscated ten years after the order.[127] After Pietro's death David was the only member of the Sceriman family still operating in Livorno. Though the diamond market recorded a gradual decline from the 1730s onwards, he continued trading with precious stones. However, like his cousins in Venice, he expanded his banking activities and acquired properties in the city as well as in the countryside. David dealt in all types of loans: risky ones with high rates of interest and safer ones that were guaranteed by jewels or property.[128] The family branches in Livorno and Venice permanently exchanged experiences and information about customers in order to minimize the risk connected with their banking business. On the other hand, failed payments secured by pledges offered a favourable occasion to acquire properties or rental incomes. In 1729 Pietro da Silva, for instance, had purchased jewels on credit and given in pledge the rental of an estate in the country. When he failed to repay the loan, David obtained the income. As this rent, which he received, was not sufficient to pay the interest rate of 6 per cent, he became the owner of the property in 1741.[129] Strong ties between the family members in Livorno and Venice are also evidenced by David's last will, which he made in March 1757 and which preceded his death by four months.[130] Being without progeny, he appointed two nephews as his heirs: Paolo, son of Leon, and Giovanni Stefano, son of Salvatore. Paolo had been living in David's house for some years and had assisted him with the business.[131] Paolo's cousin Giovanni Stefano resided in Venice, where he was involved in the gem trade. Unlike most members of the Sceriman family, he was not very successful and had accumulated several debts. Thus he allowed his cousin Diodato, son of Michele, to pay a debt of 10,517 ducats and gave him jewellery and diamonds worth 16,082 ducats in pledge. In 1769 Diodato moved from Venice to Livorno and used this jewellery as seed capital in order to enter into commercial activities.[132] His decision to settle in Livorno was sound because, since the 1760s, the Tuscan port had regained its importance as a trading centre and turnover hub.

Usually Armenian merchants did not establish strong ties with non-Armenians but instead operated within their own commercial networks. The Scerimans, in contrast, had long-lasting business relations with the Sephardic Franco family that was based in Livorno. It is likely that this collaboration resulted from pragmatic considerations. The Armenian community in the Tuscan port was not only smaller than the Jewish one but had also weaker ties with both England and Portugal.[133] As the main part of the coral trade to India was managed through these countries, the Scerimans were able to strengthen their commercial activities in this field by cooperating with Jewish partners. The Franco family used its office in London for the exchange of Mediterranean coral and Indian diamonds. Jacob and Abraham Franco served the Scerimans as correspondents in London and provided them with information about market trends. As mentioned above, they assisted them in organizing illegal cargos to India, if necessary. In general, however, Jacob and Abraham legally shipped coral and diamonds from and to India on account of the Scerimans. The two brothers operated with powers of attorney, which were granted to them by the family's headquarters in Livorno.[134] Naturally, David also had commercial relations with their brothers Joseph and Raphael, who resided in the Tuscan port and managed the Franco firm. In 1735, for example, they financed the expedition of several coral boats to Cap d'Agde in Languedoc as a joint venture.[135] Since the 1720s Joseph and Raphael had owned one of the most important coral workshops in Livorno.[136] Though they were also David's business rivals, this had no negative impact on their cooperation. The Livorno market offered sufficient opportunities to benefit from coral trade since the port had emerged as the worldwide leader in coral trading and finishing.

Conclusion

The Scerimans were an Armenian family of merchant bankers who had resided in New Julfa since the beginning of the seventeenth century. They specialized in the long-distance trading of luxury goods. In contrast to other Julfan merchants, who operated mainly as silk traders, the Scerimans became famous gem dealers who supplied courts in Europe and Asia. Retaining their headquarters in New Julfa, they established a worldwide commercial network with factors residing in all-important markets. All family members were involved in the business and established company branches in different locations depending on the current political and mercantile trends. The younger members were sent abroad to learn the business of trading. All collaborators – family members, factors and agents travelling on account of the Scerimans – continuously provided the headquarters with information about market shifts and price changes. As the traditional Armenian trade system was characterized by a high degree of flexibility, open transactions could be adapted to changing market structures. This made profits of up to 600 per cent possible. The Scerimans showed flexibility not only in terms of their trade practices but also with regard to their residences. So they moved to the locations that promised to strengthen their gem trading activities. When Venice became the centre for finishing diamonds, they settled there. Since Livorno had emerged as the main centre for trading and processing coral, the Scerimans established a company branch in this port as well. As the focus of diamond trading and finishing shifted to Amsterdam, they sent a family member there. However, when London acquired a share of the diamond trade, they did not settle there, preferring instead to commission correspondents and cooperate with other networks, such as the Sephardic one.

In Persia the Scerimans had received trade privileges, served as court financiers and were granted titles of nobility. When, at the end of the seventeenth century, the political situation in New Julfa changed, parts of the family moved to Venice, where they had established commercial relations for at least eight decades. Nonetheless, the Venetian branch of the family maintained intense contact with the headquarters in New Julfa. Though the Sceriman continued to follow Armenian traditions regarding their business and family affairs, they sought to integrate themselves into the upper class of Venetian society. Thus they stressed their Catholic faith and made large loans to the Venetian Republic as well as to several European courts in order to obtain privileges and titles of nobility. They also arranged marriages into noble families, sometimes by accepting less profitable matrimonial agreements, as in the case when Stefano wedded Lucrezia, who descended from an ancient noble family.[137] More often their partners belonged to wealthy families who were involved in trade as well. Therefore kinship increased mercantile activities and expanded the commercial network. The opposite happened even more frequently: business relations resulted in family ties. In both cases the commercial network was strengthened. With gradual integration into the host society, ethnic ties became less important. Evidence of the Scerimans' social standing is also provided by their cultural assimilation. They adapted to the lifestyle of the local nobility. When Diodato came into property of a country house near Riscossa, which belonged to Elisabetta's dowry, he transformed the building into a prestigious typical Venetian villa.[138] Other residences, such as the Palazzo Dolce acquired by Stefano, were also renovated in accordance with the prevailing taste of the upper class. They commissioned the same renowned artists who worked for the noble families. There is even evidence of a kind of artistic network, which confirms the ties based on business and kinship. In addition, the members of the Sceriman family who settled in Venice and Livorno followed the same economic strategies as the local upper classes: they had accumulated wealth through their trading activities, yet when profit margins from international commerce diminished they expanded their banking business and invested in property.

NOTES

Introduction

1. D. Calabi and S. Turk Christensen (eds), *Cities and Cultural Exchange in Europe, 1400–1700* (Cambridge: Cambridge University Press, 2007).

2. S. R. Lopez, *The Commercial Revolution of the Middle Ages, 950–1350* (Englewood Cliffs, NJ: Prentice Hall, 1971); for a short overview, see M. Fusaro, *Reti commerciali e traffici globali in età moderna* (Rome and Bari: Laterza, 2008).

3. The literature is extensive; some recent collections include V. N. Zakharov, G. Harlaftis and O. Katsiardi-Hering (eds), *Merchant Colonies in the Early Modern Period* (London: Pickering & Chatto, 2012); A. Crespo Solana (ed.), *Comunidades transnacionales. Colonias de mercaderes extranjeros en el Mundo Atlántico (1500–1830)* (Aranjuez: Doce Calles, 2010).

4. P. Duguid, 'Introduction: The Changing Organization of Industry', *Business History Review*, 79 (2005), pp. 453–66, on p. 459.

5. M. Casson, 'Networks in Economic and Business History: A Theoretical Perspective', in P. Fernández Pérez and M. B. Rose (eds), *Innovation and Entrepreneurial Networks in Europe* (New York and London: Routledge, 2010), pp. 14–40; H. Berghoff and J. Sydow (eds), *Unternehmerische Netzwerke. Eine historische Organisationsform mit Zukunft?* (Stuttgart: Kohlhammer, 2007).

6. See for example P. D. McLean, *The Art of the Network: Strategic Interaction and Patronage in Renaissance Florence* (Durham, NC: Duke University Press, 2007).

7. D. Hancock, 'The Trouble with the Networks: Managing the Scots' Early-Modern Madeira Trade', *Business History Review*, 79 (2005), pp. 467–91.

8. See M. Burkhardt in this volume and his *Der hansische Bergenhandel im Spätmittelalter. Handel – Kaufleute – Netzwerke* (Cologne, Weimar and Vienna: Böhlau, 2009).

9. D. Hancock, *Oceans of Wine: Madeira and the Emergence of American Trade and Taste* (New Haven, CT: Yale University Press, 2009).

10. For some systematic considerations, see W. von Stromer, 'Wirtschaftsgeschichte und Personengeschichte', *Zeitschrift für Historische Forschung*, 2 (1975), pp. 31–42.

11. R. de Roover, *The Rise and the Decline of the Medici Bank, 1397–1494* (Cambridge, MA: Harvard University Press, 1963).

12. F. Melis, *Aspetti della Vita Economica Medievale (Studi nell'archivio Datini di Prato)* (Siena: Monte dei Paschi di Siena, 1962).

13. On the extensive literature on the Fuggers, see M. Häberlein, *The Fuggers of Augsburg: Pursuing Wealth and Honor in Renaissance Germany* (Charlottesville, VA: University of Virginia Press, 2012).

14. J. Scott, *Social Network Analysis*, 3rd edn (Thousand Oaks, CA and London: SAGE, 2013), pp. 11–39; see also J. Scott and P. J. Carrington (eds), *The SAGE Handbook of Social Network Analysis* (Thousand Oaks, CA and London: SAGE, 2011).

15. See for example the chapters of Müller and Wegener Sleeswijk in C. Lesger and L. Noordegraf (eds), *Entrepreneurs and Entrepreneurship in Early Modern Times: Merchants and Industrialists within the orbit of the Dutch Staple Market* (The Hague: Stichting Hollandse Historische Reeks, 1995); and J. F. Padgett and C. K. Ansell, 'Robust Action and the Rise of the Medici, 1400–1434', *American Journal of Sociology*, 98:6 (1993), pp. 1259–1319.

16. L. Müller, *The Merchant Houses of Stockholm, c. 1640–1800: A Comparative Study of Early-Modern Entrepreneurial Behaviour* (Uppsala: Uppsala University Library, 1998), esp. pp. 221–51.

17. M. Häberlein, *Brüder, Freunde und Betrüger. Soziale Beziehungen, Normen und Konflikte in der Augsburger Kaufmannschaft um die Mitte des 16. Jahrhunderts* (Berlin: Akademie Verlag 1998).

18. David Hancock discussed the analytical value of networks in his 2005 article 'The Trouble with the Networks', but he does not seem to have worked with quantifying analytical approaches; see his *Oceans of Wine*.

19. E. Crailsheim, 'Seville and the European Atlantic Trade: A Network Study of French and Flemish Merchant Communities in Early Modern History (1580–1640)' (PhD dissertation, University of Graz, 2008).

20. Q. Van Dooselaere, *Commercial Agreements and Social Dynamics in Medieval Genoa* (Cambridge: Cambridge University Press, 2009).

21. M. Kalus, *Pfeffer – Kupfer – Nachrichten. Kaufmannsnetzwerke und Handelsstrukturen im europäisch-asiatischen Handel am Ende des 16. Jahrhunderts* (Augsburg: Wißner, 2010).

22. J. Haggerty and S. Haggerty, 'Visual Analytics of an Eighteenth-Century Business Network', *Enterprise and Society*, 11:1 (2009), pp. 1–25.

23. S. Haggerty, 'I Could "Do for the Dickmans": When Family Networks Don't Work', in A. Gestrich and M. Schulte-Beerbühl (eds), *Cosmopolitan Networks in Commerce and Society, 1600–1914* (London: German Historical Institute, 2011), pp. 317–42.

24. A. S. Vieira Ribeiro, 'Mechanisms and Criteria of Cooperation in Trading Networks of the First Global Age: A Case Study of the Simon Ruiz Network, 1557–1597' (PhD dissertation, University of Porto, 2011). See also the project 'Dynamic Complexity of Cooperation-Based Self-Organizing Networks in the First Global Age', at http://www.dyncoopnet-pt.org/ [accessed 1 December 2013], and A. Crespo Solana and D. A. Garcia (eds), 'Self-Organizing Networks and GIS Tools: Cases of Use for the Study of Trading Cooperation (1400–1800)', *Journal of Knowledge Management, Economics and Information Technology* special issue (June 2012).

25. P. Gervais, 'Crédit et filières marchandes au XVIIIe siècle', *Annales. Histoire, Sciences Sociales*, 67:4 (2012), pp. 1011–48.

26. C. S. McWatters and Y. Lemarchand, 'Merchant Networks and Accounting Discourse: The Role of Accounting Transactions in Network Relations', *Accounting History Review*, 23:1 (2013), pp. 49–83.

27. U. C. Ewert and S. Selzer, 'Wirtschaftliche Stärke durch Vernetzung. Zu den Erfolgs-faktoren des hansischen Handels', in M. Häberlein and C. Jeggle (eds), *Praktiken des Handels. Geschäfte und soziale Beziehungen europäischer Kaufleute in Mittelalter und früher Neuzeit* (Konstanz: UVK, 2010), pp. 39–69.

28. For the commerce of the Hanse area, a large amount of data are being systematically col-lected and edited. Most studies are not designed for a social network analysis, and some authors consider their material insufficient: J. Wubs-Mrozwicz, *Traders, Ties and Ten-sions: The Interaction of Lübeckers, Overijsslers and Hollanders in Late Medieval Bergen* (Hilversum: Verloren, 2008), p. 22. See also J. Wubs-Mrozewicz and S. Jenks (eds), *The Hanse in Medieval and Early Modern Europe*, (Leiden, MA: Brill, 2012).

29. C. Jahnke, 'Netzwerke in Handel und Kommunikation an der Wende vom 15. zum 16. Jahrhundert am Beispiel zweier Revaler Kaufleute' (Habilitation, University of Kiel, 2004).

30. Burkhardt, *Der hansische Bergenhandel im Spätmittelalter* and in this volume.

31. D. W. Poeck, *Die Herren der Hanse. Delegierte und Netzwerke* (Frankfurt am Main: Peter Lang, 2010).

32. See the critical assesment in the review of M. Burkhardt, *Zeitschrift für Historische Forschung*, 40 (2013), pp. 285–6.

33. In some cases authors writing on commercial history explicitly note that their material would not allow a historical network analysis: Wubs-Mrozwicz, *Traders, Ties and Ten-sions*, p. 22, and J. Poettering, *Handel, Nation und Religion. Kaufleute zwischen Hamburg und Portugal* (Göttingen: Vandenhoeck & Ruprecht, 2013), pp. 254–7.

34. The idea of structural holes was introduced by R. S. Burt, *Structural Holes: The Social Structure of Competition* (Cambridge MA: Harvard University Press, 1992) and refers to actors that connect to two networks with single ties.

35. Harrison C. White, *Identity and Control: A Structural Theory of Social Action* (Princeton, NJ: Princeton University Press, 1991); a second throughly revised edition appeared as *Identity and Control: How Social Formations Emerge* (Princeton, NJ: Princeton Univer-sity Press, 2008). See also M. Emirbayer and J. Goodwin, 'Network Analysis, Culture, and the Problem of Agency', *American Journal of Sociology*, 99 (1994), pp. 962–93; and M. Emirbayer, 'Manifesto for a Relational Sociology', *American Journal of Sociology*, 103:2 (1997), pp. 281–317; H. Knox, M. Savage and P. Harvey, 'Social Networks and the Study of Relations: Networks as Method, Metaphor and Form', *Economy and Society*, 35:1 (2006), pp. 116–40.

36. See for example McLean, *The Art of the Network*; and A. Mische, 'Relational Sociology, Culture and Agency', in Scott and Carrington (eds), *The SAGE Handbook of Social Net-work Analysis*, pp. 80–97.

37. There is a tendency towards more comprehensive models based on networks; see also J. F. Padgett and W. W. Powell, *The Emergence of Organizations and Markets* (Princeton, NJ: Princeton University Press, 2012).

38. See Chapter 2 in this volume, 'Interactions, Networks, Discourses and Markets' by C. Jeggle.

39. J.-Y. Grenier, 'Une économie de l'indentification. Juste prix et ordre des marchandises dans l'Ancien Régime', in A. Stanziani (ed.), *La qualité des produits en France (XVIIIe–XXe siècles)* (Paris: Belin, 2003), pp. 25–54.

40. See for example F. Trivellato, *The Familiarity of Strangers: The Sephardic Diaspora, Livorno, and Cross-Cultural Trade in the Early Modern Period* (New Haven, CT: Yale University Press, 2009).

41. J. W. Veluwenkamp, 'Familiennetwerken binnen de Nederlandse koopliedenge-meenschap van Archangel in de erste helft van de achttiende eeuw', *Bijdragen en Mededelingen betreffende de Geschiedenis der Nederlanden*, 108:4 (1993), pp. 655–72; A.-L. Head-König, 'Typologie et fonctionnement des entreprises commerciales dans le monde préalpin. Les spécialisations glaronaises, le rôle des réseaux sociaux et famil-iaux, du clientélisme et du patronage (XVIe–XVIIIe siècles)', *Itinera*, 24 (2002), pp. 73–94; M. Sugiura, 'Heiratsmuster der *wijnkopers* in Amsterdam 1660–1710', in M. Häberlein and C. Jeggle (eds), *Praktiken des Handels. Geschäfte und soziale Beziehun-gen europäischer Kaufleute in Mittelalter und früher Neuzeit* (Konstanz: UVK, 2010), pp. 407–47; F. Trivellato, 'Marriage, Commercial Capital and Business Agency: Transre-gional Sephardic (and Armenian) Families in the Seventeenth- and Eighteenth-Century Mediterranean', in C. H. Johnson, D. W. Sabean, S. Teuscher and F. Trivellato (eds), *Transregional and Transnational Families in Europe and Beyond: Experiences since the Middle Ages* (New York and Oxford: Berghahn Books, 2011), pp. 107–30.
42. Häberlein, *Brüder, Freunde und Betrüger*; Müller, *The Merchant Houses of Stockholm*; R. Grassby, *Kinship and Capitalism: Marriage, Family, and Business in the English-Speak-ing World, 1580–1740* (Cambridge: Cambridge University Press, 2001); J. Adams, *The Familia State: Ruling Families and Merchant Capitalism in Early Modern Europe* (Ithaca, NY: Cornell University Press, 2005); C. Reves, *Vom Pomeranzengängler zum Großhändler? Netzwerke und Migrationsverhalten der Brentano-Familien im 17. und 18. Jahrhundert* (Paderborn: Schöningh, 2012).
43. On this subject, see M. Häberlein and C. Kuhn (eds), *Fremde Sprachen in frühneuzeitli-chen Städten. Lernende, Lehrende und Lehrwerke* (Wiesbaden: Harrassowitz, 2010); D. Couto and S. Péquignot (eds), *Les langues de la négociation du Moyen Âge à l'époque con-temporaine* (Rennes: Presses Universitaires de Rennes, in press); G. Buti, M. Janin-Thivos and O. Raveaux, *Langues et langages du commerce en Méditerranée et en Europe à l'époque moderne* (Aix-en-Provence: Presses universitaires de Provence, 2013).
44. O. E. Williamson, *The Economic Institutions of Capitalism: Firms, Markets, Relational Contracting* (New York: Free Press; London: Collier Macmillan, 1985); W. W. Powell, 'Neither Market Nor Hierarchy: Network Forms of Organization', *Research in Organi-zational Behavior*, 12 (1990), pp. 295–336.
45. M. Belfanti, 'Guilds, Patents and the Circulation of Technical Knowledge: Northern Italy during the Early Modern Age', *Technology and Culture*, 45 (2004), pp. 569–89; K. Hofmeester, 'Working for Diamonds from the 16th to the 20th Century', in M. van der Linden and L. Lucassen (eds), *Working on Labor: Essays in Honor of Jan Lucassen* (Lei-den: Brill, 2012), pp. 19–46.
46. J. A. Marino, 'Mediterranean Studies and the Remaking of Premodern Europe', *Journal of Early Modern History*, 15 (2011), pp. 385–412.
47. Trivellato, *The Familiarity of Strangers*, esp. ch. 4 and 8; S. D. Aslanian, *From the Indian Ocean to the Mediterranean: The Global Trade Networks of Armenian Merchants from New Julfa* (Berkeley, CA: University of California Press, 2011); G. Riello, *Cotton: The Fabric that Made the Modern World* (Cambridge: Cambridge University Press, 2013), esp. pp. 169–81; see also M. Fusaro, C. Heywood and M.-S. Omri (eds), *Trade and Cul-tural Exchange in the Early Modern Mediterranean: Braudel's Maritime Legacy* (London: I. B. Tauris, 2010).

1 Burkhardt, 'Networks as Social Structures in Late Medieval and Early Modern Towns: A Theoretical Approach to Historical Network Analysis'

1. Y. Hasselberg, 'Nätverk är ingen tebjudning', in P. Aronsson, S. Fagerlund and J. Sam-uelson (eds), *Nätverk i historisk forskning – metafor, metod eller teori?* (Växjö: Växjö Universitet, 1999), pp. 12–16, on p. 13.
2. J. Scott, *Social Network Analysis: A Handbook* (London: SAGE, 1991; 3rd edn, 2012), p. 2–3; D. Knoke and J. H. Kuklinski, 'Network Analysis: Basic Concepts', in G. Thomp-son, J. Frances, R. Levacic and J. Mitchell (eds), *Markets, Hierarchies and Networks: The Coordination of Social Life* (London: SAGE, 1991), pp. 173–82, on p. 173.
3. A. Brinkmann, 'Über Vernetzungen im Mathematikunterricht – eine Untersuchung zu linearen Gleichungssystemen in der Sekundarstufe I' (PhD dissertation, University of Duisburg, 2002), p. 34.
4. J. C. Mitchell, 'The Concept and Use of Social Networks', in J. C. Mitchell (ed.), *Social Networks in Urban Situations* (Manchester: Manchester University Press, 1969), pp. 1–50; B. Wellman, 'Network Analysis: Some Basic Principles', *Sociological Theory*, 1 (1983), pp. 155–200; S. Wasserman and K. Faust, *Social Network Analysis: Methods and Applications* (Cambridge: Cambridge University Press, 1994); G. F. Thompson, *Between Hierarchies and Markets: The Logic and Limits of Network Forms of Organiza-tion* (Oxford: Oxford University Press, 2003), p. 54.
5. M. Burkhardt, *Der hansische Handel im Spätmittelalter. Handel, Kaufleute, Netzwerke* (Cologne, Weimar and Vienna: Böhlau, 2009), p. 47f.
6. My thanks go to Stuart Jenks, who, after a longer discussion, came up with this term as an appropriate expression.
7. Burkhardt, *Bergenhandel*, pp. 32–45; Scott, *Social Network Analysis*.
8. Cf. Scott, *Social Network Analysis*; Wasserman and Faust, *Social Network Analysis*.
9. Burkhardt, *Bergenhandel*, pp. 316–46.
10. The following is based on Burkhardt, *Bergenhandel*.
11. In English, 'faithfulness and trust'. Reputation and certification by a third party were essential parts of this instrument. *Treu und Glaube* is one of the most important institu-tions for mutual trust in the economic system of the Hanse merchants.
12. Compare the thesis of Carsten Jahncke on the typical pattern of a Hanseatic career: com-merce – wealth – secure investment (immovable property) – political career; C. Jahnke, 'Handelsnetze im Ostseeraum', in G. Fouquet and H.-J. Gilomen (eds), *Netzwerke im europäischen Handel des Mittelalters* (Ostfildern: Thorbecke, 2010), pp. 189–212.
13. Verein für Lübeckische Geschichte und Alterthumskunde (ed.), *Urkundenbuch der Stadt Lübeck*, 11 vols (Lübeck, 1843–1932), vol. 8, no. 125.
14. Ibid., vol. 9, no. 60.
15. Archiv der Hansestadt Lübeck, Personenkartei.
16. *Urkundenbuch der Stadt Lübeck*, vol. 9, no. 68.
17. Burkhardt, *Bergenhandel*, pp. 255–61.
18. Ibid., pp. 261–4; see also W. Brehmer, 'Verzeichnis der Mitglieder der Zirkelkompanie', *Zeitschrift des Vereins für Lübeckische Geschichte und Altertumskunde*, 5 (1888), pp. 393–454; S. Dünnebeil, *Die Lübecker Zirkel-Gesellschaft. Formen der Selbstrepräsenta-tion einer städtischen Oberschicht* (Lübeck: Schmidt-Römhild, 1996).

19. See M. Burkhardt, 'Testing a Traditional Certainty: The Social Standing of the *Bergen-fahrers* in Late Medieval Lübeck', in G. A. Ersland and M. Trebbi (eds), *Neue Studien zum Archiv und zur Sprache der Hanseaten* (Bergen: Det Hansetiske Museum, 2008), pp. 83–100.
20. R. Hammel-Kiesow, 'Häusermarkt und wirtschaftliche Wechsellage in Lübeck von 1384 bis 1700', *Hansische Geschichtsblätter*, 106 (1988), pp. 41–107.
21. J. R. McNeill and W. H. McNeill, *The Human Web: A Bird's-eye View of World History* (New York: Norton, 2003), pp. 5–7.

2 Jeggle, 'Interactions, Networks, Discourses and Markets'

1. See Introduction in this volume.
2. The literature is extensive; see for example S. Cavaciocchi (ed.), *Fiere e Mercati nella Integrazione delle Economie Europee secc. XIII–XVIII, Istituto Internazionale di Storia Economica 'F. Datini' Prato, Atti della 'Trentaduesima Settimana di Studi', 8–12 maggio 2000* (Florence: Le Monnier, 2001).
3. Cf. B. P. Priddat, *Theoriegeschichte der Wirtschaft 'oeconomia/economics'* (Munich: Fink, 2002), pp. 99–225; A. Engel, *Farben der Globalisierung. Die Entstehung moderner Märkte für Farbstoffe 1500–1900* (Frankfurt am Main: Campus, 2009); see also M. Storper and R. Salais, *Worlds of Production: The Action Frameworks of the Economy* (Cambridge, MA: MIT Press, 1997), pp. 9–12, 305–9.
4. In addition to the German historical school of economics, see M. Rutherford, *The Institutionalist Movement in American Economics 1918–1947: Science and Social Control* (Cambridge: Cambridge University Press, 2011).
5. For a critical assessment, see F. Boldizzoni, *The Poverty of Clio: Resurrecting Economic History* (Princeton, NJ: Princeton University Press, 2011).
6. E. G. Furubotn and R. Richter, *Institutions and Economic Theory: The Contribution of the New Institutional Economics*, 2nd edn (Ann Arbor, MI: University of Michigan Press, 2005); E. G. Furubotn and R. Richter (eds), *The New Institutional Economics of Markets* (Cheltenham and Northampton: Elgar, 2010).
7. W. Abel, *Agrarkrisen und Agrarkonjunktur. Eine Geschichte der Land- und Ernährungswirtschaft Mitteleuropas seit dem hohen Mittelalter. Dritte Auflage* (Hamburg and Berlin: Paul Parey, 1978); F. Braudel and F. Spooner, 'Prices in Europe from 1450–1750', in E. E. Rich and C. H. Wilson (eds), *The Cambridge Economic History of Europe, IV* (Cambridge: Cambridge University Press, 1967), pp. 374–486; B. Lepetit, 'Sur les Denivellations de l'Espace Économique en France dans les Années 1830', *Annales. Économies, Sociétés, Civilisations*, 41:6 (1986), pp. 1243–72; Engel, *Farben der Globalisierung*.
8. See also Abel, *Agrarkrisen und Agrarkonjunktur*; U. Dirlmeier, *Untersuchungen zu Einkommensverhältnissen und Lebenshaltungskosten in oberdeutschen Städten des Spätmittelalters (Mitte 14. bis Anfang 16. Jahrhundert)* (Heidelberg: Carl Winter Universitätsverlag, 1978); H.-J. Gerhardt and A. Engel, *Preisgeschichte der vorindustriellen Zeit. Ein Kompendium auf Basis ausgewählter Hamburger Materialien* (Stuttgart: Franz Steiner, 2006).
9. F. Braudel, *Civilisation Matérielle, Économie et Capitalisme, XVe–XVIIIe siècles*, 3 vols (Paris: Armand Colin, 1979). On Braudel and markets, see G. Garner and M. Midell (eds), *Aufbruch in die Weltwirtschaft. Braudel wiedergelesen* (Leipzig: Leipziger Universitätsverlag, 2012).

10. A. Desrosières and L. Thévenot, *Les Catégories Socio-Professionelles* (Paris: La Découverte, 1988; 5th edn, 2002).

11. For introductions, see N. J. Smelser and R. Swedberg (eds), *The Handbook of Economic Sociology* (Princeton, NJ: Princeton University Press, 1994; 2nd edn, 2005). For France, see A. Orlean (ed.), *Analyse Économique des Conventions* (Paris: Presses Universitaires de la France, 1994; 2nd edn, 2004); F. Eymard-Duvernay (ed.), *L'Économie des Conventions. Méthodes et Résultats*, 2 vols (Paris: La Découverte, 2006). On the reception in economic history, see C. Jeggle, 'Pre-industrial Worlds of Production: Conventions, Institutions and Organizations', in R. Diaz-Bone and R. Salais (eds), 'Conventions and Institutions from a Historical Perspective', *Historical Social Research*, special issue, 36:4 (2011), pp. 125–49, on 125–7.

12. For a recent overview, see for example J. Scott and P. J. Carrington (eds), *The SAGE Handbook of Social Network Analysis* (Thousand Oaks, CA and London: SAGE, 2011).

13. N. Elias, *Was ist Soziologie?* (Munich: Juventa, 1970); H. C. White, *Identity and Control* (Princeton, NJ: Princeton University Press, 1992; 2nd edn, 2008); M. Emirbayer and J. Goodwin, 'Network Analysis, Culture, and the Problem of Agency', *American Journal of Sociology*, 99 (1994), pp. 962–93; M. Emirbayer, 'Manifesto for a Relational Sociology', *American Journal of Sociology*, 103:2 (1997), pp. 281–317.

14. For example L. Müller, 'The Role of the Merchant Network: A History of two Swedish Trading Houses, 1650–1800', in C. Lesger and L. Noordegraf (eds), *Entrepreneurs and Entrepreneurship in Early Modern Times: Merchants and Industrialists within the Orbit of the Dutch Staple Market* (The Hague: Stichting Hollandse Historische Reeks, 1995), pp.147–63; A. Wegener Sleeswijk, 'Social Ties and Commercial Transactions of an Eighteenth-Century French Merchant', in Lesger and Noordegraf (eds), *Entrepreneurs and Entrepreneurship in Early Modern Times*, pp. 203–21. M. Häberlein, *Brüder, Freunde und Betrüger. Soziale Beziehungen, Normen und Konflikte in der Augsburger Kaufmannschaft um die Mitte des 16. Jahrhunderts* (Berlin: Akademie Verlag, 1998) has conducted a formal social network analysis.

15. M. Casson, 'Networks in Economic and Business History: A Theoretical Perspective', in P. Fernández Pérez and M. B. Rose (eds), *Innovation and Entrepreneurial Networks in Europe* (New York and London: Routledge, 2010), pp. 14–40, on pp. 22, 36; see also the Introduction to this volume.

16. H. C. White, 'Where Do Markets Come From?', *American Journal Sociology*, 87 (1981), pp. 517–47.

17. H. C. White, *Markets from Networks: Socioeconomic Models of Production* (Princeton, NJ: Princeton University Press, 2002).

18. U. Dirlmeier, *Mittelalterliche Hoheitsträger im wirtschaftlichen Wettbewerb* (Wiesbaden: Steiner, 1966); R. H. Britnell, *The Commercialisation of English Society, 1000–1500* (Cambridge: Cambridge University Press, 1993); P. Lanaro, *I Mercati nella Repubblica Veneta. Economie Cittadine e Stato Territoriale (secoli XV–XVIII)* (Venice: Marsilio, 1999); S. R. Epstein, *Freedom and Growth: The Rise of States and Markets in Europe, 1300–1750* (London and New York: Routledge, 2000).

19. T. Heerdegen, *Das Merkantil-, Friedens- und Schiedsgericht der Stadt Nürnberg* (Nuremberg: Bieling-Dietz, 1897), pp. 6–9.

20. See for example A. Montenach, *Espaces et Pratiques du Commerce Alimentaire a Lyon au XVIIe siecle. L'Économie du Quotidien* (Grenoble: Presses Universitaires de Grenoble, 2009).

21. M. Fenske, *Marktkultur in der Frühen Neuzeit. Wirtschaft, Macht und Unterhaltung auf einem städtischen Jahr- und Viehmarkt* (Cologne, Weimar and Vienna: Böhlau, 2006); M. Fortunati, 'Le Giurisdizioni Mercantili nel Commercio di Antico Regime', in A. Bonoldi and M. A. Denzel (eds), *Bozen im Messenetz Europas (17.–19. Jahrhundert) / Bolzano nel Sistema Fieristico Europeo (secc. XVII–XIX)* (Bolzano: Athesia, 2007), pp. 85–100; D. De Ruysscher, *'Naer het Romeisch recht alsmede den stiel mercantiel'. Handel en recht in de Antwerpse rechtbank (16de–17de eeuw)* (Kortrijk-Heule: UGA, 2009).

22. For introductions to the sociology of markets, see A. Preda, *Information, Knowledge, and Economic Life: An Introduction to the Sociology of Markets* (Oxford: Oxford University Press, 2009); P. Aspers, *Markets* (Cambridge: Polity Press, 2011).

23. The case of a supplier who was the only one to offer a certain good and could provide all his customers sufficiently without having any competition among them did not constitute a market but simply the selling of goods.

24. Since not only material goods but also services and property rights on goods which are not present on the marketplace are being exchanged, and furthermore payments are often made with bookings and transfers of abstracted values rather than in specie, the notion of rights seems to be appropriate to generalize the object of exchange.

25. P. Aspers, 'Sociology of Markets', in J. Beckert and M. Zafirovski (eds), *International Encyclopedia of Economic Sociology* (London and New York: Routledge, 2006), pp. 427–32, on 427.

26. J. Beckert, 'Social Order of Markets', *Theory and Society*, 38 (2009), pp. 245–69.

27. The price-building mechanism of standard economic theory is based on the premise of the equivalence of the traded goods. The qualities are taken as a substantial fact, while the way they are constituted is rather seen as an external factor or a factor of cost; cf. Y. Barzel, 'Measurement Cost and the Organization of Markets', *Journal of Law and Economics*, 25 (1982), pp. 27–48.

28. P. Aspers. 'Knowledge and Valuation in Markets' *Theory and Society*, 38 (2009), pp. 111–31. Though most markets are not organized as exchange markets, economic theory strongly draws on these as an implicit standard model; cf. Aspers, *Markets*, pp. 83–5.

29. Not all kinds of factor markets can be classified as status markets because certain kinds of services like transport were not necessarily tied to the personality of single operators and were offered as standardized services.

30. C. Geertz, 'The Bazaar Economy: Information and Search in Peasant Marketing', *American Economic Review*, 68 (1978), pp. 28–32; F. S. Fanselow, 'The Bazar Economy or How Bizarre is the Bazar Really?', *Man*, 25 (1990), pp. 250–65.

31. J. W. Veluwenkamp, *Ondernemersgedrag op de Hollandse stapelmarkt in de tijd van de Republiek. De Amsterdamse handelsfirma Jan Isaac de Neufville & Comp., 1730–1764* (Meppel: Krips Repro, 1981), pp. 22–30; P. Gervais, 'Crédit et Filières Marchandes au XVIIIe Siècle', *Annales. Histoire, Sciences Sociales*, 67:4 (2012), pp. 1011–48.

32. These investments covered all kinds of production that afforded large fixed investments, like mills, or investments in raw materials and the provisioning of the producers. See for example of the Fugger: M. Häberlein, *The Fuggers of Augsburg: Pursuing Wealth and Honor in Renaissance Germany* (Charlottesville, VA: University of Virginia Press, 2012).

33. S. W. Mintz, *Sweetness and Power: The Place of Sugar in Modern History* (New York: Viking Penguin, 1985).

34. H. Cools, M. Keblusek and B. Noldus (eds), *Your Humble Servant: Agents in Early Modern Europe* (Hilversum: Uitgeverij Verloren, 2006); M. Häberlein and M. Bayreuther,

Agent und Ambassador. Der Kaufmann Anton Meuting als Vermittler zwischen Bayern und Spanien im Zeitalter Philipps II (Augsburg: Wissner, 2013).

35. See the important considerations by P. Gervais, 'Crédit et Filières Marchandes au XVIIIe Siècle'.

36. Since the nineteenth century a shift has taken place in retail trade, and the sale of standardized goods increased significantly. Today probably most goods sold to end consumers are standardized goods, and the personal qualities of the seller have lost most of their significance as long as the goods are handled properly.

37. In economic terms, many goods were dealt as fungible goods by quantity in an economy of scale.

38. R. Reith, 'Praxis der Arbeit. Überlegungen zur Rekonstruktion von Arbeitsprozessen in der handwerklichen Produktion', in R. Reith (ed.), *Praxis der Arbeit. Probleme und Perspektiven der handwerksgeschichtlichen Forschung* (Frankfurt am Main and New York: Campus, 1998), pp. 11–54, on pp. 22–4; C. Jeggle, 'Gewerbliche Produktion und Arbeitsorganisation: Perspektiven der Forschung', in M. Häberlein and C. Jeggle (eds), *Vorindustrielles Gewerbe. Handwerkliche Produktion und Arbeitsbeziehungen in Mittelalter und Früher Neuzeit* (Konstanz: UVK, 2004), pp. 19–35, on pp. 22–3. We could also refer to the models of commodity and value chains, but that discussion is primarily directed to the global division of labour by multinational companies and not to markets; see J. Bair (ed.), *Frontiers of Commodity Chain Research* (Stanford, CA: Stanford University Press, 2009).

39. J. F. Porac and H. Thomas, 'Taxonomic Mental Models in Competitor Categorization', *Academy of Management Review*, 15 (1990), pp. 224–40; G. P. Hodkinson and G. Johnson, 'Exploring the Mental Models of Competitive Strategists: The Case for a Processual Approach', *Journal of Management Studies*, 31 (1994), pp. 525–51; J. A. Rosa, K. M. Judson and J. F. Porac, 'On the Sociocognitive Dynamics between Categories and Product Models in Mature Markets', *Journal of Business Research*, 58 (2005), pp. 62–9.

40. White, *Markets from Networks*, pp. 14–16.

41. Ibid., p. 213.

42. For a more detailed introduction and further references, see Jeggle, 'Pre-Industrial Worlds of Production'. The discussion here is based on R. Salais and M. Storper, *Les Mondes de Production. Enquête sur l'Identité Economique de la France* (Paris: Éditions de EHESS, 1993), pp. 12–55, 328–82; revised and abridged English edition: Storper and Salais, *Worlds of Production*, pp. 26–43, 269–306. Due to the different versions, references to both books are provided.

43. Cf. P. C. Reynard, 'Manufacturing Quality in the Pre-Industrial Age: Finding Quality in Diversity', *Economic History Review*, 53 (2000), pp. 493–516. Even present industries have trouble with producing generic products, as the offers of 'second selections' and the problem of large volumes of wasted products show. The rate of deficient products can be a significant factor in the competition among industrial producers.

44. I. Schwanke, '… den wir haßen die unangenehme Corespodenz … Handelspraktiken der Brüder Castell in Elzach im Schwarzwald (1814–1843)', in M. Häberlein and C. Jeggle (eds), *Praktiken des Handels. Geschäfte und soziale Beziehungen europäischer Kaufleute in Mittelalter und früher Neuzeit* (Konstanz: UVK, 2010), pp. 605–30.

45. For illustrative examples, see F. Edler de Roover, 'The Van der Molen, Commission Merchants of Antwerp: Trade with Italy, 1538–1544', in J. L. Cate and E. N. Anderson (eds), *Medieval and Historiographical Essays in Honor of James Westfall Thompson* (Chicago, IL: University of Chicago Press, 1938), pp. 78–145, on the trade in textiles in mid-sixteenth-century Antwerp.

46. In textile production, merchants developed several strategies to exploit producers to their advantage. See examples in Jeggle, 'Pre-industrial Worlds of Production', pp. 144–5; P. Minard, 'Normes et Certification des Qualités: Les Règles du Jeu Manufacturier au XVIIIe Siècle', in J.-C. Cassard (ed.), *Bretagnes. Art, Négoce et Société de l'Antiquité à nos Jours. Mélanges Offerts au Professeur Jean Tanguy* (Brest: Association des Amis de Jean Tanguy, 1996), pp. 173–90; M. Boldorf, *Europäische Leinenregionen im Wandel. Institutionelle Weichenstellungen in Schlesien und Irland (1750–1850)* (Cologne: Böhlau, 2006), pp. 122–32.

47. Salais and Storper, *Les Mondes de Production*, pp. 44, 51; Storper and Salais, *Worlds of Production*, pp. 32–4.

48. Salais and Storper, *Les Mondes de Production*, pp. 34–5, 44, 51–2; Storper and Salais, *Worlds of Production*, pp. 34–5. On fashionable products, see Edler de Roover, 'The Van der Molen'; C. Poni, 'Mode et Innovation: Les Strategies des Marchands en Soie de Lyon au XVIIIe Siècle', *Revue d'Histoire Moderne et Contemporaine*, 45:3 (1998), pp. 589–625; M. Berg, *Luxury and Pleasure in Eighteenth-Century Britain* (Oxford: Oxford University Press, 2005); C. M. Belfanti, *Civiltà della Moda* (Bologna: Mulino, 2008); B. Blondé, N. Coquery, J. Stobart and I. Van Damme (eds), *Fashioning Old and New: Changing Consumer Patterns in Western Europe (1650–1900)* (Turnhout: Brepols, 2009).

49. Salais and Storper, *Les Mondes de Production*, pp. 45, 52–3; Storper and Salais, *Worlds of Production*, pp. 35–6.

50. C. Muldrew, *The Economy of Obligation: The Culture of Credit and Social Relations in Early Modern England* (Basingstoke: Macmillan, 1998); L. Fontaine, *L'Économie Morale. Pauvreté, Crédit et Confiance dans l'Europe Préindustrielle* (Paris: Gallimard, 2008).

51. See for example B. Blondé, P. Stabel, J. Stobart and I. Van Damme (eds), *Buyers and Sellers: Retail Circuits and Practices in Medieval and Early Modern Europe* (Turnhout: Brepols, 2006); I. Van Damme, *Verleiden en verkopen. Antwerpse kleinhandelaars en hun klanten in tijden van crisis (ca. 1648–ca. 1748)* (Amsterdam: Aksant, 2007); Montenach, *Espaces et Pratiques du Commerce Alimentaire a Lyon au XVIIe Siècle*; G. Stöger, *Sekundäre Märkte? Zum Wiener und Salzburger Gebrauchtwarenhandel im 17. und 18. Jahrhundert* (Vienna: Verlag für Geschichte und Politik; Munich: Oldenbourg, 2011).

52. R. Käs, 'Der Markt zu Nürnberg', Museen der Stadt Nürnberg (eds), *Schaustück des Monats* (Nuremberg: Museen der Stadt Nürnberg, 2009).

53. For the example of colonial goods, see A. Menninger, *Genuss im kulturellen Wandel. Tabak, Kaffee, Tee und Schokolade in Europa (16.–19. Jahrhundert)*, 2nd edn (Stuttgart: Steiner, 2008) and more generally Berg, *Luxury and Pleasure in Eighteenth-Century Britain*.

54. T. Vanneste, *Global Trade and Commercial Networks: Eighteenth-Century Diamond Merchants* (London: Pickering & Chatto, 2011); F. Trivellato, *The Familiarity of Strangers: The Sephardic Diaspora, Livorno, and Cross-Cultural Trade in the Early Modern Period* (New Haven, CT: Yale University Press, 2009), pp. 224–70; Häberlein and Bayreuther, *Agent und Ambassador*; E. Korsch's essay in this volume.

55. See C. Jeggle, 'Economies of Quality as a Concept for Research on Luxury', in R. C. Rittersma (ed.), *Luxury in the Low Countries: Miscellaneous Reflections on Dutch and Flemish Material Culture (1400–2000)* (Brussels: Pharo Publishing, 2010), pp. 26–44.

56. Cools, Keblusek and Noldus (eds), *Your Humble Servant*; Häberlein and Bayreuther, *Agent und Ambassador*.

57. D. Calabi, *Il Mercato e la Città. Piazze, Strade, Architetture d'Europa in Età Moderna* (Venice: Marsilio, 1993).

58. Veluwenkamp, *Ondernemersgedrag op de Hollandse stapelmarkt in de tijd van de Republiek*, pp. 22–30; Gervais, 'Crédit et Filières Marchandes au XVIIIe Siècle', pp. 1017–26.

59. C. Reves, *Vom Pomeranzengängler zum Großhändler? Netzwerke und Migrationsverhalten der Brentano-Familien im 17. und 18. Jahrhundert* (Paderborn: Schöningh, 2012).

60. L. Molà, *The Silk Industry of Renaissance Venice* (Baltimore, MD and London: Johns Hopkins University Press, 2000).

61. P. Aspers, 'How are Markets Made?', Max Planck Institute for the Study of Societies, Working Paper 09/2 (Cologne, 2009).

62. Jeggle, 'Pre-industrial Worlds of Production', pp. 130–46.

63. C. Hochmuth, 'Distinktionshändler. Die Integration des Kolonialwarenhandels im frühneuzeitlichen Dresden', in P. Schmidt and H. Carl (eds), *Stadtgemeinde und Ständegesellschaft. Formen der Integration und Distinktion in der frühneuzeitlichen Stadt* (Berlin: LIT, 2007), pp. 225–51; Reves, *Vom Pomeranzengängler zum Großhändler?*

64. Aspers, 'How are Markets Made?'

65. S. Schmidt, 'Kommunikationsrevolution oder Zweite Kommerzielle Revolution? Die Neuen Geschäftsmedien des 16. Jahrhunderts und ihr Einfluss auf die Praktiken des frühneuzeitlichen Börsenhandels am Beispiel der Nürnberger Preiscourants (1586–1640)', in M. Häberlein and C. Jeggle (eds), *Praktiken des Handels. Geschäfte und soziale Beziehungen europäischer Kaufleute in Mittelalter und früher Neuzeit* (Konstanz: UVK, 2010), pp. 245–82, on pp. 256–68; M. Häberlein, 'Firmenbankrotte, Sozialbeziehungen und Konfliktlösungsmechanismen in süddeutschen Städten um 1600', *Österreichische Zeitschrift für Geschichtswissenschaft*, 19:3 (2008), pp. 10–35.

66. Here only a very brief outline of the concept can be introduced; for details, see White, *Markets from Networks*.

67. Ibid., pp. 43–6.

68. Ibid., pp. 14–16, 27–32.

69. Ibid., pp. 33–4; S. Mützel, 'Marktkonstitution durch narrativen Wettbewerb', *Berliner Journal für Soziologie*, 17 (2007), pp. 451–64.

70. White, *Markets from Networks*, p. 12; Porac and Thomas, 'Taxonomic Mental Models in Competitor Categorization'.

71. For a comparison of both approaches, see O. Favereau, O. Biencourt and F. Eymard-Duvernay, 'Where Do Markets Come From? From (Quality) Conventions!', in O. Favereau and E. Lazega (eds), *Conventions and Structures in Economic Organization: Markets, Networks and Hierarchies* (Cheltenham: Elgar, 2002), pp. 213–52; and White, *Markets from Networks*, pp. 153–7.

72. White, *Markets from Networks*, pp. 211–20.

73. For an example, see Jeggle, 'Pre-Industrial Worlds of Production', pp. 143–5.

74. Aspers, 'How are Markets Made?'

75. See for example M. A. Denzel, 'Das Maklerwesen auf den Bozner Messen im 18. Jahrhundert', *Vierteljahrschrift für Sozial- und Wirtschaftsgeschichte*, 96 (2009), pp. 297–319, especially the brief general introduction with further references on pp. 297–9; K. L. Reyerson, *The Art of the Deal: Intermediaries of Trade in Medieval Montpellier* (Leiden: Brill, 2002), pp. 96–102; A. Greve, 'Brokerage and Trade in Medieval Bruges: Regulation and Reality', in P. Stabel, B. Blondé and A. Greve (eds), *International Trade in the Low Countries (14th–16th Centuries): Merchants, Organisation, Infrastructure* (Leuven-Apeldoorn: Garant, 2000), pp. 37–44; on English brokers in Antwerp, O. De Smedt,

De engelse natie te Antwerpen in de 16e eeuw, 2 vols (Antwerpen: De Sikkel, 1950/4), vol. 2, pp. 457–62; on the Portuguese in Antwerp, H. Pohl, *Die Portugiesen in Antwerpen (1567–1648). Zur Geschichte einer Minderheit* (Wiesbaden: Franz Steiner, 1977), pp. 243–70; for Nuremberg, Schmidt, 'Kommunikationsrevolution oder Zweite Kommerzielle Revolution?', pp. 268–75; and on German brokers in London, M. Schulte Beerbühl, *Deutsche Kaufleute in London. Welthandel und Einbürgerung, 1680–1815* (Munich: Oldenbourg, 2007), pp. 390–9.

76. H. Simonsfeld, *Der Fondaco dei Tedeschi in Venedig und die deutsch-venezianischen Handelsbeziehungen*, 2 vols (Stuttgart: Cotta, 1887); U. Israel, 'Fondaci – Microcosmen für Fremde', in P. Bell, D. Suckow and G. Wolf (eds), *Fremde in der Stadt. Ordnungen, Repräsentationen und soziale Praktiken (13.–15. Jahrhundert)* (Frankfurt am Main: Peter Lang, 2010), pp. 119–41.

77. White, *Markets from Networks*, pp. 245–65.

78. See for example Gervais, 'Crédit et Filières Marchandes au XVIIIe Siècle'.

3 Guidi-Bruscoli, 'Creating Networks through Languages: Italian Merchants in Late Medieval and Early Modern Europe'

1. Cited in K. Braunmüller and G. Ferraresi, 'Introduction', in K. Braunmüller and G. Ferraresi (eds), *Aspects of Multilingualism in European Language History* (Amsterdam and Philadelphia, PA: John Benjamins, 2003), pp. 1–14, on p. 2.

2. 'What taught the parrot to cry, hail? / What taught the chattering pie his tale? / Hunger; that sharpener of the wits, / Which gives ev'n fools come thinking fits'; *The Satires of Persius*, ed. W. Drummond (London: J. Ginger, 1803).

3. Braunmüller and Ferraresi, 'Introduction', p. 3.

4. See for example P. Burke, *Languages and Communities in Early Modern Europe* (Cambridge: Cambridge University Press, 2004), who also underlines that 'a record of the language used by an individual on a particular occasion ... is no more than the record of the identity that came to the fore on that occasion' (p. 6).

5. E. Re, 'Archivi Inglesi e Storia italiana', *Archivio Storico Italiano*, 71:1 (1913), pp. 272–8.

6. R. Cella, *Libri, Conti e Lettere della Compagnia Senese dei Gallerani. I Testi* (Pisa: Ets, 2005), p. 13; D. Trotter, 'Italian Merchants in London and Paris: Evidence of Language Contact in the Gallerani Accounts, 1305–08', in D. Lagorgette and T. Pooley (eds), *On Linguistic Change in French: Socio-Historical Approaches. Le Changement Linguistique en Français: Aspects Socio-Historiques. Studies in Honour of R. Anthony Lodge. Études en Hommage au Professeur R. Anthony Lodge* (Charenton-le-Pont: Éditions de L'université de Savoie, 2012), pp. 222–3.

7. Trotter, 'Italian Merchants in London and Paris', p. 214.

8. K. Weissen, 'Ci Scrive in Tedescho! The Florentine Merchant-Banker Tommaso Spinelli and his German-Speaking Clients (1435–72)', *Yale University Library Gazette*, 74 (2000), pp. 112–25, on p. 113; J. J. McCusker, 'The Italian Business Press in Early Modern Europe', in S. Cavaciocchi (ed.), *Produzione e Commercio della Carta e del Libro, secc. XIII–XVIII* (Florence: Le Monnier, 1992), pp. 797–841, on p. 800.

9. J. A. M. de Bruijn-van der Helm, *Mercé, Moneta e Monte: Termini Commerciali Italiani Attestati nei Testi Nederlandesi dei Secoli XVI e XVII* (Utrecht: LEd, 1992), p. 212. The author analysed fifty sixteenth- to seventeenth-century Dutch commercial texts and extracted a list of 194 words (pp. 59–131).

10. M. E. Soldani, '"E perché costui è uxo di qua e intende bene la lingua". Remarques sur la Communication entre Marchands au bas Moyen Âge', in D. Couto and S. Péquignot (eds), *Les Langues de la Négociation du Moyen Âge à l'Époque Contemporaine* (Rennes: Presses Universitaires de Rennes, in press).

11. R. Cella, 'Prestiti nei Testi Mercantili Toscani Redatti di là dalle Alpi. Saggio di Glossario Fino al 1350', *La Lingua Italiana. Storia, Strutture, Testi*, 6 (2010), pp. 57–99.

12. Braunmüller and Ferraresi, 'Introduction', p. 3.

13. F. Balducci Pegolotti, *La Pratica della Mercatura*, ed. A. Evans (Cambridge, MA: Mediaeval Academy of America, 1936), pp. 14–19.

14. *The King's Mirror*, translated from the old Norwegian by L. M. Larson (New York: American-Scandinavian Foundation, 1917), p. 81.

15. J. Le Goff, *Mercanti e Banchieri nel Medioevo* (Messina and Florence: D'Anna, 1976), p. 96.

16. See for example P. Rota, *Storia delle Banche* (Milan: Tipografia del giornale Il Sole, 1874), p. 76: 'La lingua italiana fu la lingua ufficiale per molto tempo dei negozi di cambio' ('For many years Italian was the official language in the exchange business'); or B. Bischoff, 'The Study of Foreign Languages in the Middle Ages', *Speculum*, 36 (1961), pp. 209–24, on p. 211: 'In the realm of the Mediterranean trade Italian, Catalan, and Greek probably were the most important languages in the late Middle Ages'.

17. A. Sapori, *La Mercatura Medievale* (Florence: Sansoni, 1972), p. 52; U. Tucci, 'La Formazione dell'Uomo d'Affari', in F. Franceschi, R. A. Goldthwaite and R. C. Mueller (eds), *Il Rinascimento Italiano e l'Europa, Vol. 4: Commercio e Cultura Mercantile* (Treviso and Costabissara: Fondazione Cassamarca-Colla Editore, 2007), pp. 481–98, on p. 496; P. Jeannin, *I Mercanti del '500* (Milan: Mondadori, 1962), pp. 103–4.

18. A. J. Gurevič, 'The Merchant', in J. Le Goff (ed.), *The Medieval World* (London: Collins & Brown, 1990), pp. 243–83, on p. 266.

19. Burke, *Languages and Communities*, p. 1.

20. F. Melis, *Aspetti della Vita Economica Medievale (Studi nell'Archivio Datini di Prato)* (Siena: Monte dei Paschi di Siena, 1962), p. 118; Soldani, 'E perché costui è uxo di qua'.

21. Tucci, 'La Formazione dell'Uomo d'Affari', pp. 485, 488.

22. B. Cotrugli, *Il Libro dell'Arte di Mercatura*, ed. U. Tucci (Venice: Arsenale, 1990), pp. 210–11.

23. Burke, *Languages and Communities*, p. 43.

24. R. Cella, 'Le Carte della Filiale Londinese della Compagnia dei Gallerani e una *Ricordanza* di Biagio Aldobrandini (ottobre 1305)', *Bollettino dell'Opera del Vocabolario Italiano*, 8 (2003), pp. 403–14, on p. 404.

25. A. M. Piemontese, 'Mignanelli, Beltramo', in *Dizionario Biografico degli Italiani*, Vol. 74 (Rome: Istituto dell'Enciclopedia Italiana, 2010).

26. Melis, *Aspetti della Vita Economica Medievale*, p. 118. Melis dismisses the possibility of the intervention of a translator after comparing the authors' handwriting with that of letters written in their mother language.

27. Ibid., pp. 255–6.

28. 'E intanto Allexandro [Rinuccini] sarà pratichato e sperto e potrà li dare poi a luogho e tenpo il conto della chassa e masime chome arà apresa la linghua, nientedimeno ordina più e meno come ti pare': R. de Roover, *Il Banco Medici dalle Origini al Declino (1397– 1494)* (Florence: Nuova Italia, 1970), pp. 135, 561 (the document is not published in the English version of de Roover's book).

29. 'Ed io sone mezzo parlare catelano, tanto che m'intendono ciò che i' dico; e così io loro':
     A. Macinghi Strozzi, *Lettere di una Gentildonna Fiorentina del Secolo XV ai Figliuoli
     Esuli*, ed. C. Guasti (Florence: Sansoni, 1877), p. 30.

30. 'Chominccio a chonprendere nello ischrittoio e a 'nparare la favella, che sono in gran
     travaglo': M. Spallanzani, *Mercanti Fiorentini nell'Asia Portoghese* (Florence: Spes, 1997),
     p. 43.

31. J. Gairdner (ed.), *The Paston Letters, AD 1422–1529*, 6 vols (London: Chatto & Win-
     dus; Exeter: Commin, 1904), vol. 1, p. 152, vol. 3, p. 132; J. Hughes, 'Stephen Scrope and
     the Circle of Sir John Fastolf: Moral and Intellectual Outlooks', in C. Harper-Bill and R.
     E. Harvey (eds), *Medieval Knighthood IV* (Woodbridge: Boydell, 1992), pp. 109–46, on
     p. 132. I am grateful to Jim Bolton for this reference.

32. C. Bec, *Les Marchands Ecrivains. Affaires et Humanisme à Florence, 1375–1434* (Paris:
     Mouton, 1967), pp. 392–3; Melis, *Aspetti della Vita Economica Medievale*, p. 32 and
     tables v–viii; Soldani, 'E perché costui è uxo di qua'.

33. J. Bottin, 'La Pratique des Langues dans L'espace Commercial de l'Europe de l'Ouest au
     début de L'époque Moderne', in G. Buti, M. Janin-Thivos and O. Raveux (eds), *Langues
     et Langages du Commerce en Méditerranée et en Europe à l'Époque Moderne* (Aix-Mar-
     seille: Presses Universitaires de Provence, 2013), pp. 77–92, on p. 86. In the 1540s the
     Florentine Salviati sent all their correspondence in Italian, with the exception of letters
     addressed to Spanish or Portuguese correspondents (p. 86 n. 29).

34. J. Richard, 'L'Enseignement des Langues Orientales en Occident au Moyen-Âge', *Revue
     des Etudes Islamiques*, 44 (1976), reprinted in J. Richard, *Croisés, Missionaires et Voya-
     geurs. Les Perspectives Orientales du Monde Latin Médiéval* (London: Variorum, 1983),
     pp. 149–64, on p. 158 n. xviii. The same applied to the Western African coast: P. D. Cur-
     tin, *Cross-Cultural Trade in World History* (Cambridge: Cambridge University Press,
     1984), pp. 12, 58.

35. G. R. Cardona, 'L'Elemento di Origine o di Trafila Portoghese nella Lingua dei Viaggia-
     tori Italiani del '500', *Bollettino dell'Atlante Linguistico Mediterraneo*, 13–15 (1971–3),
     pp. 165–219, on pp. 170–3.

36. Bischoff, 'The Study of Foreign Languages', p. 213.

37. P. W. Waentig, '*Gesprächsbücher* Bi- e Plurilingui nell'Europa Occidentale tra il Trecento
     ed il Seicento: Aspetti Lessicologici-Lessicografici della Terminologia Tessile', *Quaderni
     del CIRSIL*, 2 (2003), pp. 1–5; Bischoff, 'The Study of Foreign Languages', pp. 211–12.

38. P. Höybye, 'Glossari Italiano-Tedeschi del Quattrocento', *Studi di Filologia Italiana*, 22
     (1964), pp. 167–204, on pp. 172–204. In the mid-fifteenth century a Florentine version
     of the booklet was produced; L. Böninger, *Die deutsche Einwanderung nach Florenz im
     Spätmittelalter* (Leiden: Brill, 2006), pp. 115–16.

39. A. Rossebastiano Bart, *Antichi Vocabolari Plurilingui d'Uso Popolare: La Tradizione del
     'Solenissimo Vochabuolista'* (Alessandria: Edizioni Dell'Orso, 1984), pp. 26–7; Höybye,
     'Glossari italiano-tedeschi del Quattrocento', 22 (1964), pp. 167–204 and 32 (1974),
     pp. 143–203.

40. J. van der Helm and T. Bruni, '"Caxza in là quilli boy, mena in qua li castroni". Dialogo
     Inedito fra un Mercante Fiammingo e un suo Collega Italiano a Cavallo fra il Quattro-
     cento e il Cinquecento', *Zeitschrift für romanische Philologie*, 119 (2003), pp. 443–79.

41. E. Teza, 'Un Piccolo Glossario Italiano e Arabico del Quattrocento', *Rendiconti
     dell'Accademia Nazionale dei Lincei. Classe di Scienze Morali, Storiche e Filologiche*, 5:2
     (1893), pp. 77–88.

42. Rossebastiano Bart, *Antichi Vocabolari Plurilingui*, pp. 10–2. The author, Adamo de Rodvila, defined it as 'extremely useful for those, Germans or Italians, who travel the world' and 'extremely useful to learn how to read for those who intend to do so, without going to school' ('vtilissimo per queli che vadano apratichando per el mundo, el sia todescho o taliano' and 'vtilissimo a imparare legere per queli che desiderasen senza andare a schola'); Waentig, '*Gesprächsbücher* Bi- e Plurilingui', p. 9.
43. Soldani, 'E perché costui è uxo di qua'.
44. Weissen, '*Ci Scrive in Tedesco!*', pp. 123–5; Rossebastiano Bart, *Antichi Vocabolari Plurilingui*, p. 10.
45. R. de Roover, *The Rise and Decline of the Medici Bank, 1397–1494* (New York: Norton, 1966), p. 321.
46. D. Abulafia, 'Cittadino e Denizen: Mercanti Mediterranei a Southampton e a Londra', in M. Del Treppo (ed.), *Sistema di Rapporti ed Élites Economiche in Europa (secoli XII–XVII)* (Naples: Liguori, 1994), pp. 273–92, on pp. 288–90; L. Stone, *An Elizabethan: Sir Horatio Palavicino* (Oxford: Clarendon, 1956), pp. 31–2.
47. G. Mattingly, *Renaissance Diplomacy* (Baltimore, MD: Penguin, 1964), pp. 186, 205.
48. See for example D. Kovačević-Kojić, *Account Books of the Caboga (Kabužić) Brothers* (Belgrade: Serbian Academy of Sciences and Arts, 1999); M. Dinić (ed.), *Documenta Archivi Reipublicae Ragusinae*, Vol. 1 (Belgrade: Academia Scientiarum Serbica, 1957), pp. 33–4, 35–90.
49. R. Fontanot, 'Sulla Storia della Presenza della Lingua Italiana in Dalmazia', in M. Bastiansen et al. (eds), *Identità e Diversità nella Lingua e nella Letteratura Italiana*, Proceedings of the 18th Congress of AISLLI, Louvain-Antwerp-Brussels, 16–19 July 2003, 3 vols (Florence: Cesati, 2007), vol. 1, pp. 341–3.
50. J. Favier, *De l'Or et des Epices. Naissance de l'Homme d'Affaires au Moyen Âge* (Paris: Fayard, 1987), p. 90.
51. Richard, 'L'Enseignement des Langues Orientales', pp. 153–4. In addition to being a *lingua franca* for the overland trade across Asia, Persian had long replaced Greek as the language of commerce in the Middle East; Curtin, *Cross-Cultural Trade*, p. 107.
52. Balducci Pegolotti, *La Pratica della Mercatura*, pp. 21–2.
53. Spallanzani, *Mercanti Fiorentini*, pp. 32, 177.
54. Soldani, 'E perché costui è uxo di qua'.
55. See for example Bottin, 'La Pratique des Langues', pp. 80–5, for the situation in early modern Rouen where merchants could act as (sometimes self-appointed) interpreters.
56. J.-A. Goris, *Étude sur les Colonies Marchandes Méridionales (Portugais, Espagnols, Italiens) à Anvers de 1488 à 1567* (Louvain: Librairie Universitaire, 1925), p. 83.
57. For example, Robert Bale in the 1440s could translate from Flemish: A. F. Sutton and L. Visser-Fuchs (eds), *The Book of Privileges of the Merchant Adventurers of England, 1296–1483* (Oxford: Oxford University Press, 2009), p. 104. Furthermore, young apprentices of the main mercers would have some rudimentary knowledge of French and Dutch: A. F. Sutton, *The Mercery of London: Trade, Goods and People, 1130–1578* (Aldershot: Ashgate, 2005), p. 169.
58. Weissen, '*Ci Scrive in Tedesco!*', pp. 113–14.
59. Ibid., pp. 115–16.
60. State Archives of Florence, Compagnie religiose soppresse da Pietro Leopoldo (hereafter ASF CRSPL), 2037, fols 313, 315, Lorenzo Villani, in Frankfurt, to Francesco Carletti, in Florence, 1 November 1552 and 23 January 1553.

61. ASF CRSPL, 2037, fols 308, 322, 329, Lorenzo Villani, in Frankfurt, to Francesco Carletti, in Florence, 27 April 1554, 15 July 1554 and 20 August 1555; K. Weissen, 'I Mercanti Italiani e le Fiere in Europa Centrale alla Fine del Medioevo e agli Inizi dell'Età Moderna', in P. Lanaro (ed.), *La Pratica dello Scambio, Sistemi di Fiere, Mercanti e Città in Europa (1400–1700)* (Venice: Marsilio, 2003), pp. 161–76, on p. 175.

62. 'Chome si passa 20 in 22 anni si aprende mal questa linghua e si stenta parechi anni avanti che l'huomo se ne possa servire'; ASF CRSPL, 2037, fol. 174v, Piero Saliti, in Nuremberg, to Francesco Carletti, in Florence, 6 November 1536.

63. 'E avete a sapere che per noi non si può fare tutto sì per la lingua ... e se voi sapessi certo quanto poco ci possiamo adoperare el Bonsi e io della lingua'; ASF CRSPL, 2037, fols 351v, 352v, Alessandro Talani, in Nuremberg, to Francesco Carletti, in Florence, [?] October 1536.

64. 'Egli è ben vero che qui sarebe di bixogno a levare uno putto di 14 anni che inprendessi la lingua, acciò per di qua a 2 o 3 anni ci servisimo di lui come tedesco ... esendo giovane s'avezerà a bere cervogia come fecie el fratello di Bernardo Acaiuoli, ch'è più tedesco che 'taliano: e tutto nasce che li giovanetti inparono meglio che gl'atenpati e s'avezono meglio a' costumi tedeschi ... Certo in canbio del Bonsi aresti fatto venire uno giovanetto, ché benché noi altri inpariamo a dire 4 parole, se avesimo a piatire e a preghare santi no llo sapren fare quando qui saremo stati x anni. E questo è certo'; ASF CRSPL, 2037, fols 352r–v, Alessandro Talani, in Nuremberg, to Francesco Carletti, in Florence, [?] October 1536.

65. 'El Bonsi Piero l'à lasciato a Lipizi ... potrà dare opera a 'nparare, che qui per essere tanti 'taliani non si può inparare niente; là bixognerà parli tedesco, che non v'è 'taliani'; ASF CRSPL, 2037, fol. 352v, Alessandro Talani, in Nuremberg, to Francesco Carletti, in Florence, [?] October 1536.

66. P. Mainoni, 'La Nazione che Non C'È: I Tedeschi a Milano e a Como fra Tre e Quattrocento', in G. Petti Balbi (ed.), *Comunità Forestiere e 'Nationes' nell'Europa dei secoli XIII–XVI* (Naples: Liguori, 2001), p. 226.

67. Jeannin, *I Mercanti del '500*, pp. 101–3.

68. Weissen, '*Ci Scrive in Tedescho!*', p. 118.

69. 'Volea favellar Tedesco': F. Sacchetti, *Il Trecentonovelle*, ed. D. Puccini (Turin: Utet, 2008), Novel LXXVIII, p. 230.

70. Ibid., Novel LXXXVII, p. 259.

71. 'Mi penso siate diventato buon tedesco e che abiate preso tutti li loro buoni costumi'; ASF CRSPL, 2037, fol. 264r, Giovanni Olivieri, in Florence, to Francesco Carletti, in Venice, 19 May 1543.

72. Böninger, *Die deutsche Einwanderung nach Florenz*, p. 116.

73. A. Borlandi (ed.), *Il Manuale di Mercatura di Saminiato de' Ricci* (Genoa: Di Stefano, 1963), pp. 48 (fn. 46), 163.

74. L. Molà, *La Comunità dei Lucchesi a Venezia: Immigrazione e Industria della Seta nel Tardo Medioevo* (Venice: Istituto Veneto di Scienze, Lettere ed Arti, 1994), pp. 245–6.

75. Soldani, 'E perché costui è uxo di qua'.

76. R. Mazzei, *Itinera mercatorum. Circolazione di Uomini e Beni nell'Europa Centro-Orientale, 1550–1650* (Lucca: Pacini Fazzi, 1999), pp. 233–5.

77. R. de Roover, *Money, Banking and Credit in Mediaeval Bruges*, (Cambridge, MA: The Mediaeval Academy of America, 1948), p. 21.

78. de Roover, *The Rise and Decline of the Medici Bank*, p. 93.

79. Ibid., p. 339.

80. 'Uno quaderno da imparare il fiamingo'; L. Galoppini, *Mercanti toscani e Bruges nel tardo medioevo*, (Pisa: Plus, 2009), p. 290.
81. Jeannin, *I Mercanti del '500*, p. 103.
82. 'I terrazzani d'Anversa ... insino a molte donne quantunque non sieno stati fuora del paese sono dotati di tre & di quattro lingue, senza quegli che n'hanno cinque, sei & sette'; L. Guicciardini, *Descrittione di tutti i Paesi Bassi, altrimenti detti Germania inferiore* (Antwerp: Christofano Plantino, 1588), pp. 155–6.
83. Ibid., pp. 40, 143.
84. Ch. Verlinden, 'Lettres Commerciales Italiennes d'une Firme Anversoise (1586)', *Bulletin Institut Historique Belge de Rome*, 27 (1952), pp. 507–34.
85. De Bruijn-van der Helm, *Mercé, moneta e monte*, pp. 34–8.
86. M. E. Soldani, 'A Firenze Mercanti, Cavalieri nella Signoria dei Re d'Aragona. I Tecchini-Taquí tra XIV e XV secolo', *Anuario de Estudios Medievales*, 39 (2009), pp. 575–604; p. 580 shows the examples of 'foreigners' in Catalonia.
87. D. R. Holeton, 'Fynes Moryson's *Itinerary*: A Sixteenth Century English Traveller's Observations on Bohemia, its Reformation, and its Liturgy', in Z. V. David and D. R. Holeton (eds), *The Bohemian Reformation and Religious Practice*, Vol. 5, pt 2 (Prague: Academy of Sciences of the Czech Republic, 2005), pp. 379–410, on pp. 381–2.
88. Bottin, 'La Pratique des Langues', pp. 77–8.
89. S. Jenks, 'Zum hansischen Gästerecht', *Hansische Geschichtsblätter*, 114 (1996), pp. 3–59, on p. 36.
90. Molà, *La Comunità dei Lucchesi a Venezia*, p. 246 (fn. 121).

4 Orlandi, 'Networks and Commercial Penetration Models in the Late Medieval Mediterranean: Revisiting the Datini'

1. I am referring here to the work of Federigo Melis, Fernand Braudel, Edoardo Grendi, Frederic Lane and, starting from the 1980s, the conference proceedings of the Gruppo Interuniversitario per la Storia dell'Europa Mediterranea, and in particular those edited by G. Rossetti (1989), M. Del Treppo (1994) and G. Petti Balbi (1996).
2. See P. Braunstein, 'Réseaux Familiaux, Réseaux d'Affaires en Pays d'Empire: Les Facteurs des Société Fugger (1380–1520)', in F. Crouzet (ed.), *Le Négoce International, XIIIe–XXe siècle* (Paris: Economica, 1989), pp. 23–34; B. Bailyn, *The New England Merchants in the Seventeenth Century* (Cambridge, MA: Harvard University Press, 1955); K. N. Chauduri, *Trade and Civilisation in the Indian Ocean: An Economic History from the Rise of Islam to 1750* (Cambridge: Cambridge University Press, 1985); M. Fusaro, 'Les Anglais et les Grecs. Un Réseau de Coopération Commerciale en Méditerranée Vénitienne', *Annales, Histoire, Sciences Sociales*, 58:3 (2003), pp. 605–25; J. Gentil da Silva, *Stratégie des Affaires* à Lisbonne *Entre 1595 et 1607. Lettres Marchandes des Rodrigues d'Evora et Veiga* (Paris: A. Colin, 1956); A. Greif, 'The Organisation of Long-Distance Trade: Reputation and Coalitions in the Geniza Documents During the Eleventh and Twelfth Centuries', *Journal of Economic History*, 49:4 (1989), pp. 847–82; H. Lapeyre, *Simon Ruiz et les 'Asientos' de Philippe II* (Paris: A. Colin, 1953); H. Lapeyre, *Une Famille de Marchands, les Ruiz. Contribution à l'Étude du Commerce entre la France et l'Espagne* (Paris: A. Colin, 1955); V. M. Godinho, *L'Économie de l'Empire Portugais aux XVe et XVIe siècles* (Paris: SEVPEN, 1969); A. Molho and D. Ramanda Curto, 'Les Réseaux Marchands à l'Époque Moderne', *Annales, Histoire, Sciences Sociales*, 58:3

(2003), pp. 569–79; D. Studnicki-Gizbert, 'La 'Nation' Portugaise. Réseaux Marchands dans l'Espace Atlantique à l'Époque Moderne', *Annales, Histoire, Sciences Sociales*, 58:3 (2003), pp. 627–48; F. Trivellato, 'Juifs de Livourne, Italiens de Lisbonne, Hindous de Goa. Réseaux Marchands et Échanges Interculturels à l'Époque Moderne', *Annales, Histoire, Sciences Sociales*, 58:3 (2003), pp. 581–603; F. Trivellato, *The Familiarity of Strangers: The Sephardic Diaspora, Livorno and Cross-Cultural Trade in the Early Modern Period* (New Haven, CT and London: Yale University Press, 2009).

3.   Among the many social network analyses, see A. Degenne and M. Forsé, *Introducing Social Networks* (Los Angeles, CA: Sage, 2007); A. Degenne and M. Forsé, *Les Réseaux Sociaux. Une Approche Structurale en Sociologie* (Paris: A. Colin, 1994); E. Lazega, *Réseaux Sociaux et Structures Relationnelles* (Paris: PUF, 1998); P. Merckle, *Sociologie des Réseaux Sociaux* (Paris: La Découverte, 2004); P. McLean, *The Art of the Network: Strategic Interaction and Patronage in Renaissance Florence* (Durham, NC: Duke University Press, 2007); J. L. Molina, *El Análisis de Redes Sociales: una Introducción* (Barcelona: Ediciones Bellaterra, 2006); F. Requena Santos, *Análisis de Redes Sociales: Orígenes, Teorías y Aplicaciones* (Madrid: Centro de Investigaciones Sociológicas-Siglo XXI de España, 2003); L. Sanz Menéndez, 'Análisis de Redes Sociales: o Como Representar las Estructuras Sociales Bubyacentes', *Apuntes de Ciencia y Tecnología*, 7 (2003), pp. 21–9; S. Wassermann and K. Faust, *Social Network Analysis: Methods and Applications* (New York: Cambridge University Press, 1994). With regard to the potential applications of social network analysis in the historical context (limited to studies that are most relevant to the contents of this essay), see B. H. Erickson, 'Social Networks and History: A Review Essay', *Historical Methods*, 30:3 (1997), pp. 149–57; J. M. Imízcoz Beunza, 'Familia y Redes Sociales en la España Moderna', in F. J. Lorenzo Pinar (ed.), *La Familia en la Historia* (Salamanca: Ediciones Universidad de Salamanca, 2009), pp. 135–86; J. M. Imízcoz Beunza, 'Redes, Grupos, Clases. Una Perspectiva Desde el Análisis Relacional', in S. Molina Puche and A. Irigoyen López (eds), *Territorios Distantes, Comportamientos Similares. Familias, Redes y Reproducción Social en la Monarquía Hispánica (siglos XIV–XIX)* (Murcia: Universidad de Murcia, 2009), pp. 45–88, J. F. Padgett and C. K. Ansell, 'Robust Action and the Rise of the Medici, 1400–1434', *American Journal of Sociology*, 98:6 (1993), pp. 1259–319; F. Trivellato, 'Merchants' Letters across Geographical and Social Boundaries', in F. Bethencourt and F. Egmond (eds), *Correspondence and Cultural Exchange in Europe, 1400–1700* (Cambridge: Cambridge University Press, 2007), pp. 80–103.

4.   S. Zukin and P. DiMaggio, *Structures of Capital: The Social Organization of Economy* (Cambridge: Cambridge University Press, 1990), pp. 3–13.

5.   K. P. Polanyi, *The Great Transformation* (Boston, MA: Beacon Press 1957).

6.   G. Nigro, 'The Merchant', in G. Nigro (ed.), *Francesco di Marco Datini: The Man, the Merchant* (Prato and Florence: Fondazione Istituto Internazionale di Storia Economica 'F. Datini', FUP, 2010), pp. 81–104.

7.   M. Granovetter, 'Problems of Explanation in Economic Sociology', in N. Nohria and R. Eccles (eds), *Networks and Organizations: Structure, Form and Action* (Boston, MA: Harvard Business School Press, 1992), pp. 25–56, on p. 33; M. Granovetter, 'Economic Action and Social Structure: The Problem of Embeddedness', *American Journal of Sociology*, 91:3 (1985), pp. 481–510, esp. on pp. 483–7.

8.   To the centres identified by Federigo Melis, we should add Ostale in Narbonne and Traiguera in the Maestrazgo region. A. Orlandi, *Mercaderies i Diners: La Corre-*

spondència Datiniana entre València i Mallorca (1395–1398) (Valencia: Publicaciones Univesitat de València, 2008), p. 17.

9. These data come from the Datini Fund LAN database. This figure does not include letters written in the last few days of 1399, which reached their destination in the early days of 1400. I would like to thank the director of the Prato State Archive, Dr Maria Raffaella de Gramatica, who allowed me to consult these.

10. A note on the criteria used in the preparation of the data: if a letter had more than one sender or addressee, I attributed the sent or received letter to each of the interested parties. However, where the writer simply indicated 'Francesco Datini' or the name of his working partner with the intention of sending the letter to the company, it has been counted as received by the company.

11. I would like to thank my friend and colleague Bruno Bertaccini, who introduced me to the use of this programme.

12. Unlike private letters, company letters were almost always signed with the sending company's whole name and were not addressed to a single partner. Company letters dealt with issues around company life or the economic context, while 'own' letters contained private considerations of both a commercial and personal nature. F. Melis, *Documenti per la Storia Economica dei secoli XIII–XVI* (Prato: Istituto Internazionale di Storia Economica 'F. Datini', 1973), pp. 14–27.

13. In *Melanges de l'École Française de Rome-Moyen Age, Le Carteggio Datini et les Correspondances Pratiques des XVIe–XVIe siècles*, 117:1 (2005): M. Arnoux, C. Bourlet and J. Hayez, 'Les Lettres Parisiennes du Carteggio Datini. Première Approche du Dossier', pp. 193–222; J. Hayez, 'Avant-propos', pp. 115–20; J. Hayez, 'L'Archivio Datini, de l'Invention de 1870 à l'Exploration d'un Système d'Écrits Privés', pp. 121–91. See also C. Verna, 'Quelles Sources pour Quelles Entreprises du XIIIe au XVe Siècle?', in F. Ammannati (ed.), *Dove Va la Storia Economica? Metodi e Prospettive secc. XIII–XVIII / Where is Economic History Going? Methods and Prospects from the 13th to the 18th centuries*, Atti della 'Quarantaduesima Settimana di Studi', 18–22 April 2010 (Prato and Florence: Fondazione Istituto Internazionale di Storia Economica 'F. Datini' Prato-FUP, 2011), pp. 339–71.

14. Orlandi, *Mercaderies*, p. 11.

15. M. Berti, 'The Pisa Company: A Difficult Political Context', in Nigro (ed.), *Francesco di Marco Datini*, pp. 281–320, on pp. 310–11.

16. M. Giagnacovo, 'The Genoa Company: Disappointed Expectations', in Nigro (ed.), *Francesco di Marco Datini*, pp. 321–46, on pp. 348–9.

17. Ibid.

18. Our businessmen used the word Catalonia for the three areas of Catalonia, Valencia and the Balearics.

19. Simone Bellandi was the manager of the Barcelona company.

20. Luca del Sera was partner and manager of the Valencia company.

21. Cristofano Carocci was partner and manager of the Majorca company.

22. Archivio di Stato di Prato (hereafter ASPo), *Datini*, Francesco Datini to Simone Bellandi, Prato–Barcelona, 1 March 1398, fol. 1r; ibid., Francesco Datini to Simone Bellandi, Florence–Barcelona, 8 March 1399, fol. 1r.

23. From Pisa he wrote a single letter to Guido Pieri in Prato.

24. 'perché sono le 11 di notte e òne anchora a fare parecchi e non mi sento bene con tanta faccenda che io afogho'. ASPo, *Datini*, Francesco Datini to Luca del Sera, Flor-

ence–Valencia, 10 May 1399. In the time measurement system used in Datini's day, astronomical midnight corresponded to 6 pm (sunset).

25. F. Ammannati, 'Francesco di Marco Datini's Wool Workshops', in Nigro (ed.), *Francesco di Marco Datini*, pp. 497–523, on p. 520.

26. G. Nigro, 'Francesco and the Datini Company of Florence in the Trading System', in Nigro (ed.), *Francesco di Marco Datini*, pp. 235–354, on p. 238.

27. This number includes his wife, Margherita.

28. 'Tu sai che per le schonoscienze e per le ingiurie si partono e' fratelli l'uno da l'altro, e chosì per seghuenza figl(i)uoli dal padre, nipoti dal zio, chonpagni, fattori e maestri'. ASPo, *Datini*, Francesco Datini to Cristofano Carocci, Florence–Valencia, 10 April 1406, fol. 2v; quoted in P. Nanni, *Ragionare tra mercanti. Per una rilettura della personalità di Francesco Datini (1335ca–1410)* (Pisa: Pacini, 2010), p. 158.

29. D. Toccafondi and G. Tartaglione (eds), '"Per la tua Margherita": Le Lettere di Una Donna del Trecento', CD-Rom, at http://www.archiviodistato.prato.it/margherita/ [accessed 25 November 2013].

30. Nanni, *Ragionare*, p. 159.

31. ASPo, *Datini*, Francesco Datini to Luca del Sera, Florence–Valencia, 16 March 1399.

32. ASPo, *Datini*, Luca del Sera to Francesco Datini, Valencia–Florence, 21 January 1399.

33. To give a few examples: from Avignon, Francesco Datini received one letter from Anna, the wife of a silversmith, whom Datini must have known when he lived in France and who trusted in his generous help in the face of the poverty into which she had fallen after the death of her husband. From Vico Fiorentino, Salvestra, the wife of the Avignon company employee Tommaso di Ser Giovanni, wrote four letters to Datini complaining that her husband was neglecting her and was no longer writing to her. Datini received a letter from Nastasia Ridolfi in Bibbiena recommending her son Scolaio, who had moved to Florence to learn trading, to him. ASPo, *Datini*, Anna to Francesco Datini, Avignon–Florence, 27 June 1399, fol. 1r; ibid., Salvestra to Francesco Datini, Vico Fiorentino–Prato, 11 March 1399, fol. 1v; ibid., Nastasia to Francesco Datini, Bibbiena–Florence, 5 August 1399, fol. 1r; ibid., Anna to Francesco Datini, Avignon–Florence, 27 June 1399, fol. 1r.

34. Datini received as many as 103 letters from Avignon, of which only 10 were sent by his company there.

35. ASPo, *Datini*, Otto Difensori del Popolo di Prato to Francesco Datini, Prato–Florence, 14 November 1399, fol. 1r.

36. On Rinforzato Mannelli, see G. Nigro, 'Usura e Banca nei Documenti Contabili Toscani fino alla Introduzione de Monti di Pietà', in M. Carboni and M. G. Muzzarelli (eds), *I Conti dei Monti. Teoria e Pratica Amministrativa nei Monti di Pietà fra Medioevo ed Età Moderna* (Venice: Marsilio, 2008), pp. 15–33; A. Orlandi, 'Economia e Devozione a Pistoia fra Tre e Quattrocento', in *Pistoiesi sul Cammino di Santiago* (Pistoia: Settegiorni Editore, 2009), pp. 17–30.

37. On Margherita and the relationship between her and Datini and Lapo, in addition to F. Melis, *Aspetti della Vita Economica Medievale (Studi nell'Archivio Datini di Prato)* (Siena: Monte dei Paschi di Siena, 1962), chapter 1, see, among others, E. Bensa, 'Margherita Datini', *Archivio Storico Pratese*, 6 (1926), pp. 1–14; E. Cecchi (ed.), '*Le Lettere di Francesco Datini alla Moglie Margherita (1385–1410)*', (Prato: Società Pratese di Storia Patria, 1990); C. James, 'A Woman's Work in a Man's World. The Letters of Margherita Datini', in Nigro (ed.), *Francesco di Marco Datini*, pp. 53–72; J. Hayez, 'Le Rire du marchand. Francesco di Marco Datini, sa Femme Margherita et les "Gran Maestrí" Florentins', in I. Chabot, J. Hayez and D. Lett (eds), *La Famille, les Femmes et le Quotidien (XIVe–XVIIIe*

siècle). Textes offerts à Christiane Klapisch-Zuber (Paris: Publications *de* la Sorbonne, 2006), pp. 407–58; V. Rosati (ed.), *'Le Lettere di Margherita Datini a Francesco di Marco (1384–1410)'*, (Prato : Cassa di Risparmi e Depositi, 1977).

38. The addressees of the letters to Barcelona and Valencia included three external subjects: Baldo Villanuzzi and the Alessandri and Soldani families in Barcelona, and Baldo Villanuzzi in Valencia; these are letters that the addressees may have given to their managers to read and which remained with them.

39. Orlandi, *Mercaderies*, p. 39.

40. 'à fatto danno a ssé ed altri e messo i danari in borsa a questi mori'. A. Orlandi, 'The Catalonia Company: An Almost Unexpected Success', in Nigro (ed.), *Francesco di Marco Datini*, pp. 357–87, on p. 380.

41. 'wool and cloth from England ... which are living things'. F. Melis, 'La Diffusione nel Mediterraneo Occidentale dei Panni di Wervicq e delle altre Città della Lys attorno al 1400', in G. Barbieri (ed.), *Studi in Onore di Amintore Fanfani* (Milan: Giuffrè, 1962), pp. 219–43.

42. 'L'isola è pocha e chome vi va un uccello tutti il sanno'. A. Orlandi, 'A Man from Prato in the Maestrazgo. Tuccio di Gennaio, Wool Merchant', in Nigro (ed.), *Francesco di Marco Datini*, pp. 389–96, on p. 390.

43. Orlandi, *Mercaderies*, p. 38.

44. ASPo, *Datini*, Tuccio di Gennaio to Francesco Datini, San Mateo–Florence, 19 November 1398.

45. Orlandi, 'A Man from Prato', pp. 391–2.

46. On the role of these two towns on the Barbary Coast, its marketplaces and more generally on trade in these emporiums, see the fundamentally important volume by M. D. López Pérez, *La Corona de Aragón y el Magreb en el siglo XIV (1331–1410)* (Barcelona: Consejo Superior de Investigaciones Científicas, 1995). I have also written on the subject in 2008 in Orlandi, *Mercaderies* and in 2010 in Orlandi, 'The Catalonia Company'.

47. The same writer from the Albertis who, in a letter sent from Tunis to the manager of the Palma company, wrote: 'Because you are there Majorca in the midst of so many Catalans who trade with the Barbary Coast, I think that if you wanted to trade with the Barbary Coast you would do it through them but if it should happen that we can do something for you, say the word and we'll serve you willingly' ('Perché voi sete chostì tra tanti chatalani c'àno a fare qui che penso che se avesi l'animo a farci nulla il faresti cho loro, ma se vi schadese, a le volte, che voi faciesomo nula, chometteteci serverenvi volentieri'). Orlandi, 'The Catalonia Company', p. 378.

48. ASPo, *Datini*, Magaluff ben Atllon to Cristofano Carocci, Honaine–Majorca, 4 July 1402.

49. Melis, *Aspetti*, p. 256.

50. The group's results and geographical reach have been examined in depth in various studies, beginning with Federigo Melis's *Aspetti* (1962) and culminating in the volume edited by Giampiero Nigro, *Francesco di Marco Datini* (2010).

51. As I was finalizing this essay, I had the opportunity to read – albeit cursorily – the volume by Ingrid Houssaye Michienzi, *Datini, Majorque et Le Maghreb (14e–15e siècles), Réseaux, Espaces Méditerranéens et Strategies Marchands* (Leiden and Boston, MA: Brill, 2013). It is a long work that deals with the issue of the Datini group's trading relations with the Maghreb. I do not share many of its conclusions. I will concentrate here on one of the many observations that I had made: Michienzi claims that because it was weak, the Datini group was not successful in finding a role for itself in Maghreb trade

with its own representatives, as the Albertis, a powerful Florentine family, did. In actual fact, the Datini, both partners and employees, in contrast to the Albertis, considered a permanent presence in Majorca to be more important and profitable and thus opened a limited company there. Deciding against employing a Maghreb agent, as was the case in the Maestrazgo, was anything but a forced decision.

52. These aspects (authorizations to practice trade, citizenship and exemption papers) are fully dealt with in Orlandi, *Mercaderies*, pp. 36–7.

5 Lang, 'Networks and Merchant Diasporas: Florentine Bankers in Lyon and Antwerp in the Sixteenth Century'

1. R. A. Goldthwaite, *The Economy of Renaissance Florence* (Baltimore, MD: Johns Hopkins University Press, 2009), p. 32.
2. Ibid., pp. 38–48. This argument is quite different from that given on the growing demand for artwork in R. A. Goldthwaite, *Wealth and the Demand for Art in Italy 1300–1600* (Baltimore, MD and London: Johns Hopkins University Press, 1993), pp. 33–40, where he refers to the 'accumulation of wealth'.
3. This is the conclusion Christiane Eisenberg draws from a dialogue between historians and sociologists: C. Eisenberg, 'Embedding Markets in Temporal Structures: A Challenge to Economic Sociology and History', in K. Nathaus and D. Gilgen (eds), 'Change of Markets and Market Societies: Concepts and Case Studies', *Historical Social Research*, special issue, 36:3 (2011), pp. 55–78, on p. 56.
4. M. Granovetter, 'Economic Action and Social Structure. The Problem of Embeddedness', *American Journal of Sociology*, 91 (1985), pp. 481–510.
5. R. Richter, 'Institutional Economics of the "Market itself": An Attempted Answer to a Complaint by Ronald Coase', in K. Nathaus and D. Gilgen (eds), 'Change of Markets and Market Societies: Concepts and Case Studies', *Historical Social Research*, special issue, 36:3 (2011), pp. 34–54, on p. 35; D. C. North, 'Transaction Costs in History', *Journal of European Economic History*, 14 (1985), pp. 557–76.
6. Remarks on the employment of 'network analysis' for historical evidence: M. Häberlein, 'Netzwerkanalyse und historische Elitenforschung. Probleme, Erfahrungen und Ergebnisse am Beispiel der Reichsstadt Augsburg', in R. Dauser, S. Hächler, M. Kempe, F. Mauelshagen and M. Stuber (eds), *Wissen im Netz. Botanik und Pflanzentransfer in europäischen Korrespondenznetzen des 18. Jahrhunderts* (Berlin: Akademie Verlag, 2008), pp. 315–28; M. Reitmayer and C. Marx, 'Netzwerkansätze in der Geschichtswissenschaft', in C. Stegbauer and R. Häußling (eds), *Handbuch Netzwerkforschung* (Wiesbaden: VS Verlag, 2010), pp. 869–80.
7. This summary is offered by Maria Fusaro for defining 'a commercial network' with reference to C. Schnurmann, *Atlantische Welten: Engländer und Niederländer im amerikanisch-atlantischen Raum 1648–1713* (Cologne: Böhlau 1998) in M. Fusaro, 'Cooperating Mercantile Networks in the Early Modern Mediterranean', *Economic History Review*, 65 (2012), pp. 701–18, on p. 702.
8. On the multiplicity of networks in economic contexts, see the well-structured and illuminating study by M. Casson, 'Networks in Economic and Business History: A Theoretical Perspective', in P. Fernández Pérez and M. B. Rose (eds), *Innovation and Entrepreneurial Networks in Europe* (New York: Routledge, 2010), pp. 14–40.

9. K. Nathaus and D. Gilgen, 'Analysing the Change of Markets', in K. Nathaus and D. Gilgen (eds), 'Change of Markets and Market Societies: Concepts and Case Studies', *Historical Social Research*, special issue, 36:3 (2011), pp. 34–54; J. Beckert, 'How Do Fields Change? The Interrelations of Institutions, Networks, and Cognitions in the Dynamics of Markets', *Organization Studies*, 31 (2010), pp. 605–27.

10. P. Bourdieu, 'Principles of an Economic Anthropology', in N. J. Smelser and R. Swedberg (eds), *The Handbook of Economic Sociology*, 2nd edn (Princeton, NJ and New York: Princeton University Press, 2005), pp. 75–89; B. Latour, *Reassembling the Social: An Introduction to Actor-Network-Theory* (Oxford: Oxford University Press 2005).

11. Granovetter, 'Economic Action and Social Structure'.

12. B. Moeran, 'Trade Fairs, Markets and Fields: Framing Imagined as Real Communities', in K. Nathaus and D. Gilgen (eds), 'Change of Markets and Market Societies: Concepts and Case Studies', *Historical Social Research*, special issue, 36:3 (2011), pp. 79–98, on pp. 80–1. Moeran refers particularly to Erving Goffman.

13. Cf. the interpretation of network analysis offered by P. D. McLean, *The Art of the Network: Strategic Interaction and Patronage in Renaissance Florence* (Durham, NC and London: Duke University Press, 2007).

14. M. Häberlein, 'Kaufmannsdiaspora', in J. Jäger (ed.), *Enzyklopädie der Neuzeit*, Vol. 6 (Stuttgart and Weimar: Metzler, 2007), coll. 483–511; see in particular H. Lang, 'Kaufmannsdiaspora. 6. Florentinische', in ibid., coll. 499–502.

15. L. Galoppini, 'Lucchesi e Uomini di Communità a Bruges nel tardo Medioevo', in L. Tanzini and S. Tognetti (eds), *Mercatura è Arte. Uomini d'Affari Toscani in Europa e nel Mediterraneo Tardomedievale* (Rome: Viella, 2012), pp. 45–80, on pp. 58–75; the *Libro della Communità* kept by the Lucchese in Bruges describes some of the merchants as 'non è lucchese' or 'erano strani [stranieri] e non di nostra comunitade' (pp. 64–5).

16. M. E. Soldani, 'Mercanti, "factori di facciende grosse": Fiorentini, Pisani e Lucchesi a Barcellona nel tardo Medioevo', in L. Tanzini and S. Tognetti (eds), *Mercatura è Arte. Uomini d'Affari Toscani in Europa e nel Mediterraneo tardomedievale* (Rome: Viella, 2012), pp. 115–47, on pp. 142–4.

17. R. Cohen, *Global Diasporas: An Introduction* (London: Routledge, 1997), pp. 83–104.

18. F. Mauro, 'Merchant Communities, 1350–1750', in J. D. Tracy (ed.), *The Rise of Merchant Empires: Long-Distance Trade in the Early Modern World, 1350–1750* (Cambridge: Cambridge University Press, 1990), pp. 255–86; A. Brown, 'Insiders and Outsiders: The Changing Boundaries of Exile', in W. J. Connell (ed.), *Society and Individual in Renaissance Florence* (Berkeley, CA: University of California Press, 2002), pp. 337–83; Soldani, 'Mercanti, "factori di facciende grosse"', p. 132; for exceptions, see K. Weissen, 'I Banchieri Fiorentini ai Concili di Costanza e Basilea', in L. Tanzini and S. Tognetti (eds), *Mercatura è Arte. Uomini d'Affari Toscani in Europa e nel Mediterraneo Tardomedievale* (Rome: Viella, 2012), pp. 81–96. The theory is explained by Mark Casson when he describes the impact of networks on 'a market in trust' in Casson, 'Networks in Economic and Business History', pp. 19–20.

19. M. Cassandro, 'Le Élites Internazionali a Ginevra e Lione nei secoli XV–XVI', in M. Del Treppo (ed.), *Sistema di Rapporti ed Élites Economiche in Europa (secoli XII–XVII)* (Naples: Liguori 1994), pp. 231–48; G.-R. Tewes, *Kampf um Florenz. Die Medici im Exil 1494–1512* (Cologne, Weimar and Vienna: Böhlau, 2011).

20. F. Bayard, 'Les Bonvisi, Marchands Banquiers à Lyon, 1575–1629', *Annales. Économies, Sociétés, Civilisations*, 26 (1971), pp. 1234–69.

21. J. Boucher, *Présence Italienne à Lyon à la Renaissance* (Lyon: Editions LUGD, 1994), pp. 15–22.
22. R. Doucet, *Finances Municipales et Crédit Public à Lyon au XVIe siècle* (Paris, 1937; repr. Geneva: Mégariotis Repr., 1980), pp. 7–17; P. Hamon, *L'Argent du Roi. Les Finances sous Francois Ier* (Paris: Comité pour l'histoire économique et financière Ministère de l'Économie, 1994), pp. 156–9.
23. V. Pinchera, 'L'Archivio Salviati. La Storia degli Affari Attraverso un Archivio Familiare', *Società e Storia*, 13 (1990), pp. 979–86. Averardo Salviati's company came to an end in 1561 when it was wound up and handed over to Piero Salviati and Lionardo Spina from early 1558 onwards: Archivio Salviati (hereafter AS), I, 604, fol. 227. Since Lionardo Spina held the ledgers of the new company as well, it is very probable that he kept the books in his name and did not send them back to the Salviati patriarchs.
24. P. Hurtubise, 'L'Implantation d'une Famille Florentine à Rome au début du XVIe siècle: Les Salviati', in S. Gensini (ed.), *Roma Capitale (1447–1527). Atti del Convegno di Studio del Centro Studi sulla Civiltà del Tardo Medioevo, San Miniato, 27–31 ottobre 1992* (Pisa: Pacini, 1994), pp. 253–71.
25. J. L. Bolton and F. Guidi-Bruscoli, 'When did Antwerp Replace Bruges as the Commercial and Financial Centre of North-Western Europe? The Evidence of the Borromei Ledger for 1438', *Economic History Review*, 61 (2008), pp. 360–79.
26. A. Pallini-Martin, 'L'installation d'une Famille de Marchands-Banquiers Florentins à Lyon au début du XVIe siècle, Les Salviati', in J.-L. Gaulin and S. Rau (eds), *Lyon vu/e d'ailleurs (1245–1800) Echanges, Compétitons et Preceptions* (Lyon: Presses Universitaires de Lyon, 2009) pp. 71–90 ; and her recent approach, A. Pallini-Martin, 'La Gestion et la Maîtrise du Temps et de L'espace dans la Pratique Marchande de la Compagnie Salviati de Lyon Autour de 1500', *Mélanges de l'École Française de Rome – Italie et Méditerranée Modernes et Contemporaines*, 125:1 (2013), at http://mefrim.revues.org/1245 [accessed 11 November 2013]. However, Agnès Pallini-Martin does not recognize studies published in English and German and, hence, some of the material she refers to have already been published elsewhere and her arguments remain incomplete.
27. Pinchera, 'L'Archivio Salviati', pp. 979–86; V. Pinchera, 'Mercanti toscani ad Anversa nel Cinquecento. Il Banco Salviati dal 1540 al 1544' (Master's thesis, University of Pisa, 1987–8).
28. My 'Herrscherfinanzen und Bankiers unter Franz I' is the first attempt to study a particular economic field – government finance – as practised by Florentine merchant bankers in France in the early sixteenth century, using the records preserved in the Salviati archives: H. Lang, 'Herrscherfinanzen der französischen Krone unter Franz I. aus Sicht italienischer und oberdeutscher Bankiers. Die Rolle der Florentiner Salviati als Financiers der französischen Regierung', in P. Rauscher, A. Serles and T. Winkelbauer (eds), *Das Blut des Staatskörpers. Forschungen und Perspektiven zur Finanzgeschichte der Frühen Neuzeit* (Munich and Wien: Oldenbourg, 2012), pp. 457–508; cf. Goldthwaite, *The Economy of Renaissance Florence*, pp. 230–62. Other studies refer to the fifteenth century and do not concentrate on a particular economic field, for example G. Holmes, 'Anglo-Florentine Trade in 1451', *English Historical Review*, 108 (1993), pp. 371–86; A. Carlomagno, 'Il Banco Salviati di Pisa: Commercio e Finanza di una Compagnia Fiorentina tra il 1438 e il 1489' (PhD thesis, University of Pisa, 2009), at http://etd.adm.unipi.it/theses/available/etd-11112009-115303/ [accessed 11 November 2013].
29. Goldthwaite, *The Economy of Renaissance Florence*; J.-F. Bergier, *Genève et l'Économie Européenne de la Renaissance* (Paris: SEVPEN, 1963); R. Gascon, *Grand Commerce et*

vie Urbaine au XVIe siècle. Lyon et ses Marchands (environs de 1520 – environs de 1580) (Paris: SEVPEN, 1971).

30. Tewes, *Kampf um Florenz*, pp. 163–7.
31. The *scudi di marchi* (écu de marc) is money in account used at the fairs in Lyon; the *ducato di camera* is money in account in Italy, particularly in Rome; in Antwerp the *libre di grossi* (*lb di grossi*), the Flemish pound, was the money in account: cf. A. Orlandi, *Le Grand Parti. Fiorentini a Lione e il Debito Pubblico Francese nel XVI secolo* (Florence: Olschki, 2002), pp. 5–6.
32. Lang, 'Herrscherfinanzen und Bankiers unter Franz I', p. 477.
33. For the establishment of the Bartolini, Lanfredini and Salviati compagnies in Lyon and the role of the 'economic network', see Tewes, *Kampf um Florenz*. For the multiple networks of the Florentine elite, see McLean, *The Art of the Network*.
34. Lang, 'Herrscherfinanzen und Bankiers unter Franz I', pp. 479–80.
35. J. F. Padget and P. McLean, 'Organizational Invention and Elite Transformation: The Birth of Partnership Systems in Renaissance Florence', *American Journal of Sociology*, 111 (2006), pp. 1463–568.
36. Goldthwaite, *The Economy of Renaissance Florence*, p. 48.
37. B. Dini, 'Aspetti del Commercio di Esportazione di Panni di Lana e di Drappi di Seta Fiorentini in Costantinopoli, negli Anni 1522–1532', in L. de Rosa (ed.), *Studi in Memoria di Federigo Melis*, 5 vols (Naples: Giannini, 1978), vol. 4, pp. 1–52. For a broader context, see S. Tognetti, 'I Drappi di Seta', in F. Franceschi, R. A. Goldthwaite and R. C. Mueller (eds), *Il Rinascimento Italiano e l'Europa, Vol. 4: Commercio e Cultura Mercantile* (Treviso and Costabissara: Angelo Colla, 2007), pp. 143–70; Pallini-Martin, 'L'Installation d'une Famille de Marchands-Banquiers'; H. Lang, 'Seide aus Florenz. Eine Luxusindustrie am Beispiel der Florentiner Salviati im 16. Jahrhundert', in M. Häberlein, M. Herzog, C. Jeggle, M. Przybilski and A. Tacke (eds), *Luxusgegenstände und Kunstwerke vom Mittelalter bis zur Gegenwart: Produktion – Handel – Formen der Aneignung* (Konstanz: UVK, forthcoming).
38. Lang, 'Herrscherfinanzen und Bankiers unter Franz I', pp. 490–7.
39. AS, III, 9.
40. F. P. Geffcken, 'Die Welser und ihr Handel 1246–1496', in J. Burckhard and M. Häberlein (eds), *Die Welser. Neue Forschungen zur Geschichte und Kultur des oberdeutschen Handelshauses* (Berlin: Akademie Verlag, 2002), pp. 27–167, on 142–3.
41. Tewes, *Kampf um Florenz*, pp. 642–3; Lang, 'Herrscherfinanzen und Bankiers unter Franz I', pp. 477–8.
42. H. Lang, 'Fremdsprachenkompetenz zwischen Handelsverbindungen und Familiennetzwerken. Augsburger Kaufmannssöhne aus dem Welser-Umfeld in der Ausbildung bei Florentiner Bankiers um 1500', in M. Häberlein and C. Kuhn (eds), *Fremde Sprachen in frühneuzeitlichen Städten. Lernende, Lehrende und Lehrwerke* (Wiesbaden: Harrassowitz, 2010), pp. 75–91.
43. These examples are from ibid. On aspects of theory, see Casson, 'Networks in Economic and Business History', pp. 18–19.
44. P. Hurtubise, *Une Famille-Témoin. Les Salviati* (Vatican City: Biblioteca Apostolica Vaticana, 1985), pp. 205–10.
45. AS, I, 761, fols XXIII–IIII; fols 81v–82r.
46. AS, I, 485, fol. 419/CCCCXVIIII; fol. 392; fol. 422/CCCCXXII (*fiera di pasqua* 1542).

47. *Anton Welser und Mitverwandte* in Bruges: AS, I, 437; *Bartholomäus Welser und Mitverwandte* in Antwerp: AS, I; Frescobaldi: AS, I; Giambattista Guicciardini e co d'Anversa: AS, I, 522, fol. 94/LXXXXIIII; 107/CVII (1534–5).
48. V. Pinchera, 'Mercanti fiorentini ad Anversa nel Cinquecento: I Salviati', *Incontri. Rivista di Studi Italo-Nederlandesi*, 4 (1989), pp. 157–65; Pinchera, 'Mercanti toscani ad Anversa', pp. 76–9.
49. Tewes, *Kampf um Florenz*, pp. 1006–7.
50. Pinchera, 'Mercanti toscani ad Anversa', pp. 79–86; Tewes, *Kampf um Florenz*, pp. 1007–8 Lang, 'Herrscherfinanzen und Bankiers unter Franz I', pp. 503–7.
51. L DebCred P (AS, I, 542), fol. 37/xxxvii (*conti del corpo*): *utile* auf *corpo* on 25 January 1546 *scudi* 6003.4.9. The rise of the primary capital in late 1539 did not lead directly to a more profitable performance, as it had in the previous decades.
52. Pinchera, 'Mercanti toscani ad Anversa', pp. 76–9.
53. Ibid., p. 87.
54. Cf. P. Stabel, 'Italian Merchants and the Fairs in the Low Countries (12th–16th Centuries)', in P. Lanaro (ed.), *La Pratica dello Scambio. Sisteme di Fiere, Mercanti e Città in Europa (1400–1700)* (Venice: Marsilio, 2003), pp. 131–60, on p. 157.
55. The listed merchant bankers active in Antwerp and particularly on the axis between Flanders and Castile were not only among the most influential ones but were also closely linked: J. Denucé, *Italiaansche Koopmansgeslachten te Antwerpen in de XCIe–XVIIIe eeuwen* (Mechelen and Amsterdam: De Spieghel, 1940), pp. 27–42.
56. H. van der Wee, *The Growth of the Antwerp Market and the European Economy (Fourteenth–Sixteenth Centuries), Vol. II: Interpretation* (The Hague: Martinus Nijhoff, 1963), especially pp. 166–207 (general tendencies), p. 181 (spediteurs on land routes, particularly Italians), pp. 202–5 (the Antwerp money market), pp. 344–7 (negotiating of bills of exchange); W. Brulez, 'L'Exportation des Pays-Bas vers l'Italie par Voie de Terre au Milieu du XVIe siècle', *Annales. Économies, Sociétés, Civilisations*, 14 (1959), pp. 451–91.
57. Pinchera, 'Mercanti toscani ad Anversa', pp. 93–4.
58. Ibid., pp. 93–101.
59. Ibid., pp. 104–7; Pinchera, 'Mercanti fiorentini ad Anversa nel Cinquecento', p. 159. In 1544 Guaspare Ducci signed the contract for the alum monopoly together with Sebastian Neidhart and Alexis Grimel; Denucé, *Italiaansche Koopmansgeslachten te Antwerpen in de XCIe–XVIIIe eeuwen*, pp. 29–30.
60. Pinchera, 'Mercanti toscani ad Anversa', pp. 120–1.
61. Lang, 'Herrscherfinanzen und Bankiers unter Franz I'.
62. AS, I, 523.
63. AS, I, 558, fol. 316/CCCXVI; fol. 320/CCCXX; Lang, 'Herrscherfinanzen und Bankiers unter Franz I', pp. 488–9.
64. H. Lang, 'La Pratica Contabile come Gestione del Tempo e dello Spazio. La Rete Transalpina tra i Salviati di Firenze e i Welser d'Agusta dal 1507 al 1555', *Mélanges de l'École Française de Rome – Italie et Méditerranée Modernes et Contemporaines*, 125:1 (2013), at http://mefrim.revues.org/1217 [accessed 11 November 2013].

6 Ammannati and González Talavera, 'The Astudillo Partnership and the Spanish "Nation" in Sixteenth-Century Florence'

1. F. Mauro, 'Merchant Communities, 1350–1750', in J. D. Tracy (ed.), *The Rise of Merchant Empires: Long-Distance Trade in the Early Modern World, 1350–1750* (Cambridge: Cambridge University Press, 1999), pp. 255–86, on p. 285; S. Ogilvie, *Institutions and European Trade: Merchant Guilds, 1000–1800* (New York: Cambridge University Press, 2011), p. 25; G. Rossetti, 'Nazione l'Italia o gli Italiani? Breve profilo di un mito che fa riflettere', *Scienza and Politica*, 22 (2000), pp. 23–31, on p. 30; P. Racine, 'Les Débuts des Consulats Italiens Outre-Mer', in M. Balard (ed.), *Etat et Colonisation au Moyen Age* (Lyon: La Manufacture, 1989), pp. 267–76. This aspect is explicitly absent, for example in the case of Florence: Florentine merchants, though present in the main economic centres of the late Middle Ages, never had a formal collective organization in their homeland. See R. A. Goldthwaite, *The Economy of Renaissance Florence* (Baltimore, MD: Johns Hopkins University Press, 2009), pp. 108–9; M. Fusaro, 'Gli Uomini d'Affari Stranieri in Italia', in F. Franceschi, R. A. Goldthwaite and R. C. Mueller (eds), *Il Rinascimento Italiano e l'Europa, Vol. 4: Commercio e Cultura Mercantile* (Costabissara: Angelo Colla Editore, 2007), pp. 369–95, on p. 379. E. Ferreira Priegue, 'Cónsules de Castellanos y cónsules de Españoles en el Mediterráneo Bajomedieval', in H. Casado Alonso (ed.), *Castilla y Europa. Comercio y Mercaderes en los siglos XIV, XV y XVI* (Burgos: Excma. Diputación Provincial de Burgos, 1995), pp. 191–240.

2. See, to cite but a few, the works of C. Rahn Phillips, 'Spanish Merchants and the Wool Trade in the Sixteenth Century', *Sixteenth Century Journal*, 14 (1983), pp 259–82; H. Casado Alonso, *El Triunfo de Mercurio: La Presencia Castellana in Europa, siglos XV y XVI* (Burgos: Cajacírculo, 2003); H. Kellenbenz, 'Mercanti Lucchesi a Norimberga, Francoforte, Colonia e Lipsia nel XVI e nella Prima Metà del XVII secolo', in R. Mazzei and T. Fanfani (eds), *Lucca e l'Europa degli Affari. Secoli XV–XVII* (Lucca: Maria Pacini Fazzi Editore, 1990), pp. 209–28; R. Sabbatini, *'Cercar Esca'. Mercanti Lucchesi ad Anversa nel Cinquecento* (Florence: Salimbeni, 1985).

3. See the classic study by J.-A. Goris, *Étude sur les Colonies Marchandes Méridionales (Portugais, Espagnols, Italiens) à Anvers de 1488 à 1567. Contribution à L'histoire des Débuts du Capitalisme Moderne* (Louvain: Librairie Universitaire, 1925) and the more recent A. Crespo Solana (ed.), *Comunidades transnacionales. Colonias de Mercaderes Extranjeros en el Mundo Atlántico (1500–1830)* (Aranjuez: Doce Calles, 2010); V. N. Zakharov, G. Harlaftis and O. Katsiardi-Hering (eds), *Merchant Colonies in the Early Modern Period* (London: Pickering & Chatto, 2012); R. Zaugg, *Stranieri di Antico Regime. Mercanti, Giudici e Consoli nella Napoli del Settecento* (Rome: Viella, 2011)

4. G. Pinto, 'Forestieri e stranieri nell'Italia Comunale: Considerazioni sulle Fonti Documentarie', in *Forestieri e Stranieri nelle Città Basso-Medievali – Atti del Seminario Internazionale di Studio, Bagno a Ripoli (Firenze), 4–8 giugno 1984* (Florence: Salimbeni, 1988), pp. 19–27, on p. 20; L. Molà, *La Comunità dei Lucchesi a Venezia: Immigrazione e Industria della Seta nel Tardo Medioevo* (Venice: Istituto Veneto di Scienze, Lettere ed Arti, 1994).

5. See the essays collected in *Annales. Histoire, Sciences Sociales*, 58:3 (2003), pp. 569–672, with an introduction by A. Molho and D. Ramada Curto, 'Les Réseaux Marchands à l'Époque Moderne', on pp. 569–79, and the more recent D. Carvajal de la Vega, J. Aníbarro Rodríguez and I. Vítores Casado (eds), *Redes Sociales y Económicas en el Mundo Bajomedieval* (Valladolid: Castilla Ediciones, 2011); F. Trivellato, *The Familiar-*

ity of Strangers: The Sephardic Diaspora, Livorno, and Cross-Cultural Trade in the Early Modern Period (New Haven, CT and London: Yale University Press, 2009).

6. J. M. Imízcoz Beunza, 'Actores y Redes Sociales en Historia', in *Redes Sociales y Económicas en el Mundo Bajomedieval*, pp. 21–33, on p. 26; P. D. McLean, *The Art of the Network: Strategic Interaction and Patronage in Renaissance Florence* (Durham, NC and London: Duke University Press, 2007), pp. 7, 12–13.

7. These, among others, are issues raised by G. Petti Balbi, 'Introduzione', in G. Petti Balbi (ed.), *Comunità Forestiere e 'Nationes' nell'Europa dei secoli XIII–XVI* (Genoa: GISEM-Liguori Editore, 2001), pp. xi–xxiii, on p. xii; Fusaro, 'Gli Uomini d'Affari Stranieri in Italia', p. 376.

8. On this approach, see Trivellato, *The Familiarity of Strangers*, p. 8.

9. H. Hoshino, *L'Arte della Lana in Firenze nel Basso Medioevo. Il Commercio della Lana e il Mercato dei Panni Fiorentini nei Secoli XIII–XV* (Florence: Olschki, 1980), p. 281.

10. F. Ammannati, 'Francesco di Marco Datini's Wool Workshops', in G. Nigro (ed.), *Francesco di Marco Datini: The Man, the Merchant* (Florence: Firenze University Press, 2010), pp. 489–514.

11. Hoshino, *L'Arte della Lana in Firenze*, p. 281.

12. For details, see B. Dini, 'Mercanti Spagnoli a Firenze (1480–1530)', in *Saggi su una Economia-Mondo: Firenze e l'Italia fra Mediterraneo ed Europa. Secc. 13–16* (Pisa: Pacini, 1995), pp. 289–310.

13. W. D. Phillips Jr and C. Rahn Phillips, 'Spanish Wool and Dutch Rebels: The Middelburg Incident of 1574', *American Historical Review*, 82:2 (1977), pp. 312–30.

14. P. Chorley, 'Rascie and the Florentine Cloth Industry during the Sixteenth Century', *Journal of European Economic History*, 32:3 (2003), pp. 487–526; J. Munro, 'The Rise, Expansion, and Decline of the Italian Wool-Based Textile Industries, 1100–1730: A Study in International Competition, Transaction Costs, and Comparative Advantage', *Studies in Medieval and Renaissance History*, 3rd ser., 9 (2012), pp. 45–207, on pp. 131–2.

15. This data can be found in H. Lapeyre, *El Comercio Exterior de Castilla a Través de las Aduanas de Felipe II* (Valladolid: Universidad de Valladolid, Facultad de Filosofía y Letras, 1981); F. Ruiz Martín, *Lettres Marchandes Échangées entre Florence et Medina del Campo* (Paris: SEVPEN, 1965); F. Braudel and R. Romano, *Navires et Marchandises à l'Entrée du Port de Livourne (1547–1611)* (Paris: Armand Colin, 1951).

16. M. Basas Fernández, 'Burgos en el Comercio Lanero del siglo XVI', in P. García Martín and J. M. Sánchez Benito (eds), *Contribución a la Historia de la Trashumancia en España* (Madrid: Ministerio de Agricultura, Pesca y Alimentación, Secretaría General Técnica, 1986), pp. 303–42; M. Basas Fernández, 'Relaciones Económicas entre Burgos y Florencia en el siglo XVI', *Boletín de la Institución Fernán González*, 165 (1965), pp. 689–713.

17. The Michon-Pecori Archives in Carmignano (AMPC), *Suarez de la Concha*, 313, fol. 46.

18. See P. Chorley, 'The Volume of Cloth Production in Florence 1500–1650: An Assessment of the Evidence', in G. L. Fontana and G. Gayot (eds), *Wool: Products and Markets (13–20 Century)* (Padua: CLEUP, 2004), pp. 551–71; F. Ammannati, 'L'Arte della Lana a Firenze nel Cinquecento: Crisi del Settore e Risposte degli operatori', *Storia Economica*, 11 (2008), pp. 5–39; D. Sella, 'L'industria della Lana in Venezia nei secoli Sedicesimo e Diciassettesimo', in C. M. Cipolla (ed.), *Storia dell'Economia Italiana. Saggi di Storia Economica, Vol. 1, Secoli settimo-diciassettesimo* (Turin: Einaudi, 1959), pp. 533–56.

19. Ogilvie, *Institutions and European Trade*, p. 97.

20. C. Rahn Phillips and W. D. Phillips Jr, *El Toisón de Oro Español. Producción y Comercio de Lana en las Épocas Medieval y Moderna* (Valladolid: Junta de Castilla y León, Consejería de Cultura y Turismo, 2005), pp. 243–4, 332.

21. Ibid., p. 233.

22. Ruiz Martín, *Lettres Marchandes*, pp. xxxvii–xxxviii.

23. H. Lapeyre, 'Les Exportations de Laine de Castille sous le Règne de Philippe II', in M. Spallanzani (ed.), *La Lana come Materia Prima: I Fenomeni della sua Produzione e Circolazione nei secoli 13–7 – Atti della prima Settimana di Studio, 18–24 aprile 1969* (Florence: Olschki, 1974), pp. 221–39, on p. 233.

24. R. L. Lee, 'American Cochineal in European Commerce, 1526–1625', *Journal of Modern History*, 23:3 (1951), pp. 205–24.

25. The details of the dynamics of international Castilian trade in this period are set out clearly in Ruiz Martín, *Lettres Marchandes*, pp. xxxv–lx.

26. Ibid., pp. xxxix–lx.

27. Some Astudillo family history can be found in B. González Talavera, 'Mecenazgo español en Florencia: Lesmes de Astudillo e la villa de Montughi (1589–1592)', *Cuadernos de Arte e Iconografía*, 19:38 (2010), pp. 405–28.

28. The Naldini del Riccio Archives in Florence (ANDRF), *Naldini*, Ragione cantante in Melchior de Astudillo, 21. Copias de Chartas de Burgos et Castilla (1559–1560).

29. Ibid., pp. 21–49.

30. Ibid., pp. 22, 23.

31. B. González Talavera, *Presencia y Mecenazgo Español en la Florencia Medicea: de Cosme I a Fernando I de Médicis (1539–1609)* (Granada: Editorial Universidad de Granada, 2011), pp. 188–9.

32. Ruiz Martín, *Lettres Marchandes*, pp. xi, 203–5 (n. 254).

33. Florence State Archives (ASFi), *Libri di Commercio e Famiglia*, 923, 924.

34. Ruiz Martín, *Lettres Marchandes*, p. lxxiv. Another source has him living, during his first Florentine year, with Pietro di Montoya. See AMPC, *Notizie di Nobiltà di Casa Suares: Traduttione dallo Spagnolo in Italiano di un Figlio di Memorie Scritte di Propria Mano dal S.r Baldassarre Suarez della Concia primo Balì di Firenze* (not paginated).

35. E. Lorenzo Sanz, *Comercio de España con América en la época de Felipe II* (Valladolid: Institución Cultural Simancas, de la Diputación Provincial de Valladolid, 1986), p. 263.

36. ANDRF, *Naldini*, Ragione cantante in Melchior de Astudillo, 22, letters of 20 November 1562.

37. C. Polanco Melero, *Muerte y sociedad en Burgos en el siglo XVI* (Burgos: Excma. Diputación Provincial de Burgos, 2001), pp. 242, 244, 262, 300.

38. See González Talavera, *Presencia y Mecenazgo Español en la Florencia Medicea*, p. 156 (nn. 516, 517, 519) for further details about this wedding, celebrated on 28 November 1578.

39. On 16 December 1588 Baldassarre's surname and inheritance were legitimized by a privilege granted by Grand Duke Ferdinand as 'if he had been procreated in a legitimate marriage'. ASFi, *Pratica Segreta*, 189, fol. 73v.

40. Baldassarre's name was inscribed in the baptismal records of Santa Maria del Fiorene on the date of 14 May 1572; the Archives of the Opera di Santa Maria del Fiore in Florence (AOSMFF), *Registri battesimali*, 15, fol. 41. That Lesmes died in 1594 is confirmed by the account opened for his funeral expenses on 22 September. ANDRF, *Naldini*, 53, fol. 491.

41. For more about the Spanish chapel in the convent of Santa Maria Novella, see B. González Talavera, 'Imagen y Poder Español en la Florencia Medicea: La Capilla de los Españoles de Santa María Novella', in *Actas de la XI Reunión Científica de la Fundación Española de Historia Moderna*, 2 vols (Granada: Editorial Universidad de Granada, 2012), vol. 1, pp. 361–72.

42. V. Fineschi, *Memorie sull'antico Cimitero della Chiesa – Il Forestiero Istruito* (Rome: Multigrafica Editrice, 1977), p. 59. For an iconographic study of the frescoes commissioned by Lesmes de Astudillo in the Great Cloister, see González Talavera, *Presencia y Mecenazgo Español en la Florencia Medicea*, pp. 395–8, 401–3.

43. M. Basas Fernández, *El Consulado de Burgos en el siglo XVI* (Burgos: Diputación Provincial de Burgos, 1994), p. 29: 'e porqe los dichos mercaderes e fatores y los consules pasados que estan en el Consulado de Flandes y en Enberes y en La Rochela y en Nantes y en Londres y en Florencia'.

44. A. Crespo Solana, 'Comunidad y familia versus nación en el marco atlántico. Cooperación y competencia en las redes de negociantes flamencos (1690–1760)', in Crespo Solana (ed.), *Comunidades Transnacionales*, pp. 55–62, on p. 57.

45. G. M. Mecatti, *Notizie Istoriche Riguardanti il Capitolo Esistente nel Convento de' Padri Domenicani di Santa Maria Novella della citta di Firenze detto comunemente il Cappellone degli Spagnuoli da Diversi Autori Compilate e Raccolte e Date alla Luce dall'abate Giuseppe Maria Mecatti e da Esso Dedicate al Merito Sempre Grande dell'eminentissimo e reverendissimo Principe Lodovico Belluga Moncada* (Florence: Bernardo Paperini, 1737), pp. 37–41: 'Por entonces, el "Consul Nationis praedictae" era el "Magnificus D. Balthassar Suares" (Baltasar Suárez de la Concha) y los cuatro diputados eran los señores "D. Lesmes de Astudillo, D. Petrus de Montorio, D. Diegus Lopes de Castro, et D. Gabriel de Castro"'.

46. ASFi, *Mediceo del Principato*, 5080, fol. 411r.

47. The data on the map and the analysis which follows covers in particular the years 1591–4, resulting from these letter books: ANDRF, *Naldini*, 37: 'Copias de cartas para Leon y Bisançon, I' (1591–4); *Naldini*, 38: 'Copie di lettere' (1592–7); *Naldini*, 39: 'Copias de Cartas para Italia, I' (1593–4); *Naldini*, 40: 'Copias de Cartas para Italia, I' (1593–4); and from the Libro Mayor, the ledger (ANDRF, *Naldini*, 53, labelled I, 1591–8) together with the corresponding Libro Manual, the journal (ANDRF, *Naldini*, 54, labelled I, 1591–8).

48. Braudel and Romano, *Navires et Marchandises*.

49. The most important evidence of this activity is the presence, in the Libro Mayor, of specific accounts named 'Encomiendas generales' which summarized all the fees concerning each trade or financial operation that had been charged to the commissioners of Astudillo a year at a time. ANDRF, *Naldini*, 53: see 'Economiendas generales' in the accounts list attached to the Libro Mayor.

50. Casado Alonso, *El Triunfo de Mercurio*.

51. M. Casson, 'An Economic Approach to Regional Business Networks', in J. F. Wilson and A. Popp (eds), *Industrial Cluster and Regional Business Networks in England, 1750–1970* (Aldershot: Ashgate, 2003), pp. 19–43.

52. ASFi, *Libri di Commercio e Famiglia*, 919, fol. 73r; 920, fols 3v, 11r.

53. In 1586 there were 114 wool workshops active in Florence, a number that was down to 100 in 1596. See P. Malanima, *La Decadenza di un'Economia Cittadina. L'Industria di Firenze nei secoli XVI–XVI* (Bologna: Il Mulino, 1982), p. 292.

54. ANDRF, *Naldini*, 53, fols 30 3, 44, 54, 71, 78, 95, 107, 119, 131, 140, 153, 162, 165, 192, 237, 251, 259, 319, 325, 337, 344, 397, 411, 421, 422, 424, 520.
55. Ibid., fols 140, 237, 298, 482, 483, 494.
56. Ibid., fols 316, 336, 426, 473, 473, 516.
57. Ibid., fols 48, 166, 195, 222, 266, 324, 396.
58. Ibid., fol. 182; *Naldini*, 39, letter of 6 March 1593 to Paolo Donati.
59. Ibid., *Naldini*, 53, fols 43, 45, 152, 156, 171, 408, 420, 440, 450.
60. Ibid., *Naldini*, 39, letter of 27 March 1593 to Francesco and Bartolomeo Berzighetti.
61. Ibid., *Naldini*, 53, fols 127, 280.
62. ASFi, *Miscellanea Medicea*, 27/III, fols 1095r–1097r.
63. ANDRF, *Naldini*, 37, the many letters to Arnolfini Micheli from November 1591 onwards.
64. Ibid., the many letters to Gioacchino Berardi and Paolo Piero Bebo from February 1593 onwards. Ibid., *Naldini*, 53, fol. 83.
65. Ibid., fols 50, 84, 151, 241, 254, 257, 338, 379, 395, 478.
66. Ibid., fols 266, 267.
67. Ibid., fols 44, 197, 397, 500, 509.
68. R. A. Goldthwaite, 'Le aziende seriche e il mondo degli affari a Firenze alla fine del '500', *Archivio Storico Italiano*, CLXIX, 62:2 (2011), pp. 281–341, on p. 304.
69. ANDRF, *Naldini*, 53, fols 71, 362, 426, 514.
70. Ibid., fols 128, 154, 177, 227, 253, 496, 519.
71. Ibid., fol. 128.
72. See, among many others, C. Sánchez Silva and M. Suárez Bosa, 'Evolución de la producción y el comercio mundial de la grana cochinilla, siglos XVI–XIX', *Revista de Indias*, 66:237 (2006), pp. 473–90.
73. It must therefore be stressed that the Casa de la Contratación in Seville never permitted the creation of a monopoly of only one merchant, or a group of merchants, over the cochineal trade. Ruiz Martín, *Lettres Marchandes*, p. ccxvii–ccxviii.
74. ANDRF, *Naldini*, 53, fols 117, 148, 198, 203, 251, 261, 332, 438.
75. Ibid., fols 126, 142.
76. Ibid., fols 177, 196, 221, 222, 242, 281, 299, 310, 335, 352, 370, 386, 386, 451, 470, 477, 510.
77. In the vast bibliography about fairs in Europe in the sixteenth and seventeenth centuries, see M. Cassandro, *Le Fiere di Lione e gli Uomini d'Affari Italiani nel Cinquecento* (Florence: Baccini & Chiappi, 1979); H. Lapeyre, *Une Famille de Marchands: Les Ruiz* (Paris: Armand Colin, 1955).
78. The Federigo di Ruberto de' Ricci company was one of the most prominent banks active on the local market: see Goldthwaite, *The Economy of Renaissance Florence*, p. 477. See the huge account opened for the 'Redi de Federigo de' Ricci de banco' in the Libro Mayor. ANDRF, *Naldini*, 53, fols 35ff.
79. Ruiz Martín, *Lettres Marchandes*, pp. lxiv–xciii.
80. The Astudillo corresponded with Giuseppe and Bernardo Arnolfini & Girolamo and Bonaventura Micheli in Antwerp, Francesco and Giuseppe Arnolfini & Girolamo and Alessandro Micheli in Lyon, Battista Arnolfini & Baldassarre Fardini in Ancona, and Francesco Arnolfini and Girolamo Diodati, and with Giuseppe Arnolfini alone in Lucca. For Bonvisi and Balbani, see ANDRF, *Naldini*, 53, the accounts list attached to the Libro Mayor. See also F. Bayard, 'Les Bonvisi, Marchands Banquiers à Lyon, 1575–1629', *Annales. Histoire, Sciences Sociales*, 26:6 (1971), pp. 1234–69; F. Bayard, 'Après les Buon-

visi. Les Lucquois à Lyon aux XVIIe et XVIIIe siècles', in R. Mazzei and T. Fanfani (eds), *Lucca e l'Europa degli Affari. Secoli XV–XVII* (Lucca: Maria Pacini Fazzi Editore, 1990), pp. 193–208.

81. ANDRF, *Naldini*, 53, fols 39, 98, 187, 259, 264, 381, 351, 407.
82. See the accounts of Iacopo Carpiani in Rome in ibid., fols 142, 241.
83. Emanuel De Fonseca, Juan Enriquez de Herrera & Ottavioe Costa, Gaspar Gomez de la Serra, Juan Lerma, Gaspar Manriques Loyola, Francisco De Melgosa, Hieronimo Miranda. See the accounts list attached to the Libro Mayor in ibid.
84. This is the full list of bankers corresponding from Bisenzone with the partnership: Giovanbattista Segni, Cristoforo and Giovanni Balbani, Niccolò Del Bene, Francesco Fratini & Gherardo Arrighi, Lorenzo Furieti & Lorenzo Pamizoli, Antonio Galilei, Jorge Gentil and Paulo Batista Serra, Iacopo di Giunta and Pier Filippo Gianfigliazzi, Filippo Spinola and Melchiorre Negroni, Giovanni Francesco Viviano, Filippo Cattaneo and Adamo Centurione, Giovan Pietro Cattaneo Serra and Giovan Benedetto Spinola, Alessandro Ottaviano and Niccolò Diodati, Giorgio Giulio Gentil and Mario Paravicino, Girolamo and Francesco Mazini, Niccolò Paravicino and Paulo and Battista Serra. See the accounts list attached to the Libro Mayor in ibid.
85. Malanima, *La Decadenza*; Ammannati, 'L'Arte della Lana a Firenze'. However there were exceptions, such as Ascanio Saminiati's (1624–84) companies with their wide-ranging business activities; see S. Groppi, *L' archivio Saminiati-Pazzi* (Milan: Egea, 1990).
86. ANDRF, *Naldini*, Ragione cantante in Melchior de Astudillo, 142.
87. ASFi, *Ceramelli Papiani*, n. 227, and *Manoscritti*, 320.
88. J. I. Pulido Serrano, 'Procesos de Integración y Asimilación: El Caso de los Portugueses en España durante la Edad Moderna', in Crespo Solana (ed.), *Comunidades Transnacionales*, pp. 189–206, on pp. 193–6.
89. F. Ruiz Martín, *Pequeño Capitalismo, Gran Capitalismo. Simón Ruiz y sus Negocios en Florencia* (Barcelona: Crítica, 1990), p. 74.
90. C. Sebregondi, *Famiglie Patrizie Fiorentine I (Ramirez de Montalvo, Suárez de la Concha y Ximenes de Aragona)* (Florence: C. Cya, 1940), Suárez de la Concha, table I. This path was also followed by other members of the Suárez de la Concha family: Fernando, Baltasar's son, 'married in 1618 Maria de' Medici, son of Cosimo *patrizio* of Florence, Captain under the Imperial service, Commissioner in Pisa and Senator of the Grand Duke Cosimo II'. A few years later, in 1627, he married his second wife, Eleonora degli Albizzi, 'daughter of Piero, *patrizio* of Florence and granddaughter of Eleonora degli Albizzi, a *favourite* of Grand Duke Cosimo I'.
91. González Talavera, *Presencia y Mecenazgo Español en la Florencia Medicea*, p. 260.
92. R. Bizzocchi, 'Cultura e Sociabilità Nobiliare', in E. Fasano Guarini (ed.), *Storia della Civiltà Toscana*, 6 vols (Florence: Le Monnier, 2003) vol. 3, pp. 485–504, on p. 495; D. Barsanti, 'Presenze spagnole a Firenze nel secolo XVI: Le commende di Padronato Sastri e Suarez nell' "Ordine di Santo Stefano"', *Toscana e Spagna nel secolo XVI. Miscellanea di studi storici* (Pisa: ETS, 1996), pp. 189–222.
93. ASFi, *Mediceo del Principato*, 1163, fol. 472.
94. ASFi, *Panciatichi Ximenes d'Aragona*, fols 221–7.
95. H. Casado Alonso, 'Las Colonias de Mercaderes Castellanos en Europa (siglos XV y XVI)', in Casado Alonso (ed.), *Castilla y Europa*, pp. 15–56, on p. 26; A. Vandewalle, 'El consulado de Burgos en los Países Bajos', in *Actas del V Centenario del Consulado de Burgos (1494–1994)*, (Burgos: Diputación Provincial de Burgos, 1994) vol. 1, pp. 283–300, on p. 291.

96. González Talavera, *Presencia y Mecenazgo Español en la Florencia Medicea*, pp. 132–55.

97. AMPC, *Notizie della Nobiltà di Casa Suares* (unpaginated).

98. C. Demeulenaere-Douyère, 'Les Espagnols et la Société Rouennaise au XVIe Siècle', *Etudes Normandes*, 3 (1981), pp. 65–83.

99. For the changing structure of the Florentine wool industry between the sixteenth and the seventeenth century, see F. Ammannati, 'Forentine Woollen Manufacture in the Sixteenth Century: Crisis and New Entrepreneurial Strategies', *Business and Economic History On-Line*, 7 (2009), pp. 1–9, on pp. 6–9; Malanima, *La Decadenza*.

100. G. M. Mecatti, *Storia Genealogica della Nobiltà e Cittadinanza di Firenze Divisa in Quattro Parti* (Naples, 1754), part I, introduction.

101. P. Molas, *La Burguesía Mercantil en la España del Antiguo Régimen* (Madrid: Cátedra, 1985), p. 125.

102. Lapeyre, *Une Famille de Merchands: Les Ruiz*, p. 95, n. 294, and pp. 116–20.

103. See, among many others, P. Malanima, *I Riccardi di Firenze. Una Famiglia e un Patrimonio nella Toscana dei Medici* (Florence: Olschki, 1977), pp. 43–5; S. Berner, 'Florentine Society in the Late Sixteenth and Early Seventeenth Centuries', *Studies in the Renaissance*, 18 (1971), pp. 203–46; R. Burr Litchfield, 'Les Investissements Commerciaux des Patriciens Florentins au XVIIIe siècle', *Annales. Économies, Sociétés, Civilisations*, 24:3 (1969), pp. 685–721.

104. J. Goodman, 'Financing Pre-Modern European Industry: An Example from Florence, 1580–1660', *Journal of European Economic History*, 10:2 (1981), pp. 415–35; M. Carmona, 'Aspects du Capitalisme Toscan aux XVIe et XVIIe Siècles', *Revue d'Histoire Moderne et Contemporaine*, 11:2 (1964), pp. 81–108.

105. 'a avido siempre un consul nombrado por los Hombres de negocios residentes en ella, pero por averse ydo desminuyendo las casas de españoles de manera que no han quedado sino dos: no ay quien concurra a la elección del dicho consul que solian hacer'. AMPC, *Notizie di nobiltà di Casa Suares* (not paginated), quoted in González Talavera, *Presencia y Mecenazgo Español en la Florencia Medicea*, p. 178.

7 Carvajal de la Vega, 'Merchant Networks in the Cities of the Crown of Castile'

1. On medieval legacies, see S. R. Duplessis, *Transitions to Capitalism in Early Modern Europe* (Cambridge and New York: Cambridge University Press, 1997), pp. 14–43; and on Castile, see M. Á. Ladero Quesada, *Ciudades en la España Medieval* (Madrid: Dykinson, 2010), pp. 30–2.

2. C. H. Parker, 'Introduction: Individual and Community in the Early Modern World', in C. H. Parker and J. H. Bentley (eds), *Between the Middle Ages and Modernity: Individual and Community in the Early Modern World* (Lanham, MD: Rowman & Littlefield, 2007), pp. 1–9, on pp. 8–9.

3. S. Subrahmanyam, 'Introduction', in S. Subrahmanyam, *Merchant Networks in the Early Modern World* (Aldershot: Ashgate Variorum, 1996), pp. xiii–xxvi, on p. xxii.

4. J. F. Padgett and C. K. Ansell, 'Robust Action and the Rise of the Medici, 1400–1434', *American Journal of Sociology*, 98:6 (1993), pp. 1259–319.

5. J. M. Imízcoz Beunza, 'Actores y Redes Sociales en la Historia', in D. Carvajal de la Vega, J. Añíbarro Rodríguez and I. Vítores Casado (eds), *Redes Sociales y Económicas en el Mundo Bajomedieval* (Valladolid: Castilla Ediciones, 2011), pp. 21–33.

6.   The importance of financial networks as credit suppliers in the Spanish monarchy was studied by J. P. Dedieu, *Grupos Financieros al Servicio del Rey de España. Fines del siglo XVII – Principios del XVIII* (Laboratoire de Recherche Historique Rhone-Alpes, 2009), at http://halshs.archives-ouvertes.fr/docs/00/44/45/81/PDF/Entreprises_esp.pdf [accessed 13 March 2013]. On the 'social network analysis' approach in studies of the Spanish Middle Ages, see M. Á. Martín Romera, 'Nuevas Perspectivas para el Estudio de las Sociedades Medievales: El Análisis de Redes Sociales', *Studia Histórica. Historia Medieval*, 28 (2010), pp. 217–39.

7.   H. Casado Alonso, *El Triunfo de Mercurio: La Presencia Castellana in Europa, siglos XV y XVI* (Burgos: Cajacírculo, 2003); H. Casado Alonso, 'Una familia de la oligarquía burgalesa en el siglo XV: los Alonso de Burgos-Maluenda', in *La ciudad de Burgos* (Madrid: Junta de Castilla y León, 1985), pp. 143–62; H. Casado Alonso, 'Los flujos de información en las redes comerciales castellanas de los siglos XV y XVI', *Investigaciones de Historia Económica: Revista de la Asociación Española de Historia Económica*, 10 (2008), pp. 35–68; B. Caunedo del Potro, 'Los Negocios de Diego de Soria, Mercader Burgalés', in *La Ciudad de Burgos* (Madrid: Junta de Castilla y León, 1985), pp. 163–71; B. Caunedo del Potro, 'Operaciones Comerciales del Grupo Familiar Castro', *En la España Medieval*, 8 (1986), pp. 289–98; B. Caunedo del Potro, 'Factores Burgaleses, ¿Privilegiados o Postergados?', *En la España Medieval*, 21 (1988), pp. 39–60; B. Caunedo del Potro, 'Acerca de la Riqueza de los Mercaderes Burgaleses: Aproximación a su Nivel de Vida', *En la España Medieval*, 16 (1993), pp. 97–118; B. Caunedo del Potro, 'Compañías Mercantiles Castellanas a Fines de la Edad Media', *Medievalismo*, 3 (1993), pp. 39–58; B. Caunedo del Potro, 'La Disgregación de una Rica Hacienda: El Ocaso Mercantil de los Descendientes de Diego de Soria. ¿Un problema político?', *Espacio, Tiempo y Forma. Serie III. Historia Medieval*, 19 (2007), pp. 77–97; M. Basas Fernández, 'El Mercader Burgalés Gómez de Quintanadueñas', *Boletín de la Institución Fernán González*, 155 (1961), pp. 561–76; Y. Guerrero Navarrete, 'Elites urbanas en el siglo XV: Burgos y Cuenca', *Revista d'historia medieval*, 9 (1998), pp. 81–104; Y. Guerrero Navarrete, 'Hacia una prosopografía de los grupos financieros burgaleses', in Y. Guerrero Navarrete (ed.), *Fiscalidad, sociedad y poder en las ciudades castellanas en la Baja Edad Media* (Madrid: Universidad Autónoma de Madrid, 2006), pp. 203–39.

8.   C. Muldrew, 'Credit and the Courts: Debt Litigation in a Seventeenth-Century Urban Community', *Economic History Review*, 46 (1993), pp. 23–38, and C. Muldrew, *The Economy of Obligation: The Culture of Credit and Social Relations in Early Modern England* (Basingstoke: Macmillan, 1998), pp. 218–32.

9.   D. Carvajal de la Vega, 'Flujos financieros Norte-Sur en Castilla a fines de la Edad Media', in J. Añíbarro Rodríguez, I. Vítores Casado and D. Carvajal de la Vega (eds), *Relaciones Norte-Sur en la Edad Media* (Santander: AMEA, forthcoming).

10.   We could appreciate the creation of networks around the taxation business in 1440; see P. Ortego Rico, 'Financieros y Redes Financieras en Tiempos de Juan II: Posibilidades de Estudio del Libro de Recepta de 1440', in Carvajal de la Vega, Añíbarro Rodríguez and Vítores Casado (eds), *Redes Sociales y Económicas en el Mundo Bajomedieval*, pp. 105–21. On the royal tax administration networks, see P. Ortego Rico, 'Arrendadores mayores y arrendadores menores. La configuración de redes socioeconómicas a través de la gestión de la hacienda real a fines del siglo XV: Algunos ejemplos', in Á. Galán Sánchez and E. García Fernández (eds), *En busca de Zaqueo: Los Recaudadores de Impuestos en las Épocas Medieval y Moderna* (Madrid: Instituto de Estudios Fiscales – Arca Comunis, 2012), pp. 99–116.

11. M. Á. Martín Romera, 'Las Redes Sociales de la Oligarquía de la Villa de Valladolid (1450–1520)' (PhD dissertation, Universidad Complutense de Madrid, 2012).
12. Archivo de la Real Chancillería de Valladolid (hereafter ARChV), Pleitos Civiles, Masas (Fenecidos), box 3174,3.
13. F. A. Al-Hussein, 'Estrategia de los Mercaderes en Matrimonio y Herencia', pp. 175–90, and 'Las Compañías o Asociaciones de Mercaderes', pp. 193–211, both in E. Lorenzo Sanz (ed.), *Historia de Medina del Campo y su Tierra, Volume II* (Valladolid: Ayto. Medina del Campo – Junta de Castilla y León – Exma. Dip. de Valladolid, 1986)
14. Guerrero Navarrete, 'Elites Urbanas en el siglo XV'.
15. Casado Alonso, *El Triunfo de Mercurio*, p. 45.
16. Ibid., pp. 73–5; H. Casado Alonso, 'Oligarquía urbana, comercio internacional y poder real: Burgos a fines de la Edad Media', in A. Rucquoi (ed.), *Realidad e imágenes del poder: España a fines de la Edad Media* (Valladolid: Ámbito, 1988), pp. 325–48.
17. See Mike Burkhardt's essay in this volume.
18. The case of Diego de Soria was a perfect example on this process. His fortune was based on weapons commerce with Italy and his good relations with kings; Caunedo del Potro, 'Los Negocios de Diego de Soria'.
19. Some of the best examples to understand the importance of family structures are R. A. Goldthwaite, 'The Medici Bank and the World of Florentine Capitalisme', *Past & Present*, 114 (1978), pp. 3–31; and Padgett and Ansell, 'Robust Action'.
20. D. Carvajal de la Vega, 'Redes Socioeconómicas y Mercaderes Castellanos a Fines de la Edad Media e inicios de la Moderna', in Carvajal de la Vega, Añíbarro Rodríguez and Vítores Casado (eds), *Redes Sociales y Económicas en el Mundo Bajomedieval*, pp. 81–101.
21. N. Palenzuela, *Los Mercaderes Burgaleses en Sevilla a Finales de la Edad Media* (Seville: Universidad de Sevilla, 2003), p. 17.
22. On the diversification of Burgalese merchant families, see Caunedo del Potro, 'Operaciones Comerciales'.
23. Archivo General de Simancas (hereafter AGS), Registro General del Sello (hereafter RGS), legajo 148712,76; ARChV, Registro de Ejecutorias, box 311–39; and F. A. Al-Hussein, 'Las Ferias de Medina y el Comercio de la Lana: 1514–1573', in Lorenzo Sanz (ed.), *Historia de Medina del Campo Volume II*, pp. 15–42, on p. 32.
24. See Mike Burkhardt's essay, above.
25. Carvajal de la Vega, 'Redes Socioeconómicas y Mercaderes Castellanos', pp. 87–100.
26. The common family, Burgos, was divided into different groups: López de Burgos, García de Burgos and Alonso de Burgos. Guerrero Navarrete, 'Hacia una prosopografía de los grupos financieros burgaleses', pp. 220–1, and Casado Alonso, 'Una familia de la oligarquía burgalesa'.
27. Y. Guerrero Navarrete, *Organización y Gobierno en Burgos durante el Reinado de Enrique IV de Castilla (1453–1476)* (Madrid: Universidad Autónoma de Madrid, 1986), pp. 146–93.
28. M. Basas Fernández, *El Consulado de Burgos en el siglo XVI* (Madrid: CSIC, 1963), pp. 29–36.
29. ARChV, Pleitos Civiles, Alonso Rodríguez (Fenecidos), box 3545,1.
30. This lawsuit was studied by Caunedo del Potro in 'La Disgregación de una Rica Hacienda'.
31. Basas Fernández, *El Consulado de Burgos*, pp. 36–9.
32. J. D. González Arce, 'La Universidad de Mercaderes de Burgos y el Consulado Castellano en Brujas durante el siglo XV', *En la España Medieval*, 33 (2010), pp. 161–202.

33. P. Spufford, *How Rarely Did Medieval Merchants Use Coin?* (Utrecht: Geldmuseum, 2008).
34. E. Otte, 'Los Instrumentos Financieros', in E. Aznar Vallejo and A. Collantes de Terán (eds), *Andalucía 1492: Razones de un Protagonismo* (Seville: Sociedad Estatal para la Exposición Universal Sevilla, 1992), pp. 157–65.
35. Á. García Sanz, 'El Crédito a Principios del siglo XVI en una Ciudad de Castilla: La Nobleza como Financiadora del Comercio y de la Industria en Segovia, 1503–1508', *Studia Historica. Edad Moderna*, 5 (1987), pp. 77–88; and D. Carvajal de la Vega, 'Crédito Privado en Castilla (1480–1521)', *X Congreso Internacional de la Asociación Española de Historia Económica* (2011), at http://www.aehe.net/xcongreso/pdf/sesiones/tesis/david-carvajal.pdf [accessed 29 November 2013].
36. The social role of credit between merchants was studied by Muldrew, *The Economy of Obligation*, p. 123 (see the chapter 'The Sociability of Credit and Commerce').
37. In this essay I do not consider credit operations with institutions like the city council, but it is well known that strong financial ties existed between these agents in order to finance institutional expenditures. B. Caunedo del Potro, 'Operaciones Comerciales', p. 295, and Caunedo del Potro, 'Los Negocios de Diego de Soria'.
38. D. Carvajal de la Vega, 'Crédito Privado y Deuda en Castilla (1480–1521)' (PhD dissertation, Universidad de Valladolid, 2013).
39. Casado Alonso, 'Los flujos de información en las redes comerciales'.
40. F. Trivellato, 'Marriage, Commercial Capital, and Business Agency: Transregional Sephardic (and Armenian) Families in the Seventeenth- and Eighteenth-Century Mediterranean', in C. H. Johnson, D. Warren Sabean, S. Teuscher and F. Trivellato (eds), *Transregional and Transnational Families in Europe and Beyond: Experiences since the Middle Ages* (New York and Oxford: Berghahn Books, 2011), pp. 107–30.
41. ARChV, Pleitos Civiles, Quevedo (Depósito), box 47–1.
42. ARChV, Reales Ejecutorias, box 41–14.
43. ARChV, Reales Ejecutorias, box 38–14.
44. Caunedo del Potro, 'La Disgregación de una Rica Hacienda', p. 79.
45. ARChV, Pleitos Civiles, Alonso Rodríguez (Depósito), box 10–6.
46. ARChV, Pleitos Civiles, Fernando Alonso (Fenecidos), box 202–7.
47. ARChV, Pleitos Civiles, Moreno (Olvidados), box 949,2 and Pleitos Civiles, Moreno (Olvidados), box 544,1.
48. For example, in 1493 Andrés de Escobar and his father demanded their economic rights to different neighbours from Almazán (Soria). In 1494 García de Fuentedueña and Bernaldino de Cuéllar, merchants from Segovia, demanded some credit sales to Andrés de Escobar and his father. AGS, RGS, leg. 149312,154 and leg. 149467,397.
49. Caunedo del Potro, 'Acerca de la Riqueza de los Mercaderes Burgaleses'.
50. AGS, RGS, leg. 149907,340.
51. Andrés de Escobar could not pay his debt. For this reason, the local judges ordered houses that Fernán López de Calatayud had in the centre of Valladolid to be confiscated. 13 October 1506. ARChV, Pleitos Civiles, Lapuerta (Fenecidos), box 488–2.
52. ARChV, Pleitos Civiles, Lapuerta (Fenecidos), box 488–2.
53. ARChV, Pleitos Civiles, Pérez Alonso (Fenecidos), box 986,2.
54. García de Quintanadueñas was Isabel de la Torre's uncle; and Isabel was married to Luis de Burgos, a member of the García de Burgos family. ARChV, Pleitos Civiles, Fernando Alonso (Fenecidos), box 770,1.
55. ARChV, Reales Ejecutorias, c.32–29/30.

56. We know well their business in Rouen; Basas Fernández, 'El Mercader Burgalés Gómez de Quintanadueñas'.
57. R. Muñoz Solla, 'Judeoconversos Burgaleses a Fines de la Edad Media', *Espacio, Tiempo y Forma. Serie III. Historia Medieval*, 22 (2009), pp. 207–27, on p. 210.
58. Guerrero Navarrete, 'Elites urbanas en el siglo XV', p. 103.

8 Montemezzo, 'Galley Routes and Merchant Networks between Venice and the North Sea in the Fifteenth Century'

1. For a general reference, see among others F. C. Lane, *Venice. A Maritime Republic* (Baltimore, MD: Johns Hopkins University Press, 1973), pp. 66–81 and 124–31.
2. P. Lanaro, 'At the Centre of the Old World: Reinterpreting Venetian Economic History', in P. Lanaro (ed.), *At the Centre of the Old World. Trade and Manufacturing in Venice and the Venetian Mainland, 1400–1800* (Toronto: Centre for Reformation and Renaissance Studies, 2006), pp. 19–21.
3. J. C. Hocquet, 'I Meccanismi dei Traffici', in G. Arnaldi, G. Cracco and A. Tenenti (eds), *Storia di Venezia. Dalle Origini alla Caduta della Serenissima*, Vol. III, *La Formazione dello Stato Patrizio* (Rome: Centro per l'Enciclopedia Italiana, 1997), pp. 529–616; C. Judde de Larivière, *Naviguer, Commercer, Gouverner. Économie Maritime et Pouvoirs à Venise (XVe–XVIe siècles)* (Leiden: Brill, 2008), pp. 63–122; M. Fusaro, 'Cooperating Mercantile Networks in the Early Modern Mediterranean', *Economic History Review*, 65:2 (2012), pp. 701–18; B. Arbel, 'Venice's Maritime Empire in the Early Modern Period', in E. Dursteler (ed.), *A Companion to Venetian History, 1400–1797* (Leiden: Brill, 2013), pp. 125–253; L. Pezzolo, 'The Venetian Economy', in E. Dursteler (ed.), *A Companion to Venetian History, 1400–1797* (Leiden: Brill, 2013), pp. 255–89.
4. A transcript of the books is published in S. Montemezzo (ed.), *Giovanni Foscari. Viaggi di Fiandra, 1463–1464 e 1467–1468* (Venice: La Malcontenta, 2012).
5. See among others A. A. Ruddock, *Italian Merchants and Shipping in Southampton, 1270–1600* (Southampton: University College, 1951); A. Wandewalle and N. Geirnaert, 'Bruges and Italy', in V. Vermeersch (ed.), *Bruges and Europe* (Antwerp: Fonds Mercator, 1992), pp. 182–205; D. Abulafia, 'Cittadino e Denizen: Mercanti Italiani a Southampton e Londra', in M. Del Treppo (ed.) *Sistema di Rapporti ed Élites Economiche in Europa (secoli XII–XVII)* (Napoli: Liguori, 1994), pp. 273–92; J. A. Van Houtte, 'L'attività delle Élites Meridionali nei Grandi Centri Commerciali dei Paesi Bassi tra il XIII e il XVI secolo', in M. Del Treppo (ed.) *Sistema di Rapporti ed Élites Economiche in Europa (secoli XII–XVII)* (Napoli: Liguori, 1994), pp. 259–72; P. Stabel, 'Venice: Where North Meets South', in B. Akema and B. L. Brown (eds), *Renaissance Venice and the North: Crosscurrents in the Time of Bellini, Dürer and Titian* (London: Thames & Hudson, 2000), pp. 31–43; A. Vandewalle, 'Les Nations Étrangères à Bruges', in *Les Marchands de la Hanse et la Banque de Médicis. Bruges Marché d'Échanges Culturels en Europe* (Oostkamp: Stichting Kunstboek, 2002), pp. 27–42; G. Nordio, 'La Colonia Mercantile Veneziana nella Londra di Metà Quattrocento: Attività Commercial e Movimento Anti-Alien', in G. Boschiero and B. Molina (eds), *Politiche del credito. Investimenti, Consumo, Solidarietà: Atti del Congresso Internazionale, Asti 20–22 marzo 2003* (Asti: Arti Grafiche TSG, 2004), pp. 222–40; B. Blondé, O. Gelderblom and P. Stabel, 'Foreign Merchant Communities in Bruges, Antwerp and Amsterdam', in D. Calabi

(ed.), *Cultural Exchange in Early Modern Europe*, Vol. 2, *Cities and Cultural Exchange in Europe, 1400–1700* (Cambridge: Cambridge University Press, 2007), pp. 154–74.

6.   Stabel, 'Venice: Where North Meets South', pp. 31–3; J. M. Murray, *Bruges: Cradle of Capitalism, 1280–1390* (Cambridge: Cambridge University Press, 2005), pp. 223–4.

7.   Judde de Larivière, *Naviguer, Commercer, Gouverner*; B. Doumerc, 'Le Galere da Mercato', in A. Tenenti and U. Tucci (eds), *Storia di Venezia. Dalle Origini alla Caduta della Serenissima*, Vol. 12, *Il mare* (Rome: Istituto della Enciclopedia italiana, 1991), pp. 357–96; D. Stöckly, *Le Système de l'Incanto des Galées du Marché à Venise (fin XIIIe–milieu XVe siècle)* (Leiden: Brill, 1995).

8.   The State Archive of Venice experienced heavy losses of private documents, particularly in relation to accounting, at the end of the nineteenth century. The choice not to retain private documents was dictated by the prevailing interests during the period, which were mostly oriented to public documents as testimony to the conduct of the Republic.

9.   Among others, see F. J. Apellániz de la Galarreta, *Pouvoir et Finance en Mediterrenée Prémoderne. Le Deuxième État Mamelouk et le Commerce des Épices (1382–1517)* (Barcelona: Consejo Superior de investigaciones científicas, 2009); M. Fusaro, *Uva Passa. Una Guerra Commerciale fra Venezia e l'Inghilterra, 1540–1640* (Venice: Il Cardo, 1996); F. Trivellato, *The Familiarity of Strangers: The Sephardic Diaspora, Livorno, and Cross-Cultural Trade in the Early Modern Period* (New Haven, CT and London: Yale University Press, 2009); M. van Gelder, *Trading Places: The Netherlandish Merchants in Early Modern Venice* (Leiden: Brill, 2009).

10. Accounting documentation, in particular the ledgers I consider in this essay, does not provide the information necessary for the reconstruction of a network. There are three reasons: the first is the short-term and sporadic nature of the data; second, the point of view offered by the source is unilateral and does not address the relations between actors; and third, as the data concern a seasonally mobile merchant, the entry to or exit from a network cannot be defined as totally voluntary. For references, see Mike Burkhardt's contribution in this volume.

11. Lane, *Venice*, pp. 96 and 124–7; E. R. Dursteler, 'Introduction: A Brief Survey of Histories of Venice', in E. Dursteler (ed.), *A Companion to Venetian History, 1400–1797* (Leiden: Brill, 2013), pp. 1–24.

12. The private sector was still very important, and crucial for the supply of essential and bulky goods (such as salt, wheat, timber, wine, etc.). Furthermore, there was a difference in the use of ships in the two sectors: while the public navy was based on the use of galleys, the private sector based its trade on the cogs. Lane, *Venice*, pp. 122–4.

13. For more detailed information on the Venetian merchant navy, see F. C. Lane, *Venetian Ships and Shipbuilders in the Renaissance* (Baltimore, MD: Johns Hopkins University Press, 1934), pp. 1–53.

14. Ibid., p. 14; Judde de Larivière, *Naviguer, Commercer, Gouverner*, pp. 13–34; Stöckly, *Le Système de l'Incanto*, pp. 28–32.

15. Hocquet, 'I Meccanismi dei Traffici'; Doumerc, 'Le Galere da Mercato'.

16. Capacity of 600–700 tonnes for the cogs against 150–250 tonnes for the galleys; Lane, *Venetian Ships*, pp. 15 and 47.

17. Lane, *Venice*, pp. 124–6 and pp. 337–42; Judde de Larivière, *Naviguer, Commercer, Gouverner*, pp. 44–8.

18. Continental Europe was covered with a series of routes connecting Northern Italy with the principal markets through the Alpine passages. These routes were primarily used

until the end of the thirteenth century and passed through the Champagne and the Rhine valleys.

19. For an overview, see A. Tenenti and C. Vivanti, 'Le film d'un grand système de navigation: les galères marchandes vénitiennes, XIVe–XVIe siècles', *Annales. Histoire, Sciences Sociales*, 16:1 (1961), pp. 83–6.

20. One of the last lines to be created was one of the *Trafego* (literally 'traffic') routes in the 1460s, linking North Africa, Modone and Beirut. This line is unlike the others, as it was not created only for the Venetians' advantage but at the express request of commercial partners (such as the Hafsids). The purpose was, of course, to offer a service to the south Mediterranean powers that would help Venetians with local affairs. B. Doumerc, *Venise et l'émirat hafside de Tunis (1231–1535)* (Paris: Montreal 1999).

21. Judde de Larivière, *Naviguer, Commercer, Gouverner*, p. 25; Lane, *Venice*, pp. 144–6; 337–42.

22. H. Van Werveke, *Bruges et Anvers. Huit siècles de commerce flamand* (Brussels: Editions de la librairie encyclopedique, 1944), pp. 32–3; E. Aerts, 'Bruges, a European Trading Centre', in V. Vermeersch (ed.), *Bruges and Europe* (Antwerp: Fonds Mercator, 1992), pp. 56–72.

23. F. Franceschi, R. A. Goldthwaite and R. C. Mueller (eds), *Il Rinascimento Italiano e l'Europa, Vol. 4: Commercio e Cultura Mercantile* (Treviso and Costabissara: Angelo Colla, 2007); see in particular the section 'La Pratica degli Affari'.

24. Van Werveke, *Bruges et Anvers*, pp. 40–1.

25. Goods transported in Venetian galleys could apply for a special reduction on duty. These privileges were renewed from time to time, for example in 1468. Stabel, 'Venice: Where North Meets South', pp. 32–3; Van Werveke, *Bruges et Anvers*, pp. 32–40.

26. J. A. Van Houtte, *Bruges. Essai d'histoire urbaine* (Brussels: La Renaissance du livre, 1967), pp. 62–3; Vandewalle, 'Les Nations', pp. 183–4; Stabel, 'Venice: Where North Meets South', pp. 32–3.

27. R. Flenley, 'London and Foreign Merchants in the Reign of Henry VI', *English Historical Review*, 25:100 (1910), pp. 644–55; L. W. Archer, 'Responses to Alien Immigrants in London c. 1400–1650', in S. Cavaciocchi (ed.), *Le Migrazioni in Europa: Secc. XIII–XVIII, Atti della 'Venticinquesima Settimana di Studi', 3–8 maggio 1993* (Florence: Le Monnier, 1994), pp. 755–74.

28. D. Romano, *The Likeness of Venice: A Life of Doge Francesco Foscari* (New Haven, CT and London: Yale University Press, 2007); G. Gullino, *La saga dei Foscari. Storia di un enigma* (Sommacampagna: CIERRE, 2005).

29. Goods sent by boat were frequently divided among different ships in order to avoid the loss of the whole shipment in the case of shipwreck.

30. The two accounting books are gathered together in a unique ledger (composed of 145 folios assembled in a leather-bound book) at the State Archives of Venice: Archivio di Stato di Venezia, *Gradenigo rio Marin* (hereafter ASV, *GRM*), b. 250/2.

31. Usually written by the *scrivano*, who was appointed by the Senate.

32. Montemezzo, *Giovanni Foscari*, pp. 113, 165, 206–9, 335, 391–5.

33. Foscari does not mention these traders at all. As it is not possible to know their exact number, they are not considered in the essay. The amounts of money in which unknown sellers or buyers were involved were 13,439 ducats in 1463–4 and 7,073 ducats in 1467–8.

34. This is probably the reason why they were copied down and survived in the archive.

35. In the case of Bruges, a local courtier tended to be placed with the foreign merchant. Van Werveke, *Bruges et Anvers*, pp. 32–3.
36. This number would be much higher had unnamed partners been included.
37. The data used for these elaborations do not include transactions for food, salaries or galley expenses. The sums related to goods include duties, taxes and the expenses for unloading and transportation to the markets. The total amount of expenses Foscari incurred for supplying the ship was more than 8,000 ducats for the first voyage and almost 7,000 ducats for the second trip, including salaries and nourishment for the crew. The food designated for the officials was recorded separately.
38. This is probably because of the effects of the Ottomon–Venetian Wars, which started in 1463.
39. Stöckly, *Le Système de l'Incanto*, pp. 32–6.
40. The two companies, or societies, are composed of Genoese merchants: one was formed by Chierico Cattaneo and Benedetto Imperiale, the other by Chierico Cattaneo, Benedetto Imperiale and Giovanni Pinello. See Table 8.3.
41. Foscari paid him the sum of 1,192 ducats by draft, probably for these services and some currency exchanges.
42. The relationship with Marino Dandolo was later compromised by a suit pursued by the same Dandolo against Foscari, for the allegedly improper *nolo* charged by the *patrono*. ASV, *GRM*, b. 196/6.
43. Bankers are mentioned only in relation to payments by draft and deposits and withdrawals on their banks.
44. ASV, *GRM*, b. 246, unnumbered folio, letter to Giovanni Foscari from Damascus (1476); ASV, *GRM*, b. 246/5, statement of Marco Foscari during the lawsuit for the allegedly bad management of the Giovanni Foscari's inheritance (undated).
45. The total turnover for the second voyage (only for those exchanges concerning goods) amounts to more than 32,000 ducats. Purely for comparison, the salary of the chief clerk (the man appointed to keep the official accounting books of the galley) was 50 ducats.
46. Van Werveke, *Bruges et Anvers*, p. 79.

9 Miranda, 'Network Takers or Network Makers? The Portuguese Traders in the Medieval West'

1. J. M. Murray, *Bruges: Cradle of Capitalism, 1280–1390* (Cambridge: Cambridge University Press, 2005), p. 219.
2. It is impossible to perform a study on socio-economic dynamics for the Portuguese case in the same manner as the one done for the Genoa case, by Q. Van Doosselaere, *Commercial Agreements and Social Dynamics in Medieval Genoa* (Cambridge: Cambridge University Press, 2009).
3. These are almost the same sources used in F. Miranda, 'Portugal and the Medieval Atlantic: Commercial Diplomacy, Merchants, and Trade, 1143–1488' (PhD dissertation, University of Porto, 2012).
4. The absence of these records is usually explained by the consequences of Lisbon's earthquake of 1755, which destroyed part of the city and many of the records at the Torre do Tombo (Portugal's national archives).
5. *Calendar of the Close Rolls* (hereafter *CCR*), Henry IV, vol. 2, p. 107.

6. J. Paviot (ed.), *Portugal et Bourgogne au XVe Siècle (1384–1482): Recueil de Documents Extraits des Archives Bourguignonnes* (Paris: Centre culturel Calouste Gulbenkian, 1995), doc. 21; *CCR*, Henry IV, vol. 2, pp. 236, 242.
7. A. de M. Basto (ed.), *Vereaçoens. Anos de 1390–1395* (Porto: Camâra Municipal do Porto, 1937), pp. 147–51; A. Cruz, *O Porto nas Navegações e na Expansão*, 2nd edn (Lisbon: Instituto de Cultura e Língua Portuguesa, 1983), pp. 37–8; National Archives, London, 'Particulars of Customs Accounts' (hereafter NA), E122/16/15.
8. *Calendar of the Patent Rolls* (hereafter *CPR*), Henry III, vol. 2, pp. 43, 52–3.
9. V. M. Shillington and A. B. W. Chapman, *The Commercial Relations of England and Portugal* (New York: Burt Franklin, 1907), p. 27; A. H. de O. Marques, 'A Diversificação Económica', in M. H. de C. Coelho and A. L. de C. Homem (eds), *Portugal em Definição de Fronteiras. Do Condado Portucalense à Crise do Século XIV*, Nova História de Portugal (Lisbon: Presença, 1996), p. 514.
10. V. de Santarém, *Quadro Elementar das Relações Políticas e Diplomáticas de Portugal*, 17 vols (Paris: J. P. Aillaud, 1842–63), vol. 3, pp. xix, 5; V. M. Godinho, *A Expansão Quatrocentista Portuguesa*, 2nd edn (Lisbon: Dom Quixote, 2008), p. 101; P. Connolly and G. Martin (eds), *The Dublin Guild Merchant Roll, c. 1190–1265* (Dublin: Dublin Corporation, 1992), p. 1.
11. T. D. Hardy (ed.), *Rotuli Litterarum Clausarum* (London: G. Eyre and A. Spottiswoode, 1833), p. 419; T. D. Hardy (ed.), *Rotuli Litterarum Patentium* (London: Record Commission, 1835), p. 87; see also W. R. Childs, 'Anglo-Portuguese Relations in the Fourteenth Century', in J. L. Gillespie (ed.), *The Age of Richard II* (New York: Sutton Publishing, 1997), pp. 27–49, on pp. 28–9.
12. A. Pinheiro and A. Rita (eds), *Lei de Almotaçaria, 26 De Dezembro de 1253* (Porto: Banco Pinto & Sotto Mayor, 1983); A. M. P. Ferreira, *A Importação e o Comércio Têxtil em Portugal no Século XV (1385 a 1481)* (Lisbon: Imprensa Nacional Casa da Moeda, 1983), pp. 18–25.
13. M. de Laurière (ed.), *Ordonnances des Rois de France*, Vol. 2 (Paris: Imprimerie Royale, 1723), pp. 157–8.
14. Ibid., pp. 157–61; J. Thieury, *Le Portugal et la Normandie Jusqu'à la fin du XVIe siècle* (Paris: A. Aubry, 1860), p. 71.
15. T. Rymer (ed.), *Fœdera, Conventiones, Literæ, Et Cujuscunque Generis Acta Publica, Inter Reges Angliæ*, 10 vols (London, 1869), vol. 5, pp. 763–4.
16. S. Ogilvie, *Institutions and European Trade: Merchant Guilds, 1000–1800* (Cambridge: Cambridge University Press, 2011), p. 1; A. Greif, P. Milgrom and B. R. Weingast, 'Coordination, Commitment, and Enforcement: The Case of the Merchant Guild', *Journal of Political Economy*, 102:4 (1994), pp. 745–76, on p. 755.
17. Greif, Milgrom and Weingast, 'Coordination, Commitment, and Enforcement', p. 755.
18. M. Farelo, 'A Oligarquia Camarária de Lisboa (1325–1433)' (PhD dissertation, University of Lisbon, 2008), p. 192. See also F. Miranda, 'The Portuguese and the Sea: Urban Interaction and Exchange in the Late Middle Ages', in J. Á. Solórzano Telechea, M. Bochaca and A. A. Andrade (eds), *Gentes de Mar en la Ciudad Atlántica Medieval* (Logroño: Instituto de Estudios Riojanos, 2012), pp. 275–92.
19. T. V. de Faria and F. Miranda, '"Pur Bone Alliance Et Amiste Faire": Diplomacia e Comércio Entre Portugal e Inglaterra no Final da Idade Média', *CEM: Revista do CITCEM*, 1 (2010), pp. 109–28.
20. *CPR*, Richard II, vol. 6, p. 102; J. A. P. Ferreira (ed.), *Vereaçoens. Anos de 1401–1449* (Porto: Câmara Municipal do Porto, 1980), p. 87.

21. A. de Sousa, *As Cortes Medievais Portuguesas (1385–1490)*, 2 vols (Porto: Instituto Nacional de Investigação Científica, 1990), vol. 1, pp. 181–242, 517–36.
22. M. M. Postan, *Medieval Trade and Finance* (Cambridge: Cambridge University Press, 1973), p. 66.
23. K. Höhlbaum (ed.), *Hansisches Urkundenbuch*, 11 vols (Halle, 1882), vol. 3, p. 474.
24. A. H. Thomas (ed.), *Calendar of Plea and Memoranda Rolls Preserved among the Archives of the Corporation of the City of London at the Guildhall, A.D. 1413–1437* (Cambridge: Cambridge University Press, 1943), pp. 49–50.
25. J. Paviot (ed.), *Les Portugais à Bruges au XVe Siècle*, Vol. 38 (Paris: Arquivos do Centro Cultural Calouste Gulbenkian, 1999), docs 83, 102, 05, 18, 23, 27, 28, 31; J. Finot, Étude Historique sur les Relations Commerciales Entre la Flandre et *L'espagne au Moyen*-Âge (Paris: A. Picard, 1899), p. 199.
26. Murray, *Bruges*, p. 216; F. Miranda, 'Portugal y las redes mercantiles en la Europa atlántica a finales de la Edad Media', in J. Añíbarro Rodríguez, D. Carvajal de la Vega and I. Vítores Casado (eds), *Redes Sociales y Económicas en el Mundo Bajomedieval* (Valladolid: Castilla Ediciones, 2011), pp. 151–71, on pp. 157ff.
27. K. G. Persson, *An Economic History of Europe: Knowledge, Institutions and Growth, 600 to the Present* (Cambridge: Cambridge University Press, 2010), p. 4; P. D. Curtin, *Cross-Cultural Trade in World History* (Cambridge: Cambridge University Press, 1984), pp. 1ff. See also K. L. Reyerson, *The Art of the Deal: Intermediaries of Trade in Medieval Montpellier* (Leiden: Brill, 2002).
28. G. M. Hodgson, 'What Are Institutions?', *Journal of Economic Issues*, 40:1 (2006), pp. 1–25, on p. 2.
29. Percentages calculated in Miranda, 'Portugal and the Medieval Atlantic', pp. 203–4.
30. J. T. Landa, *Trust, Ethnicity, and Identity: Beyond the New Institutional Economics of Ethnic Trading Networks, Contract Law, and Gift-Exchange* (Ann Arbor, MI: University of Michigan Press, 1994); Miranda, 'Portugal y las redes mercantiles', pp. 171–4.
31. The causes for these variations have been discussed in an unpublished paper presented in 2010: F Miranda, 'Portuguese trade and traders in medieval England', *English and Portuguese in Exchange, 1100–1500*, St John's College, Oxford, 28 May 2010.
32. *CPR*, Henry VI, vol. 2, pp. 128–9.
33. S. Tognetti, *Il Banco Cambini: Affari e Mercati di una Compagnia Mercantile-Bancaria nella Firenze del XV Secolo* (Florence: L. S. Olschki, 1999).
34. The ongoing research project ENPRESA ('Entreprise, Négoce et Production en Europe (XVe–XVIe siècles). Les Compagnies Salviati'), coordinated by Mathieu Arnoux, and developed in Portugal by Joana Sequeira, will surely bring new insights on the role of the Italians in Lisbon. This project was recently presented in Pisa: J. Sequeira, 'La Compagnie Salviati-Da Colle dans la Lisbonne du XVe siècle', *Archivio Salviati: Due Giornate di Studi*, Pisa, Italy, 15–16 March 2013.
35. NA, E122/16/11 fol. 4; 20/9 fols 23, 24v; H. S. Cobb (ed.), *The Overseas Trade of London: Exchequer Customs Accounts, 1480–1* (London: London Record Society, 1990), pp. 101, 303, 446.
36. Bibliothèque Nationale de France, 'Chambre de Comptes de Paris', MS français, 25999, n. 166.
37. M. Mollat, 'Choix de Documents Relatifs à la Normandie Pour Servir à l'Histoire du Commerce Maritime, XVe–XVIe Siècles', in M. Mollat (ed.), *Études d'Histoire* (Turin: Bottega d'Erasmo, 1977), pp. 112–14; *CPR*, Henry IV, vol. 2, p. 281; NA, 'Ancient Petitions', SC8/335/15825.

38. NA, SC8/248/12396.

39. *CPR*, Henry IV, vol. 3, pp. 301, 50; NA, SC8/185/9210; D. M. Gardiner (ed.), *A Calendar of Early Chancery Proceedings Relating to West Country Shipping, 1388–1493* (Exeter: Devon and Cornwall Record Society, 1976), pp. 9–10; Archivo del Reino de Valencia, 'Protocolos', n. 2604, in F. T. Barata, 'Portugal e o Mediterrâneo: Resumo de Documentos de Arquivos de Espanha e de Itália', *Fontes do Sul e do Mediterrâneo* (Évora: CIDEHUS), p. 10.

40. F. T. Barata, *Navegação, Comércio e Relações Políticas. Os Portugueses no Mediterrâneo Ocidental (1385–1466)* (Lisbon: Fundação Calouste Gulbenkian, Junta de Investigação Científica e Tecnológica, 1998), pp. 265–72.

41. J. de S. Marques (ed.), *Descobrimentos Portugueses. Documentos Para a Sua História*, 2 vols (Lisbon: Instituto Nacional de Investigação Científica, 1944), vol. 1, pp. 427–34, doc. 337; I. Elbl, 'Nation, Bolsa, and Factory: Three Institutions of Late-Medieval Portuguese Trade with Flanders', *International History Review*, 14:1 (1992), pp. 1–22, on p. 10.

42. F. Miranda, 'Before the Empire: Portugal and the Atlantic Trade in the Late Middle Ages', *Journal of Medieval Iberian Studies*, 5:1 (2013), pp. 69–85.

43. E. M. Carus-Wilson, 'The Overseas Trade of Bristol', in E. Power and M. M. Postan (eds), *Studies in English Trade in the Fifteenth Century* (London: Routledge, 1933), pp. 183–246, on p. 222.

44. P. Spufford, *Power and Profit: The Merchant in Medieval Europe* (New York: Thames & Hudson, 2003), p. 309.

45. R. Van Answaarden (ed.), *Les Portugais Devant le Grand Conseil des Pays-Bas (1460–1580)* (Paris: Fondation Calouste Gulbenkian, Centre culturel portugais, 1991) (hereafter *GCPB*), doc. 11.

46. Murray, *Bruges*, p. 219.

47. *GCPB*, doc. 4.

48. See Cátia Antunes's project *Challenging Monopolies, Building Global Empires in the Early Modern Period*, Leiden University, at http://www.hum.leiden.edu/history/research/projects-mgi/challenging-monopolies.html [accessed 25 November 2013].

10 Crivelli, 'Pepper and Silver between Milan and Lisbon in the Second Half of the Sixteenth Century'

1. See M. Bustos Rodríguez, 'La Problemática Acerca de los Comerciantes de la Carrera de Indias', in A. Crespo Solana (ed.), *Comunidades Transnacionales. Colonias de Mercaderes Extranjeros en el Mundo Atlántico* (Madrid: Ediciones Doce Calles, 2010), pp. 29–46, on pp. 40–1; and D. Alonso García, 'Una Nación, Diferentes Familias, Múltiples Redes. Genoveses en Castilla a Principio de la Edad Moderna', in A. Crespo Solana (ed.), *Comunidades Transnacionales. Colonias de Mercaderes Extranjeros en el Mundo Atlántico* (Madrid: Ediciones Doce Calles, 2010), pp. 65–82, on pp. 72–3.

2. The images most commonly used are the 'hub-and-spokes' metaphor and the 'nodes-and-ties' metaphor, depending on whether the analysis focuses on location or on individuals. A concise discussion of these issues can be found in G. Grabher, 'Trading Routes, Bypasses, and Risky Intersections: Mapping the Travels of "Networks" between Economic Sociology and Economic Geography', *Progress in Human Geography*, 30 (2006), pp. 163–89. See J. B. Owens, 'Social Networks of Milanese Merchants in Sixteenth-century Castile',

in R. Mukherjee (ed.), *Networks in the First Global Age, 1400–1800* (New Delhi: Indian Council for Historical Research & Primus, 2011), pp. 159–82.

3. This concept is developed by the French philosophers Félix Guattari and Gilles Deluze in their *A Thousand Plateaus: Capitalism and Schizophrenia* (Minneapolis, MN: University of Minnesota Press, 1987). See also Grabher, 'Trading Routes', p. 18.

4. Fernand Braudel had already insisted on the necessity of integrating the spatial aspect into historical analysis; see F. Braudel, *Civilisation Matérielle, Économie et Capitalisme, XVe–XVIIIe siècles*, 3 vols (Paris: Armand Colin, 1979). Regional economic analysis has since been developed further in spatial economic theory by I. Wallerstein's classic study, *The Modern World-System II. Mercantilism and the Consolidation of the European World-Economy, 1600–1750* (New York: Academic Press, 1980), and the more recent C. Martínez Shaw and J. M. Oliva Melgár (eds), *El Sistema Atlántico Español (siglos XVII–XIX)* (Madrid: Marcial Pons, 2005).

5. The emphasis on the space-time dimension has allowed the development of theoretical and epistemological models that are confirmed by the research conducted with geospatial technologies and lines of investigation adopted by geographically integrated history. For a useful summary, see A. Crespo Solana, 'La historia geográficamente integrata y los sistemas de información geográfica (SIG): concepto y retos metodológicos', *Tiempos Modernos*, 26 (2103), pp. 1–33.

6. See in particular a number of studies on complex, dynamic, non-linear systems and geographically integrated history: J. B. Owens, 'Dynamics of Trade Networks: The Main Research Issues on Space-Time Representations', in A. Crespo Solana and D. A. Garcia (eds), 'Self-Organizing Networks and GIS Tools: Cases of Use for the Study of Trading Cooperation (1400–1800)', *Journal of Knowledge Management, Economics and Information Technology* special issue (June 2012), pp. 53–80.

7. Grabher, 'Trading Routes', p. 20.

8. H. C. White, *Markets from Networks: Socioeconomics Models of Production* (Princeton, NJ: Princeton University Press, 2002).

9. F. Ruiz Martín, *Pequeño Capitalismo, Gran Capitalismo. Simón Ruiz y sus Negocios en Florencia* (Barcelona: Crítica, 1990); H. Lapeyre, *Simón Ruiz et les 'Asientos' de Philippe II* (Paris: Colin, 1953); H. Lapeyre, *Une Famille de Merchands: les Ruiz* (Paris: Collin,1955).

10. J. Gentil da Silva, *Marchandises et Finances. Lettres de Lisbonne (1563–1578)*, 3 vols (Paris: SEVPEN, 1959), vol. 2, and (Paris: SEVPEN, 1961), vol. 3; J. Gentil da Silva, *Stratégie des affaires à Lisbonne entre 1595 et 1607. Lettres marchandes des Rodrigues d'Evora et Veiga* (Paris: Collin, 1956); F. Ruiz Martín, *Lettres marchandes échangées entre Florence et Medina del Campo* (Paris: SEVPEN, 1965).

11. F. Trivellato, *The Familiarity of Strangers: The Sephardic Diaspora, Livorno and Cross-Cultural Trade in the Early Modern Period* (New Haven, CT and London: Yale University Press, 2009), pp. 153–76.

12. See H. Casado, 'Los flujos de información en las redes comerciales castellanas de los siglos XV y XVI', *Investigaciones de Historia Económica*, 10 (2008), pp. 35–68, on pp. 52–9.

13. See G. Sabatini and J. J. Ruiz Ibañez, 'Monarchy as Conquest: Violence, Social Opportunity, and Political Stability in the Establishment of the Hispanic Monarchy', *Journal of Modern History*, 3 (2009), pp. 501–39.

14. B. Yun Casallilla, '"Localism", Global History and Transnational History. A Reflection from the Historian of Early Modern Europe', *Historisk Tidskrift. Sweden*, 127 (2007), pp. 659–78, on p. 671.

15. G. Barrett, 'An Exploration of the Role of Portugal in the Economic Integration of Asia and Europe with a Focus on the Pepper Market', Asian-Pacific Economic and Business History Conference, 16–18 February 2012, ANU, Canberra, Australia, p. 4.

16. J. Boyajian, *Portuguese Trade in Asia under the Habsburgs, 1580–1640* (Baltimore, MD and London: Johns Hopkins University Press, 1992), pp. 167–70.

17. L. Freire Costa, P. Lains and S. Münch Miranda, *História Economica de Portugal (1143–2010)* (Lisbon: A esfera dos livros, 2011), pp. 105–6.

18. J. M. Pedreira, 'Cost and Financial Trends in the Portuguese Empire, 1415–1822', in F. Bethencourt and D. Ramada Curto, *Portuguese Oceanic Expansion, 1400–1800* (New York: Cambridge University Press, 2007), pp. 49–87, on p. 81.

19. Freire Costa, Lains and Münch Miranda, *História Economica de Portugal*, pp. 137–9.

20. C. Álvarez Nogal and C. Chamley, 'Debt Policy under Constraints between Philip II, the Cortes and Genoese Bankers', WP–11–06 (2011), at http://e-archivo.uc3m.es/bitstream/10016/11634/1/wp%2011-06.pdf [accessed 20 August 2013], p. 2.

21. C. de Carlos Morales, *Felipe II: El Imperio en Bancarrota. La hacienda real de Castilla y los Negocios Financeiros del rey prudente* (Madrid: Dilema, 2008), p. 204.

22. See G. Felloni, 'All'Apogeo delle Fiere Genovesi: Banchieri ed Affari di Cambio a Piacenza nel 1600', in *Studi in Onore di Gino Barbieri*, 3 vols (Pisa: IPEM edizioni, 1983), vol. 2, pp. 883–901.

23. G. de Luca, 'Strutture e Dinamiche delle Attività Finanziarie Milanesi tra Cinquecento e Seicento', in E. Brambilla and G. Muto (eds), *La Lombardia Spagnola Nuovi Indirizzi di Ricerca* (Milan: UNICOPLI, 1997), pp. 31–75, on p. 35; Archivio Storico Civico Milano (hereafter ASCM), Fondo Materie, Banche e banchieri, 7 May 1584, box 49.

24. G. Tonelli, *Affari e Lussuosa Sobrietà. Traffici e Stili di Vita dei Negozianti Milanesi nel XVII Secolo (1600–1659)* (Milan: Franco Angeli, 2012), p. 50.

25. For the rules that define these commercial companies, see B. Crivelli, 'Le compagnie mercantili dei Litta in Spagna nella seconda metà del XVI secolo. Forme di finanziamento e relazione tra soci', *Studi Storici Luigi Simeoni*, 63 (2013), pp. 63–74.

26. C. Villanueva Morte, 'La Empresa Familiar de los "Litta": Negocios e Intereses entre Milán y España desde Mediados del siglo XV', *Edad Media. Revista Histórica*, 10 (2009), pp. 307–41.

27. ASCM, Fondo Famiglia, Litta, 10 July 1567, box 864. Agostino Litta was elected in 1567 to replace Giovanni Battista Taverna who died thus leaving his position vacant.

28. Archivio di Stato di Milano (hereafter ASM), Fondo Notarile, Ottaviano Castelletto, 2 December 1582, cart. 14944.

29. ASM, Fondo Notarile, Giovanni Paolo Pellizzari, 30 September 1584, cart. 17564. See G. de Luca, *Commercio del Denaro e Crescita Economica a Milano tra Cinquecento e Seicento* (Milan: Il Polifilo, 1996), p. 96.

30. G. de Luca, 'Hombres de Negocios e Capitale Mercantile: Verso il Nuovo Equilibrio dell'Economia Milanese (1570–1612)', in J. Martinez Millán (ed.), *Felipe II (1527–1593). Europa y la Monarquía Católica* (Madrid: Parteluz, 1998), pp. 527–51, on p. 534.

31. Archivio della Camera di Commercio di Milano (hereafter ACCM), 26 October 1575, box 40, 7.

32. ACCM, box 24, 6: 'Libretto dove restano registrati al foglio 3 sino al foglio 5 li SS. Mercanti descritti e dal foglio 6 al foglio 31 le nomine degli abati della Camera dei Mercanti come pure dal foglio 33 sino al foglio 40 li ssr. Mercanti utenti delle strade come diffusamente accade dal medesimo libretto coperto di cartone bianco.'

33. Archivio dell'Ospedale Maggiore di Milano (hereafter AOMM), box 413, 52.

34. AOMM, Archivio Litta, 10 January 1583, box 11, 63.

35. Alonso García, 'Una Nación, Diferentes Familias', pp. 72–4.

36. AOMM, Archivio Litta, cart. 413, 51 and cart. 405, 27. The same happened with Cesare Negrolo and his business in Paris.

37. Alonso García, 'Una Nación, Diferentes Familias', p. 73.

38. J. Denucé, *Inventaire des Affaitadi Banquiers Italiens a Anvers de l'année 1568* (Antwerp and Paris: Éditions de Sikkel, 1934), pp. 20–7.

39. H. Kellenbenz, 'I Borromeo e le Grandi Casate Mercantili Milanesi', in *San Carlo e il Suo Tempo*, Vol. 2 (Rome: Edizioni di Storia e Letteratura, 1986), pp. 825–8.

40. Denucé, *Inventaire*, pp. 24–5.

41. Gentil da Silva, *Marchandises*, vol. III, letter no. 34, Lisbon, 24 December 1576, p. 96, and vol. III, letter no. 38, Lisbon, 28 January 1577, p. 104.

42. Arquivo Nacional Torre do Tombo, Lisbon (hereafter ANTTL), Chancelaria Regia, Privilégios, 27 August 1586, liv. 1, fl. 134.

43. AOMM, Archivio Litta, 16 June 1609, box 405, d. 27.

44. The agreed interest rate was 5 per cent for 12 years. Cf. ASM, Fondo Notarile, Cristoforo Castelletto, 17 February 1584, cart. 16195.

45. AOMM, Archivio Litta, cart. 413, 52. The document is dated 1560, but it is likely that the speculative operation had occurred between 1566 and 1567 as evidenced by a bill of exchange issued by the Milanese Federico Cusani and Geronimo Tavola to pay Ippolito Affaitati and Giacomo de Bardi at the October fair of Medina del Campo in 1567.

46. Gentil da Silva, *Marchandises*, vol. III, letter no. 57, Lisbon, 22 November 1577, p. 147.

47. ASM, Fondo Notarile, Cristoforo Castelletto, 17 February 1584, cart. 16195.

48. Gentil da Silva, *Marchandises*, vol. III, letter no. 39, Lisbon, 11 February 1577, p. 104.

49. AOMM, Archivio Litta, cart. 405, 27.

50. AOMM, Archivio Litta, cart. 413, 51.

51. AOMM, Archivio Litta, 16 June 1609, cart. 405, 27.

52. Gentil da Silva, *Marchandises*, vol. III, letter no. 64, Lisbon, 25 February 1578, p. 166.

53. 1 Malacca cruzado was worth 400 reis.

54. ANTTL, Cartório Notarial 15A, 5 March 1583, box 11, 53, fl. 122v.

55. The history of Rott's companies and his activity as a speculator in the pepper trade have been dealt with in several works, including H. Kellenbenz, 'Autor de 1600: Le commerce du poivre des Fugger et le marché international du poivre', *Annales: Économies, Sociétés, Civilisations*, 11 (1956), pp. 1–28; and R. Hildebrandt, 'Wirtschaftsentwicklung und Konzentration im 16. Jahrhundert: Konrad Rot und die Finanzierungsprobleme seines interkontinentalen Handels', *Scripta Mercaturae*, 4 (1970), pp. 25–50. Here we restrict our analysis to Rott's relation with Giovanni Battista Rovellasca and the pepper trading contract in Lisbon.

56. ASM, Fondo Notarile, Ottaviano Castelletto, 2 December 1582, cart. 14944.

57. Gentil da Silva, *Marchandises*, vol. III, letter no. 99, Lisbon, 4 August 1577, p. 263; vol. III, letter no. 103, Lisbon, 5 September 1577, p. 266; and vol. III, letter no. 120, Lisbon, 4 December 1577, p. 277. Archivo Historico y Provincial de Valldolid (hereafter AHPV), Archivo Simón Ruiz (hereafter ASR), Genoa, 27 November 1577, box 39, 6, and Piacenza, 7 March 1581, box 70, 58.

58. See K. S. Mathew, 'Indo-Portuguese Trade under Dom Philip I of Portugal and the Fuggers of Germany', in A. Teodoro de Matos and L. F. Thomaz (eds), *A carreira da Índia e as rotas dos estreitos* (Lisbon: CHAM, CEPCEP, IICT, 1996), pp. 563–80.

59. AHPV, ASR, Lisbon, 1590, box 144, 231–36.

60. Archivo de Nossa Senhora de Loreto de Lisboa, 'Libro B dell'amministrazione della Chiesa e confraternita di Ittaliani dell'Invocazione di Nra S.ra de Loreto'. Giovanni Battista was administrator in 1587 and 1601, and his brother Francesco in 1589.

61. Lapeyre, *Une Famille de Merchands*, pp. 271–2.

62. AHPV, ASR, Piacenza, 8 August 1584, box 95, 172.

63. Ibid.

64. AHPV, ARS, Lisbon, 6 January 1590 and 27 January 1590, box 144, 226–7. It may be assumed that they included members of Italian and German communities, including Giovanni Battista Rovellasca.

65. AHPV, ARS, Piacenza, 8 August 1591, box 151, 26.

66. Ibid.

67. AHPV, ARS, Milan, 1594, box 169, 1–24, and Milan, 1593, box 175, 1–27.

68. AHPV, ARS, Lisbon 19 February 1590, box 144, 231.

69. AHPV, ASR, Lisbon, 24 February 1590, box 144, 232.

70. APHV, ASR, Lisbon, 30 March 1591, box 152, 130.

71. Ibid.

72. APHV, ASR, Genoa, 23 February 1594, box 168, 337.

73. ANTTL, Collecção São Vicente, 10 March 1591, fl. 94.

74. AHPV, ASR, Lisbon, 30 March 1591, box 152, 130.

75. APHV, ASR, Lisbon, 11 September 1593, box 164, 202.

76. APHV, ASR, Lisbon, 29 June 1591, box 152, 137.

77. Owens, 'Social Networks', p. 11.

78. The date of death of Giovanni Battista Rovellasca is not documented. However, it may be inferred from a request, dated 1610, sent to King Philip II asking him to grant a loan to the merchant, who was now ill and without resources, in order for him to have a respectable burial. Arquivo Historico Ultramarino, Conselho do Ultramar, São Tomé e Príncipe, 17 March 1610, box 1, 15.

11 Caracausi, 'The Wool Trade, Venice and the Mediterranean Cities at the End of the Sixteenth Century'

1. See especially A. Molho and D. Ramanda Curto, 'Les Réseaux Marchands à l'Époque Moderne', *Annales, Histoire, Sciences Sociales*, 58:3 (2003), pp. 569–80; A. Greif, *Institutions and the Path to the Modern Economy: Lessons from Medieval Trade* (Cambridge: Cambridge University Press, 2006); S. Ogilvie, *Institutions and European Trade: Merchant Guilds, 1000–1800* (Cambridge: Cambridge University Press, 2011).

2. For a discussion of the concept 'trading diaspora' and its limitations, see F. Trivellato, *The Familiarity of Strangers: The Sephardic Diaspora, Livorno and Cross-Cultural Trade in the Early Modern Period* (New Haven, CT and London: Yale University Press, 2009); S. D. Aslanian, *From the Indian Ocean to the Mediterranean: The Global Trade Networks of Armenian Merchants from New Julfa* (Berkeley, CA: University of California Press, 2011), pp. 7–16.

3. F. Trivellato, 'Juifs de Livourne, Italiens de Lisbonne, Hindous de Goa. Réseaux Marchands et Échanges Interculturels à l'Époque Moderne', *Annales, Histoire, Sciences Sociales*, 58:3 (2003), pp. 581–603, on pp. 584–5.

4. As Francesca Trivellato has recently stated, Fernand Braudel already challenged the 'conventional notion that a sequence of European state powers (the Dutch, then the English,

and finally the French) replaced the Italian (especially the Venetian) domination of the eastern Mediterranean'; Trivellato, *The Familiarity of Strangers*, pp. 102–3. On 'formal' and 'informal' institutions, see D. C. North, *Institutions, Institutional Change and Economic Performance* (Cambridge: Cambridge University Press, 1990).

5. Trivellato, *The Familiarity of Strangers*; D. Hancock, *Oceans of Wine: Madeira and the Emergence of American Trade and Taste* (New Haven, CT: Yale University Press, 2009); M. Fusaro, 'Cooperating Mercantile Networks in the Early Modern Mediterranean', *Economic History Review*, 65:2 (2012), pp. 701–18.

6. On this approach, see especially Hancock, *Oceans of Wine*, pp. xiv–xxv.

7. On this subject, and especially on the direct participation of Genoese merchants in the western Mediterranean in the late medieval period, see A. García Porras and A. Fábregas García, 'Genoese Trade Networks in the Southern Iberian Peninsula: Trade, Transmission of Technical Knowledge and Economic Interactions', *Mediterranean Historical Review*, 25:1 (2010), pp. 35–51, on pp. 39–47.

8. On the role of states and merchants in sustaining technological development, see M. Belfanti, 'Between Mercantilism and Market: Privileges for Invention in Early Modern Europe', *Journal of Institutional Economics*, 2:1 (2006), pp. 1–20; L. Molà, 'States and Crafts: Relocating Technical Skills in Renaissance Italy', in E. Welch and M. O'Malley (eds), *The Material Renaissance* (Manchester: Manchester University Press, 2007), pp. 133–53.

9. D. J. Harreld, 'Foreign Merchants and International Trade Networks in the Sixteenth-Century Low Countries', *Journal of European Economic History*, 39:1 (2010), pp. 11–32.

10. Hancock, *Oceans of Wine*, p. xiv.

11. S. R. Epstein, 'Labour Mobility, Journeyman Organizations and Markets in Skilled Labour Europe, 14th–18th Centuries', in M. Arnoux and P. Monnet (eds), *Le technicien dans la cité en Europe occidentale 1250–1650* (Rome: École Française de Rome, 2004), pp. 251–69.

12. J. Munro, 'South German Silver, European Textiles, and Venetian Trade with the Levant and Ottoman Empire, c. 1370 to c. 1720: A Non-Mercantilist Approach to the Balance of Payment Problem', in S. Cavaciocchi (ed.), *Relazione economiche tra Europea e mondo islamico, secoli XII–XVII* (Florence: Le Monnier, 2007), pp. 905–60.

13. M. Greene, 'Beyond the Northern Invasion: The Mediterranean in the Seventeenth Century', *Past & Present*, 174:1 (2000), pp. 41–70; Fusaro, 'Cooperating Mercantile Networks'; M. van Gelder, *Trading Places: The Netherlandish Merchants in Early Modern Venice* (Leiden and Boston, MA: Brill, 2009).

14. D. Sella, 'L'economia', in G. Cozzi and P. Prodi (eds), *Storia di Venezia, Vol. 6: Dal Rinascimento al Barocco* (Rome: Istituto dell'Enciclopedia Italiana, 1994), pp. 651–711.

15. U. Tucci, 'Mercanti veneziani in India alla fine del XVI secolo', in *Studi in onore di Armando Sapori*, 2 vols (Milan: A. Giuffrè, 1957), vol. 2, pp. 1091–111.

16. D. Sella, 'The Rise and Fall of the Venetian Woollen Industry' in B. Pullan (ed.), *Crisis and Change in the Venetian Economy in the 16th and 17th Centuries* (London: Methuen, 1968), pp. 106–26; P. Sardella, 'L'épanouissement industriel de Venise au XVIe siècle', *Annales, Histoire, Sciences Sociales*, 2:2 (1947), pp. 195–6.

17. W. Panciera, *L'arte matrice. I lanifici della Repubblica di Venezia nei secoli 17. e 18.* (Treviso: Canova, 1996); W. Panciera, 'Qualità e costi di produzione nei lanifici veneti (secoli XVI–XVIII)', in G. L. Fontana and G. Gayot (eds), *Wool: Products and Markets (13th–20th Century)* (Padua: Cleup, 2004), pp. 419–46, on p. 421.

18. Panciera, *L'arte matrice*.

19. Ibid.; A. Mozzato, 'The Production of Woollens in 15th and 16th Centuries Venice', in P. Lanaro (ed.), *At the Center of the Old World: Trade and Manufacturing in Venice and the Venetian Mainland (1400–1800)* (Toronto: Victoria University Press, 2006), pp. 73–107.

20. J. Munro, 'I panni di lana', in F. Franceschi, R. A. Goldthwaite and R. C. Mueller (eds), *Il Rinascimento Italiano e l'Europa, Vol. 4: Commercio e Cultura Mercantile* (Treviso and Costabissara: Angelo Colla, 2007), pp. 105–41, on pp. 135–6, 139–40.

21. Fusaro, 'Cooperating Mercantile Networks'; van Gelder, *Trading Places*.

22. Panciera, 'Qualità', p. 421; E. Demo, *L' 'anima della citta'. L'industria tessile a Verona e Vicenza (1400–1550)* (Milan: Unicopli, 2001); P. Chorley, 'Rascie and the Florentine Cloth Industry during the Sixteenth Century', *Journal of European Economic History*, 32:3 (2003), pp. 487–526; A. Caracausi, *Dentro la bottega. Culture del lavoro in una città d'età moderna* (Venice: Marsilio, 2008).

23. I do not consider the role of the Italian wool (especially from Southern Italy) and those imported from the Balkans. However, despite their importance, their role in those years was less remarkable than that of Spanish wool. See, however, Panciera, *L'arte matrice*, pp. 39–66; E. Demo, 'Wool and Silk: The Textile Urban Industry of the Venetian Mainland (15th–17th Centuries)', in P. Lanaro (ed.), *At the Centre of the Old World: Trade and Manufacturing in Venice and on the Venetian Mainland, 1400–1800* (Toronto: Victoria University Press, 2006), pp. 217–43, on p. 220; Mozzato, 'The Production of Woollens', pp. 78–9; B. Braude, 'The Rise and Fall of Salonica Woollens, 1500–1650: Technology Transfer and Western Competition', *Mediterranean Historical Review*, 6:2 (1991), pp. 216–36.

24. J. Klein, *The Mesta: A Study in Spanish Economic History* (Cambridge, MA: Harvard University Press, 1920); H. Lapeyre, 'Les exportations de laine de Castille sous le règne de Philippe II', in M. Spallanzani (ed.), *La lana come materia prima. I fenomeni della sua produzione e circolazione nei secoli XIII–XVII* (Florence: Olschki, 1974), pp. 212–39, on pp. 225–7; F. Ruiz Martín, 'Pastos y Ganaderos en Castilla; la Mesta (1450–1600)', in M. Spallanzani (ed.), *La lana come materia prima. I fenomeni della sua produzione e circolazione nei secoli XIII–XVII* (Florence: Olschki, 1974), pp. 271–85; J. P. le Flem, 'Las Cuentas de La Mesta', *Moneta y Credito*, 121 (1972), pp. 23–104; C. R. Philips, 'The Spanish Wool Trade, 1500–1780', *Journal of Economic History*, 42:2 (1982), pp. 775–95.

25. Lapeyre, 'Les exportations', pp. 225–7; Philips, 'The Spanish Wool Trade', pp. 777, 782, 790–1.

26. Lapeyre, 'Les exportations', pp. 231–2.

27. G. Doria, 'Conoscenza del mercato e sistema informativo: il "know-how" dei mercanti-finanzieri genovesi nei secoli XVI e XVII', in A. de Maddalena and H. Kellenbenz, *La Repubblica internazionale del denaro tra XV e XVIII secolo* (Bologna: Il Mulino, 1986), pp. 57–121; Lapeyre, 'Les exportations', pp. 231–2.

28. See also the essay by Ammannati and González Talavera in this volume.

29. E. Grendi, *I Balbi una famiglia genovese fra Spagna e Impero* (Turin: G. Einaudi, 1997), p. 24.

30. Lapeyre, 'Les exportations'.

31. Doria, 'Conoscenza del mercato'.

32. See the State Archive of Venice (hereafter ASV), *Notarile atti* (hereafter *NA*), Luca e Giulio Gabrieli, 6524, fol. 192v, 14 June 1580; fol. 288v, 18 August 1580; fol. 289r, 18 August 1580.

33. On woollen production in the Balkans, see Braude, 'The Rise and Fall of Salonica Woollens'.

34. E. Demo, 'Dall'auge al declino: manifattura, commercio locale e traffici internazionali a Cremona in età moderna', in G. Politi (ed.), *Storia di Cremona. L'età degli Asburgo di Spagna (1535–1707)* (Bergamo: Bolis Edizioni, 2006), pp. 262–87.

35. I have indicated only those merchants who appear in more than one *fides* between 1580 and 1595. See ASV, *NA*, Luca e Giulio Gabrieli, 6523–42.

36. F. Ruiz Martín, *Lettres marchandes échangées entre Florence et Medina del Campo* (Paris: SEVPEN, S1965), p. xv.

37. ASV, *NA*, Pietro Partenio, 10675, fol. 403r, 18 July 1586.

38. Ruiz Martín, *Lettres marchandes*, p. xv. See also Philips, 'The Spanish Wool Trade', p. 792; R. Goldthwaite, 'The Florentine Wool Industry in the Late Sixteenth Century', *Journal of European Economic History*, 32:3 (2003), pp. 527–54, on p. 535.

39. Ruiz Martín, *Lettres marchandes*, p. cvii.

40. Ibid., pp. 378–9, 23 May 1585.

41. Ibid., p. cxv.

42. Ibid., p. 414.

43. Ibid., p. 300.

44. ASV, *NA*, Luca e Giulio Gabrieli, 6542, fol. 1r, 3 January 1595.

45. On the ability to recognize the wool, especially in case of damages, see ASV, *NA*, Luca e Giulio Gabrieli, 6525, fol. 300r–v, 18 August 1580; 6525, fol. 328v, 13 October 1581; 6532, fol. 90v, 12 March 1585.

46. ASV, *NA*, Luca e Giulio Gabrieli, 6526, fol. 328v, 21 October 1581.

47. ASV, *NA*, Luca e Giulio Gabrieli, 6532, fol. 311v, 15 November 1585.

48. ASV, *NA*, Luca e Giulio Gabrieli, 6533, fol. 177v, 16 May 1586.

49. ASV, *NA*, Luca e Giulio Gabrieli, 6532, fol. 189r, 13 June 1585.

50. Ibid.

51. ASV, *NA*, Pietro Partenio, 10663, fol. 581v, 15 September 1580; 10661, fol. 470v, 5 September 1579.

52. ASV, *NA*, Pietro Partenio, 10675, fol. 403r, 18 July 1586.

53. ASV, *NA*, Pietro Partenio, 10670, fol. 235v, 19 May 1585.

54. ASV, *NA*, Luca e Giulio Gabrieli, 6535, fol. 33v, 26 January 1588.

55. ASV, *NA*, Luca e Giulio Gabrieli, 6541, fol. 252v, 27 November 1585.

56. See for instance ASV, *NA*, Pietro Partenio, 10683, fol. 318v, 16 June 1590; 10760, fol. 1v, 29 December 1584; 10698, fol. 325v, 9 September 1600; 10668, fol. 455v, 14 August 1582.

57. For Vicenza, see E. Demo, 'Le manifatture tra Medioevo ed Età moderna', in G. L. Fontana (ed.), *L'industria vicentina dal Medioevo ad oggi* (Padua: Cleup, 2004), pp. 21–126, on pp. 106–14.

58. ASV, *NA*, Pietro Partenio, 10682, fol. 292r, 5 June 1590.

59. ASV, *NA*, Pietro Partenio, 10701, fol. 69v, 18 March 1603.

60. L. Molà, 'Il mercante innovatore', in F. Franceschi, R. A. Goldthwaite and R. C. Mueller (eds), *Il Rinascimento Italiano e l'Europa, Vol. 4: Commercio e Cultura Mercantile* (Treviso and Vicenza: A. Colla, 2007).

61. See above, nn. 44–55.

62. ASV, *NA*, Luca e Giulio Gabrieli, 6543, fol. 136v, 6 January 1597; 6544, fol. 136v, 6 January 1598.

63. ASV, *NA*, Pietro Partenio, 10662, fol. 42v, 16 January 1580.

64. See below, n. 100. For the Spanish wool in Padua, see Caracausi, *Dentro la bottega*, p. 43. For the Venetian mainland, see Demo, 'Wool and Silk', p. 219.
65. See for instance ASV, *NA*, Pietro Partenio, 10661, fols 487r–488r, 18 September 1579.
66. State Archive of Padua (hereafter ASP), *Università della lana* (hereafter UL), 342, fols 155v–233v; 336, fols 163r–178v.
67. ASP, *Notarile*, 3181, fol. 7r, 23 February 1594; ASP, *Estimo miscellanea*, 22, 'traffichi'; ASP, *UL*, 350, fol. 93r; ASP, *UL*, 8, years 1598–1607; ASP, *UL*, 96, fol. 319r, 22 May 1627.
68. ASP, *UL*, 68, fol. 143r, 29 February 1556.
69. A. Caracausi, 'Mercanti e manifatture tessili fra Padova e Venezia. Reti di scambio e specializzazioni produttive fra Padova e Venezia', *Cheiron*, 25:1 (2008), pp. 19–30, on pp. 22–5.
70. ASP, *UL*, 349, 1575, fol. 20r.
71. ASV, *Cinque savi alla mercanzia* [hereafter CSM], ser. I, 142, 16 January 1607. See also ASV, *CSM*, ser. I, 143, fol. 81v and fol. 162v, 31 August 1613.
72. ASV, *CSM*, ser. I, 137, fols 92v–93r, 4 September 1583.
73. ASV, *NA*, 10679, fol. 304r, 7 July 1588; fol. 416r, 13 September 1588.
74. ASV, *Senato Terra*, 65, fol. 82r, 27 June 1584.
75. ASV, *CSM*, ser. I, 141, 1 August 1604.
76. ASV, *NA*, Luca and Giulio Gabrieli, 6519, fols 76r–84v, 29 April–11 May 1575. I would like to thank Edoardo Demo, who suggested this document to me. See also Mozzato, 'The Production of Wollens', p. 84. Mozzato, 'The Production of Wollen', p. 86 shows that around one-third of the workforce was made by foreigners between the end of the fifteenth and the beginning of the sixteenth centuries. For similar considerations for Florence, see Chorley, 'Rascie'; p. 495; Goldthwaite, 'The Florentine Wool Industry', pp. 543–4.
77. ASP, *UL*, 80, fols 304v–305r.
78. A. Bellavitis, '"Per cittadini metterete..." La stratificazione della società veneziana cinquecentesca tra norma giuridica e riconoscimento sociale', *Quaderni storici*, 30:2 (1995), pp. 359–84.
79. ASV, *CSM*, ser. I, 138, fol. 108r, 22 March 1590.
80. See, among others, the Genoese Agostino di Marini (26 January 1459), Pasquale Spinola (27 January 1584), Francesco and Giovanni Ambrogio Marini (23 August 1590); the Florentine Andrea Oste (29 January 1579), Niccolò and Giacomo Berti (13 September 1586) and Alvise Scarlatti (19 March 1588); the drapers Francesco de Piero *laner* (18 May 1545), P. Antonio and Orlando Rizzoli (17 November 1587), Alvise Poccobello (17 November 1588), Gregorio Maccarelli (10 March 1590). For the complete list of Venetian citizenship *de intus* and *de intus et extra*, see A. Bellavistis, '"Ars meccanica" e gerarchie sociali a Venezia tra XVI e XVII secolo', in M. Arnoux and P. Monnet (eds), *Le technicien dans la cité en Europe occidentale, 1250–1650* (Rome: École Française de Rome, 2004), pp. 161–79.
81. Sella, 'L'economia', p. 680.
82. J. Delumeau, *L'Alun de Rome 15.–19. Siècle* (Paris: SEVPEN, 1962). At the end of the sixteenth century the Capponi played an important role in the import of alum from the port of Civitavecchia, near Rome. See ASV, *NA*, Andrea Spinelli, 11915, fol. 77v, 22 February 1597; 11917, fol. 221v, 1 June 1596; 11918, fol. 503v, 28 December 1597. On Genoese merchants in the alum trade in the mid-sixteenth century, see ASV, *CSM*, ser. I, 135, fols 78v, 80r and 101v. See also ASV, *CSM*, ser. I, 143, fol. 81v, 31 March 1612.

83. U. Tucci, *Mercanti, navi, monete nel Cinquecento veneziano* (Bologna: Il Mulino, 1981), pp. 99. Filippo Sassetti in his *Ragionamento* of 1577 highlighted the comparative advantage the Venetians enjoyed with respect to the Florentines in Aleppo and Alexandria. See Chorley, 'Rascie', p. 491, n. 19. See also Munro, 'I panni di lana', pp. 131–2.

84. Tucci, 'Mercanti veneziani', p. 1095, n. 9.

85. See for instance ASV, *CSM*, ser. I, 138, fol. 191r, 27 February 1592.

86. Ruiz Martín, *Lettres marchandes*, p. cvii.

87. Caracausi, 'Mercanti e manifatture', pp. 23–4.

88. Ruiz Martín, *Lettres marchandes*, p. 361–2, 28 February 1585.

89. Ibid., p. 53.

90. Ibid., p. 106.

91. Sella, 'L'economia', p. 686. On the relevance of the public galley system (the *mude*) at the end of the sixteenth century, see ASV, *NA*, Pietro Partenio, 10673, fol. 64r, 8 February 1585, Zaccaria de Zuanne in Aleppo to Bernardino Fonda in Venice.

92. G. Gullino, 'I patrizi veneziani e la mercatura negli ultimi tre secoli della Repubblica', in G. Borelli (ed.), *Mercanti e vita economica nella Repubblica veneta (secoli XIII–XVIII)* (Verona: Banco popolare di Verona, 1985), pp. 403–51.

93. ASV, *NA*, Giovanni Andrea Catti, 3360, fol. 90v, 23 March 1589.

94. ASV, *NA*, Giovanni Andrea Catti, 3363, fol. 483v, 11 September 1592. On Levantine Jews in late sixteenth-century Venice, see especially B. Arbel, *Trading Nations: Jews and Venetians in the Early Modern Eastern Mediterranean* (Leiden: Brill, 1995).

95. ASV, *NA*, Giovanni Andrea Catti, 3361, fol. 219v, 26 January 1590.

96. See for instance ASV, *NA*, Giovanni Andrea Catti, 3361, fol. 348v, 21 September 1590; 3362, fols 254v–255r, 12 August 1591; fol. 298v, 31 August 1591; 3363, fol. 104r; 3364, fol. 102v, 23 February 1593; fol. 381v, 11 August 1593; 3365, fols 80r–82r, 25 February 1594.

97. ASV, *NA*, Giovanni Andrea Catti, 3355, fol. 119r, 20 April 1584.

98. ASV, *NA*, Luca e Giulio Gabrieli, 6524, fol. 409r, 9 December 1580.

99. ASV, *NA*, Pietro Partenio, 10690, fol. 172r, 23 June 1595.

100. ASV, *NA*, Pietro Partenio, 10696, fol. 395r, 12 November 1599.

101. Munro, 'I panni di lana', p. 932.

102. See for instance ASV, *NA*, Giovanni Andrea Catti, 3362, fol. 190v, 28 May 1591.

103. For similar migration flows in the late Middle Ages, see Mozzato, 'The Production of Woollens', p. 87. For Florence, see Chorley, 'Rascie', p. 495; Goldthwaite, 'The Florentine Wool Industry', pp. 543–4.

104. Munro, 'I panni di lana'; Chorley, 'Rascie'; P. Chorley, *The Volume of Cloth Production in Florence 1500–1650*, in G. L. Fontana and G. Gayot (eds), *Wool: Products and Markets (13th–20th Century)* (Padua: Cleup, 2004), pp. 551–71.

105. Epstein, 'Labour Mobility'.

106. Sella, 'The Rise and Fall', pp. 113–15; Munro, 'I panni di lana', pp. 129–30. See for instance the requests for privileges in producing 'saglie' in the Florentine style in ASV, *CSM*, ser. I, 142, fols 119v–120r; 143, fols 23v–24r, 21 February 1611. See also Panciera, *L'arte matrice*. For the Florentine woollen industry, see, on the other hand, the attempts to imitate Venetian cloths: Chorley, 'Rascie', p. 501.

107. See Munro, 'I panni di lana', p. 132; Panciera, *L'arte matrice*.

108. See ASV, *NA*, Pietro Partenio, 10667, fol. 455v, 14 August 1582, on the selling of the wool and the purchasing of woollen cloths after they were sold to Venetian merchants.

109. Ruiz Martín, *Lettres marchandes*, p. cxv. The trajectory, evolution and patterns in the Spanish wool trade during the seventeenth century still require in-depth analysis. See the debate in Philips, 'The Spanish Wool Trade', pp. 784–5, 794–5; J. I. Israel, 'Spanish Wool Exports and the European Economy, 1610–40', *The Economic History Review*, 33:2 (1980), pp. 193–211. Munro, 'I panni di lana', p. 135, rightly discusses in terms of comparative costs the matter of the Spanish wool trade's competition with Venetian and British manufacturers. Nevertheless, we don't have sufficient evidence on the role of the merchant-capitalists (probably Genoese) who controlled the supply of the raw material from Spain and their commercial networks in general in this period. Moreover, some researches on the Genoese merchant-bankers during the seventeenth century are currently in progress: see C. Marsilio, 'The Genoese and Portuguese Financial Operators' Control of the Spanish Silver Market (1627–1657)', *Journal of European Economic History*, 41:3 (2012), pp. 67–89.

110. Panciera, *L'arte matrice*, p. 60 refers to the high prices of the wool (as well as the highest cost of labour and of cochineal).

111. Ibid.; G. Pizzorni, *La Marcantonio Bonduri di Gandino un'impresa laniera in controtendenza tra Sei e Settecento* (Milan: Franco Angeli, 2005); Caracausi, *Dentro la bottega*; R. Rossi, *La lana nel Regno di Napoli nel 17. Secolo: produzione e commercio* (Turin: G. Giappichelli, 2007).

12 Korsch, 'The Scerimans and Cross-Cultural Trade in Gems: The Armenian Diaspora in Venice and its Trading Networks in the First Half of the Eighteenth Century'

1. I. Baghdiantz McCabe, *The Shah's Silk for Europe's Silver: The Eurasian Trade of the Julfa Armenians in Safavid Iran and India (1530–1750)* (Atlanta, GA: Scholars Press, 1999), pp. 327–8; H. Furber, *Rival Empires of Trade in the Orient 1600–1800* (Minneapolis, MN: University of Minnesota Press, 1976), pp. 260–2.

2. S. Mentz, *The English Gentleman Merchant at Work: Madras and the City of London 1660–1740* (Copenhagen: Museum Tusculanum Press, 2005), pp. 111–12.

3. K. Siebenhüner, 'Kostbare Güter globaler Herkunft. Der Juwelenhandel zwischen Indien und Europa', in M. North (ed.), *Kultureller Austausch. Bilanz und Perspektiven der Frühneuzeitforschung* (Cologne, Weimar and Vienna: Böhlau, 2009), pp. 327–42, on p. 336.

4. F. Trivellato, *The Familiarity of Strangers: The Sephardic Diaspora, Livorno, and Cross-Cultural Trade in the Early Modern Period* (New Haven, CT and London: Yale University Press, 2009), p. 226.

5. G. Yogev, *Diamonds and Coral: Anglo-Dutch Jews and Eighteenth-Century Trade* (Leicester: Leicester University Press, 1978), pp. 103–4; G. Tescione, *Italiani alla pesca del corallo ed egemonie marittime nel Mediterraneo* (Naples: Industrie Tipografiche Editoriali Assimilate, 1940), pp. 105–27.

6. R. W. Ferrier, 'The Armenians and the East India Company in Persia in the Seventeenth and Early Eighteenth Centuries', *Economic History Review*, new ser., 26 (1973), pp. 38–62.

7. E. Herzig, 'Venice and the Julfa Armenian Merchants', in B. L. Zekiyan and A. Ferrari (eds), *Gli Armeni e Venezia. Dagli Sceriman a Mechitar: il momento culminante di una consuetudine millenaria* (Venice: Cierre Grafica, 2004), pp. 141–64, on p. 163.

8. L. Frattarelli Fischer, 'Per la storia dell'insediamento degli Armeni a Livorno nel Seicento', in B. L. Zekiyan and C. Bonardi (eds), *Gli Armeni lungo le strade d'Italia. Atti del convegno internazionale. Torino, Genova, Livorno, 8–11 marzo 1997. Giornata di studi a Livorno* (Pisa and Rome: Istituti Editoriali Poligrafici Internazionali, 1998), pp. 23–41, on p. 38.

9. V. Baladouni and M. Makepeace (eds), *Armenian Merchants of the Seventeenth and Early Eighteenth Centuries: English East India Company Sources* (Philadelphia, PA: Armenian Philosophical Society, 1998), p. xxxiv.

10. Trivellato, *The Familiarity of Strangers*, p. 156.

11. I. Baghdiantz McCabe, 'Global Trading Ambitions in Diaspora: The Armenians and their Eurasian Silk Trade 1530–1750', in I. Baghdiantz McCabe, G. Harlaftis and I. Pepelasis Minoglou (eds), *Diaspora Entrepreneurial Networks: Four Centuries of History* (Oxford: Berg, 2005), pp. 27–50.

12. Baghdiantz McCabe, *The Shah's Silk*; S. Babaie, K. Babayan, I. Baghdiantz McCabe and M. Farhad, *Slaves of the Shah: New Elites of Safavid Iran* (London and New York: I. B. Tauris, 2004).

13. J. Chardin, *Voyages en Perse*, ed. C. Gaudon (Paris: Union générale d'éditions, 1965); J.-B. Tavernier, *Travels in India* (1676), trans. and ed. W. Crooke, 2nd edn (New Delhi: Munshiram Manoharlal Publishers, 2001).

14. M. Aghassian and K. Kévonian, 'The Armenian Merchant Network: Overall Autonomy and Local Integration', in S. Chaudhury and M. Morineau (eds), *Merchants, Companies and Trade: Europe and Asia in the Early Modern Era* (Cambridge: Cambridge University Press, 1999), pp. 74–94.

15. The title 'grand duke' was granted to the Medici by Pius V in 1569 and confirmed by the emperor in 1575.

16. A. Rocchi, 'Il primo insediamento della nazione armena a Livorno', in G. Panessa and M. Sanacore (eds), *Gli Armeni a Livorno: L'intercultura di una Diaspora. Interventi nel Convegno 'Memoria e cultura armena fra Livorno e l'Oriente'. Catalogo della Mostra 'Gli Armeni a Livorno: Documenti e Immagini di una Presenza Secolare'* (Livorno: Debatte Otello, 2006), pp. 83–7; Frattarelli Fischer, 'Per la storia dell'insediamento', p. 26.

17. R. Ghezzi, 'Mercanti armeni in Livorno nel XVII secolo', in B. L. Zekiyan and C. Bonardi (eds), *Gli Armeni Lungo le Strade d'Italia. Atti del convegno internazionale. Torino, Genova, Livorno, 8–11 Marzo 1997. Giornata di Studi a Livorno* (Pisa and Rome: Istituti Editoriali Poligrafici Internazionali, 1998), pp. 43–53, on pp. 52–3.

18. Frattarelli Fischer, 'Per la storia dell'insediamento', p. 37; Yogev, *Diamonds and Coral*, pp. 106–9.

19. J. Chardin, *Voyages de M.r le Chevalier Chardin, en Perse, et autres lieux de l'orient*, 10 vols (Amsterdam: Jean Louis de Lorme, 1711), vol. 9, p. 7; S. D. Aslanian, *From the Indian Ocean to the Mediterranean: The Global Trade Networks of Armenian Merchants from New Julfa* (Berkeley, CA: University of California Press, 2011), pp. 149–58.

20. Biblioteca del Museo Correr di Venezia (hereafter BMCV), Cod. Cicogna 3428, Brevi Memorie, fol. 1v.

21. Ibid.

22. Baghdiantz McCabe, *The Shah's Silk*, pp. 205–14 and 245–7.

23. M. Sanacore, 'Splendore e Decadenza degli Sceriman a Livorno', in B. L. Zekiyan and C. Bonardi (eds), *Gli Armeni Lungo le Strade d'Italia. Atti del Convegno Internazionale: Torino, Genova, Livorno, 8–11 Marzo 1997. Giornata di Studi a Livorno* (Pisa and

Rome: Istituti Editoriali e Poligrafici Internazionali, 1998), pp. 127–60, on pp. 134–5; Frattarelli Fischer, 'Per la storia dell'insediamento', p. 27.

24. C. Bonardi, 'Il commercio dei preziosi', in B. L. Zekiyan (ed.), *Gli Armeni in Italia. Catalogo della mostra a Venezia, Isola di San Lazzaro, e Padova, Museo al Santo, 9 settembre 1990–20 gennaio 1991* (Rome: De Luca edizioni d'arte, 1990), pp. 110–14, on p. 110.

25. G. Lenzen, *Produktions- und Handelsgeschichte des Diamanten. Zeitlich geordnete Beiträge unter besonderer Berücksichtigung der Preisbildung und der Konzentrationsbestrebungen der Urproduktion* (Berlin: Duncker & Humblot, 1966), p. 94–5; K. Hofmeester, 'Shifting Trajectories of Diamond Processing: From India to Europe and Back, from the Fifteenth Century to the Twentieth', *Journal of Global History*, 8 (2013), pp. 25–49, on p. 30.

26. T. Vanneste, *Global Trade and Commercial Networks: Eighteenth-Century Diamond Merchants* (London: Pickering & Chatto, 2011), pp. 42–3. In 1636, 186 diamond cutters still worked in Venice. Cf. Lenzen, *Produktions- und Handelsgeschichte*, p. 111.

27. For fashion trends and the consumption of jewellery, see M. Pointon, *Brilliant Effects: A Cultural History of Gem Stones and Jewellery* (New Haven, CT and London: Yale University Press, 2009).

28. Bonardi, 'Il commercio dei preziosi', p. 110.

29. Trivellato, *The Familiarity of Strangers*, p. 232. Diamond mines were operating in Borneo too. However, only a small quantity was sold. Cf. Hofmeester, 'Shifting Trajectories', p. 27.

30. Lenzen, *Produktions- und Handelsgeschichte*, p. 111.

31. See the letters from Giacomo in Archivio di Stato di Padova (hereafter ASPD), Archivio Sceriman, b. 27/M.

32. D. M. White, *Zaccaria Seriman 1709–1784 and the Viaggi di Enrico Wanton: A Contribution to the Study of the Enlightenment in Italy* (Manchester: Manchester University Press, 1961), pp. 9 and 11.

33. Ibid., pp. 9–11.

34. BMCV, Cod. Cicogna 3428, Risultato del processo, fol. 4r. The papal bull is partly transcribed in ibid., fol. 6v–7r; the complete transcription can be found in White, *Zaccaria Seriman*, pp. 12–15.

35. BMCV, Cod. Cicogna 3428, Brevi Memorie, fol. 4r; BMCV, Cod. Cicogna 3428, Risultato del processo, fol. 7v–8r.

36. BMCV, Cod. Cicogna 3428, Brevi Memorie, fol. 1r.

37. Ibid., fol. 2v.

38. For details, see BMCV, Cod. Cicogna 3428, Informatione sopra il Memorial presentato li 18 settembre 1751 dal Sig.r Co. Gio. Steffano [*sic*] Seriman per nome suo, e del Co. David Seriman suo zio e del Conte Emanuel Seriman nell'Ecc.mo Coleggio [*sic*].

39. White, *Zaccaria Seriman*, p. 16.

40. BMCV, Cod. P.D. C. 2711/1, Carte della Famiglia Tornimben, pp. 43–4.

41. ASPD, Archivio Sceriman-Cumani, b. 4/9; BMCV, Cod. P.D. C.2711/1, Carte della Famiglia Tornimben, pp. 43–4.

42. White, *Zaccaria Seriman*, p. 22. Later Emanuel had to flee too. Cf. BMCV, Cod. Cicogna 3428, Risultato del Processo, fol. 13v.

43. ASPD, Archivio Sceriman, b. 27/M, p. 9.

44. BMCV, Cod. Cicogna 3428, Risultato del Processo, fols 5v and 8r–v; C. Bonardi, 'Gli Sceriman di Venezia da mercanti a possidenti', in B. L. Zekiyan (ed.), *Ad limina Italiae. In*

viaggio per l'Italia con mercanti e monaci armeni (Padua: Editoriale Programma, 1996), pp. 229–50, on p. 230.

45. ASPD, Archivio Sceriman, b. 27/K, pp. 5–8.
46. Ibid., b. 27/M, p. 95.
47. Ibid., p. 10.
48. Ibid., pp. 10–1 and 93.
49. Ibid., p. 94.
50. Ibid., p. 14.
51. Ibid., p. 14.
52. Ibid., pp. 11 and 15; ASPD, Archivio Sceriman-Cumani, b. 4/1, p. 19.
53. ASPD, Archivio Sceriman, b. 27/L, p. 58.
54. Ibid., b. 27/M, p. 13.
55. Ibid., pp. 10 and 15.
56. Ibid., p. 13.
57. ASPD, Archivio Sceriman-Cumani, b. 4/1, p. 20.
58. ASPD, Archivio Sceriman, b. 27/M, p. 93.
59. Ibid., pp. 10 and 13–14; ASPD, Archivio Sceriman-Cumani, b. 4/1, p. 20.
60. ASPD, Archivio Sceriman, b. 27/M, pp. 66–7. This was a traditional Indian technique. Cf. Hofmeester, 'Shifting Trajectories', p. 32.
61. For the bankers, cf. ASPD, Archivio Sceriman, b. 27/M, p. 11.
62. A. Mariuz and G. Pavanello, 'La chiesetta di Bernardo Nave a Cittadella', *Arte Veneta*, 50 (1997), pp. 68–85, on p. 69.
63. ASPD, Archivio Sceriman, b. 27/M, pp. 12 and 15; b. 27/L, p. 59.
64. G. Cunial, 'Palazzo Contarini-Seriman a Venezia' (MA thesis, University of Padua, 1977/8), p. 50.
65. Archivio di Stato di Venezia (hereafter ASV), Notarile, Atti, b. 3607: Giovanni Garzoni Paulini, fols 304r–307r and 313v.
66. Bonardi, 'Gli Sceriman di Venezia', p. 236.
67. BMCV, Cod. Cicogna 3428, Risultato del processo, fols 2r and 10r–v; ASPD, Archivio Sceriman, b. 27/M, pp. 93–4.
68. ASV, Avogaria di comun, b. 348, fols 8r–12r.
69. Ibid., capitolo 8, unpaginated.
70. ASPD, Archivio Sceriman, b. 27/M, pp. 25–7. I am grateful to Jan-Christoph Rössler for indicating the kinship between Giorgio Corner and Pietro Capello.
71. ASV, Notarile, Testamenti, b. 1169: Francesco Dies, no. 112.
72. ASV, Avogaria di comun, reg. 94 (= Matrimoni patrizi per nome di donna, reg. 7), fols 27r and 172v.
73. I thank Jan-Christoph Rössler for indicating the kinship between Giorgio Bembo and the Sarotti family.
74. ASPD, Archivio Sceriman, b. 27/M, p. 96.
75. Ibid.
76. ASV, Notarile, Atti, b. 3607: Giovanni Garzoni Paulini, fols 304r–307r and 313v.
77. ASPD, Archivio Sceriman, b. 27/M, p. 24.
78. BMCV, Cod. Cicogna 3428, Risultato del processo, fols 3r–v.
79. ASPD, Archivio Sceriman, b. 27/M, p. 66.
80. Hofmeester, 'Shifting Trajectories', p. 40.
81. BMCV, Cod. Cicogna 3428, Risultato del processo, fol. 3v.
82. ASPD, Archivio Sceriman, b. 27/L, pp. 87–8.

83. Ibid., b. 27/M, pp. 15–20; ASPD, Archivio Sceriman-Cumani, b. 4/1, pp. 16–21.
84. Vanneste, *Global Trade and Commercial Networks*, p. 46–8; Hofmeester, 'Shifting Trajectories', p. 38.
85. ASPD, Archivio Sceriman, b. 27/L, pp. 56–9 and b. 27/M, p. 13.
86. ASPD, Archivio Sceriman-Cumani, b. 4/1, pp. 17–21.
87. ASPD, Archivio Sceriman, b. 27/M, pp. 15–20.
88. Hofmeester, 'Shifting Trajectories', pp. 37–8; Bonardi, 'Il commercio dei preziosi', p. 110; Sanacore, 'Splendore e Decadenza', p. 137.
89. ASPD, Archivio Sceriman-Cumani, b. 4/9. Murat distributed the cash holdings among his six sons. Seriman received 90,000 ducats while Nazar, Sarat, Giovanni and Pietro received 33,000 ducats each and Giacomo 32,500 ducats.
90. For instance, ASV, Avogaria di Comun, Civile, b. 17, n. 7 and b. 299, n. 2; ASV, Inquisitori di Stato, b. 204, p. 1042; ASPD, Archivio Sceriman-Cumani, b. 5/5 and b. 5/7.
91. BMCV, Cod. Cicogna 3428, Risultato del processo, fol. 9r; ASPD, Archivio Sceriman, bb. 13–14, bb. 49–53; ASPD, Archivio Sceriman-Cumani, bb. 1–2.
92. ASPD, Archivio Sceriman, bb. 3–8.
93. This expansion to Livorno was so common among Venice-based merchants that the area where they settled was called 'Nuova Venezia'. Another successful Armenian family, the Mirmans, established their business in the same three locations as the Scerimans: New Julfa, Venice and Livorno. For the Mirman family, see P. Castignoli, 'I Mirman a Livorno', in B. L. Zekiyan and C. Bonardi (eds), *Gli Armeni lungo le strade d'Italia. Atti del convegno internazionale: Torino, Genova, Livorno, 8–11 marzo 1997. Giornata di studi a Livorno* (Pisa and Rome: Istituti Editoriali e Poligrafici Internazionali, 1998), pp. 103–20.
94. R. Ciorli, 'Gli insediamenti degli Armeni', in G. Panessa and M. Sanacore (eds), *Gli Armeni a Livorno: L'intercultura di una Diaspora. Interventi nel Convegno 'Memoria e Cultura Armena fra Livorno e l'Oriente'. Catalogo della Mostra 'Gli Armeni a Livorno. Documenti e Immagini di una Presenza Secolare'* (Livorno: Debatte Otello, 2006), pp. 121–6.
95. Archivio di Stato di Livorno (hereafter ASL), Decima, 214, no. 2697. The sale contract is in part transcribed by R. Ciorli, 'L'insediamento urbano della nazione armena a Livorno', in B. L. Zekiyan and C. Bonardi (eds), *Gli Armeni Lungo le Strade d'Italia. Atti del Convegno Internazionale: Torino, Genova, Livorno, 8–11 marzo 1997. Giornata di studi a Livorno* (Pisa and Rome: Istituti Editoriali e Poligrafici Internazionali, 1998), pp. 161–77, on p. 174.
96. Sanacore, 'Splendore e Decadenza', p. 127.
97. R. Ciorli, 'Gli insediamenti degli Armeni', in G. Panessa e M. Sanacore (eds.), *Gli Armeni a Livorno: l'intercultura di una diaspora. Interventi nel convegno "Memoria e cultura armena fra Livorno e l'Oriente". Catalogo della mostra "Gli Armeni a Livorno. Documenti e immagini di una presenza secolare"* (Livorno: Debatte Otello, 2006), pp. 69–79.
98. A. A. Kharadian, 'Le relazioni economico-commerciali degli Armeni di Smirne con le città italiane (secc. XV–XIX)', in B. L. Zekiyan (ed.), *Ad limina Italiae. In Viaggio per l'Italia con Mercanti e Monaci Armeni* (Padua: Editoriale Programma, 1996), pp. 251–66.
99. Sanacore, 'Splendore e Decadenza', p. 129.
100. Ibid., p. 135; Rocchi, 'Il primo insediamento', p. 84.
101. Sanacore, 'Splendore e Decadenza', p. 129.
102. Ibid., p. 128.

103. Ibid., p. 130, mentions the artisan Giacomo Rinaldi, who invented a new cut for emeralds at the beginning of the eighteenth century.
104. Trivellato, *The Familiarity of Strangers*, p. 230.
105. ASL, Capitano poi Governatore poi Auditore vicario (hereafter CGA), 485, nos 879–80; Sanacore, 'Splendore e Decadenza', p. 130.
106. ASL, CGA, 747, no. 260.
107. Ibid., 610, no. 691.
108. Bodleian Library, Oxford, MS Ital. d.9, fols 108r–v, quoted in Trivellato, *The Familiarity of Strangers*, p. 254.
109. ASL, CGA, 472, no. 408.
110. E.g. ibid., 584, no. 536; 596, no. 523; 668, no. 356; Sanacore, 'Splendore e Decadenza', p. 131.
111. ASPD, Archivio Sceriman, bb. 27/K–M.
112. Sanacore, 'Splendore e Decadenza', p. 131.
113. ASL, CGA, 747, no. 260.
114. Sanacore, 'Splendore e Decadenza', p. 131.
115. David's wealth is revealed in the records of a lawsuit of 1716; ASL, CGA, 571, no. 333; Trivellato, *The Familiarity of Strangers*, p. 151.
116. Sanacore, 'Splendore e Decadenza', p. 134.
117. ASL, CGA, 2211, no. 121.
118. Sanacore, 'Splendore e Decadenza', p. 135.
119. ASPD, Archivio Sceriman, b. 27/M, p. 59.
120. Trivellato, *The Familiarity of Strangers*, p. 108.
121. Ibid., p. 151.
122. Sanacore, 'Splendore e Decadenza', p. 136.
123. ASL, CGA, 694, no. 645; 777, no. 541; Sanacore, 'Splendore e Decadenza', p. 136.
124. ASL, CGA, 742, no. 326.
125. Sanacore, 'Splendore e Decadenza', p. 137.
126. ASL, CGA, 2211, no. 121.
127. Ibid., 610, no. 694; Sanacore, 'Splendore e Decadenza', p. 136, points out that Zorab and the merchant Giuseppe di Giovanni residing in Lisbon were the same person.
128. ASL, CGA, 712, no. 727; 769, no. 248; 923, no. 165; Sanacore, 'Splendore e Decadenza', pp. 138–40.
129. Sanacore, 'Splendore e Decadenza', p. 140.
130. ASL, CGA, 1215, no. 848.
131. Sanacore, 'Splendore e Decadenza', p. 142.
132. Ibid., pp. 144–5. Michele was one of the sons of Diodato Sceriman and Elisabetta Tornimben.
133. Trivellato, *The Familiarity of Strangers*, p. 230.
134. Archivio di Stato di Firenze (hereafter ASF), Notarile Moderno, Protocolli, Nicolò Mazzinghi, 27111, fols 3r–v; Trivellato, *The Familiarity of Strangers*, p. 161.
135. ASF, Notarile Moderno, Protocolli, Giovanni Giuseppe Mazzanti, 23705, fols 177v–179r, no. 149; Trivellato, *The Familiarity of Strangers*, p. 229.
136. ASF, Mediceo del Principato, 2474, fol. 380; Trivellato, *The Familiarity of Strangers*, p. 230.
137. ASV, Avogaria di comun 348, capitolo 2, fols 13r–v.
138. ASV, Notarile, Atti, b. 7402: Gio. Antonio Generini, fasc. April 1746, no. 2, fols 3r–5r.

INDEX

Speculum regale, 68
spices, 56, 99, 103, 117, 153, 155, 163, 190,
    193, 196, 217, 230
    pepper, 130–1, 187–90, 194–200
Spina, Lionardo, 116, 117, 119
Spinelli, Tommaso, 75
Spinola, Pasquale, 212
'standard markets', 49
standardized goods, 52–3, 55–6
stockfish, 19
Strauch, Lorenz, 54–5
Strozzi, Lorenzo, 69
Struwe, Brun, 31
Suarez, Baldassarre, 211, 213, 217–18
Suárez, Baltasar, 124, 125, 133, 135–6
sugar, 50, 130–1, 180, 182, 184, 230
Suleiman I, Shah, 226

Taddeo Gaddi (di), Zanobi, 100
Talani, Alessandro, 74–5
Tana, 94
Tani, Agnolo, 72
Tavernier, Jean-Baptiste, 225
Tavola, Geronimo, 194
Tavora (de), Cristoforo, 194
Tecchini, Piero, 95
Thessaloniki, 176
tin, 100, 164
Toledo, 139, 142, 145, 150, 194, 204–5
Treaty of Tordesillas (1494), 190
Treaty of Windsor (1386), 178, 182
Treu und Glauben, 28
Trevisan, Domenico, 163
Treviso, 214, 216, 221–2
Tucci, Ugo, 68
Tunis, 159–62, 164, 167–8, 169
Tuscany, 69–70, 83, 86, 90, 93–4, 105 , 107,
    110–1, 123–6, 129, 131–5, 223–5,
    237–8

Ugleimer, Pieter, 75

Valencia, 87, 90, 93, 95–106, 140, 192
Valladolid, 138–9, 142, 149–51, 192
Van Dooselaere, Quentin, 3
Venice, 61–2, 67, 71, 75–6, 100–1, 124
    129–31, 153–69, 194–5, 201–39
Verona, 216, 230, 232
Vicenza, 214

Vienna, 223, 225, 226, 231
Villalón, 139
Villani, Lorenzo di Bernardo, 74
Visconte, Ludovico, 200
Visconti, Gian Galeazzo, 89
Vitoria, 139

wax, 167–8, 229
    Berber wax, 168
weapons, 144
Weldon, Henry, 182
Welser, Anton, 114–15
Welser, Bartholomäus, 119
Welser, Hans, 115, 119
Wentmeyer, Sander, 20
White, Harrison C., 5, 7, 45, 52, 58–60,
    62–3, 188
    Markets from Networks, 47
wills, 29, 31–5
wine, 182–5, 219, 229
wineskins, 148
wool, 99–105, 122–5, 127–30, ,135, 140–2,
    144, 152, 167–8, 201–222
    bresvatter, 168
    Merino wool, 123, 127
    Florentine wool cloth, 99
    Maestrazgo wool, 100
    rascie, 123, 127, 129, 211
    perpignani, 129
    panni alti (fine heavy broadcloths),
        203–4, 211, 215, 217
    panni bassi, 217
    panni bastardi, 164
    panni larghi (English wool cloth), 168
    pannina veneziana, 217
    saglie, panni da, 204
    saglie alla fiorentina, 215
    sex larghi (English wool cloth), 168
    sex stretti (English wool cloth), 168
Worcester, William, 70
Wulff, Hans, 20
Wykinghoff, Lambert, 31

Ximenes, Francesco, 130
Ximénez de Aragón, Sebastián, 133

Zareale, Piero, 102
Zorzi, Bartolomeo, 162